17 ⁹⁵

HI/FRANCE

BLENHEIM

BLENHEIM

BATTLE FOR EUROPE

Charles Spencer

WEIDENFELD & NICOLSON

For Ned

Weidenfeld & Nicolson

The Orion Publishing Group Ltd
Orion House, 5 Upper Saint Martin's Lane, London WC2H 9EA

Copyright © Charles Spencer 2004
First published 2004

Second impression 2004

British Library Cataloguing-in-Publication Data
A catalogue record for this book is available from the British Library

ISBN 0-297-84609-4

Printed and bound in Great Britain by
Clays Ltd, St Ives plc

ACKNOWLEDGEMENTS

MANY MODERN ACADEMICS HAVE contributed to my research, and their works are listed at the end of this book. However, it is to the soldier-diarists of both sides that I am particularly grateful, for bringing their experiences to life so vividly, and for managing to bring a less haughty voice to events otherwise dominated by the Titans of the age – Marlborough, Eugène, and the focal figure of Europe for more than half a century: Louis XIV.

To history teachers and tutors of my past – especially Alec Porch, Timothy Connor, the late Angus Macintyre, and Laurence Brockliss – I owe many thanks, for their quiet encouragement at a time when I was often impatient with academic work.

I would like to thank the staff of the British Library for all their help in the research stages of this book, particularly Dr Frances Harris for gaining me access to the Manuscripts Department.

Above all I would like to thank my darling wife, for her patience and understanding as I became increasingly immersed in this work. It has dominated my waking hours for so long – and has frequently taken a stake in my dreams – that I am sure the intensity of it all has sometimes made her wonder at the wisdom of my undertaking such a book, which has stretched my limited scholarly pretensions to the full. However, whether at my most distracted, or my most enthused, she has quietly encouraged and understood me, and I will never forget the level of love and loyalty that she has displayed, unstintingly, and so generously, throughout all stages of this book.

AUTHOR'S NOTE

DATES
At the time of Blenheim, England used the Old Style of dates, whereas the rest of Europe used the Gregorian Calendar. The Old Style was ten days behind the New. To avoid confusion, I have used the New Style throughout.

SPELLING
This was not standardised. At the risk of being accused of meddling, I have modified spelling in diaries and letters that may confuse the general, modern, reader.

CONTENTS

LIST OF MAPS

PREFACE

IF IT WERE NOT FOR THE VAST and impressive palace of the same name, it's doubtful whether many people outside the academic world would be aware of the Battle of Blenheim. Agincourt and Waterloo still have a distant and satisfying echo in the modern British psyche, but Blenheim, where the British helped win a victory that changed the course of history, is all but forgotten. Historians have breathed life into the reign of Queen Anne, and written biographies of John and Sarah Marlborough, yet the battle itself seems to have slunk off into the background, overtaken by the more glamorous exploits of Napoleon and the large-scale carnage of the twentieth century's wars.

Ironically, Napoleon believed that his contemporaries undervalued Marlborough's generalship, and he commissioned authors to make good the neglect. But still in Europe you find the battle, most frequently referred to as Höchstädt, as a mere footnote, even though so many different nationalities took part. Austrians, Belgians, British, Danes, Dutch, French, Irish, Swiss, and many different German states all contributed soldiers to this, one of the greatest battles in Europe's history.

When I went to see the battle site, in the spring of 2003, I could find only one specific memorial in the village of Blindheim, whose Anglicised name has given the engagement its identity. A small plaque in the ground gives a few basic details. Wandering the lines where the Irish

'Wild Geese' nearly turned the battle in favour of their master, King Louis XIV; where the French generals were stunned to see the elite horsemen of their *Gendarmerie* utterly defeated by British cavalry, there is little to see except neat dormitory communities surrounded by sweeping fields of highly mechanised agriculture. I had assumed that the churchyard at Blenheim, where some of the most intense fighting took place, would have gravestones pockmarked by musket balls: instead, I was confronted by the shininess of modern tombstones that had seen no battle, and witnessed no war. I found it immensely sad that the sacrifice of so many men on the surrounding battlefield could be distilled down into a marble tablet, and nothing more.

The tercentenary of Blenheim seems set to return the battle to its rightful prominence. The Bavarian state government, previously reluctant to remember a crushing defeat of its army on home turf, has chosen to honour the event with an exhibition. This will be in nearby Höchstädt Castle and is intended to be permanent. It will show how Louis XIV's overweening ambition drove neighbouring countries to form a coalition that was at last strong enough to check the mighty army of the 'Sun King'.

The exhibition at Höchstädt Castle will mirror the message of this book: that the Battle of Blenheim ended King Louis's plans to dominate Europe, and to extend his brand of absolute royal power from Spain to the Low Countries, and from Germany to Italy. The battle took place as a mighty transition was underway in Europe. France, Austria and an enfeebled Spain were still major powers in European affairs; Sweden and the Netherlands, giants of the seventeenth century, were slipping towards secondary status; Prussia's gathering strength hinted at its dramatic future.

British soldiers made up only a fifth of the victorious allied army at Blenheim, but their contribution was decisive. They shrugged off a reputation for idle incompetence and showed uncommon ability and bravery. In the wake of Blenheim, the greatest land victory won under an English commander on foreign soil since Henry V's Agincourt, the British took their first faltering steps towards empire.

This tale unfolds at a time when the Age of Reason combined with increasingly lethal weaponry to produce a unique period of military history: one when heavy bloodshed was shunned. The violent excesses of the Thirty Years' War (1618–48) were still fresh in the memory, and the increased reliability and rate of fire of muskets and cannon ensured that casualties were extraordinarily high if armies met head-on. Monarchs and generals shrank from the cost of defeat and preferred wars of manoeuvre and sieges where the stakes were relatively low. Only the boldest commanders were prepared to gamble everything in open battle.

Blenheim left some 40,000 men dead or wounded. The consequences of this bloody battle were far-reaching: Southey wrote a poem decrying the futility of war, arguing that the bloodshed of 13 August 1704 settled nothing. However, the nineteenth-century historian, Sir Edward Creasy, included Blenheim in his magnum opus, *The Fifteen Decisive Battles of the World*, alongside such pivotal actions as Marathon, Hastings and Saratoga. The reason for this was the effect that the battle had on Louis XIV's ambitions: 'Blenheim had dissipated for ever his once proud visions of almost universal conquest.' Winston S. Churchill believed Blenheim was an event that 'changed the political axis of the world'. Placing the battle in a wider context, he wrote: 'The destruction of the Armada had preserved the life of Britain: the charge at Blenheim opened to her the gateways of the modern world.'

Such assessments provide, I hope, justification enough for returning to the background and the expression of a dynamic moment in Europe's history, three hundred years ago, when the hitherto invincible army of a monstrous tyrant was destroyed in an afternoon.

PROLOGUE

PICTURE THE PRINCE AT THE PEAK of his power.

He has, in the course of an already monumental reign, transformed his nation's status from one of fragile potential to that of feared military juggernaut. For France, for Louis XIV, the future looks not only secure; it also holds the promise of even greater glory. It seems certain that the empire historically at the heart of Europe will, within days, be superseded by his own Gallic hegemony. Louis knows that his armies are closing in on Vienna, poised to deliver the final blow to the Habsburgs and their decrepit Holy Roman Empire. Once the sword arm of Catholic Europe, the Empire had lost most of its power and survived only by default. The imminent French victory will compel all Europe to accept that Louis XIV holds the true imperial power and his Bourbon dynasty reigns supreme. This summer of 1704 is a glorious time indeed, for a third generation of heirs now stands in the direct line: after his son the Dauphin, then his grandson the Duke of Burgundy, there is now the reassuring consolidation of a great-grandson, the newborn Duke of Brittany.

To Louis, 'the Catholic King', this continuation of his seed is a clear demonstration of divine support for him and the Bourbon line. With confidence Louis writes that this latest royal birth '… is one of the most visible signs that I have yet received of [God's] protection. I am aware that such is without example in any of my regal predecessors' reigns, and that this long succession of Kings assures the perpetuation of the good fortune of my lands.'[1] He asks for the *Te Deum* to be sung across France in acknowledgement of the divine blessing afforded his family and nation.

With the boy's June birth, Louis has declared the summer of 1704 a season of general celebration. The Duke of Saint Simon, courtier and diarist, records disapprovingly in his secret journal: 'This event caused great joy to the King and the Court. The town [of Paris] shared their delight, and carried their enthusiasm almost to madness, by the excess of their demonstration, and their festivities.'[2]

It is at Versailles, where Saint Simon is one of the myriad drones in attendance on the Sun King, that the festivities reach their zenith. The day there habitually culminates in colourful evening amusements – balls, concerts, operas – but this being summer, it is the season for Louis's beloved outdoor '*fêtes*'. A keen and accomplished actor in his youth, when an addiction to amateur theatricals was formed, Louis still basks in the opulence of such displays: they allow him to reclaim the thespian limelight, without demeaning his regal status. The *fête*, like so much at Versailles, is part play-acting, part propaganda, and wholly for Louis's pleasure.

Most of the *fêtes* take place outdoors, in the regimented grounds. The water bobs with tributes from across Europe, some from countries that are now France's bitterest enemies: 'On the mile-long cross-shaped grand canal glided a hundred swans from Denmark, two little yachts from England, carved and gilded galleys decked with red and white streamers and hangings fringed with gold, a small warship and a fleet of gondolas, manned by fourteen Venetian gondoliers.'[3]

Tonight, see Louis sitting in customary splendour above the courtiers on his royal dais, a periwig on his head, modish high heels on his feet. A classically based triumph is accorded him, led by Mars. The God of War is atop a chariot, drawn forward by soldiers. Fawning nymphs are in attendance, testimony to Mars' military virility. Louis takes the salute with studied precision. He may never have led his troops into battle, his wartime experience confined to observing sieges, but that is of no matter. He has been the figurehead through decades of glory.

After the triumphal procession there follows an allegory, further pandering to the royal ego. It is a representation of how Europe – in French eyes – is currently arranged. In a position of unquestioned dominance stands the Seine, the main artery of Paris; and, here, the symbol of France. The river expects and receives cowered homage from six major waterways: the Thames, the Meuse, the Neckar, the Scheldt, the Rhine, and the Danube. The Danube has a central role in our tale, far removed from further French triumphalism. Tonight, though, the prospect beckons of domination of the continent that is criss-crossed by these rivers.

For Louis, this was an evening that he would look back on as a watershed in his reign. Before it stood years of victorious wars, and mounting dynastic solidity. After it came repeated hammer-blows of disappointment, both military and familial. Our eyewitness Saint Simon marked the moment everything changed: 'Even while these rejoicings were being celebrated, news reached us which spread consternation in every family, and cast a gloom over the whole city.'[4] The first reports of Blenheim were reaching Paris.

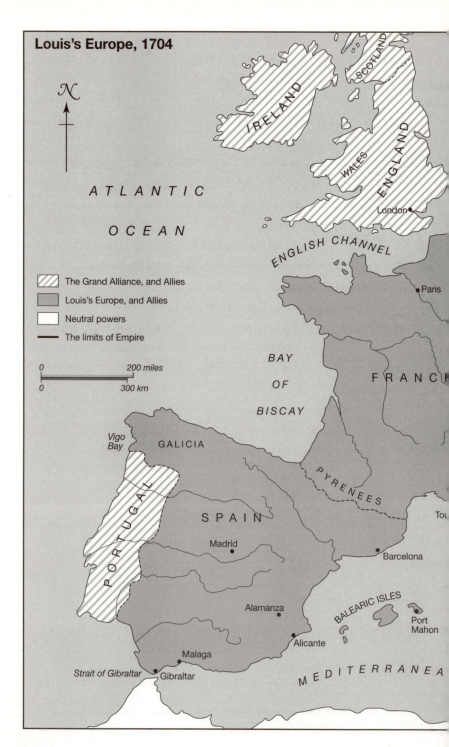

Louis's Europe, 1704

N

ATLANTIC

OCEAN

IRELAND

SCOTLAND

WALES

ENGLAND

London

ENGLISH CHANNEL

Paris

The Grand Alliance, and Allies
Louis's Europe, and Allies
Neutral powers
The limits of Empire

0   200 miles
0   300 km

BAY

OF

BISCAY

FRANCE

Vigo
Bay

GALICIA

PYRENEES

Tou

PORTUGAL

SPAIN

Madrid

Barcelona

BALEARIC ISLES

Port
Mahon

Alamanza

Alicante

Malaga

Strait of Gibraltar   Gibraltar

MEDITERRANEA

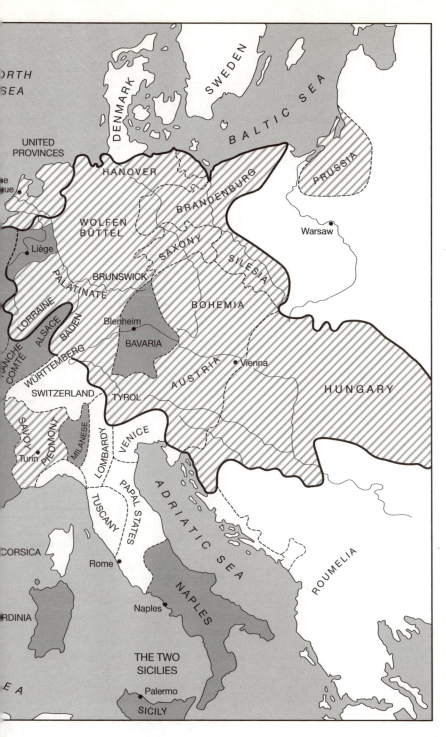

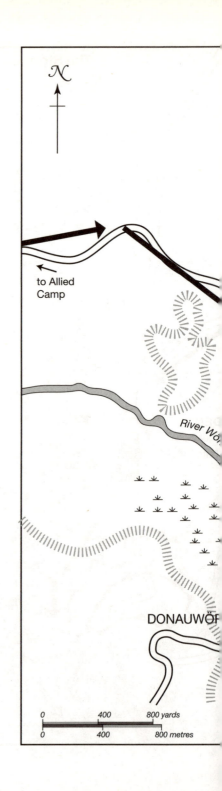

to Allied
Camp

River Wö

DONAUWÖ

| 0 | 400 | 800 yards |
| 0 | 400 | 800 metres |

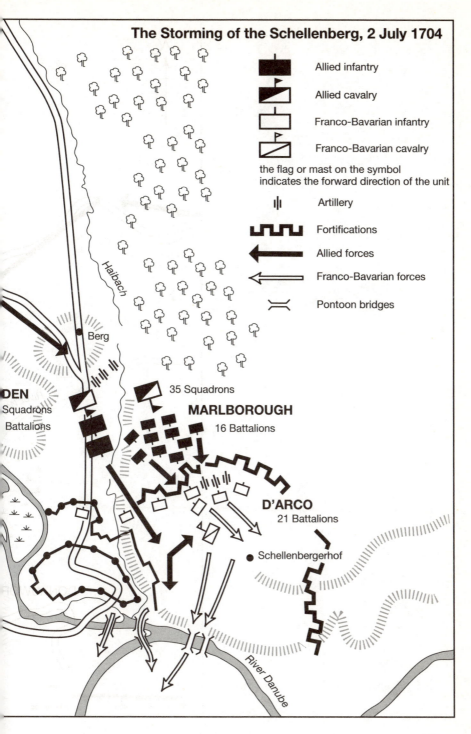

The Storming of the Schellenberg, 2 July 1704

Allied infantry

Allied cavalry

Franco-Bavarian infantry

Franco-Bavarian cavalry

the flag or mast on the symbol
indicates the forward direction of the unit

Artillery

Fortifications

Allied forces

Franco-Bavarian forces

Pontoon bridges

Haibach

Berg

DEN

Squadrons

Battalions

35 Squadrons

MARLBOROUGH

16 Battalions

D'ARCO

21 Battalions

Schellenbergerhof

River Danube

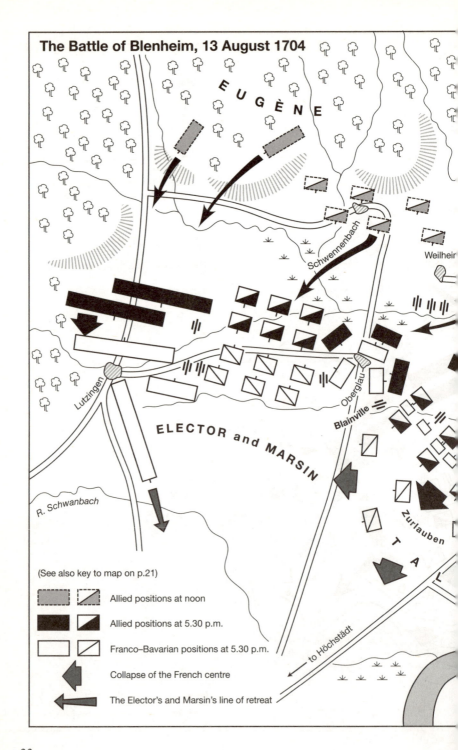

The Battle of Blenheim, 13 August 1704

EUGÈNE

Schwennenbach

Weilheir

Lutzingen

Oberglau

Blainville

ELECTOR and MARSIN

R. Schwanbach

Zurlauben

T A
L

to Höchstädt

(See also key to map on p.21)

Allied positions at noon

Allied positions at 5.30 p.m.

Franco–Bavarian positions at 5.30 p.m.

Collapse of the French centre

The Elector's and Marsin's line of retreat

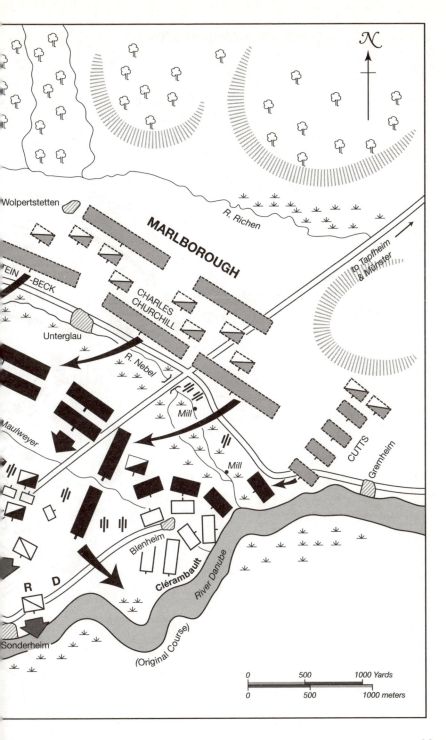

Wolpertstetten

R. Richen

MARLBOROUGH

to Tapfheim
& Münster

EIN -BECK

Unterglau

CHARLES
CHURCHILL

R. Nebel

Maulweyer

Mill

Mill

CUTTS

Gremheim

Blenheim

R D

Clérambault

River Danube

Sonderheim

(Original Course)

N

| 0 | 500 | 1000 Yards |
| 0 | 500 | 1000 meters |

PART ONE

LOUIS'S EUROPE

CHAPTER ONE

A ROD FOR HIS OWN BACK

'That spirit of infatuation and error
The fatal avant-courier of the fall of kings.'
FROM RACINE'S *ATHALIE*

LOUIS XIV BESTRODE THE END of the seventeenth and the opening of the eighteenth centuries with a mixture of menace and panache. He was as dominating a figure then as Napoleon was to be a hundred years later. Like Bonaparte, Louis relied on military might to impose his will; at home and abroad, he cajoled the unwilling and crushed the openly hostile. However, whereas Napoleon's control was limited to less than twenty years, Louis's pungent brand of autocracy wafted through seven decades of European history.

France had twenty million inhabitants: three times the population of Spain, four times that of England, and nine times that of the Netherlands. Louis harnessed this numerical advantage, building a huge, efficient, army. In a ferocious quest for personal glory and national security, he unleashed it on France's neighbours one after another.

Louis was the insecure and poorly educated son of an unremarkable king. His inadequate childhood tutoring left him with an outlook that was underpinned by two intertwined prejudices: a passionate belief in the divine right of kings, and a violent abhorrence of Protestantism. His historical knowledge, which might have lent context to his reign, was limited. He was proud to be a grandson of Henry IV, one of France's greatest rulers. He was also aware that his father had yielded much respect and power during a disappointing 23-year reign. He wanted to emulate his grandfather, and put right his father's failings. Louis's life's aim was to create a homogenous force in the centre of Europe, which he could lead with distinction.

The instinct for greatness was evident early in Louis's rule. In September 1651, the thirteen-year-old boy-king gamely announced to *Parlement* that he was assuming his place as active head of state. However, this was a case of premature posturing, for the real power still resided with Cardinal Mazarin, Louis's first minister. This Macchiavellian cleric remained the de facto ruler of France until his death in 1661. Only then did Louis wrest the power that his self-esteem so craved. Confident in his regal status, the king informed his politicians: 'You will assist me with your advice when I ask for it.' This was to be less often than they could possibly have envisaged.

It was the start of an autocratic reign that led Winston S. Churchill to accord Louis a unique place in historical infamy: 'No worse enemy of human freedom has ever appeared in the trappings of polite civilisation. Insatiable appetite, cold, calculating ruthlessness, monumental conceit, presented themselves armed with fire and sword.'[1] The year he assumed real power, the twenty-three-year-old king married Maria Theresa, a daughter of King Philip IV of Spain. The dynastic potential of this union between Bourbon and Habsburg, the two most powerful dynasties of Western Europe, was enormous, but he could not capitalise on the match straightaway. As he explained in his *Mémoirs*, Louis's domestic problems came first: in his kingdom 'disorder reigned every-where'.[2] Indeed, at the time of the wedding, international pressure persuaded Louis to renounce any future rights to the Spanish throne. The concession was accepted – Louis had no alternative – on condition that France receive the compensation of a sizeable dowry. This was not paid.

To the rest of Europe, this was a mere detail – an unfortunate reflection of Spain's parlous finances, which had brought bread riots to her cities and creeping paralysis to her industry. However, to Louis, the non-payment constituted a clear breach of contract. It kept alive his hopes that, in the right circumstances, he could lop off various branches of the huge Spanish empire for French consumption.

His opportunity came in 1665 when Philip IV of Spain died, leaving the throne to four-year-old Carlos II, a sickly boy not expected to see adulthood. Better yet, Carlos had no obvious heir – although Philip had fathered more than thirty illegitimate children, neither of his two queens had been able to provide him with another son. Louis decided that the Spanish Netherlands (roughly equating to modern-day Belgium) would be fitting compensation for the unpaid dowry. The region had been the springboard for Spanish invasions during the fifteenth and sixteenth centuries, so its annexation would solve a long-standing strategic problem for France. Louis informed his mother-in-law, the Queen Regent of Spain, and negotiations began. They ended in 1667 when Louis ordered his army to attack.

Marshal Turenne, perhaps Louis's most able commander, led 50,000 French troops on campaign, accompanied by his king. Thirsting to be in at the kill, Louis travelled in characteristic style, accompanied by his queen and two of his mistresses. Turenne captured half-a-dozen towns before laying siege to the city of Lille. Vauban, the king's renowned siege expert, cracked the Spanish defences within a month. The keys of the city were presented to Louis in a ceremony that emphasised his role as all-conquering king.

Louis had expected support from the Dutch United Provinces, whose savage and protracted war of liberation from Spanish control had made them instinctive opponents of the Habsburgs. Only five years previously they had signed a treaty with France, guaranteeing mutual armed assistance in attack or defence for the next twenty-five years. However, the Dutch had since realised that Spanish power was fading. Their international trading network reported Spanish ships rotting at anchor, while the garrisons were unpaid, under-equipped and sometimes only partially clothed. The Dutch had signed the treaty with France without realising the intensity of Louis's ambitions. Now, many men of influence in the United Provinces pointed to the unprecedented increase in the size of the French army. Instead of joining Louis in the invasion, the Dutch reneged on the treaty.

The United Provinces sought help from two fellow Protestant nations, England and Sweden. The union with the English was surprising, since the two nations had recently been at war – Dutch warships had stormed up the Thames to burn a British fleet at anchor. Nevertheless, this new confederacy, the 'Triple Alliance', informed Louis that it would take up arms against him unless he withdrew from the Spanish Netherlands forthwith.

Louis was outraged by this betrayal, but he had no choice but to cease hostilities. France emerged from the Peace of Aix-la-Chapelle in possession of a handful of towns and cities, including Tournai, Oudenarde and Lille. However, Louis was convinced that the perfidy of the Dutch had denied him the lordship of the whole of the Spanish Netherlands. He swore revenge.

Louis eschewed renewed armed conflict, instead plotting his vengeance through sinuous diplomacy. First, he exploited his ties with Charles II of England. The two kings were first cousins and Charles, albeit secretly, shared Louis's Catholic faith. Charles's sister Henrietta was married to Louis's brother, the Duke of Orléans, and she acted as the conduit between the two Courts, in negotiations that led to the secret Treaty of Dover in May 1670. England and France agreed 'their joint resolution to humble the pride of the States-General [the Dutch Parliament], and to destroy the power of a people which has ... shown ingratitude to those who have helped to create its republic.'[3] The alliance was cemented by massive bribery: Louis paid Charles a secret pension of £225,000 a year for the duration of the war. Charles's chief minister, the Earl of Sunderland, also pocketed vast sums. Louis insisted on a clause that committed Charles to re-establishing Catholicism in Britain – promising further payments and the provision of 6,000 French troops if it met with resistance. Charles II took the money, but shrank from challenging the staunch Protestantism of his people.

Sweden proved equally receptive to French gold. For years the Protestant champion of Europe, the Swedes were beginning to place territorial ambition over religious solidarity. Already in control of Finland, Estonia, Livonia and West Pomerania, Swedish ambitions now extended to Denmark and Poland. The Dutch could fend for themselves.

Having torn the wings off the triple alliance, Louis entrusted his most seasoned and dynamic marshals with the avenging invasion. In 1672 Turenne and Condé marched through the Bishopric of Liège with 120,000 troops, before advancing along the Rhine on separate banks. Facing just 25,000 Dutch soldiers, the French swarmed over the southern areas of the United Provinces. Louis ordered a war of dark aggression: 'Go, my children,' Marshal Luxembourg exhorted his men, 'plunder, murder, destroy – and if it be possible to commit yet greater cruelties, be not negligent therein. Let me see that I am not deceived in my choice of the flower of the King's troops.'[4]

The Dutch took desperate measures. In coastal Holland the dykes' sluice gates were opened, flooding the low-lying land to form the defensive Water Line. With their fields and roads submerged, the peasants retreated out of reach of the invader, behind fortified town walls. This held the French back through the autumn, but in late December winter frosts turned the expanses of water into walkways of ice. Marshal Luxembourg issued skates to his foot soldiers, so they could speed across the frozen flats. French soldiers raped the women of Bodegraven and Zwammerdam before herding them into their homes with their families. They then set the buildings alight, razing both towns to the ground, and burning alive many of their inhabitants. Louvois, the leading French military administrator of the age, recorded with relish his part in such an atrocity: 'We lit the town and grilled all the Hollanders in it.'[5]

Louis's policy of deliberate terror won him Leiden, whose citizens forced their mayor to greet the invaders outside the walls, bearing the city's keys in cowed surrender. But the atrocities were ultimately counterproductive, inspiring lasting hatred of France. Saint Simon recognised French savagery to be counter-productive, since it 'caused such fear to all Europe that France never recovered from it.'[6] The de Witt brothers, key Dutch apologists of Louis's before the war, had refused to heed warnings that invasion was imminent. They were seized by the mob, shot, and then torn into pieces: their ripped-out hearts were placed on public display. In the de Witts' place emerged William of Orange, the leading member of what had been the Dutch ruling family before the advent of the republic.

By blood a prince, William was now created *Stadholder*, the generalissimo of the republic's forces. In their desperation the States-General were prepared to proclaim this living vestige of their nation's royal past Captain- and Admiral-General for life; this despite William's being, in Voltaire's estimation, merely 'a young Prince in poor health, who had seen neither siege nor combat'.[7]

William was aware of his shortcomings. To compensate for his military inexperience, he appointed the redoubtable Count von Waldeck as his second-in-command. The contrast of the charismatic, if sickly, young prince and the ill-humoured, but able, Prussian general gave the Dutch focus and hope. Waldeck inspired the troops, while William's diplomatic skills brought allies to the aid of his people. Spain and the Holy Roman Empire joined the fight against France, forcing Louis to quit the United Provinces. After 1673 the Dutch War was mainly fought in the Spanish Netherlands.

The strong Dutch navy, under the brilliant admirals van Tromp and de Ruyter, stopped the English and French from landing invasion forces. By now William was being hailed as the 'Redeemer of the Fatherland': a young and dogged Protestant champion had emerged, who would stand against Louis for the remainder of the century.

William's life's work was a resolute refusal to bow to Louis's military strength. It is a tale of brave resistance that takes us from the ravaged Lowlands of the 1670s to the brink of the war that produced the Battle of Blenheim. The influence of William – as Holland's prince, England's king, and France's enemy – is a backdrop to our tale.

WILLIAM'S HATRED OF LOUIS PREDATED the rape of the United Provinces. His family inheritance included small, autonomous Orange,

'which country and principality', John Evelyn noted, 'had no dependence on France these 500 years,'[8] despite being surrounded by French
territory. To Louis, Orange's independence was an accident that needed
correction. The principality's Protestantism was a further affront to
Louis's Catholic zeal. In 1660, Louis overran Orange, and made a
triumphal entrance to establish his lordship of the new acquisition. His
progress concluded at Orange's fortifications, which he climbed.
Reaching the top, he pulled a fragment of stone from the battlements,
and tossed it over the walls to the ground below. The king's retinue
were quick to interpret this gesture, demolishing the fortress soon afterwards. Louis sent word to the ten-year-old William that he would
oversee Orange as its protector, until the boy attained his majority. In the
meantime, Louis explained, France would enjoy the principality's
revenues. William never forgave the confiscation of his patrimony.

The Dutch War ended in victory for Louis, recognised in a series of
treaties from 1678–80. The Dutch had assembled a potent coalition to
oppose him, but the combined forces of the United Provinces, Spain,
the Holy Roman Empire and several German states failed to defeat
France. Franche-Comté and a dozen key cities were ceded to France,
shortly followed by Alsace and Lorraine. In France, Louis was referred to
as *Louis le Grand*, a sobriquet that he wholeheartedly embraced.

To cover his territorial ambitions with a veneer of legality, Louis
established offices, *Chambres de Réunion*. There his lawyers sifted through
ancient treaties and agreements, in search of long-forgotten clauses
which might justify French territorial claims abroad. The 1680s saw the
relentless combination of Louis, his court lawyers and his soldiers continue
to identify and then seize cities and lands to which often only tenuous pretensions could be made. In 1681 the *Chambres de Réunion* identified
Louis's claim to the county of Chiny, in Spanish-owned Luxembourg.
Three years of strong resistance followed, leading to the brief but bloody
War of the Reunions. In 1684, however, blockaded Luxembourg was
plucked from Spain, to become a French possession. Weeks later, Strasbourg was similarly added to France's dominions. The same year, Louis
ordered the bombardment of Genoa without declaration of war, because

of the city's pro-Habsburg leanings. No longer was Louis's pretext simply to add francophone areas to his French dominions: German and Italian lands were also in his sights.

Louis emerged from the concluding Treaty of Ratisbon with his two major acquisitions, Strasbourg and Luxembourg, intact. Austria and Spain were obliged to recognise France's new frontiers for twenty years. From The Hague, William of Orange watched Louis's apparently unstoppable advance with despair: 'If God does not take upon himself the protection of this poor people and her neighbours, in a short time all will be over.' [9] Evelyn, in England, agreed, recognising that Louis was within reach of establishing a 'Fifth Universal Monarchy'. [10]

IN THE AUTUMN OF 1685, LOUIS developed an agonising and persistent toothache, and his doctors decided to extract the offending molar. However, they were ignorant of the importance of post-operative hygiene, and infection set in: the king's gums, jawbone and sinuses became dangerously inflamed. A committee of nervous physicians concluded that drastic measures were called for. Louis underwent a truly terrible ordeal: they removed all the teeth from the top layer of his mouth, then punctured his palate and broke his jaw. This was all completed without anaesthetic, the king being fully awake throughout the procedure. The most powerful man in Western Europe was helpless before the primitive medical knowledge of his time. At least the wounds were kept clean on this occasion – cauterised with red-hot coals.

The Sun King never fully regained his former dignity. He had to be careful when drinking, in case the contents of his goblet reappeared out of his nose. The English poet Matthew Prior was later to observe that: 'The monarch as to his health is lusty enough, his upper teeth are out ... and he picks and shows his under teeth [with] a good deal of affectation, being the vainest creature alive even as to the least things.' [11] Similar mismanagement of another chronic irritant led to more than mere embarrassment at the dinner table.

To Louis, the continued tolerance of France's Huguenots was a betrayal of his deepest beliefs, and triggered his most heart-felt prejudices. The nation's one million Protestants had been left relatively untroubled since the bloody religious and civil wars that preceded Louis's personal rule. This was a pragmatic recognition of the material benefits that the Huguenots brought to the economy. They were conspicuously prominent in specialist areas of trade, commerce, and manufacture. Their rights to freedom of worship had been enshrined in the Edict of Nantes.

Now, with some of his key advisers encouraging a policy of intolerance, Louis resolved to rid the country of what he viewed as heresy. Louis's bigotry, instilled during his scanty childhood education, was stoked by his mistress, Madame de Maintenon, herself a convert to Catholicism. She argued that the acceptance of divergent Christian views was untenable, and would stain her lover's soul.

Louis had given vent to his religious prejudices in 1679, withdrawing some of the Protestants' rights to worship. In 1680 he sent a regiment of dragoons to Poitou, ordering its soldiers to be billeted on the richer households. The expense of this was dire; but it was nothing compared with the deprivations meted out to the poorer Protestants in the region. They were raped and brutalised, whilst encouraged to end their torment by embracing Catholicism. Thirty thousand Poitevin conversions were recorded, convincing the king of his policy's effectiveness. The *dragonnades* became a valued weapon against the Huguenots.

In the autumn of 1685, the season of his gruesome encounter with his dentists, Louis revoked the Edict of Nantes. Protestant worship was deemed a criminal activity, with imprisonment – even death – the penalty for those who refused to turn to Catholicism. Unless they were protected by noble status, women who rejected the *religion du roi* were whipped, and their faces branded with the *fleur de lis*. Men were broken at the wheel: each bone in their body systematically smashed by the executioner. To ensure that there could be no escape, Louis declared it illegal to seek sanctuary from his religious tyranny abroad.

Despite this, over 200,000 Huguenots fled France, many leaving behind all their possessions rather than slow their flight. The fugitives were enthusiastically welcomed in the United Provinces, Denmark, and Prussia. Many came to England, too, although there they were tolerated rather than fêted. Nevertheless, the English listened to the refugees' tales of horror with deep concern. John Evelyn recorded with disgust: 'The French persecution ... raging with the utmost barbarity, exceeded even what the very heathens us'd ... on a sudden demolishing all their churches, banishing, imprisoning and sending to the galleys all the ministers; plundering the common people ... taking away their children; forcing people to the Mass, and then executing them as relapsers ...'.[12] Throughout Protestant Europe, such tales were received with horror. Since Louis was clearly intent on expanding France's frontiers, many wondered if they would be next to experience such brutality.

In 1686, the United Provinces joined Spain and Prussia to form the League of Augsburg: a defensive alliance against Louis. He remained deaf to the fear and exasperation evoked by the rasping tone of his kingship, thrusting himself into the affairs of Cologne, where the incumbent ruler, Archbishop-Elector von Wittelsbach, was seriously ill. Louis wanted to be certain that his successor would be a friend to France, as von Wittelsbach had been: for Cologne, situated between France, several Germanic states, and the United Provinces, controlled bridgeheads across the area's major rivers. The king informed Cologne that he had chosen its new archbishop-elector, who would take office when the current incumbent died. Louis's choice was Cardinal von Fürstenberg, the Bishop of Strasbourg, who had cravenly served France's interests for thirty years. However, Pope Innocent ignored Louis, installing Joseph Clement, brother to the Elector of Bavaria, instead.

Louis ordered his troops to invade, and they laid siege to Philippsburg. Hostilities quickly escalated: the French ravaged the Rhineland, provoking the Prussians, Saxons and Hanoverians into action. The Emperor sent a strong force under the Elector of Bavaria to assist them. War was inevitable, Louis knew that; but its form and scale was to surprise all of Europe.

Louis asserted rights over the Palatine from Strasbourg through to Mainz, in the name of his sister-in-law, Liselotte. Once more he anticipated speedy victory. The invading troops surpassed the litany of war crimes associated with the Dutch War of the 1670s, when Turenne had pillaged the electorate. In 1688, the Second Devastation of the Palatinate saw the destruction of a dozen historic cities, including Heidelberg, Worms, Mannheim and Speyer. Hundreds of towns and villages shared treatment of unspeakable savagery: murder, rape, torture and looting.

The French atrocities recalled the worst excesses of the Thirty Years' War: and this in the so-called Age of Reason. Louis XIV's state-sanctioned terror ran contrary to every tenet of 'civilised' warfare. Across Europe it was generally accepted that civilian losses should be kept to a minimum and that private property should be respected.

WILLIAM OF ORANGE NOW SAW that it was not just his Dutchmen who looked to him for leadership, but also the majority of German princes. Emperor Leopold found common cause with the confederacy, bolstering the standing of the League of Augsburg by joining its ranks. He was uncomfortable about helping Protestant forces against a divinely anointed king, but political considerations overrode religious sensibilities. Besides, Leopold was comforted by the Pope's encouragement: Innocent was furious that Louis had dismissed the papal claim to infallibility, and denied the Pontiff's right to excommunicate princes. He, too, joined the anti-French coalition. So it was that by the end of 1688 only one power stood aloof from the forthcoming European war: England.

CHAPTER TWO

AN ISLAND NO MORE

'Yes, mighty Prince, our fear and danger's fled,
Error and ignorance by thee struck dead,
No more th'old chaos o'er our world shall spread.
Thy words bid there be light, and strait a ray,
All heavenly bright, calls forth a new-born day.'

'A CONGRATULATORY POEM TO HIS HIGHNESS THE PRINCE
OF ORANGE ON HIS ARRIVAL AT LONDON', 1688

ENGLAND'S LACK OF MILITARY pretensions in the quarter century following the Restoration was marked. Charles II was a hedonist, not a soldier. His energies were most happily deployed in his pleasures, such as race horses and mistresses – he kept a generous stable of both. Since 1660 British politics had been dominated by domestic considerations. The Civil Wars might be over, but instead of military campaigns, Court, Country, and Parliament engaged in political conflict. In Churchill's phrase, 'there had been *sides* in the Great Rebellion; henceforward there would be *parties*, less picturesque but no less fierce.'[1] Whigs and Tories would trace their family trees back to Charles's reign: factions that could still clash with lethal force well into the eighteenth century.

By European standards, Charles maintained a tiny army; little more than 5,000 strong in 1661. Ten years later it still only numbered 8,000, but supporting this force consumed a quarter of the king's revenue, a key reason he took the secret bribe from Louis. English attitudes to the army were coloured by the discord and destruction of the Civil War, and by the hated military government of Cromwell's major-generals in the 1650s. People and Parliament were united in their opposition to a standing army that they feared was as likely to be turned on them as on the country's enemies.

Charles died in 1685 and the throne passed to his controversial younger brother James, Duke of York. James II faced a rebellion within months, when his illegitimate nephew, the Duke of Monmouth, landed at Lyme Regis but failed to garner sufficient support before he was brought to battle at Sedgemoor. He was beheaded and his followers summarily dealt with at the 'Bloody Assizes'.

James's shrill Catholicism soon cost him popularity, since, in stark contrast to Charles's covert faith, it was construed as a blatant threat to the Anglican Church. The Whigs had shown their intense distrust of James – and their political clout – by forcing Charles to send him into exile. His enforced spells in Scotland and on the Continent had not mellowed James: if anything they stiffened his resolve. Early in the new reign, James tired of hiding his strong beliefs.

At the end of 1686, Lord Chesterfield summed up the sadness of a people who could see its king's qualities, but regret their misapplication: 'Though we have now a Prince, whose study is his country's glory, whose courage would give him lustre without a throne, whose assiduity in business makes him his own chief minister, yet heaven, it seems, hath found a way to make all this more terrible than lovely.'[2]

The English knew James's talents included a gift for military leadership: as Duke of York, he had overseen the overhaul of the Navy and gained it parity with the Dutch fleet. On a personal level, he was also respected as a brave and accomplished fighter. When James began to expand the army, the suspicion spread that he was preparing to impose his own religious faith on England by force of arms. It was unfortunate for James that his efforts coincided with Louis's revocation of the Edict of Nantes. The terrifying events unfolding across the Channel stoked fears that James planned to establish a similar absolutist and Catholic monarchy in England. By 1688, James had trebled the size of the army he had inherited to 25,000 men, its ranks swelled by Scottish and Irish soldiers and – most worryingly – by Catholic officers. Was this the precursor to England's own *dragonnades*?

One more, diminutive, reinforcement to James's forces tipped the scale. In 1688 his second, Catholic, queen, Mary of Modena, gave birth to a son. To the Protestants, the baby's gender caused consternation: he supplanted the two Protestant princesses by James's first marriage, in the line of succession. The king's opponents in England looked to the husband of James's eldest daughter, Princess Mary, to intervene. He was William of Orange.

Although he was a foreign prince, whose navy was England's great rival, William was the obvious candidate to save England from James and his Catholicism. The Dutchman's links to the English throne were manifold. His mother was a Stuart princess, sister to Charles II and James II. As a boy William had been a great favourite with his uncles, during their exile from Commonwealth England. In 1677, William married his first cousin, Princess Mary. Charles II approved the match, which was an acknowledgement of improved English relations with the United Provinces since the conclusion of the Dutch War. Louis XIV was furious. 'You have given your daughter to my mortal enemy,'[3] he fumed, in a letter to the Duke of York. Louis had correctly guessed that William's motives for the match were tactical, rather than sentimental. The Prince of Orange was marrying the heir apparent to the Stuart crown because England's wealth would be welcome in his European wars. Furthermore, Louis could not hope to equal the combined Dutch and English fleets.

William was not a risk-taker, but a man of unyielding practicality. He only agreed to seek the English crown after much thought. If he allowed James's infant prince to take his wife's place in the succession, the United Provinces would be denied the support of England's ships and coffers in the forthcoming war with France. Despite his status as a Protestant saviour, William would not invade in order to save England from a potential Catholic tyrant. His intention was to harness the country's capabilities against the Papist autocrat who had long possessed the throne of France. Before committing himself, William took soundings from trusted Dutch aides, who were encouraging about his prospects. He also received a letter inviting his immediate intervention, which had been signed by seven English magnates. Comfortingly, they represented the Anglican Church and the two dominant parliamentary factions, the Whigs and the Tories.

William invaded England in November 1688, while Louis's forces were terrorising the upper Rhine. His polyglot army, which included Dutchmen, Swedes, Prussians, Danes, and French Huguenots, landed to negligible opposition. Senior political and military figures scrambled to join William; even Princess Anne slipped away from London in the night, deserting her Catholic father in favour of her Calvinist brother-in-law. It was an unexpectedly smooth end to James's reign, and the English congratulated themselves on their 'Glorious Revolution'.

Louis was surprised and disappointed by the success of William's gamble. When the possibility of an invasion had first been mooted, earlier in the year, Louis had volunteered to come to James's aid. He had offered money, 30,000 soldiers, and the French Channel fleet. In return for Louis's support, James had to agree to align his nation with France in the pending European war. However, James would not consent to this, so the disgruntled Louis left him to fend for himself.

The view at Versailles had been that the invasion of England would bring nothing but ill to the Prince of Orange. It seemed inevitable that William's army would be embroiled in another English Civil War. The French had failed to foresee a successful invasion without battle on sea or land. Neither had James's speedy flight to the Continent been predicted: his many royal supporters dared not act when their leader had already deserted them.

William never felt enamoured of his new kingdom, nor did he trust many of those who had aided the toppling of his predecessor. Although he was the prime beneficiary of this treachery, he realised that it could be repeated to his cost. During his reign he remained focused on the war with Louis: England's involvement could add a new and promising element to the hotch potch of anti-French nations that he had brought together. Little did he realise that these first faltering steps, made under his gaze, were to take his island kingdom away from isolation, towards Empire.

CHAPTER THREE

JOHN CHURCHILL

*'No one in this world could possibly have done better
than Mr Churchill has done and M. de Turenne is very
well pleased with all our nation.'*

LETTER OF LORD DURAS (LATER THE EARL OF FEVERSHAM)
TO THE ENGLISH GOVERNMENT, 1674

THE FRENCH ENJOYED BELITTLING William of Orange's generalship. They knew that his personal courage on the field of battle, whilst admirable, had rarely brought him victory. A contemporary joke in Paris suggests widespread disdain for a hapless foe: 'The Prince of Orange can at least boast', it was said, 'that no general of his age had raised so many sieges and lost so many battles.'[1] William was bitterly aware of his limitations, blaming them on his lack of training at the side of the great generals of his youth. 'I would', he said wistfully, 'willingly give part of my provinces to have served some campaigns under the Prince of Condé.'[2]

At the outbreak of war in 1689, William turned to an apprentice of Turenne – Condé's brother-in-arms – to make something of his English troops. His name was John Churchill, and he had recently been promoted to lieutenant-general.

John was the son of Sir Winston Churchill, a Royalist cavalry officer during the Civil War. Sir Winston had suffered financially for having supported the king: the Churchill family endured confiscation and impoverishment during Cromwell's Commonwealth. After the restoration of the Stuarts, however, Sir Winston retrieved some status, even if money continued to elude him. He became a Tory Member of Parliament, and a junior courtier. These posts left him time to write a sycophantic history of the kings of England, further testimony to his pronounced loyalty to the Crown.

Eight of John's eleven siblings died young. His two surviving brothers followed him into the armed services, with success: George Churchill became an admiral, and younger brother Charles a general. The only surviving sister, Arabella, was also to enjoy prominence in adulthood.

In common with other daughters of impoverished Royalists, Arabella Churchill was despatched to the Restoration Court to become a teenaged maid of honour. Her mistress was the former Anne Hyde, a commoner who had caught the eye of James, Duke of York, whilst in-waiting to his sister Mary, the mother of William of Orange. To the chagrin of James's family, the couple married. The new duchess quickly discovered that her duties included a tacit acceptance of her husband's roving eye. The duke's particular penchant was for her own female retinue, from which he drew fresh conquests at will.

Sir Peter Lely's luscious portraits tell us that Charles II liked ravishing mistresses, with generous bosom and ringletted hair. James's tastes were altogether less obvious, veering towards the plain. Bemused by his brother's series of dowdy lovers, Charles concluded that they must be a penance inflicted on James by Catholic confessors. 'My brother will lose his kingdom by his bigotry, and his soul for a lot of ugly trollops,' [3] was the king's opinion; and we know that he was right on one count, at least.

Arabella Churchill captivated the Duke of York. Their romance started when she fell from her horse in a royal riding party. As she struggled amidst her petticoats, attempting to regain her dignity, James noticed her unexpectedly fine legs. The duke, who had already shown mild interest in Arabella, was now full of lustful resolve, and it was not long before Miss Churchill became his mistress. This was 'not one of his numerous casual affairs; it was the chief affair of his life, lasting ten or twelve years.' [4] During this time Arabella bore James four illegitimate offspring. One was given the title of Duke of Berwick and was a great favourite of James's: the king later contemplated installing his natural son as the Catholic ruler of Ireland. When James lost his English throne, Berwick joined him in exile. After his father's death Berwick became one of the more successful of Louis's later marshals, thus confirming the Churchills' genetic gift for the military.

Of more immediate benefit to Arabella's family was the favour that now fell on her younger brother. After studying at St Paul's, in London, John became a page of honour to the Duke of York. Hostile historians have criticised John for benefiting from his sister's courtesan status. However, impoverished gentry during the Stuart Age had few scruples about the method of their advancement.

Having become a trusted servant, young Churchill took advantage of his master's favour to progress from Court life to soldiery. One day, when watching a parade of troops in London, James asked his page what he would most like in the world. 'A pair of colours' was the immediate reply, his words a euphemism for an ensign's commission. James approved of this ambition and in 1667 the seventeen-year-old Ensign Churchill was gazetted to the King's Regiment of Foot Guards.

In 1668, Churchill served in the Governor's Regiment in Tangier, where Moors were the enemy. This outpost had come to Britain as part of Catharine of Braganza's dowry when she married Charles II. Although the garrison cost over £100,000 per year to maintain, the king valued Tangier highly. It was certainly a useful training ground for Charles's soldiers, toughening them up and introducing them to new methods of warfare: in 1663, the Tangier Regiment was the first English unit to employ the bayonet.

Returning to London in 1671, John embarked on an affair with his cousin, Barbara Castlemaine. Almost a decade John's senior, she was one of King Charles's more promiscuous mistresses. Her passion for Churchill was intense and the king, in a surprise visit, caught the pair in a tryst. Heading a court heaving with licentious behaviour, it is strange to think of Charles as a sentimental man. However, he was reportedly hurt by Barbara's infidelity, for he had genuine feelings for the mother of five of his illegitimate tribe. The king showed magnanimity, though, dismissing the young gallant with an avuncular chiding: 'Go. You are a rascal, but I forgive you because you do it to get your bread.' [5]

Charles's comment showed an awareness of Churchill's precarious financial position. Perhaps a consequence of relative childhood poverty, Churchill displayed an unattractive relationship with money throughout his life. It later brought him ridicule and contempt, for the rich and powerful were expected to display their wealth magnanimously. Avarice was a character flaw that John Churchill never defeated, although with his famed meanness came astute management of his personal finances. This was an important skill for the ambitious young man: without it, the prospects for future advancement were limited, for Court positions and army ranks were bought and sold as commodities. When the infatuated Barbara Castlemaine gave her young lover the astonishing gift of £5,000 – enough, at the time, to have bought a colonelcy in the Foot Guards – most of it was squirreled away to become the foundation of Churchill's later extraordinary wealth and position.

A return from Court life to soldiery brought Churchill action and advancement in the early 1670s. It was soon clear that this was an officer of the highest potential. When life was breathed into Charles II's secret Treaty of Dover, in 1672, the English joined Louis against the Dutch. The Duke of York kept his protégé close to him, on board his flagship, the *Royal Prince*. The vessel was involved in the bloody Battle of Sole Bay, which was fought off the Suffolk town of Southwold within sight of a huge crowd. Churchill's conduct has not been recorded, yet it was conspicuous enough to merit a rare double-promotion, to the rank of captain.

Churchill was transferred at the end of the year to fight on land for France. Serving as a volunteer under the Duke of Monmouth, Churchill distinguished himself at the siege of Maastricht. Several notable men were present during this action, including Count d'Artagnan, the musketeer later immortalised by Alexandre Dumas; while Claude-Louis-Hector Villars, Churchill's most able military opponent in later life, fought alongside him here. Louis XIV, a proponent of siege warfare, was in the trenches as John joined in three French charges against the

Dutch defences, the last of which was successful. Churchill is credited with raising the French standard on the captured parapet, as well as with saving Monmouth's life while countering a daring but doomed Dutch counter-attack.

The taking of Maastricht was a bloody affair, the garrison of 6,000 inflicting heavy casualties on a French force that outnumbered it by eight to one. D'Artagnan was one of many attacking officers slain, shot through the head at the age of fifty-three. Churchill was among the numerous wounded. However, the capture of this fortress on the River Meuse was a significant French success, whose English participants shared the military glory. It seeems ironic in retrospect that the king singled out Churchill for congratulations, allegedly thanking him at the head of Monmouth's small force for his bravery in the cause of France. Louis wrote to Charles II recommending that he promote his brave and able captain. It was an act of patronage that Louis was later to regret.

CHURCHILL'S NEXT POSTING WAS with Marshal Turenne. In an age that favoured the gentle pace and structured format of siege warfare over the uncertainty and expense of pitched battle, Turenne was unorthodox. His bold dictum was: 'Make few sieges and fight plenty of battles; when you are master of the countryside the villages will give us the town.' [6] It is a small step from this maxim to Churchill's philosophy when a commander: winning a battle, the Englishman stated, was 'of far greater advantage to the common cause than the taking of twenty towns.' [7]

Turenne also showed Marlborough the importance of using infantry firepower to maximum effect. This ran counter to the accepted bias that engagements were won or lost by the cavalry. The matchlock muskets of Turenne's era were desperately slow and unreliable, taking more than a minute to reload and frequently misfiring. They had a range of 100 yards, but were inaccurate even at that distance: they had no sights to assist their aim and were often discharged not from the shoulder, but from the chest. However, the marshal was confident that, if used efficiently, they offered the commander the edge over chaotic infantry blocs: intermingling of pike-men and musketeers need not ape the clumsy deployments of the Middle Ages. Indeed, the trend towards larger armies in the second half of the seventeenth century resulted in the recruitment of far more foot soldiers than cavalry. This was essentially because of the cavalry's greater expense. When Turenne was first a general, his army was one-third infantry to two-thirds cavalry; but by 1675, when he died, the ratio was three to one in favour of the foot soldier. The marshal's ability to accept this development and adapt his tactics accordingly, made a lasting impression on his English apprentice.

Turenne's military talents reached their zenith in 1674, when he was in his mid-sixties. 'In that year's campaign Turenne displayed his powers both in tactics and in strategy at their highest and to have served such a campaign under him was for Churchill a great good fortune.' [8] Churchill continued in Louis's service, even though his country had agreed peace with the Dutch early in the year. The opportunities for advancement and action, neither of which Churchill ever knowingly shirked, were obvious. Aged only twenty-four, Churchill was placed in charge of a battalion of Turenne's infantry.

There were three major battles during the campaign. It remains unclear whether Churchill fought at the first, Sinzheim, where Turenne's flair and resolve upset a larger Imperial army: the marshal's deft blending of foot soldiers, dragoons and cavalry reminded Europe of the great Swedish warrior Gustavus Adolphus at his peak. English infantrymen helped to hold Turenne's flanks as the French cavalry advanced to engage Count Caprara's Imperialist force. Intense fighting led to 2,000 deaths on each side, but France claimed victory when the enemy retreated.

We know that Churchill took part in the Battle of Enzheim, near Strasbourg. Turenne, his lines of communication already vulnerable, was forced to attack a superior enemy expecting reinforcements. His unorthodox tactics included an early morning advance over a river that the Imperialists had adjudged a secure defensive barrier. There was a massive exchange of artillery fire and Turenne sustained significant casualties in attaining his goal. Half of the officers in Churchill's battalion were killed or wounded at Enzheim. Turenne praised the officer he liked to call his 'handsome Englishman' in his report to Louis.

He admired the young man's style, courage and readiness to learn.

Churchill's experiences at Enzheim proved to be of crucial importance. Thirty years afterwards, he was to attempt an aggressive river crossing under circumstances that mirrored those facing Turenne. Artillery would have a vital role in the action, and losses would have to be borne in an assault on a well-ensconced enemy. The similarities between Enzheim and Blenheim were significant. 'I durst not brag much of our victory', Churchill wrote in 1674, 'but we have three of their cannon, several of their colours and some prisoners.' [9] Even the reports of victory echoed one another. The main difference lay in the composition of forces: at Enzheim the French were his allies, while at Blenheim they would be the enemy.

It had been an extraordinary campaigning season for Turenne and he extended his good run, taking the Imperialists by surprise in their winter quarters and then defeating them at Turkheim, in January 1675. This campaign was a powerful finale by one of the great soldiers of the seventeenth century, played out in view of one who was to dominate the first decade of the eighteenth. Turenne died six months after Turkheim, felled by a cannon ball while reconnoitring an enemy gun emplacement. Churchill, having acquitted himself with distinction, returned to England an experienced, respected, young colonel, full of promise.

RESUMING HIS PLACE AT COURT, Churchill was made a Gentleman of the Bedchamber to the Duke of York. His fine looks attracted much attention in a milieu where the appeal of the physical often eclipsed the cerebral. What choice of bride would this increasingly influential man make? His father, so impoverished that he had asked John to return his share of the Churchill inheritance, encouraged a financially advantageous match. Katherine Sedley, an heiress cousin, and one of the Duke of York's plain mistresses, was Sir Winston's recommendation. For once, though, John overcame avarice and followed his heart.

Sarah Jenyns was the extremely pretty daughter of an impoverished Hertfordshire gentleman. She had followed her beautiful sister Frances to serve as an adornment at Court. The Jenynses were among many families who were prepared to despatch their daughters to the licentious world of the 'Merry Monarch', hoping that such a move might lead to an advantageous marriage which would pluck them from the ranks of the distressed gentry. Maybe their daughter would bring home to St Albans a wealthy, titled, son-in-law?

Sarah's role was lowly: when the Duke of York married Mary of Modena at the end of 1673, having lost his first wife Anne to breast cancer, Sarah became Maid of Honour to the new duchess. She must have met John Churchill soon afterwards, and she cannot have been immune to his charms. Contemporaries found Churchill extraordinarily good-looking. A Dutch contemporary, while commenting on a frightening ambition and a suspicious charm, recorded his admiration for the Englishman's physical attributes: 'He is about the middle height, and has the best figure in the world; his features are without fault, fine, sparkling eyes and good teeth. In short, apart from his legs, which are too thin, he is one of the handsomest men ever seen.' [10] It is easy to see why the teenaged Sarah found the dashing colonel, ten years her senior, intriguing.

Allied to his looks and potential was an easy manner, which was soon engaged in earnest courtship. Initially wary of the man who was so scandalously associated with Barbara Castlemaine, Sarah found she could not resist her suitor, whom she declared 'handsome as an angel'. John's emotions have largely remained impenetrable, despite the copious correspondence that has survived him. It is clear, though, that he found Sarah's uncompromising and forthright nature utterly bewitching. She was an auburn-haired beauty, yes; but beyond this the ambitious, calculating soldier was dazzled by the thrilling freeness of Sarah's spirit. The courtship was tempestuous, but the chemistry between John and Sarah eventually drew a line under the Churchill and Jenyns families' ambitions. They were quietly married in the winter of 1677–8, in the Duchess of York's apartments; a suitable venue for the solemnisation of a partnership that was to reach the zenith of its power through royal favour, before being dashed by the same capricious force.

The couple's relationship remained intense, in a marriage whose roles were clearly defined and rigidly adhered to: Sarah was passionate and wilful, often painfully so, while John was devoted and necessarily patient. He was afflicted with migraines throughout his life, many triggered by the stress of his wife's behaviour. In early 1679, Sarah wrongly accused John of having an affair while in Scotland, causing him severe headaches, and evincing from him fervent protest: 'I am not so unreasonable as to expect you should not be concerned if I were coquet, and made love to any other woman, but since I do not, and love only you above my own life, I can't but think you are unjust, and unkind, in having a suspicion of me.'[11] Churchill blamed Sarah's unfounded suspicions on his enforced absence from home. John's counter to this was to write openly of the depth of his feelings for his wife: 'Although I believe you love me, yet you do not love so well as I, so that you can not be truly sensible how much I desire to be with you. I swear to you the first night in which I was blessed in having you in my arms, was not more earnestly wish'd for by me, than now I do, to be again with you, for if ever man loved woman truly well I now do you, for I swear to you were we unmarried, I would beg you on my knees to be my wife, which I would not do, did I not esteem you, as well as love you.'[12]

The Churchills were diligent and loving parents, Sarah bearing seven children between 1679 and 1690, five of whom ('four daughters and a son, all like little angels'[13]) survived infancy. John wrote to his wife of the huge enjoyment he derived from fatherhood: 'You can not imagine how I am pleased with the children; for having nobody but their maid, they are so fond of me, that when I am at home, they will always be with me, kissing me and hugging me.' Such parental tenderness was a reflection of profound adoration of his wife: 'Miss [Henrietta, the eldest daughter] is pulling me by the arm, that she may write to her dear Mamma, so that I will say no more, only beg that you will love me always so well as I love you, and then we can not but be happy.'[14] His delight in family life was only accentuated by the demands of a career that was to take him overseas for increasingly extended periods.

In 1678 Churchill was entrusted with an apparently important piece of statecraft. He was sent on a diplomatic mission with his lifelong friend

Sidney Godolphin, a Cornishman whom he met while both were Pages of Honour to the Duke of York. They were instructed to sound out the Dutch and the Spanish about the possibility of combining forces with England against France. It came to nothing; indeed, it is doubtful whether Charles II intended any other outcome, given his links with Louis XIV. However, the choice of Churchill for this task confirms his growing importance at Court, which was mirrored in his military career. On his return to England he was given command of a new regiment of Foot. By the end of 1678 he was promoted to brigadier-general.

Churchill was by now among the group of courtiers favoured not only by the Duke of York, whose creature he was seen to be, but also by the king. He, Godolphin, and Feversham (a Huguenot nephew of Turenne's) made up the group which played 'much at tennis' with Charles II, the quartet being 'all so excellent players that if one beat the other 'tis alternately.' [15]

Religious and political tensions temporarily displaced the Churchills from their positions at Court, but not from royal friendship: after the Roman Catholic 'Popish Plot' against his life, Charles reluctantly bowed to Whig demands, and sent his brother James into exile. The Churchills loyally followed the ducal Court to Belgium and Scotland, their stead-fastness being rewarded with a Scottish peerage; in 1682 they were created Baron and Baroness Churchill of Aymouth. After the exile had been repealed, Lord and Lady Churchill returned to London to even greater royal favour. The Duke of York's second daughter, Anne, had nursed a schoolgirl crush on Sarah since childhood. The dowdy, plodding and neglected princess was entranced by Sarah's glamour, confidence, and beauty. G. M. Trevelyan poeticised the cruel contrast between the women: 'Anne's mind was slow as a lowland river, Sarah's swift as a mountain torrent.' [16] Anne married the stolid Prince George of Denmark, in 1683, after which she was allowed a modest, but independent, house-hold. Sarah was encouraged by her husband to apply for the post of the princess's Lady of the Bedchamber. Anne's Tory relatives on her maternal side resisted this, fearing the effect of Sarah's Whig sympathies on her mistress. Sarah told Anne how saddened she was by such a lack of trust, prompting an abject letter from the princess: 'Oh, dear Lady Churchill, let me beg you once more not to believe that I am in fault: do not let this take away your kindness from me, for I assure you 'tis the greatest trouble in the world to me, and I am sure you have not a faithfuller friend on earth that loves you better than I do. My eyes are full, I cannot say a word more.'[17] Such was the balance of power when Sarah was installed in Anne's affections, and her Court. These were positions of influence that Sarah was to exploit on her own and her husband's behalf for quarter of a century.

THE DEATH OF CHARLES II, in February 1685, brought John Churchill's patron to the English throne. The new king, James II, chose him to travel to France to tell Louis XIV formally of the succession. While on this mission, Churchill was instructed to negotiate a continuation of the secret 'pension' that Louis had paid Charles. If possible, an increase was to be secured.

Although the people had greeted his coronation with enthusiasm, this was an uncertain time for James. Monmouth's invasion came in the first summer of his reign. Churchill seized the moment and immediately moved against the man who had been his commanding officer at the siege of Maastricht. As soon as he heard that Monmouth had landed at Lyme (which was in his father's, Sir Winston's, parliamentary constituency), Churchill set out to head off the threat. With him went only a small column of foot and an inconsequential body of horse. However, Churchill's march echoed the approach of his mentor, Marshal Turenne, by relying on speed and decisiveness to surprise the enemy. He appreciated that the key to defeating Monmouth was to harry him. The renegade duke must not be allowed to settle, since he could then become a focal point to which the disaffected could rally. Churchill forged ahead with his cavalry, moving from London to Bridport in just two days, purloining horses, oxen and wagons along the way, his confiscations causing resentment but gaining him speed.

Monmouth's forward planning was thrown into confusion when, within a week of his arrival, Churchill appeared at his heels. The royal force lacked the manpower to attack, but Churchill reported to London that he would 'press the rebels as close as ever I can',[18] until reinforcements arrived. Otherwise, he told James, the West Country would be lost to Monmouth. He was further convinced of this by the conduct of militia drawn from the men of Devon and Somerset. Sent to tackle the invaders, they instead showed themselves sympathetic to their cause: many happily switched allegiance, proclaiming their support for 'King Monmouth'.

Churchill harried the rebels continuously with his professional troops, seeking to contain the invasive bacillus rather than allow the contagion to spread. Monmouth later conceded that he had not enjoyed a moment's peace between his arrival in England and his capture. It was Churchill's terrier force that did most to deprive him of composure or hope. Under constant pressure, the duke's campaign lost focus. Monmouth would have had more chance of success if he had ignored the attentions of Churchill's cavalry and pushed ahead. If he had captured Gloucester, for instance, he could have established a bridgehead over the River Severn. From there he could have struck out from the south-west, into the belly of England. However, wrong-footed by Churchill, and suspecting in any event that his venture was doomed, Monmouth's impetus stalled. He persuaded himself that stretching out for such a prize would leave him more vulnerable to his former colleague's needling attacks.

Its momentum lost, the invasion gradually turned in on itself. Monmouth drew back to the south, followed by Churchill's men, who had been joined by reinforcements. The royal cavalry pared away at the slow and the doubtful, till the duke was left with just the buffeted kernel of an increasingly despondent army. If he was to have a chance, Monmouth knew he must risk battle. By now significantly outnumbered, he elected to stake his success on that most uncertain of manoeuvres, a night attack.

The Earl of Feversham commanded the king's army as it camped at Sedgemoor. An unexceptional general, Feversham owed his position to his friendship with James. His involvement in the subsequent battle was secondary to Churchill's, who appears to have anticipated Monmouth's plan, and was immediately on site to lead a steely defence against the rebels. The duke's 4,000 men, some armed with nothing more than improvised agricultural implements, others toting guns but little ammunition, were brave and determined. However, the English standing army was disciplined, holding the initial attack before hurling it back on itself. Monmouth must have regretted his time as de facto captain-general of the English army a decade earlier: one of his legacies was a standardisation of the musket drill. The steadiness of James II's infantry fire, combined with Churchill's deft use of the artillery, destroyed the rebel cause that night at Sedgemoor. It was to be the last battle to be fought between Englishmen on English soil.

James II showed no mercy for the defeated. He sanctioned the execution of Monmouth, and several hundred of his followers. (Monmouth had a particularly grisly end, the executioner's axe striking seven times before his head was severed.) Churchill had hoped to garner real advancement from what was essentially his victory, but Feversham received the chief plaudits. However, Churchill was promoted to major-general. He also received the lasting respect of those who had served him at Sedgemoor and in the weeks leading up to the battle. The *London Gazette* reported that Churchill had 'performed his part with all the courage and gallantry imaginable'. He was now, in his late thirties, established as one of the foremost soldiers in England's tiny army.

This was why William of Orange turned to Churchill after his own invasion, three years later. William was reluctant to trust those who had deserted his father-in-law: the new king's reliance on Churchill at this time was a typically pragmatic gesture, based on an appreciation of his martial skill. His enthusiasm for the gifted general was tempered by a conviction that Churchill was a man of flimsy moral fibre. How else to explain his desertion from a monarch who had raised him from poverty to significant military and courtier status?

Lord Feversham, by contrast, proved loyal to James II to the end. After the king's flight, he disbanded the army rather than have it remain in good order, ready to serve the Dutch usurper. William needed someone to reconstitute his new kingdom's scattered regiments. He ordered Churchill not only to regroup, but also to reorganise, the soldiers. Although William had a low regard for English troops – preferring Dutch soldiers, Dutch officers, and Dutch generals – he wanted them as auxiliaries in the impending war in mainland Europe. Churchill was charged with improving the English army so that it could stand against the seasoned troops of France. To encourage Churchill, and to lend him the necessary authority to oversee such changes, he was confirmed in the rank of lieutenant-general. In April 1689, at the time of the coronation of William and Mary, his role in the Glorious Revolution was recognised with his elevation to an earldom.

One month later John Churchill, Earl of Marlborough, landed at Rotterdam with 8,000 men. His arrival on the Continent coincided with the declaration of war with France. His priority was to harmonise the training of the different English regiments and to coalesce with their principal allies. A letter from him while at Breda during this time shows him keen to find out which musket drill was to be adopted by his infantry: 'I desire that you will know the King's pleasure, whether he will have the Regiments of Foot learn the Dutch Exercise or else continue the English, for if he will I must have it translated into English.'[19] Marlborough wrote with urgency, shocked at the state of the troops he had found awaiting his command. He must forge them into a force that could compete with the French, the most feared enemy in Europe.

Many of the greatest improvements to the English army in the seventeenth and early eighteenth centuries date from this time, when William needed more and better troops, and Marlborough set about providing them. Marlborough would benefit from his hard work over the coming years; for, one day, these soldiers would be his to lead.

CHAPTER FOUR

FRANCE FEELS
THE STRAIN

'War, the mortality of 1693, the constant quarterings and movements of soldiery, military service, the heavy dues and the withdrawal of the Huguenots have ruined the country.'

REPORT OF THE SUPERINTENDENT OF ROUEN, 1697

THE CONFLICT THAT ENVELOPED much of Europe in the closing decade of the seventeenth century was a new trial for France. Despite her manpower, her wealth, and the galvanising capabilities of her autocratic government, by immersing herself yet again in warfare, an already stretched France was now riven with fresh and undeniable tensions. It was a watershed in Louis's reign: before the War of the League of Augsburg French victory had been expected; from this point on, the possibility of defeat became increasingly pronounced.

The breadth and strength of the forces arrayed against Louis were daunting. The war saw France confronted by a union of her two historic rivals, Spain and the Holy Roman Empire, together with the United Provinces and Britain. These four powers were aided by several predominantly Protestant states of Germany, as well as by powerful, Catholic, Bavaria. The menace of Louis's aggression had goaded these disparate interests into forming the Grand Alliance. This confederacy, if it could be held together, seemed to match – perhaps even to exceed – the might of France. It was testimony to Louis's success that he had conjured up a polyglot opponent that, for all its internal tensions, was potentially so strong. However, France was not to thank her king for provoking such a powerful antagonist.

Since 1643, and Condé's defeat of Spain at Rocroi, France had been the dominant military nation in Europe. With Louis's encouragement, his father's well-organised army had become an enormous force. Soon after the outbreak of the War of the League of Augsburg, Louis was able to call on a total of 420,000 troops; six times the size of the French army one hundred years earlier. By the end of the seventeenth century his command reached a peak of 450,000 soldiers; and a further 250,000 served in the local militia, in the navy, and in military support. This was the largest European army since the height of the Roman Empire, a millennium and a half earlier.

It was desperately difficult for a largely rural society with a rudimentary economy to sustain such a force. Even before the latest outbreak of hostilities, liberties had been taken with recruitment. Restrictions – of height, of capability, of background – were waived, as the rapacious military machine began to feed from hand to mouth. The diet was increasingly poor, for the newly enlisted could now be any males, provided they were 'neither vagabonds, nor children, nor deformed'.[1] Now, with the enemy so numerous and varied, the consumption of men and money escalated. The strain on the community and on the nation's coffers was unprecedented. Philippe Contamine, in his recent *Histoire Militaire de France*, has calculated that whereas 7 per cent of French government expenses in 1694 went to direct military costs, and 8 per cent to debt service, by 1697 the figures were 64 per cent and 23 per cent respectively. Louis had created a military state; but scrutiny of its long-term sustainability was overdue.

The growth of the French military can be linked directly to Louis's desire for territorial expansion and to his own appetite for glory. However, these were notional aims that could only be achieved if the army was reordered into an efficient and disciplined force. While England persevered with a Secretary-at-War who was essentially a senior bureaucrat, Louis demanded a more assertive role from his Minister of War. The minister must report directly to the king; but he had powers to drive through measures himself.

The king needed to find men of quality to realise his military dreams. Even as a young man he had been adept at spotting potential in his subordinates, and then delegating. Sir Edward Creasy, the nineteenth-century historian, noted: 'One of the surest proofs of the genius of Louis was his skill in finding out genius in others, and his promptness in calling it into action.'[2] In Michel Le Tellier and his son, François-Michel, Marquis de Louvois, Louis divined real talent. He relied on them with increasing confidence, which they repaid with dynamic and committed service. United by blood, they were also linked by their determination to root out the military abuses that were common to the age. In a tenure that, between them, lasted from 1643 to 1691, Le Tellier and Louvois transformed the soldiers of France. No longer would they tolerate a series of independent regiments, each with its own self-serving owner-commander. They demanded, instead, a unified royal army.

Louvois had encouraged the excesses of his troops in the Dutch War. He had also inflicted obscenities on his Huguenot compatriots during the *dragonnades*. In 1662, he was brought into the ministry to lend youthful vigour to his father's efforts. Eight years later he assumed the dominant role in the partnership; although Le Tellier had instigated reforms and most of the changes had been agreed upon by the time he retired in 1677. It was Louvois, 'haughty, brutal, coarse'[3], who rammed the programme through to its conclusion. Louis XIV benefited handsomely from the focus that Le Tellier and Louvois brought to their task. Unleashed, the two uncompromising agents of the Royal Will gradually amassed the powers needed for wholesale structural change of the military system.

The Controller-General of Finance found many of his military duties taken from him. The Ministry of War was now the body that would oversee the victualling and quartering of troops; the care of the sick and wounded; the building and running of defensive fortifications. This transfer of responsibilities seems as logical to us now as it was revolutionary then. Such a radical change was only achievable with the full support of an absolutist monarch, who could choose to ignore the protests of the losers in this power struggle. Louis backed his reformers with the full might of his autocracy.

A novel layer of control was introduced through intermediary inspectors, known as *intendants d'armée*, *commissaires de guerre*, and *contrôleurs des guerres*. The *intendants* had limited spheres of duty, sometimes only being appointed for a year, or given responsibility for a single regiment or region. However, within that time, or locality, their power was enormous: they supervised every aspect of the raising and payment of soldiers. They also provided medical facilities for the troops, and organised their fortifications. The *commissaires* helped to oversee recruitment and logistics, while the *contrôleurs* were bureaucrats who checked and logged the minutiae of army life: to them fell the task of verifying officers' claims for wages, so that non-existent soldiers did not swell the pay list. The first loyalty of *intendant*, *commissaire* and *contrôleur* was to the reforming ministry, and not to the military establishment. They were the conduits of the king's power as he set about standardising the French military system.

Le Tellier and Louvois sought control over the army through conformity. What better way of achieving this than establishing a model unit, a paragon of excellence for all to aspire to? In 1663, the *Régiment du Roi* was formed under Lieutenant-Colonel Jean Martinet, an officer whose surname has remained a byword for military pedantry. There had previously been a veneration of the long-established units. Now the insistence that a totally new body was the crack regiment of the army made it clear that the old and complacent days were over. In 1667, this message was driven home when Martinet was promoted to become inspector-general for the entire infantry.

With Martinet came the standardisation of military life. The comprehensive overhaul addressed everything from firearms and uniforms, to discipline and methods of military encampment. Instead of haphazard camps, tents were to be erected in carefully ordered rows, away from the health hazards of human waste. In place of the white sash that had been the distinguishing feature of French troops in battle, regimental uniforms were ordered. Out went the cheap ragbag of firearms ordered by cost-cutting colonels, and in came standardised muskets: these were interchangeable, all subject to the same drill, all taking the same ammunition. As a result of the demands of the Ministry of War, military manuals became hugely popular: Mallet's *Les Travaux de Mars*, first published in 1672, was required reading for officers keen to stay abreast of their new duties. It was reprinted many times; a sign that central control was recognised, even if there were difficulties in imposing it upon an army whose traditions were rooted in amateurism and corruption.

The French Ministers of War and their intermediaries were faced with problems familiar to their counterparts throughout Europe. Of these, one of the deepest-rooted was the granting of exaggerated military rank to men of high social standing, regardless of merit. Louvois wanted his professional troops led by the ablest, not merely the noblest, generals. Certainly, deference still had its place, in what was the king's army – Princes of the Blood would continue to outrank marshals in the field – but aristocrats and well-connected soldier-courtiers would have to prove their worth. Nearly five hundred officers were cashiered for incompetence between 1686 and 1693. Louvois's rebukes for those who failed to meet his standards were feared throughout the armed forces:

> 'Sir,' said Louvois one day to M. de Nogaret, 'your company is in a very bad state.'
> 'Sir,' answered Nogaret, 'I was not aware of it.'
> 'You have to be aware,' said M. de Louvois, 'have you inspected it?'
> 'No, sir,' said Nogaret.
> 'You ought to have inspected it, sir!'
> 'Sir, I will give orders about it.'
> 'You ought to have given them: a man ought to make up his mind, sir, either to openly profess himself a courtier or to devote himself to his duty when he is an officer.' [4]

No longer was it enough to buy a junior rank and then inexorably percolate upwards to high command. It was possible, from this point, to purchase up to a colonelcy, no further. A new officer hierarchy was created, based on earned seniority and merit rather than the accident of birth. In the wake of these reforms Vauban and Catinat, neither of patrician background, but both immensely talented, received marshal's batons. Lower down the scale, new ranks were introduced into the French army that were within reach of those of modest means. By 1667 it was possible to become a brigadier-general in the French army without the expense of first buying a colonelcy.

It was not just the professionalism of officers, but also the lot of the ordinary soldier that preoccupied Louis and his reforming ministers. The king felt bound by a two-way contract with his troops, writing: 'Just as the soldier owes obedience and submission to those who command him, the commander owes his troops care for their subsistence.'[5] Louvois concurred and made the provision of food and other essentials for the troops a prime concern. Using the superbly constructed fortresses of Marshal Vauban as magazines, he supplied the armies of the 1670s and 1680s with all their needs.

Each soldier of France was entitled to a daily ration of 24oz of bread, 1lb of meat and a pint of wine, beer or cider. In the field, *cintres* – easily assembled mobile ovens – were crucial parts of the baggage train. A French munitions expert at the end of the seventeenth century calculated that an army consuming 50,000 rations per day needed constant access to twenty *cintres*. The bread was transported from these to the soldiers in huge wagon-borne waterproof chests, each containing loaves for 800 men. The soldiers assembled to collect their ration every two to four days – more frequently in hot weather. The cavalry received their loaves first, at 8 a.m., then the dragoons two hours later, followed by the infantry at noon. It was a massive operation, day in, day out, to give the Leviathan its daily bread.

Louis and Louvois also combined to provide care for the wounded. Previously the view in the army had been, 'When a soldier is once down, he never gets up again'. In 1670, twenty years before London's

Chelsea Hospital and thirty-five years before the Prussians introduced the *Invalidenkasse* pension for wounded serviceman, France built its *Hôtel des Invalides*. Louis's words at the time show how he believed himself obliged to tend his nation's injured warriors: 'It were very reasonable that they who have freely exposed their lives and lavished their blood for the defence and maintenance of this monarchy, who have so materially contributed to the winning of the battles we have gained over our enemies and who have often reduced them to asking peace of us, should enjoy the repose they have secured for our subjects and should pass the remainder of their days in tranquillity.'[6] It was an example of enlightened kingship, from an autocrat whose ambitions depended on the fruits of war.

The expense of providing for the soldiers of a nation invariably at war grew, as France's military commitments multiplied. Until the end of the 1680s Louis's will, allied to Louvois's flair, ensured that this massive exercise of supply and provision succeeded. After Louvois died, in 1691, France had to face mounting problems without her ablest military administrator. This when the army's demands had already cut deep.

In 1693, for the first time in Louis's campaigns, the forward supplies for French troops were not in place at the start of the season. Tellingly, this allowed the Grand Alliance to take the field before the French. With his diligent servant dead, and the multi-fronted conflict demanding gargantuan levels of provision, Louis faced unprecedented problems. No longer was he able to supply troops at the front as smoothly as he had in earlier wars.

IT WAS THE SAME WITH THE ARMY'S manpower: an initial ability to cope with recruitment was followed by a stretching of resources and eventual crisis. Louis believed that upstanding men should fill his ranks, whenever possible, and forbad prisoners from being pressed into service because he wanted it to be an honour, not a punishment, to fight for him and his nation. Most recruitment took place in the bigger towns and cities, and their immediate surroundings. Before the War of the

League of Augsburg the majority of soldiers were from solid working-class and peasant stock.

During the glory days of Louis's reign, there was a glamour attached to service in the all-conquering army. There was also an opportunity for self-enrichment from bounty and from pillaging, both of which were sanctioned as the fruits of victory. Furthermore, in the beginning and middle of Louis's reign, registering for military service was not a long-term commitment. Demobilisation took place at the end of each war; and a discharge was attainable after four years' service, a right supposedly rendered inalienable by legislation in the mid-1660s. This could make a spell in the army an attractive alternative to the drudgery and poor pay of peasant farming or artisan apprenticeship.

The turning point came after 1685, when the revocation of the Edict of Nantes resulted in a haemorrhaging abroad of Huguenot soldiers, leaving a worrying void in the ranks. Louis's devastation of the Palatinate made widespread war ever more likely, so Louvois's concerns multiplied. How could he manage to inflate the army further, to meet the enemy confederacy that William of Orange was assembling? War in several areas – against the Dutch, the Spanish, the Imperialists, various German peoples, and now the English – demanded recruitment on an unprecedented scale. But, with traditional reserves of cannon fodder already empty, where could the extra troops be found?

Louvois met the problem with a typically far-reaching and bold plan. In 1688, he instigated a system of militia throughout France. Each parish was to provide, clothe and pay a fully equipped militiaman for two years' service. The resulting levy of 25,000 men was formed into thirty regiments, which were subject to full military discipline. Louvois initially intended to use these men to free regular soldiers from duties that were keeping them from the front line – garrisoning fortresses, guarding towns, and other time-consuming chores that semi-professionals could manage. However, the militiaman's duty broadened spectacularly as the War of the League of Augsburg sucked France dry.

We must look briefly at the chronology of the conflict, to see how the military machine envisaged by the Sun King quickly overstretched itself.

There was the customary litany of French military success in the early years, thanks largely to the brilliance of Luxembourg, the sole survivor from the trio of great marshals who had been the architects of victory through the years of conquest. The campaigns of 1691–3 were triumphant. France gained Mons, captured the supposedly impregnable Namur, marginally defeated William of Orange at Steenkirk, and won the slaughterous battle of Landen. However, Luxembourg died in the winter of 1694, and with him went an age of victory that was not to return during Louis's reign. 1695, as if to illustrate the turning of the tide, was remarkable for that most rare of military phenomena, a warrior triumph for William, when he recaptured Namur.

The results on the sea were more clear-cut, the damage done to France's navy hamstringing her war efforts for a generation. In 1692, a forty-four-strong French fleet was given a severe drubbing by ninety-nine ships of the Anglo-Dutch navy, off Cape La Hogue. For five days the allies continued their pummelling, sinking enemy warships before pursuing the defeated remnants into their harbours, where the destruction continued. Until this great battle Louis had fostered hopes both of invading England, and of dominating the oceans. After it, such aspirations were dashed. Winston S. Churchill called La Hogue 'the Trafalgar of the seventeenth century'[7]: it put the seal on British maritime supremacy over the French for a generation.

Louis was particularly aggrieved by the loss of his talismanic flagship, the 110-gun *Soleil Royal*, for which he had personally paid £200,000. With typically flamboyant arrogance, he had decorated the captain's cabin of his ship with a portrait depicting himself with 'several European Kings and princes in chains under his feet'.[8] After La Hogue it was clear that, if Louis was ever to achieve such a triumphant pose, it was not going to be through mastery of the sea.

From the 1690s onwards, France was unable to find the money to re-create a powerful fleet. Between 1695 and 1698, the Anglo-Dutch navy was boosted by sixty-six fresh ships of the line, whereas the French received just nineteen vessels of similar calibre. For the remainder of his reign, Louis's regular maritime forces were negligible. The efforts of

French privateers, especially those based in Dunkirk, provided a modicum of consolation during a period of relative impotence.

Even as the French navy lay in the doldrums, there was a diminishment in calibre of Louis's senior servicemen. Used to a bank of exceptional talent to call upon, in all spheres of public life, the king was now left with thinner pickings. This happened at a time when the habit of absolute power had begun to dull Louis's judgement and abilities. Guizot, a historian of France, recognised the passing of the great men, and the advent of lesser successors: 'Louis XIV had lost Condé and Turenne, Luxembourg, Colbert, Louvois and Seignelay; with the exception of Vauban, he had exhausted the first rank; Catinat alone remained in the second; the king was about to be reduced to the third: sad fruits of a long reign, of an incessant and devouring activity, which had speedily used up men and was beginning to tire out fortune; grievous result of mistakes long hidden by glory.'[9] His very longevity ensured that Louis experienced the downside of earlier years of acquisition and glory. He was to learn the dependence a ruler has on the quality of his lieutenants.

Courtiers at Versailles began to focus on the problems facing France, with critics attributing them to their monarch's unfettered powers. There was no authoritative representative body capable of putting their concerns to the king. As a result, more roundabout means were employed to bring grievances to the attention of the *Grande Monarque*. Fénelon chose to vent his fears via anonymous correspondence: 'The whole of France is no longer anything but one vast hospital,' he protested. 'The people who so loved you are beginning to lose affection, confidence and even respect; the allies prefer carrying on war with loss to concluding a peace which would not be observed. Whilst you in some fierce conflict are taking the battle-field and the cannon of the enemy, whilst you are storming strong places, you do not reflect that you are fighting on ground which is sinking beneath your feet, and that you are about to have a fall in spite of your victories.'[10] It was strong criticism and it was fair; but its message was ignored.

Increasingly, the king took on the responsibilities of government and generalship himself, with unhappy results. He charged men with positions that their fathers had held; a comforting tactic for a monarch keen to recapture past triumphs, but – apart from the shining examples of Le Tellier and Louvois – not successful. The appointment of the mediocre François Villeroi, a royal favourite and the son of Louis's childhood governor, to replace Marshal Luxembourg, was a downgrading of quality that delighted France's enemies. Equally, the transfer of the Ministry of War to a third generation of the Le Tellier family, in the hope that genetics would provide Louis with a further brilliant military organiser from the same stock, was doomed.

These promotions were indicative of Louis's conviction, in middle age, that a long reign had imbued him with a multitude of talents. This was a development ridiculed by the Duke of Saint Simon in his secret Versailles diary, who wrote of Louis: 'He wished to reign by himself … The superior ability of his early ministers and his early generals soon wearied him. He liked nobody in any way superior to him. Thus he chose his ministers, not for their knowledge, but for their ignorance; not for their capacity, but for their want of it. It was the same with his generals. He took credit to himself for instructing them; wished it to be thought that from the cabinet he commanded and directed all his armies. Naturally fond of trifles, he unceasingly occupied himself with the most petty details of his troops, his household, his mansions.' [11]

The king's talent in his prime had been in deciding on a course, and then finding others to pursue it on his behalf. From now on, he would attempt to be both principal and agent.

BY 1695, AFTER HALF-A-DOZEN years of hardship and famine, and with no obvious benefit from the struggle, France was crying out for peace. The *Te Deum* was sung often to mark yet another military victory, but the excited, united, joy of the triumphant years was missing. The demands of war were felt on the home front with increasing pain.

Regular troops of the French army, short of supplies and low on morale, were denied their right to retire from service. Still, there were not enough soldiers. A dreaded drawing of lots after Sunday church helped fill the ranks of the militia, which was rapidly becoming indistinguishable from the main army. Young men of the parish were prepared to avoid the draft through self-mutilation, or by fleeing their homes. Significantly, recruitment for the militia was confined as much as possible to rural areas, because the authorities feared uprisings in cities and towns. The military machine was starting to overheat.

Meanwhile the suffering of France's civilians was such that Marshal Vauban estimated that a tenth of the nation was reduced to begging for food. He beseeched Louis to lessen the load on his people. In return, the most talented marshal left to France was treated with harsh recriminations by a king aghast at his impudence. Deaf to Vauban's pleas, Louis added to his people's burden by imposing a new poll tax, the *capitation*. It garnered only half the projected revenue, while helping to incite further resentment against the war and its attendant demands.

In 1696, at last accepting that his people needed respite from warfare, Louis transformed four years of covert diplomatic soundings into a sustained quest for peace. The majority of the alliance arrayed against him were receptive, many of them equally concerned by the expense of long, inconclusive, campaigns. Some of the components of the Grand Alliance were also feeling the strain of their unnatural union, which only the diplomatic skill of William of Orange had held together for so long. 'Both the imperial and Spanish courts felt a natural unease at allying with the Protestant states of northern Europe, especially since they were, in effect, supporting a Protestant usurper against the rightful Catholic king of England.'[12] Ironically it was William's two nations, England and Holland, which were keenest to end the war, and Spain, which had shown herself militarily weak, which wished to continue the fight. With Swedish mediation, peace was signed in the Dutch town of Ryswick in the autumn of 1697. In London, news that nine years of war had ended was greeted with two months of public celebrations, the likes of which had not been seen since the Restoration.

The Peace of Ryswick marked a change in direction for Louis, for this was a treaty that was to deprive France of territory: she had to surrender her gains of the previous two decades in the Low Countries and the Holy Roman Empire, and she was also obliged to withdraw from

Lorraine. A more personal humiliation was inflicted on Louis when he was forced to return the principality of Orange to William and to recognise his old foe as rightful king of England. Louis completed the climb-down by swearing no longer to assist any enemy of William's. He was not specifically named, but the displaced James II could, if the terms of the Peace were observed, no longer be helped to retrieve his forfeited crown. Louis justified his acceptance of such terms by claiming that he was prepared 'to sacrifice the fruits of my victory to the Repose of Europe'.[13]

William suspected a more sinister reason behind Louis's eagerness for peace: perhaps Louis had calculated that a resumption of arms in a few years time would not involve such a mighty coalition against him? It must have seemed unlikely that anyone other than William could galvanise such diverse forces into a unified opposition to France; and the Prince of Orange was clearly unwell, a lifetime of conflict and respon-sibility draining his already poor constitution. In short, given breathing space and the right pretext, could France rise to the occasion yet again, and provide Louis *le Grand* with another generation of warriors? Could it be that the French were only withdrawing from this conflict to prepare for the next?

CHAPTER FIVE

THE SPANISH
SUCCESSION

*'Carlos II, king of Spain, of Naples and of Sicily, sovereign
of Flanders, of part of Italy, of several islands in the Ocean
and the Mediterranean, of the Philippines in the Indian
sea, emperor of Mexico and Peru; Carlos II, without
children, languished, threatened by approaching death.'*

HISTOIRE DE FRANCE, BY ANQUETIL, PARIS, 1832

CARLOS II WAS THE WRETCH TO whom heredity had bequeathed the
throne of Spain. The royal gene pool from which he sprang had been
soured by an unhealthily close blend: Carlos's father, Philip IV, had
married his niece, Mariana of Austria, to produce this boy, the only one
of their nine children to outlive his father. Carlos was so inbred that he
was 'more a medical curiosity than a man'.[1] His features were cruelly
pronounced versions of the distinctive Habsburg physiognomy: his eyes
had a thin pallor, and his jaw was so prominent that he was unable to
chew; his head so outsized and his balance so poor that during his first
appearance at court, as a child, his nurse suspended him from strings to
keep him from stumbling forward. It was apt, given his increasing reliance
on powerful aristocrats and churchmen, that Carlos was presented to
his people while hanging like a puppet.

Syphilitic, afflicted with dropsy and epilepsy, sick in body and mind,

69

his wan features and jerky twitches betrayed a festering inner torment. Carlos became convinced that he was the Devil's creation, a belief which fostered an obsession with death. He would linger in the royal crypt and gaze with melancholy into the opened coffins of his ancestors, before climbing into his own casket. He found solace from the trials of his earthly existence in contemplation of the afterlife. Beset by ignorant doctors and scheming advisers, his struggle through increasing infirmity was gloomily watched by some of his people, who called him Carlos the Sufferer. Others observed the plethora of his afflictions, and dubbed him Charles the Bewitched. He was never expected to see adolescence, let alone adulthood; but the invalid defied such predictions to limp into manhood, carrying the potential for massive diplomatic ructions on his frail back.

The rest of Europe was more sanguine about the deformed, feeble-minded Spaniard. The details of his treatments were titillating items of gossip – the chopped chicken giblets placed on his sternum; the brutally effective purges of his intestines; the infusions of milk and pulverised pearls. However, to the key figures in the Courts of Europe Carlos's health, throughout the four decades of his life, was of paramount concern. No matter how weak Spain had become, she retained a core importance born of her days as the premier world power. She still possessed a cornucopia of colonies and dependencies as mementoes of her heyday, from the Spanish Netherlands, the Canary Islands, California, Cuba, Florida and Mexico, to Sicily, Sardinia, Naples and Milan, and the Philippines and much of South America. However, these lands had no direct heir, despite Carlos having taken first a French queen, Marie-Louise of Orléans; then a German one, Maria-Anna of Pfalz-Neuburg. Where these prizes were destined, after the invalid king's demise, was the backdrop for some of the most complex and important diplomacy of the last decades of the seventeenth century.

CARLOS'S IMMINENT DEATH HAD been anticipated ever since his birth in 1661. From his earliest boyhood, when he was crowned king, the powers of Europe tried to contain the expected fall-out from the end of the Spanish Habsburg line. They sought an acceptable and controlled deconstruction of the Empire. The first attempt at this, in 1668, was termed the Partition Treaty. However, as Carlos progressed into manhood its provisions were rendered obsolete.

What remained unchanged was a desire among outsiders to stop the passing of Spain's possessions to a single heir, since this would destroy the balance of power in Europe. One point that France, England and the United Provinces seemed consistently to agree upon was the need to divide the spoils among the potential beneficiaries. This, it was hoped, would preclude the obvious alternative: pan-European warfare, as interested parties scrambled to gain for themselves what they could, before rivals beat them to the best prizes. How to achieve this controlled detonation, in both theory and practice, exercised the great diplomats and rulers of the day.

Towards the close of the century there were three prime candidates for the Spanish inheritance: France, the Empire, and the German Electorate of Bavaria, all of whom had strong blood links to the ailing Carlos.

The main aim of The Hague and London was to ensure that the crowns of France and Spain would remain separate and distinct. The French, for their part, feared that a union of Madrid and Vienna would leave them sandwiched between the two halves of the huge Habsburg Empire of old. The clash of interests between the great houses of Europe, Bourbon and Habsburg, left Bavaria as an intriguing option. Although powerful compared to other German states, the electorate was not in the first rank of nations; neither would she be able to seek European domination, even if festooned with Spanish dominions. Secondly, the Elector of Bavaria was son-in-law of the Holy Roman Emperor, Leopold I, whilst also being related by marriage to Louis XIV. Therefore, although an Imperial candidate, his line was not intrinsically hostile to France. The Bavarians had the classic hallmarks of the compromise candidate: acceptable to all, and threatening to none.

In 1698, Carlos II was so ill that death once more seemed imminent. France, England and the United Provinces secretly agreed to what was later known as the First Partition Treaty. The three powers consented to support the Bavarian heir, Electoral Prince Joseph Ferdinand, as Carlos's principal successor. France and the Empire would be awarded minor territorial gains, whilst England and Holland would receive generous trading rights overseas. There was a flaw in this neat dissection: neither Spain nor the Holy Roman Empire had been included in these negotiations. There was outrage in Spain when the secrecy around the First Partition Treaty was, inevitably, breached. It was quite unacceptable to the Spanish aristocracy and senior churchmen that their overseas' possessions should be parcelled off to outsiders. It was even more outrageous that people they regarded as allies against Louis – the Dutch and English – should have secretly colluded with the enemy. The Court was split as to who was the most appropriate heir to the throne, but it was united in wanting the inheritance to remain undivided.

It may well have been poison, or it could perhaps have been illness. Either way, after displaying disturbing symptoms, the young Electoral Prince died very suddenly in February, 1699. He was taken violently ill one afternoon, lapsed into a coma, and was dead within hours. With him died the First Partition Treaty. The diplomats of France, England and the United Provinces urgently reconvened. Count Tallard, one of Louis's favoured soldier-diplomats, headed the French delegation. The Earl of Portland – William's intimate favourite, and a respected figure in Paris – represented Anglo-Dutch interests. The upshot was another theoretical division of Spain's possessions: Leopold's second son, the Archduke Charles, would become king of Spain, ruler of the Spanish Netherlands and lord of most of the overseas territories. In return, he would be required to guarantee that these gains would never be incorporated into the Holy Roman Empire. France was to be consoled with the bulk of Carlos II's Italian lands, as well as Lorraine. England and Holland received their customary pay-off in the form of trading concessions.

Once Louis and William had approved Tallard's and Portland's draft terms, Emperor Leopold was presented with a *fait accompli*. He had been excluded from the Second Partition Treaty and was now given just two months to agree to the new negotiations. Angered, he dismissed the suggestion as impudent effrontery. Leopold knew that the century-and-a-half since Charles V's division of his lands had been threaded through with marital alliances between the two Habsburg families. These had been open recognition of a deeper understanding: that, if one branch of the family died off, the other would succeed it. For others to inter-fere in family matters, and questions of sovereignty, was an outrage.

Despite the proposed strictures of the Second Partition Treaty, Leopold remained optimistic that his line would succeed that of his childless cousin. The Emperor had a powerful advocate in Maria-Anna of Pfalz-Neuburg, his sister-in-law and Carlos's queen. She urged her ailing husband to leave his lands to Archduke Charles, her nephew and Leopold's son from his third wife. Maria-Anna had displayed her loyal-ties on learning about the Second Partition Treaty: she 'flew into such a towering rage that she smashed up the furniture in her apartment, paying special attention to the mirrors and other ornaments that were of French origin'.[2] The queen followed her tantrum with ceaseless intercessions on behalf of the Holy Roman Empire.

Louis XIV had influence and spies in every European Court. Nowhere were they more active than in Spain. The coded despatch that arrived at Fontainebleau, near Paris, on the morning of 9 November 1700 was from Blécourt, the French ambassador in Madrid, and it contained the news that two generations of Europeans had awaited: Carlos II had died. More excitingly, Blécourt reported, near the end, the dying monarch had signed a new Will in which he had left his territories in their entirety to Philip of Anjou, Louis's younger grandson. Sustained French lobbying and some selective bribery had helped secure this result. However, the influence of Spanish churchmen tending the king was significant. They insisted on keeping the German queen away from Carlos's deathbed while they worked on their victim. The invalid's attentions were else-where: 'The king of Spain was beginning to see the things of this world by the light alone of that awful torch which is lighted to lighten the dying.'[3]

Free from Maria-Anna's interference, the Spanish Establishment focused Carlos's distracted mind on maintaining the integrity of the empire. John Evelyn wrote in his diary that 'the Spanish Counsels dreaded nothing so much as the dismembering of [their] dominions, & this 'tis believed, induced them to make the King settle it by Will.'[4] If this meant a French prince being brought in as their king, then that was preferable to seeing their overseas territories cut up and distributed to a variety of different rulers. Alexander Stanhope, the English ambassador, believed that the Spanish 'would rather deliver themselves to the devil, so that they could all go together, rather than be dismembered.'[5] Besides, the grandees and churchmen detested the Austrians – they had been too influential in Spain for too long. Louis was unique among the rulers of Europe in having the power to guarantee the Spanish status quo, and Carlos believed it his duty to hold his inheritance together. When he looked for vindication for favouring the French, Pope Innocent XII assured him this was indeed the right choice.

The Will was signed at the beginning of October. Carlos added a codicil, asking that Anjou marry an Imperial princess, in the hope that this might avert warfare. The king then stumbled to his ancestors' tombs to plead forgiveness for handing their empire to France, the historic enemy. Four weeks later he joined them in the mausoleum, finally at peace in his longed-for coffin.

Louis now had to decide whether to honour the Second Partition Treaty and reluctantly decline his grandson's proffered inheritance, or to accept the terms of the Will, and gain huge swathes of territory. The nineteenth-century historian, Sir Edward Creasy, argued that all Louis's earlier conflicts throughout Europe were mere preludes to this crescendo, for, 'It must be borne in mind that the ambition of Louis in these wars was twofold. It had its immediate and its ulterior objects. Its immediate object was to conquer and annex to France the neighbouring provinces and towns that were most convenient for the increase of her strength; but the ulterior object of Louis, from the time of his marriage to the Spanish Infanta in 1659, was to acquire for the house of Bourbon the whole empire of Spain.'[6] After more than four decades, the opportunity to achieve his ultimate ambition had arrived. However, acceptance of the prize was bound to lead to war with Emperor Leopold.

Louis was unable to see a clear way forward. He summoned his three closest advisers, as well as his mistress Madame de Maintenon, and his heir the Dauphin, to examine the options and their implications. They concentrated on the proviso in Carlos's Will that passed everything to the Austrian Archduke Charles, should Anjou decline the inheritance. The Marquis de Torcy, Louis's Secretary for Foreign Affairs, argued that acceptance of the Will was the right course, since war with Austria seemed inevitable either way. It would therefore be folly to decline the bequeathed empire. The Dauphin agreed. Beauvillier, governor to the royal children, took a more legalistic approach. He advised Louis that he should honour the Partition Treaty, because he had given his solemn undertaking to do so. Pontchartrain, the Chancellor, merely itemised the arguments for and against each decision, without concluding which one he believed to be preferable.

Louis still could not decide. He pondered the crucial question for a few days, taking soundings from others whose opinions he valued. There was much to consider: could he persuade himself that the union of France and Spain was justifiable; that his duty as a good Christian monarch was to unite the two nations in a way that could guarantee peace in Europe in general, even if it led to a duel with Austria?

There was a further consideration. Over the previous 150 years the Habsburgs had usually held the whip hand over France. His father and grandfather had both fought off Spanish invasions, as had he, early in his reign. Was this Will therefore not a unique opportunity to put an end to the threat from across the Pyrenees, as well as from the Spanish Netherlands? Practicality, honour, logic and temptation jostled for position in Louis's mind.

On 16 November, Versailles rippled with excitement. Louis, whose daily rituals were the fulcrum of court life, broke with tradition and invited all to hear his pronouncement on Carlos's bequest. The king stood by the opened double doors of his study. 'Then he ran his eyes majestically over the numerous company. "Gentlemen," he said, showing them the 17-year-old Duc d'Anjou, "here is the King of Spain. His birth called him to this crown, the late king also, by his Will. The Spanish nation has wished it and has demanded it of me: it was the command of heaven; I have granted it with joy."' [7] And thus the king of France recognised his grandson, previously a secondary figure at Versailles, as his regal equal.

While the courtiers digested the ramifications of Louis's decision Castel del Rey, the Spanish ambassador, fell to his knees before his new master. His utterance captured the enormity of the moment: 'Il n'y a plus de Pyrènées' – The Pyrenees are no more.

Louis continued, turning to Philip and exhorting him to: 'Be a good Spaniard, that is now your first duty, but remember that you were born a Frenchman to bring about the union of the two nations; that is the way to ensure both their happiness and the peace of Europe.' [8] Was this simply advice to an inexperienced grandson, encouraging him to forego aggression? Or was it a veiled threat as Louis asserted his dominance over a vassal, ordering Philip to rule for France's benefit? To the Courts of Europe, French control of Spain was a huge concern, running counter to thirty-five years of complex diplomacy.

William of Orange was in no doubt as to the correct interpretation of recent events in Madrid and Paris. He was dining at Hampton Court when informed of Louis's decision. He leaned forward, pulling his hat hard against his features to cover an angry flush. When he regained composure he received the French ambassador to London, Count Tallard, who confirmed his master's intent. The count had been one of the architects of the now worthless Second Partition Treaty. 'Tallard did not utter a single word on handing me his sovereign's letter, the contents of which are the same as of that which the States [the Dutch Parliament] have received. I said to him that perhaps I had testified too eager a desire for the preservation of peace, but that, nevertheless, my inclination in that respect had not changed. Whereupon he replied: "The king my master, by accepting the will, considers that he gives a similar proof of his desire to maintain peace." Thereupon he made a bow and withdrew.' [9]

There was little that William could do. He wrote bitterly to Grand Pensionary Heinsius, the Dutch president: 'I have never had much dependence on treaties with France, but that this solemn undertaking should be torn up in the eyes of all the world I never would have believed possible.'[10] William recognised that his two nations would accept Louis's reneging on the Second Partition Treaty. The United Provinces showed no inclination for another war; indeed, its stock market rose at the news that the Spanish succession had been settled. Meanwhile the English Parliament was more openly hostile to its own king than to France's. It contained a resentful Jacobite contingent, which intensely disliked the Dutchman on the Stuart throne. Some moderate MPs were alienated by the revelation that their foreign monarch had secretly – and, in their view, unconstitutionally – agreed the Second Partition Treaty, without reference to them.

The Tories, in power since displacing the Whigs in 1699, had little wish to become embroiled in Continental affairs. The landowners and farmers at the core of their vote had been battling with a run of poor harvests since 1693 . The four-shilling in the pound tax imposed during the War of the League of Augsburg was not an experience they were keen to repeat. They were for isolationism. The Whigs appeared to be equally wary. They feared a large, peacetime, standing army, primarily on constitutional grounds. When the Peace of Ryswick drew a line under the War of the League of Augsburg, Parliament insisted that William disband his forces.

MPs were so aggressively determined about this that they almost precipitated William's abdication and return to the United Provinces. From a war footing of 87,000 soldiers Parliament ordered the English army to be scaled down to 20,000 men. Of these, a maximum of 7,000 could be stationed in England and Scotland. William pleaded for the retention of at least 30,000 troops, but he was ignored. In a symbolic rejection of the alien king and his foreign wars, the elite Dutch Guard were ordered to quit England. William 'was aghast. Every fibre in his nature revolted at the baseness, cruelty, and ingratitude with which his faithful troops were treated, at the same time he felt his whole European nation undermined by the blotting out of England as a military factor. But he was powerless.'[11]

Just before Christmas 1700, Count Tallard triumphantly reported to

Louis that London and The Hague were prepared to recognise Anjou as king of Spain. This showed that the Dutch placed peace and trade above international politics. It was also proof that the English were prepared to believe Louis's promise that France and Spain's crowns would never be united. A Parliament composed of resentful Tories and assertive Whigs contemptuously ignored William's warnings about French duplicity. Some of the more extreme Whigs even questioned the *raison d'être* of monarchy. By 1701, the relationship between king and Parliament was so strained that a French agent was able to report: 'The Royal authority is so enfeebled that England cannot but be regarded as a Republic, and her king as an officer authorised to carry out what Parliament has ordered in the intervals between its sessions.'[12] William was no longer able to exert influence even in his own kingdom, let alone across Europe.

Anjou's succession was recognised throughout the Continent except, predictably, in Vienna. The Holy Roman Emperor railed against the usurping of what he maintained was his son's rightful inheritance. France had little to fear from Austria standing alone, though; such a conflict could only have one result. Austria would need allies. However, William, the wily enemy of French domination, could not rouse his peoples, let alone his confederates of old, to war.

LOUIS'S HUBRIS TORE AWAY THE mantle of peace cast over most of Europe. Philip V was received in his new kingdom of Spain with genuine enthusiasm, but the well-meaning youth had no experience or training in statecraft. In 1701, the Spanish Regency Council asked Louis to guide him. It should have been clear that such an overt intermeshing of French and Spanish interests would alarm the rest of Europe, yet a flattered Louis was blind to the likely consequences and accepted the invitation.

With the same disregard for international opinion, Louis sent troops to the Barrier Fortresses in the Spanish Netherlands, claiming them on his grandson's behalf. However, the 1678 Peace of Nijmegen stipulated that Dutch and Spanish forces should jointly garrison this score of important towns on the River Meuse. The arrangement had been made when the United Provinces and Spain were joined against France. Now the

Spanish occupants of the Barrier Fortresses opened up town after town to their new allies, the French. Twenty-two battalions of Dutch troops – 15,000 men – meekly quit their postings, leaving the fortifications in Louis's hands. Apart from the well-garrisoned Maastricht, all of the Meuse defences, including Mons, Namur and Venlo, surrendered. Within weeks, the fruits of William of Orange's campaigns and diplomacy had been lost, without a shot being fired. He cried out in despair: 'For twenty-eight years I have toiled unceasingly to preserve this barrier for the State and now I have to watch it swallowed up in one day without a single blow being struck.' [13]

There was further unease when the electorate of Cologne became a French puppet state. This shift in allegiance threatened lines of communications between the Dutch and the Emperor. The United Provinces realised that the loss of the Barrier Fortresses, added to Cologne's position, was ominous. They prepared to defend themselves.

England was also forced to rethink its pacifism. There was fury, in mercantile circles, when France and Spain agreed that Louis's ships should enjoy favourable trading rights in South America. The most contentious issue was the granting to the French of a monopoly of the 'Assiento', the trade in slaves. This brought to an immediate end the informal agreement that had allowed English and Dutch merchant ships to trade between Cadiz and Spanish America. Could this development be a precursor to something similarly damaging in the Mediterranean? If so, the merchant class thought, war would be a price worth paying.

Louis provoked his neighbours further by announcing that Anjou could remain in the French line of succession, despite ruling Spain. Louis, rejecting all that generations of diplomats had strived to achieve, proudly displayed the letters patent confirming his decision. Such arrogance lent credibility to William, who had predicted that Louis would renege on his word in this way. It seemed that those who had demonised William as a self-serving scaremonger had been a little hasty. He was now seen as the one man who had not been gulled by the manipulations of the Sun King.

WAR WAS ALREADY PROBABLE, but Louis's continued arrogance rendered it inevitable. The eleven-year-old Duke of Gloucester, Princess Anne's last surviving child, died in July 1700. The boy had suffered from hydrocephalus – water on the brain. (Twelve of Anne's seventeen children had miscarried, and the remaining five died young.) Gloucester was carried by servants, to protect him from bumps and falls. However, no one could protect him from a deadly attack of smallpox. After Gloucester's death it was considered unlikely that the 35-year-old Anne would produce any more children, let alone healthy ones.

There were various candidates to succeed Anne, herself the heir to King William. Few Englishmen considered welcoming back the former James II, although a handful thought a return to the main line of the Stuarts was both possible and desirable. In Jacobite eyes the exiled king's son, James Francis Edward, was the preferred future ruler. Might he not be raised by William as a Protestant prince, combining the true bloodline of England's kings with the religion demanded by her people? However, most shrunk from this proposal, fearing a return of the discord that had marred earlier Stuart reigns. Foreign monarchs had a limited appeal, a fact underlined by William's unpopularity, but there were no other credible English candidates, so it was necessary to look at overseas royal families with Stuart blood.

The dukes of Savoy had a strong claim, being descended from Charles I's popular daughter, Minette. However, they were Catholic. They were also distrusted, because Savoy had deserted the Grand Alliance for Louis's cause in the War of the League of Augsburg.

The house of Hanover presented a more attractive possibility. The Electress Sophia was a granddaughter of James I, giving her claim to the throne parity with Savoy's. Furthermore, Sophia was staunchly Protestant. With more pragmatism than joy, Hanover was accepted as a sound solution to a delicate conundrum. In March 1701, the Act of Settlement was agreed: the crown of England would pass to Sophia and her descendants, if Princess Anne remained without her own, direct, heir.

SIX MONTHS AFTER THE ENGLISH succession was agreed, the deposed James II collapsed while at prayer in his private chapel at St Germain. Louis was told to hurry to the bedside of his friend and beneficiary. He arrived to find James unconscious, surrounded by his court-in-exile. Louis had a residual affection for his deposed cousin, and reacted to the deathbed scene with pity. This, and his belief in the divine right of kings, prompted Louis to promise that he would help James's son to regain the English throne. The gasps of gratitude from the ousted queen and her attendants were as nothing compared to the intake of breath that greeted Louis's pledge, across the Channel.

The outrage that swept England surprised Louis. However, when his advisers suggested he recant his commitment to James's son, he refused. The Peace of Ryswick specifically forbad Louis from aiding William's enemies, while acknowledging the Dutchman as England's lawful king. Despite that, Louis dared to assert his views in direct con-travention to the will of the English people, as expressed by the recent Act of Settlement. Louis's judgement that day at St Germain was appalling. Stanhope, England's ambassador in Vienna, wrote of the French king's folly: 'Whom God designs to destroy he infatuates first, and makes them do their own business themselves.' [14]

At the end of 1701, a new Parliament met in London. Sir Edward Seymour, a Tory leader who had witheringly dismissed William's calls against France in the past, now moved that a clause be added to the Grand Alliance's stated aims. As a result it was agreed that the war would continue until Louis XIV recognised the Protestant succession in England. Louis's arrogance and inflexibility had once again united disparate forces against him. Leading these foes, as ever, was the Prince of Orange.

PART TWO

THE WAR

CHAPTER SIX

TAKING SIDES

'France had never before found herself in such a favourable
position for making war upon her enemies; not only could
she count upon being able to keep Philip V upon his Spanish
throne, but it seemed as if the stubbornness of the House of
Austria would furnish her with the best of opportunities
for fresh conquests.'

MEMOIRS OF MONSIEUR DE LA COLONIE, DETAILED IN
THE CHRONICLES OF AN OLD CAMPAIGNER, 1692–1717

WILLIAM MAXIMISED THE MOMENT. He terminated diplomatic relations between France and England, closing his embassy in Paris, and
banishing Count Tallard from the Court of St James's. Diplomacy
continued elsewhere, however, with real urgency, as William contacted
potential allies against France and Spain: the Empire, England and the
United Provinces would head the second Grand Alliance; but support
was also needed from as many of the German and Italian nations as
possible. William secretly wrote to the Emperor Leopold, encouraging
him to pursue Archduke Charles's claims, and in particular: 'to make an
immediate effort in Italy, with the hope that a momentary success would
encourage the well-intentioned, and rouse the European states, in defence
of their independence'.[1]

The first Grand Alliance had been too weak to defeat Louis. Now
Spain and other members of the former confederacy were on the French

side. Versailles was confident that, despite Louis's blundering into this war, there were enough allies to guarantee French victory. 'The whole universe had borne witness to the power of France. This Monarchy had fought single-handed with almost the whole of Europe leagued against her, and had been victorious,' wrote Monsieur de la Colonie, a French army officer: 'I say this, as the whole Germanic body – [and] England, Holland, Spain, Portugal, and Savoy – had combined forces against Louis XIV, and this Prince had invariably defeated them. France now thus found herself in a very favourable position, for she had just added to her forces those of Spain, Portugal, [and] Savoy.'[2]

Since the second Grand Alliance was less numerous than its predecessor, it demanded greater contributions from its leading members. In particular, England could no longer act merely as an adjunct of the Dutch; she must now become a driving force within the confederacy. When the three main powers agreed their contributions to the Grand Alliance, the Emperor committed 82,000 and the Dutch 100,000 men. William watched with satisfaction as England promised 40,000 soldiers, and a similar number of sailors.

Aware of his ailing health, William looked for someone who would keep England in the coming war after his death. Despite concerns at Marlborough's flirtation with Jacobitism, William recognised that here was the man to continue his crusade against Louis. The king knew Princess Anne's succession would establish the Marlboroughs as the most powerful couple in the land, and in 1701 William passed on his mantle, promoting Marlborough to commander-in-chief of the English forces in Holland, and ambassador extraordinary to the United Provinces.

Marlborough's experience as a general had been restricted by William's distrust, both of him personally and of his compatriots in general. Only two of the six lieutenant-generals in the standing army of 1691 were native Englishmen. However, the few opportunities afforded him since Sedgemoor had confirmed that here was a soldier of special talent. Marlborough commanded the English sector of the Anglo-Dutch-Spanish army at the Battle of Walcourt in 1689. Waldeck, the allied commander-in-chief, had already seen Marlborough transform his unpromising detachment of Englishmen into 'the finest in the Dutch army', through assiduous training. During the battle, Marlborough headed the charge of the Household Cavalry in the decisive moment of the engagement. Waldeck reported to William: 'the Earl of Marlborough is assuredly one of the most gallant men I know'.[3]

In Ireland the following year, after James II's defeat by William at the Battle of the Boyne, Marlborough again showed exceptional skill. He led masterly attacks on the Irish ports of Cork and Kinsale, through which the French supplied James's remaining supporters. Cork fell within a week, with Kinsale surrendering in the same month. This Irish campaign also demonstrated Marlborough's diplomacy as leader of a multi-national force: his 5,000 men included Huguenot, Dutch and Danish troops. One of the foreign generals was the Duke of Württemberg, who expected his social superiority to give him supreme authority over the combined forces. Marlborough, however, was not prepared to lose his command. Neither did he want to upset his ally. He therefore proposed that he and Württemberg should lead the army on alternate days, and the duke accepted the compromise. This was an early example of Marlborough's flair for diplomacy, a gift that was to prove invaluable during the Blenheim campaign.

The successes in Ireland won William's strong approval. His view was that: 'No officer living who has seen so little service as my Lord Marlborough is so fit for great commands'.[4] The Prince de Vaudemont reinforced the good impression, telling William in 1691 his estimation of England's senior officers: 'Kirke has fire, Lanier thought, Mackay skill, and Colchester bravery; but there is something inexpressible in the Earl of Marlborough. All their virtues seem to be united in this single person. I have lost my wonted skill in physiognomy, if any subject of your Majesty can ever attain such a height of military glory as that to which this combination of sublime perfections must raise him.'[5]

Despite his potential, Marlborough's career had stalled. After his Irish successes, he had hoped to be created a Knight of the Garter. Instead, in 1692, he was relieved of all his offices, without explanation. John Evelyn wrote in his diary of the commonly believed reason behind the fall from grace: 'The Lord of Marboro, L:Gen: of K.William's Army in England, Gent. Of Bedchamber, etc. dismissed from all his Charges Military and other; & given to divers others: for his excessive taking bribes & Covetousness & Extortion upon all occasions from his inferior officers.' Evelyn enjoyed the fall. 'Note this was the Lord who being entirely advanced by K.James, the merit of his father being the prostitution of his Daughter (this Lord's sister) to that King: is now disgraced; & by none pitied, being also the first who betrayed & forsook his Master K. James.'[6]

Marlborough was imprisoned in the Tower for treachery, in 1692. Although found innocent of the convoluted charges, Marlborough remained sidelined as a soldier for the rest of the War of the League of Augsburg. William had reason to be suspicious of Marlborough, however: like many powerful contemporaries, he communicated with James's court-in-exile, insuring against a second Stuart Restoration. The most serious charge levelled against Marlborough was that he betrayed English plans for an ill-fated attack on the port of Brest in 1694. Although it was eventually established that the French already had this intelligence from another source, Marlborough was indeed guilty of giving the enemy secret information. He endeared himself to nobody by applying for the position left vacant by General George Tollemache, the Brest expedition's commander, who died during the raid.

Marlborough's questionable loyalty, both past and present, damaged his position. However, the prime reason for tension between the king and the earl was his wife's hold over her mistress. William and Mary blamed the pronounced difficulties between their Court and that of Princess Anne on Sarah Marlborough's manipulations. Mary demanded that her sister dismiss this disruptive influence, but Anne repeatedly refused. When Sarah offered her resignation, Anne declared she would 'rather live in a cottage with you than reign Empress of the world without you'.[7]

Their relationship never graduated to the cordial, but William and Anne were brought closer by Queen Mary's sudden death from smallpox in 1694. This gave closure to a bitter sisterly rivalry. Marlborough, however, remained in the wilderness during the remainder of the War of the League of Augsburg. Sarah heard of the high English casualties at William's defeats, and gave thanks that her husband's disgrace had kept him from the front line.

The king's respect for Marlborough grew after the Peace of Ryswick. He was one of the few willing to listen to and agree with William's fear of France. This reassured the king that Marlborough was sound. In the summer of 1698, William agreed to the earl's appointment as governor to the Duke of Gloucester, Anne's surviving son. 'My Lord,' said William, 'teach him but to know what you are, and my nephew cannot want for accomplishments.'[8] At the same time, he restored Marlborough to his Court and army ranks. He had regained his position independent of aid from either political party. His subsequent command of the English army, and his ambassadorial status, put the seal on a remarkable comeback.

LOUIS'S IMPETUOSITY HAD LAID bare his continued threat to Protestant Europe, and to all the nations whose lands bordered French territory. The Dutch States-General welcomed Marlborough to The Hague, hoping that he would assemble an alliance strong enough to deter French aggression. If Louis could not be diverted from conflict, though, the United Provinces appreciated the need for a strong confederacy to stand against France. The Dutch installed Marlborough in the palatial Mauritshuis. This was the venue for intense diplomacy as the earl encouraged, cajoled and bribed potential signatories to join the second Grand Alliance. It was difficult and unpredictable work. Winston S. Churchill characterised this era in European history as a time of the most treacherous self-interest: 'It was an epoch of divided loyalties, of criss-cross ties, of secret reserves and much dissembling.'[9]

Of no individual was this truer than the colourful Maximilian II Emmanuel, the Elector of Bavaria. Known as the White Knight, because of his personal valour, Maximilian had succeeded the Duke of Lorraine as Supreme Commander of the Imperial armies against the Turks in 1688. Success then had been followed by a leading role against the

French in the War of the League of Augsburg: the Elector of Bavaria had been the Imperial commander who had helped William to capture Namur in 1695.

Maximilian Emmanuel's proven abilities as a general and the strength of his army made Bavaria's services desirable to Louis and the Grand Alliance. However, it was his nation's location – his domain also included the dukedom of the Upper Palatinate, and the county of Palatine of the Rhine – that made him an ally of particular interest to France. The Elector's compliance would give France a base deep inside the Empire, within striking range of the capital, Vienna. Louis sent one of his foremost diplomats, the Marquis de Ricous, to alert Maximilian Emmanuel to the many benefits that friendship with France could bring.

The Elector, was, by definition, one of the standard-bearers of the Holy Roman Empire. However, he contemplated an alliance with Louis because he believed France would win this war, and win it quickly. He had a matchless knowledge of the weakness of the Imperial forces, and he expected the Habsburg dynasty to fall during the conflict. The death of his young son before he could succeed Carlos II had deprived the Elector's family of the Spanish Empire. However, maybe there was now a chance to secure another Imperial crown, albeit as the vassal of Louis XIV, by defeating and replacing Emperor Leopold and his line?

Maximilian had been created Viceroy of the Spanish Netherlands after the War of the League of Augsburg. The Emperor had welcomed the appointment, believing his able commander would help to control this sensitive area. However, when the French overwhelmed the Barrier Fortresses, Leopold discovered that Maximilian Emmanuel was in cahoots with the Franco-Spanish. Philip V had guaranteed the Elector's continuance as viceroy, provided he allow the Barrier Fortresses to fall to Louis.

Many lesser German princes were reluctant to follow the Emperor into battle against the strength of France. They now looked to Maximilian Emmanuel to lead their cause. 'Every day the highest dignitaries of the Empire besought him to return to his own territory, as he was regarded as a prince capable of leading those who were opposed to the violent policy with which Germany was threatened by the Court of

Vienna, backed by England and Holland.'[10] Maximilian Emmanuel returned to Munich, the Bavarian capital, to hear these representations in person. However, it was soon evident that peace was not an option: the Emperor was determined on armed conflict to eject Philip V from Spain, in favour of Archduke Charles. Leopold secured the votes of the three bodies that constituted the Diet of Ratisbon – the seven electors; the hereditary Imperial princes; and the Free Cities of the Empire – then declared war against France.

Maximilian Emmanuel was now left with a stark choice: he could either support his nephew, the new king of Spain; or side with his father-in-law, Emperor Leopold. As he dithered, Louis's envoy, the Marquis de Ricous, proposed a treaty that was temptingly generous to the Elector. In return for his generalship and 45,000 troops, France would share her Germanic acquisitions in the coming war equally with Bavaria. In the very unlikely circumstance that the Grand Alliance made territorial gains inside the electorate, Maximilian Emmanuel would be compensated with sovereignty elsewhere; either in Burgundy, or in the Spanish Netherlands. These terms were agreed but they were to remain secret: the Elector would only declare his hand once he could pretend that war had been forced upon him.

Unaware that a covert deal had been reached between Maximilian Emmanuel and Louis, the Grand Alliance offered Bavaria a selection of bribes and threats. So keen was the Emperor to secure the return of the Elector to his cause, that he offered him the Supreme Commander's role in Italy. Maximilian Emmanuel pretended to be intrigued. William was unsettled by this inscrutability, declaring: 'It is time that he lifts the mask and that he openly opposes liaisons so contrary to the good of the Empire of which he is a member.'[11]

Meanwhile Joseph Clement of Bavaria shared his electoral brother's leanings. In 1688, he had been installed by the Emperor as the archbishop and and elector of Cologne, to block Louis's candidate, Cardinal von Fürstenberg. His strongholds on the Meuse and the Rhine were considerable: Bonn, Huy, Kaiserwerth, Liège, and Rheinberg. However, he felt no lasting gratitude for these acquisitions. Joseph Clement shared

Maximilian Emmanuel's view that France would win the conflict, and that further advancement lay in alliance with the victor. Self-interest held sway over historic ties to a notional overlord, whose days were surely numbered.

With the Bavarian princes failing to come to his colours, Marlborough worked harder to win over other potential allies in Germany. Each had a self-serving agenda. For the Elector of Brandenburg, the quid pro quo was enhanced status. He knew that the services of the Duke of Brunswick-Lüneburg-Hanover had been secured in the previous war, by making him the ninth Imperial Elector. Frederick of Brandenburg was a mediocrity figure whose obsession with pomp and ceremony made him an avid admirer of Louis XIV's Court life. Contemporaries sneered at him as 'Louis's monkey', and mocked him for his superficiality. However, he controlled a hardy and professional army of 43,000 men. When the price of his assistance was set at elevation from elector to king, Leopold reluctantly agreed to pay.

The Hanoverian forces had a special reason for joining the Grand Alliance, for their electoral family was in line for the English throne. They were among the first Germans to commit to the cause, providing 10,000 troops before the terms of their involvement were finalised. Their keenness for the fray was further demonstrated when they attacked their neighbours, the princes of Saxe-Gotha and Wolfenbuttel, who had been raising troops for Louis. After Hanover's intervention, they stood down their forces, and Louis lost the services of 12,000 men.

Self-interest, greed, self-aggrandisement and fear confronted Marlborough as he did William's diplomatic bidding. No wonder Marlborough called his efforts at this time 'tormenting'. However, William had chosen his special envoy wisely. Lord Chesterfield, looking back on Marlborough's career, believed the graciousness that he brought to his diplomatic missions was the key to his overall success: 'It was by this engaging graceful manner that he was enabled, during all the war, to connect the various and jarring Powers of the Grand Alliance, and to carry them on to the main object of the war, notwithstanding their private and separate jealousies and wrong-headedness. Whatever Court he went on (and he was often obliged to go to restive and refractory ones) he brought them into his measures. The Pensionary Heinsius, who had governed the United Provinces for forty years, was absolutely governed by him. He was always cool, and nobody ever observed the least variation in his countenance; he could refuse more easily than others could grant; and those who went from him the most dissatisfied as to the substance of their business, were yet charmed by his manner, and, as it were, comforted by it.' [12] These were the attributes that helped Marlborough to forge the Grand Alliance on William's behalf: Prussia, Denmark, Sweden, Hanover, Baden, and Hesse-Cassel joined the Imperialists, the Dutch and the English. Between 1701 and 1704 England was to sign fifty treaties and conventions with her allies.

WILLIAM CALLED ON HIS ADOPTIVE people to prepare for war. In January 1702, Parliament received one of his more impassioned speeches. He lashed Louis for his presumptuousness, and urged the English to stand up to the threat he represented: 'I have no doubt that the late proceedings of His Most Christian Majesty and the dangers which threaten all the powers of Europe have excited your most lively resentment. All the world have their eyes fixed upon England; there is still time, she may save her religion and her liberty, but let her profit by every moment, let her arm by land and sea, let her lend her allies all the assistance in her power, and swear to show her enemies, the foes of her religion, her liberty, her government and the king of her choice, all the hatred they deserve!' [13]

William died two months afterwards. He broke his collarbone in a fall from his horse, and his physical weakness left him prey to complications, including pneumonia. Incompetent physicians sped his passing. The reactions to the death of Protestantism's champion was mixed: in England, Jacobites toasted the mole whose molehill had caused William's mount to stumble; in Holland, consternation was widespread, and church bells were rung thrice a day, in doleful respect; in France, Louis allowed no official mourning, in order not to offend his exiled Stuart protégés at

St Germain; but he equally allowed no rejoicing at the death of a respected adversary.

Louis was disappointed if he hoped that England would now revert to isolationism: the new monarch, Queen Anne, rushed to reassure her privy council that vigorous opposition to France, and the stout defence of the Church of England, were her twin priorities. She then wrote to her allies, confirming her readiness for war, and England's acceptance of a lead role in the coming conflict. In mid-March, she wrote to the Elector Palatine and his son: 'Therefore in very friendly manner we ask and invite Your Highness and Your Highness Elect to enter into the same Alliance, and to add strength and endurance by your accession. By which act, you will be joining with His Imperial Majesty, with the most high estates of the Dutch Allies, who are very zealous for the Public Good, and especially with Ourselves, who have now solely turned Our attentions, and are about to exert all Our energies, to the end that We may vindicate the common liberty of Europe against the immoderate power of the French.'[14] Anne joined her allies in committing to a fight with France on 4 May 1702. When Louis was informed, he quipped: 'I must be getting old, if ladies are now declaring war on me.'

The new queen enjoyed the full support of her people, but there were unspoken fears that this war was against an invincible enemy. France had not lost a significant land engagement for two generations, during which time Louis XIV's professional armies had established a reputation for brilliance. However, surely the five years since the Peace of Ryswick had not been long enough for Louis's forces to regain their pre-1688 strength? The War of the League of Augsburg may have seemed a costly stalemate to the constituents of the first Grand Alliance, but it had pulled some of France's teeth. William III had fought Louis at his peak: often unsuccessfully, but always with determination. He had blunted the French military machine, imperceptibly but indubitably, and in the process sharpened up the troops under his own control. In particular, as Louis's armies had begun to wane, English forces were on the rise.

CHAPTER SEVEN

THE WAR IN FLANDERS

'If an army was completely destroyed it was impossible to make another: and behind the army there was nothing. This called for great prudence. Only when the decisive advantage was likely to be gained, could the risk be undertaken. It was in the creation of such chances that the art of the commander lay.'

GENERAL CARL VON CLAUSEWITZ, *ON WAR*

IN CONTRAST TO THE GRAND Alliance, the forces of the Two Crowns – of France and of Spain – enjoyed a centrality and a focus that promised to be a significant advantage in the ensuing war. Louis had more than 80,000 mercenaries at his disposal: Swiss, Irish, German, Italian, and Walloon. There were also the commands of his allies, the electors of Bavaria and Cologne, and the king of Spain. Louis held dominance over this confederacy. His indigenous army was so numerous that everyone standing against the Grand Alliance looked to Versailles for leadership, for policy and for coordination. There was none of the potential for debilitating fractiousness that thrived in the allied ranks. If Louis's foes were to negate his advantage, they must rally together and suppress divisive self-interest.

The priority was to find a commander-in-chief acceptable to all. Queen Anne was keen that her husband, Prince George of Denmark, be chosen. However, her high opinion of this affable but bovine man was unique, an expression of wifely love rather than of queenly wisdom. His ineffectuality had been summed up two decades earlier by Charles II, with the jovially dismissive summation: 'I've tried 'im drunk, and I've tried 'im sober, and there's nothing in 'im!' Certainly, Prince George's candidacy failed to impress the Dutch. They prided themselves on the quality and experience of their own generals, which clearly exceeded the capabilities of the well-meaning Dane. They also resisted the commitment of Dutch troops to the command of an alien prince. The States-General insisted on having Field Deputies accompany their men on campaign. It would be hard for these civilians to exert control over the husband of their greatest ally.

The suit of the new king in Prussia was also rejected. Frederick's soldiers, with their many Huguenot officers, were welcome to help the cause. However, his rank was a barrier, and his generalship was not highly regarded. Initially the Prince of Nassau-Saarbrücken was agreed upon as a compromise, stopgap, incumbent; but in July, despite his relative inexperience, command was transferred to the English captain-general, Marlborough. His appointment was recognition of England's importance in the coalition and consolation for Anne: her favourite was honoured, even if her consort could not be.

With Marborough's elevation came the jealousy of the United Provinces' senior generals: Athlone, Opdam, Overkirk and Slangenberg would each have expected supremacy over the Englishman. Marlborough's battle honours seemed, to those weaned on the endless conflicts of the Continent, distinctly limited. At the same time it was confirmed that Marlborough would remain effectively junior to the Dutch Field Deputies. These civil representatives would be his constant attendants on campaign. Even William of Orange had been obliged to accede to their restraint, during earlier wars. The States-General were bound to continue the practice with Marlborough, a foreigner of unknown ability. Two Field Deputies would accompany his army on campaign, and were 'to be consulted on all occasions'.[1] They had negligible military knowledge, and yet were able to override Marlborough's field command.

It is hard to think of a more uncomfortable encumbrance for Marl-

The Duke and Duchess of Marlborough. Oil by Johann Baptist Clostermann, 1660–1711, Blenheim Palace. *Bridgeman*

William III, 1650–1702. Oil attributed to Sir Godfrey Kneller, 1646–1723, Bank of England, London. *Bridgeman*

John Churchill, Duke of Marlborough, 1650–1722. Oil by Sir Godfrey Kneller, Althorp. *Earl Spencer*

Prince Lewis of Baden, 1655–1707. Mezzotint published by Elias Christoph Heiss, Augsburg, c. 1700. *Karl Baumann Collection, Dillingen/Donau*

Prince Eugène of Savoy, 1663–1736. Oil, circle of Sir Godfrey Kneller, Althorp.
Earl Spencer

Maximilian II Emmanuel, Elector of Bavaria, 1662–1726. Oil, 1704, by Johann
Andreas Wolff, 1652–1716. *Schloss Nymphenburg, Bayerische Schlösserverwaltung*

A Paris chez I. Mariette rue St Iacques aux Colonnes d'Hercule.

Marshal Tallard, 1652–1728. Engraving by Jean Mariette, Paris, early 18th century.
Karl Baumann Collection, Dillingen/Donau

The Battle of Blenheim tapestry, Blenheim Palace.
By kind permission of His Grace the Duke of Marlborough

The Battle of Blenheim. Oil by John van Huchtenburg, 1646–1733.
Bayerisches Armeemuseum, Ingolstadt

The Battle of Blenheim. Oil by John Wootton, c.1682–1764.
National Army Museum, London

Tallard Hands Over his Sword to Crown Prince Frederick of Hesse-Cassel.
Woodcut, c.1855, by Wilhelm Camphausen, 1818–85, coloured later. *AKG images*

The Garrison of the Village Had at Last Surrendered. Oil by Robert Alexander
Hillingford, 1825–1904, private collection. *Bridgeman*

The Duke of Marlborough Signing the Despatch at Blenheim. Oil by Robert Alexander Hillingford, private collection. *Bridgeman*

Marlborough's despatch to his wife Sarah, written in the field at Blenheim,
13 August 1704, bidding her let his queen know of her army's glorious victory.
The British Library, Add 61428 95

Anne, Queen of Great Britain and Ireland, daughter of James II, 1665–1714. Oil by William Wissing, 1656–87, private collection. *Bridgeman*

Captain Robert Parker, author of *Memoirs of the Most Remarkable Military Transactions from the Year 1683 to 1718. National Army Museum, London*

'The front View of Blenheim House'. Engraving, 1749, Sylvanus Urban, *The Gentleman's Magazine and Historical Chronical. AKG images*

The north front of Blenheim Palace today. *AKG images/Stefan Drechsel*

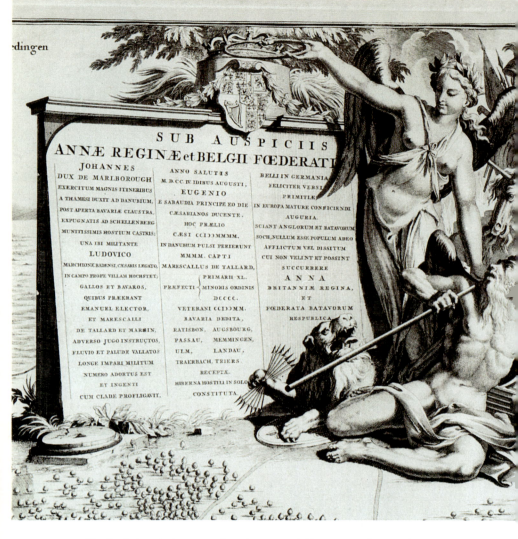

The Latin inscription recording the events following Marlborough's *magnis itineribus* from the Thames to the Danube; a fragment of the great engraving of the Battle of Blenheim by the Dutch engraver Pieter van Gunst.
Karl Baumann Collection, Dillingen/Donau

borough than these civilian masters. Here was a middle-aged general who had been sidelined against his will for much of the previous war. He was now intent on establishing the military reputation he had long thought his destiny. At fifty-two, he was already six years older than Napoleon was to be at Waterloo, but had yet to win a major battle as commanding officer. Marlborough's every instinct was to bring about, and win, engagements. However, such opportunities as arose would have to be approved by the States-General's representatives. He was the undisputed leader of the English troops and their paid auxiliaries, but his rank in the Dutch army was specific in its limitations; he was to be *Deputy* Captain-General of the Republic. For a man whose previous triumphs, such as they were, had depended on flair, pace and independence, the imposition of cautious regulators was deeply unwelcome.

The United Provinces had a history of suffering. Spanish aggression had been supplanted by the French savagery of more recent times. Their struggle for survival had fostered a mindset of the utmost defensiveness. They looked back with pride at the efforts of their saviour, Prince Maurice of Nassau: his dogged, stonewalling tactics were held up as the example from which the Dutch should draw inspiration. So, while the French remained strong along the Meuse, the Field Deputies' brief was to restrain their English ally: Marlborough must remain as the shield-bearer of the United Provinces, and not risk Dutch safety through impetuosity.

EARLY EIGHTEENTH-CENTURY European warfare was generally limited to the months from April till October. The already poor roads became impassable in winter mud and the huge quantities of supplies needed to support an army on the move were unobtainable outside of the growing seasons. A force of 60,000 men would typically be accompanied by 40,000 horses – half pack animals, the rest mounts for the cavalry and dragoons – requiring vast amounts of green feed. Although he was starting out halfway through the traditional campaigning season, in July of 1702, Marlborough was intent on early and decisive victory. He wanted to attack the Duke of Burgundy and Marshal Boufflers's army as soon as possible, delivering a knockout punch in pitched battle. He would dictate the pace of the campaign and wrong-foot opponents who would not expect his aggressive brand of warfare.

Marlborough's was an extremely unusual approach. This was an age when most generals were content to lead their large and expensive armies in stately procession around the well-supplied Flemish countryside. There they played giant games of chess, with feints and counter-feints, aware that defeat on the battlefield could spell military, financial, and personal disaster. Daniel Defoe summed up the prevailing trend with characteristic cynicism: 'Now it is frequent to have armies of fifty thousand men on a side standing at bay within sight of one another, and spend a whole campaign in dodging – or, as it is genteelly termed – observing one another, and then march off into winter quarters.' [2]

The prevalence siege warfare was indicative of this conservative caution. It was a form of engagement that Louis XIV particularly enjoyed: we have witnessed the French king, a quarter of a century earlier, watching excitedly from the trenches outside Maastricht as the young Englishmen, Monmouth and Churchill, fought bravely under Turenne. (The Sun King's enemies noted that Louis was strangely reluctant to grace the more rigorous demands of the open battlefield.) A more orderly form of conflict than the clash of armies in the open, siege warfare was governed by established rules, which allowed several gradations of honourable surrender. These made it possible to avoid the scale of bloodshed common in pitched battle; something that the spirit of the age applauded, partly in reaction to the carnage of the Thirty Years' War. To nowhere was this mode of conflict more suited than Flanders: the combination of its fertile plains, the resulting density of its population, and the importance of its network of waterways, made it an area well worth protecting. This explains the proliferation of fortified towns in the Flemish landscape.

Into this heavily protected arena, pulling against the restraining leash of the Dutch Field Deputies, charged Marlborough, looking for immediate action. With him went an army of 60,000 men, to the rolling accompaniment of a seventy-piece artillery train. His was a concept of dashing leadership that had all but died out a generation before with the passing of Turenne and Condé. As the hapless Monmouth had learnt, this was a general who liked to harass the enemy. Marlborough refused to let the opposition set the pace. Equally dangerously for the enemy, he savoured action and hungered for glory. His proposal in the summer of 1702 was to march directly at the French, threatening their lines of communication, in order to panic them into battle. At first the Field Deputies approved the plan. Then, in what was to become their signature reflex, they lost their nerve and insisted on referring the decision to the States-General. The States, in turn, sent for the advice of their generals on the ground. Marlborough reacted with superficial good grace to the resulting delays, but he was demoralised. His frustration is shown in private correspondence with his great friend and ally, Lord Treasurer Godolphin: 'I am ashamed to write from this camp, for we ought to have marched from hence three or four days ago; but the fears of the Dutch for Nijmegen and the Rhine have created such difficulties when we were to take a resolution, that we were forced to send to the Hague, and the States would not come to any resolution, but have made it more difficult by leaving it to the general officers, at the same time recommending, in the first place, the safety of the Rhine and Nijmegen.'[3]

Marlborough feared that the chance to dictate the campaign's pace had already been squandered. He would now have to pursue the French hard in the hope of bouncing them into battle. His spirits revived when the Field Deputies gave permission for their troops to advance. Riding within sight of the French camp while on a reconnaissance mission, the English commander called out to his Dutch companions: 'I shall soon deliver you from these troublesome neighbours!'[4] With such optimism the allies crossed the Meuse and pushed forward. Marlborough's aggression indeed caused alarm in the French high command, and made them react in ways that he had foreseen. Boufflers's army moved gingerly forward to identify the precise nature of the threat. Marlborough anticipated that the French would now seek to protect the towns in their control, and would therefore march between the towns of Sonhoven and Beringhen. If he was right, this would present the opportunity to force a battle: either by ambushing Boufflers in transit, on one of the open heaths so suited to sweeping cavalry attack, or by surprising him in his encampment. Allied spies confirmed that the French were on the expected route, crossing the heaths of Peer.

However, the Dutch Field Deputies derailed Marlborough's plan to attack: 'Lord Marlborough had his men under arms, and just ready to march, when the Field Deputies came to him, and prayed him to desist,' wrote Robert Parker, a British infantry captain. 'This greatly surprised him, as they had agreed to his scheme the night before. But being a man of great temper and prudence and being determined not to do anything this first campaign without their approbation, at their earnest entreaty he desisted. Whereupon the tents and baggage were sent for and the army pitched their camp again. However, he desired that they would ride out with him to see the enemy pass the heath, which they and most of the general officers did and saw them hurrying over it in the greatest confusion and disorder imaginable; upon this they all acknowledged that they had lost a fair opportunity of giving the enemy a fatal blow.' [5]

The French knew they had enjoyed a very fortunate escape. The young Duke of Berwick – James II's illegitimate son by Marlborough's sister, Arabella – was serving as one of Boufflers's lieutenant-generals. He wrote in his memoirs of the panic at the probable allied attack: 'but the Deputies of the States-General, never wished to consent to it, any more than to attacking us in our camp at Sonhoven; which was lucky for us, because we were positioned in a way that meant we would have been beaten without being able to stir, our left being very high, and our right sunk into a cul-de-sac between two rivulets.' [6] Marlborough was so angered by the Field Deputies' actions that he wrote to the French generals, explaining that the decision to shirk battle had not been his.

Marlborough now planned to force the Field Deputies into battle by engineering a situation which would force them to fight, in self-defence. It seemed that Boufflers might engage, even though his was the smaller army, because he was stung by Louis XIV's criticisms of the ineffectuality of his campaign to date: thanks to Marlborough's aggressive manoeuvring, he had already ceded areas previously under control.

Moreover, in the War of the League of Augsburg, Boufflers had become the first French marshal to surrender in battle. Louis expected the commander to make amends for this ignominy.

Noting with satisfaction that Boufflers and Berwick were advancing toward the allied line, Marlborough tried to lure them further out of their defensive positions. His ruse was to march an apparently isolated Dutch army, of a few thousand men, across the French front. This was an irresistible fly, cast across a hungry nose. Boufflers, keen to re-establish his reputation, pursued the Dutch across the Lowlands for several days, confident that when he overhauled the allied troops, he would utterly destroy them. However, when the French caught up with the detachment, at the heath of Helchteren, their confidence evaporated. The massed ranks of Marlborough's grand army stretched before them, ready for battle.

Boufflers's men, outnumbered and frightened, struggled to fall into battle order, their efforts hampered by the boggy terrain. Marlborough, keen to capitalise on the enemy's milling confusion, instructed his generals to prepare for immediate action. He ordered the artillery to open fire. It was mid-afternoon, and Marlborough was anticipating triumph by nightfall. He had the support of the Field Deputies: their military knowledge was limited, but sufficient to recognise the huge advantage enjoyed by their well-ordered ranks over the awkwardly placed enemy. But the opportunity to fight slipped by. This time the culprit was Opdam, one of the four Dutch generals who had so resented Marlborough's promotion. He refused to advance, insisting on assessing the forward terrain before committing his men to battle. His disobedience led to a disastrous delay, which made it impossible for the allies to strike that evening. Under cover of night the French brought order to their position. The next morning Marlborough observed across the heath an imposing foe, far removed from the chaotic lines that had been at his mercy the previous day.

The Deputies wavered as they took stock of the French lines. All day the two armies faced one another. Marlborough was unable to secure permission to attack, while Boufflers was reluctant to engage a superior force, after his exhausting march and nervous standoff. In the afternoon the two Dutchmen implored their general to postpone his attack until the next morning. Marlborough objected, determined not to give the enemy a chance to avoid battle and slip away unharmed. But he was forced to concede to the Field Deputies' concerns and stood his men down.

As predicted, Boufflers took the opportunity to steal away in the darkness. Marlborough was enraged, but again had to hide his anger. He relayed his furious disappointment in a letter to Godolphin: 'The enclosed letter to the States will let you see the account I have given of the two days being in presence of the enemy. I have but too much reason to complain. However, I have thought it much for Her Majesty's service to take no notice of it, as you see by my letter to the States. I am in so ill humour that I will not trouble you, nor dare I trust myself to write more.'[7]

To his beloved wife, Sarah, Marlborough revealed that he was wracked with migraines, the physical manifestation of his stress: 'I thought I should not have been able to write so much, my head aching extremely. The minute I seal this I shall go to bed.'[8] His British officers shared Marlborough's frustration. Brigadier-General Rowe wrote with disdain for the Dutch: 'We had all the advantage a tired, disorderly and inferior army could give to good troops, but the States were against fighting.'[9] Their timidity and ignorance had combined to deny a nigh certain allied victory.

The French had avoided defeat, but at the cost of retreat. The Barrier Fortresses, whose acquisition by Louis had helped to precipitate the war, were left exposed. The recapture of these would secure the vulnerable south-eastern frontiers of the United Provinces. Then, Marlborough believed, the Deputies might be more adventurous and loosen his leash. He decided to make the remainder of the 1702 campaign a period of siege warfare against the key fortresses on the Meuse.

THIS WAS THE ERA WHEN THE English army consolidated a reputation as a proud and able fighting force. Its international stock, before William III's reign, was low: English soldiers had been renowned for gluttony, for slovenliness and for indiscipline. William introduced Continental standards that made the most of his kingdom's resources.

A reflection of the English army's low standing was provided by the calibre of its personnel. Domestic recruitment was a trawling through the dregs of society – debtors, the unemployed and drifters. It was hard to encourage men to embrace the grim conditions of a service controlled by administered brutalities, such as the lash. The primary reward for service was a laissez-faire attitude to 'roistering', the tradition of boisterous womanising and heavy drinking, which further lowered the soldier in public esteem. Recruiting officers were reduced to bribing and tricking men into enlisting: a shilling slipped into a drunk's pocket was proof of his having 'volunteered' to serve the Crown; the promise of easy women and foreign plunder was enticement enough for the gullible and the greedy. Some chose to serve in the ranks, grateful for regular food and an escape from poverty, but they rarely anticipated how hard life in the army would be. Pay was infrequent and reached the soldier after deductions both open and covert: contributions towards rations, medical services, even weaponry, left very little cash for the soldier, especially after corrupt officers had pilfered what they could.

These were the unprofessional standards that would have appalled Le Tellier and Louvois in France, but would not have surprised other European ministers of war. M. S. Anderson, in his book *War and Society in Europe of the Old Regime*, tells how, in 1699, a Bavarian colonel confined thirty of his men to bed, day and night, because they were without clothes. Fifteen years later sixty-nine German children died of starvation because their fathers' military pay had been so long delayed. Armies of the seventeenth century were frequently subject to scandalous management, self-serving officers, and fractured administration. Until William III imposed stricter standards, this was particularly true of England's forces.

The main problem in the late seventeenth-century English army was administrative. French reformers could summon the authority of an all-powerful king, when seeking greater efficiency. English bureaucrats trying to improve their standing army, however, were obstructed by parliamentary distrust. There was consequently no encouragement for the key officers to be united in a centralised war ministry. Offices of the

Secretary at War, of Master-General of the Ordnance, of Paymaster-General or of the Commissioners for the Sick and Wounded, remained disjointed parts of the whole.

The result was confusion, inefficiency, and a lack of standardisation. A survey in the mid-1680s showed the English infantry was using more than a dozen different types of musket, complicating the supply of ammunition (the guns had varying gauges), and drill. Similarly, there were more than ten manoeuvres for that newfangled invention, the bayonet. Meanwhile the basics of army life were absent: uniforms were not mandatory, and there was no permanent barracks or convalescent home for the military in the whole of England. In the field, troops had no battlefront hospitals, while regimental surgeons were limited in number and ability.

At the same time – as in France before the influence of Le Tellier and Louvois – senior ranks were bought and sold. In the seventeenth and early eighteenth centuries, regiments bore the names of their colonels, emphasising their identity as possessions, rather than units of a cohesive army. Their officers were men of wealth, but of varying skill. For many, a commission was not so much a military rank as a generator of income: the corrupt sought payment for non-existent soldiers in their regiments. These phantoms helped boost the return on their investment. In turn, Parliament often held up payment to the regiments for the benefit of its own bookkeeping – sometimes soldiers' pay was delayed by years. Troops were as likely to be defrauded by their government as they were by their officers.

Despite these manifold flaws, William needed his island army in the struggle against Louis XIV. Dramatic changes were required and Marlborough proved to be the perfect lieutenant to see his plans through. In 1689, when the English contingent arrived in Holland to bolster the Dutch troops, Field Marshal Waldeck reported disapprovingly to William: 'The English suffer from sickness, slackness, wretched clothing and the worst of shoes.'[10] Marlborough set to work on this rabble with gusto: he could even be seen out on the parade ground, personally controlling his troops by signal of flag and drum.

The recruits from Marlborough's intense military training proved their mettle at the battle of Walcourt, mere months after receiving Waldeck's criticism. This time, his report was one of astonished admiration: 'I never would have believed so many of the English would show such a "joie de combattre".'[11] During the engagement 600 English infantrymen held off the main French attack for two hours while the rest of the allied force prepared for action. 2,000 Frenchmen died that day – seven times the English losses – in the only Anglo-Dutch success of 1689. Europe took note of England's fledgling military capabilities.

The rest of the War of the League of Augsburg confirmed the Englishman's steadiness under fire. At Steenkirk, in 1692, outnumbered by five to one, the English infantry were cut down by Marshal Luxembourg's Household troops. Half the division was lost; but the survivors stood their ground, defending themselves doggedly from behind a hedgerow. William watched the pitiful scene with tears in his eyes. 'Oh, my poor English!'[12], he was heard to say, as they fell by the hundred. Parliament was outraged that so many native troops had been left to die. The Dutch, they claimed, had been sheltered from the worst of the French attack. There was a feeling that English troops were: 'hated in Flanders, abused at all rates by the Dutch, exposed upon all accounts as Forlorns'.[13] Some consolation was found in the bravery the fallen had shown in defeat.

There were further plaudits, and further casualties, for the English at Landen, in July 1693. Again they remained unbroken, this time in a bloodbath that was concluded by a decisive French bayonet charge. William narrowly avoided joining the 20,000 allied casualties when bullets ripped through the folds of his clothes. Another passed through his periwig, temporarily deafening him. However, the French also suffered and many of their casualties were credited to the steadfast English troops.

The War of the League of Augsburg provided valuable experience for the coming war. Marlborough knew his men's capabilities and a Prussian general recalled his eagerness to show them off: 'We had become acquainted, and as between soldiers it is customary to talk shop, Marlborough showed me his English, smart troops and brisk. He asked me if I did not believe them invincible and whether with such men were we not sure to beat the French? "Sir", I said, "you may see on the other side troops who believe themselves apparently equally invincible, and if that be so, there is clearly a conflict of opinion".[14] Marlborough's fall from favour prevented him from proving his case in the remainder of that war. Supreme command in the War of the Spanish Succession now handed him the opportunity to test his men against the supposed invincibility of the French.

THE FIGHTING PEDIGREE OF THE English army that Marlborough led into the new war was limited, but proud. Moreover, its morale was high under a captain-general that the men respected. Sergeant Millner of the Royal Irish Regiment confided in his diary how, in the lead-up to the opening campaign, the British troops were: 'waiting Lord Marlborough's Arrival, which was long'd for, and expected every Day'.[15] Marlborough did not disappoint, displaying customary charm and energy on reaching his forces.

He realised that if his men were to be recognised as the finest soldiers in Europe, they must be prepared for the role. This necessitated control of every aspect of their life in camp. Whores were forbidden to ply their trade, regular Christian worship was provided, and a strict but fair code of discipline was imposed. Equally, supplies were always on hand, and Marlborough insisted on the best medical care available. The men were mindful of the efforts made on their behalf, nicknaming Marlborough 'Corporal John', and rewarding him with uncommon devotion. Sergeant Millner's journal gives an insight into the men's feelings for their commander: 'Each and every soldier under his ... command, being animated by his graceful presence and inviting example, did in like manner, with heroical spirits and undaunted courage, unanimously fully imitate the steps of the same leader.'[16] Millner's admiration is echoed in all the surviving journals of Marlborough's men.

The transformation was swift and dramatic: the unpromising raw material delivered by recruiting officers became a self-respecting, efficient, army. The intricacies of parade-ground displays took time to master, but the fundamental training schedule adhered to from the 1690s was easily digestible. Formal inspections became customary, and familiarity with weaponry and tactics were instilled in mock battles fought during the months spent in winter quarters.

From 1702, for nearly a decade, Marlborough achieved mastery of England's military machine. The captain-general relied on two men in particular to help push through organisational reforms. William Cadogan had impressed Marlborough with his flair for administration during the Irish campaign of 1690, and he became quartermaster to the British army. Adam Cardonnel was the earl's Huguenot private secretary, an efficient transmitter and receiver of commands and requests. Marlborough charged this duo with helping to eradicate age-old abuses in the army. Where colonels had been responsible for clothing their men and for extracting pay for them, from 1703 these duties passed to efficient boards, answerable to the Comptroller of Army and Accounts. Their powers overrode those of senior regimental officers, who might prove less diligent in their bookkeeping.

Marlborough also improved his officer class. Recommendations for promotion were checked to see if money rather than merit were the motives behind the proposals. Although the purchase of ranks continued for a further century-and-a-half, a new professionalism took root during the War of the Spanish Succession. As a result of these administrative and structural improvements, the English army was to become better clothed, better paid and better led than ever before. C. T. Atkinson sums up the transformation that Marlborough's innovations and energies imparted: 'Before his day British soldiers had won victories abroad as well as at home. But the British Army was a thing of but little reputation or standing before the days of John Churchill. It was unpopular and suspected at home. It was little feared or regarded abroad. Under Marlborough it did not altogether live down the atmosphere of suspicion with which politicians and plotters had managed to surround it, though the popular dread of the Army was based not on what it had done but on what James II had failed to make it do. But it did effectively dispel any misapprehensions as to its fighting capacities.' [17]

ENGLAND'S NEWFOUND MARTIAL skill was evident in the 1702 campaign. From mid-August, the British were in the front-line of the siege of Venlo, an imposing fortified city on the Meuse. The Prince of Nassau-Saarbrücken led the operation, his force consisting of 32 infantry battalions and 36 cavalry squadrons. The key to the siege was Fort St Michael, 'a fortification of five bastions'[18] garrisoned by 1,500 men. Baron van Coehoorn, Holland's senior siege tactician, was meticulously planning Venlo's fall. However, Marlborough had instructed Nassau-Saarbrücken to secure the city before the campaign's end so, when Coehoorn had shown little progress by mid-September, the prince attacked.

The assault on the fort was a brave but fortunate affair, entrusted to Lord Cutts, who had a reputation for extreme bravery against well-defended positions. While serving as Adjutant-General to the Duke of Lorraine, in 1686, he had taken a prominent part in the capture of the Turks' citadel at Buda. His reputation for always being where the heat of an engagement was at its fiercest had resulted in his nickname, 'the Salamander'. At Venlo, Cutts briefed his officers to push the enemy back from the covered way of Fort St Michael, a protected area in the defences from where they were inflicting serious casualties on Coehoorn's engineers. If an opportunity then presented itself to carry the assault further, it was to be seized. This was unconventional leadership: usually, with an attack of this sort, a clear goal was agreed upon first. However, Cutts was a brave and flexible leader, who enjoyed the full confidence of his commander. He saw an opportunity and we have an eyewitness's account of the assault of his three regiments (two English and one Irish):

> About four in the afternoon the signal was given, and according to our orders, we rushed up to the covert-way; the enemy gave us one scattering fire only, and away they ran. We jumped into the covert-way, and ran after them. They made to a ravelin [outwork], which covered the curtain of the fort, in which were a captain and sixty men. We seeing them get into the ravelin, pursued them, got in with them, and soon put most of them to the sword. They that escaped us, fled over a small wooden bridge, that led over the moat to the fort; and

here like madmen without fear or wit, we pursued them over that tottering bridge, exposed to the fire of the great and small shot of the body of the fort. However we had nothing for it, but to take the fort or die. [19]

The garrison fled before the charging British. The fort fell, 200 French soldiers were taken prisoner and hundreds of their colleagues were slain; some died in the fighting, while many were drowned trying to swim the Meuse. Only 27 British troops were killed. The success of such a hazardous operation was greeted with 'the great surprise of the whole army'[20]. From this point the British were treated with increased respect.

After the engagement, Marlborough's men pondered what else they might have achieved during the campaign, if they had been unleashed in open battle: 'By these things you may judge what probability there was of success when we might have engaged with a superiority of numbers on our side, no stone walls, nor any impediments but a morass in M. Dopt's noddle.'[21] Dopt was one of the Dutch Field Deputies, who had become figures of ridicule in the British ranks. Marlborough and his soldiers were aware that, 'by the great caution of the Dutch in not hazarding a battle ... opportunities of ruining the French army in Flanders'[22] had been squandered.

The townsfolk of Venlo noted the ferocity of the attack on the fort with terror. They dreaded the next phase of the allied operations, which they feared would be an assault on their walls. However, three days after the fall of Fort St Michael, news reached the allies that Landau had fallen to their colleagues in Germany. Prince Nassau-Saarbrücken ordered a celebratory salvo to mark this victory: three rounds of cannon, mortar and small arms fire were discharged into the air. Unnerved by what they assumed to be the prelude to all-out attack, the burghers of Venlo called on their military governor to surrender. Marlborough's soldiers' newly won reputation had secured its first dividend.

The allies garnered further significant honours in 1702, capturing Ruremond, Stevenswaert and Maaseik. Marlborough now controlled the River Meuse all the way to Maastricht; but still he wanted more.

Determined to eke out every day from the twilight of the campaigning season, he turned to Liège. Marlborough quickly overran the lightly defended town, before offering surrender terms to the governor of the fortified citadel. The Frenchman declined, inviting Marlborough to repeat his offer in a month's time. By the rules of siege engagement, the governor's rebuff forfeited his men's right to clemency. The next day, 23 October 1702, Marlborough ordered an assault, again led by his British troops. It started at noon and the action was completed in less than an hour, 'Our men giving no quarter for some time, so that the greater part of the garrison was cut to pieces'.[23] Three hundred British fell in the action, during which the 9th Foot regiment showed particular bravery. Marlborough reported with pride to London 'the very vigorous behaviour of the Queen's subjects'.[24] Around Europe the stock of Anne's army was rising.

IN THE AUTUMN OF 1702, Marlborough headed by boat for The Hague. With him travelled the two Dutch Deputies, while a cavalry detachment rode alongside on the bank of the River Meuse. After they passed Venlo, the escort became separated from their charges. This allowed a French raiding party, led by an Irish deserter called Farewell, to waylay the boat. The two Deputies carried passes guaranteeing their safe passage home, signed by the Duke of Burgundy. Marlborough, however, had not secured a passport. His quick-thinking clerk, Stephen Gell, pressed a document into his master's hand and this he presented to the raiding party. It was a pass in the name of Lieutenant-General Charles Churchill, Marlborough's younger brother. Farewell failed to recognise the allied commander, but he noticed that the pass was out of date and thus invalid. Nine hours of negotiation followed, before the raiding party alighted from the vessel with lesser prisoners of war – Marlborough's prized chef amongst them – and some booty.

But word reached The Hague that Marlborough had been captured. There was panic. Without him, the United Provinces' hopes for the war seemed crushed. The allied garrisons of Venlo and Nijmegen immediately marched on Geldern, the likeliest prison for the captive general, and demanded his return. The French governor of Geldern was mystified, agreeing to hand over Marlborough's chef to the besieging force. As for the English captain-general, the governor said he was unable to assist the enemy, since he knew nothing of his whereabouts.

Marlborough then made his way to The Hague where the reaction of the inhabitants amazed him: 'My room is full at this time,' he wrote to his wife. 'Till they saw me, they thought me a prisoner in France, so that I was not ashore one minute, before I had great crowds of the common people, some endeavouring to take me by the hands, and all crying out welcome. But that which moved me most was, to see a great many of both sexes cry for joy.'[25] The depth of Dutch relief at Marlborough's deliverance was conveyed by Grand Pensionary Heinsius: 'Your captivity was on the point of causing the slavery of these provinces, and restoring to France the power of her extending her uncontrollable dominion over all Europe. No hope was left, if she retained in bondage the man whom we revere as the instrument of Providence, to secure independence to the greater part of the Christian world.'[26]

Marlborough was flattered by the effusive welcome. It gave him hope that, the following year, he might be able to act with a freedom that the Field Deputies had denied him in 1702.

In England, Queen Anne marked the end of the campaign with generous rewards. Marlborough's earldom was superseded by a dukedom, an increase in status that was supported by an annual pension of £5,000. Sarah was reluctant to accept the new title, fearing others' jealousy; but her husband was eager for the elevation. He wrote to his wife of how Heinsius had: 'said to me, that it was not reasonable to expect ever to have so much success in any other campaign as in this, so that he ended in begging me for the good of the common cause, the queen's service, and my own sake, that I would think this the proper time of being distinguished.'[27] Yet Sarah had been correct: John Evelyn recorded the envy aroused by Anne's treatment of Marlborough. He had, it was believed, received an excessive reward for his achievements, and the diarist could not forget the humble origins from which the new duke had risen. His sudden 'rising was taken notice of & displeased those who had him till now in great esteem: he is indeed a very handsome, proper, well-spoken, & affable person, & supplies his want of acquired knowledge by keeping good Company: in the meantime, [his] ambition and love of riches have no end.'[28] The Tory-dominated Commons voted to clip his wings a little. The Members insisted that the pension voted Marlborough be restricted to the duke's lifetime, and not – as Anne had intended – in perpetuity for his heirs.

Their patriotism allowed the Tories to join in the celebrations of Marlborough's military successes. However, they remained committed to a policy of limited naval action, rather than the continental warfare that had brought Marlborough gains in Flanders. Balancing the mood of the moment with their historic prejudices, the Tories offered the sovereign their congratulations on a fine campaign. As they did so, they pointedly contrasted Marlborough's triumphs with William III's litany of setbacks in the previous war. The Commons' tribute to Queen Anne emphasised how: 'the vigorous support of Your Majesty's Allies and the wonderful progress of Your Majesty's arms under the conduct of the Earl of Marlborough have signally retrieved the ancient honour and glory of the English nation.'[29] The word 'retrieved' was a calculated insult. The 1690s, when William had enjoyed few successes, were years when the Whigs had supported his continental endeavours with vigour. It was to this hapless time that the Tories referred, keen to remind England of the failure of the Whigs' war policy then.

The point was driven home further. When the queen ordered national thanksgiving for Marlborough's grand sweep along the Meuse, the Tory leaders tacked a lesser naval victory at Cadiz on to the celebrations. This devalued the army's triumphs, while exaggerating the navy's achievement. Political one-upmanship was more important to the rival factions than an honest appraisal of successes overseas. The enmity between Whig and Tory in the early eighteenth century was every bit as intense as that between Royalist and Parliamentarian sixty years earlier; it was just that the clashes would remain centred on the Houses of Parliament, rather than progressing to the battlefield. This was not only a point of bitter regret for Marlborough, but also a source of potential danger for him and his plans.

CHAPTER EIGHT

FRIENDS LIKE THESE

*'If both parties agree that the war must not be offensive in
this country, I am very much afraid the Dutch will not think
themselves very safe in our friendship. However, I cannot but
be much concerned; for if this country is ruined, we are
undone. May God preserve me and my dearest love from
seeing this come to pass.'*

LETTER OF MARLBOROUGH TO SARAH, HIS WIFE, SEPTEMBER 1703

IN OCTOBER 1702 THE HOUSE of Commons assembled, the Tories
returning to power with a majority of 133 seats. The Whigs' secondary
position in the Commons was a true reflection of their standing in the
nation. Attachment to the Tories, 'the Church Party', was the natural
reflex of an electorate that, in the main, valued royal authority, and the
dominance of Anglicanism. There were many who identified dissenting
sects, such as Presbyterians, with republicanism. For them, the Tories
were the upholders of stability in a world made dangerous by the revo-
lutions of the 1640s and 1688.

The Tories berated those who had opposed the Crown in the Civil
War, associating the regicides of the past with continued resistance to
royal authority. In a sermon to the Commons in 1697 William Lancaster
thundered: 'I know not but there may be men in the world, thus left to
themselves, who instead of repenting of a most horrid murder and of
shedding innocent blood, have themselves and their posterity justified

the doing it, and advanced from the blood of one king, to maintain the lawfulness of resisting all kings.'[1] This level of invective played well in the shires.

William III, reassured by Tory respect for the monarchy, initially sided with their cause. However, the party's unhelpful attitude to the War of the League of Augsburg gradually alienated him. The Earls of Nottingham and Danby, high Tory leaders, denied him sufficient funds to supply the army. In 1694, the king turned to the Whigs, for they promised to support him in his foreign ventures. However, when the Peace of Ryswick concluded the war three years later, the Whigs were seen as the enablers of a foreign policy that had become hugely unpopular. They lost power and only became electable again once Louis XIV's provocations had restored the English to fighting mode.

Throughout William's and Anne's reigns, regardless of the pendulum of popularity in the Commons, the Whigs remained a considerable force in the Lords. There they were controlled by a clique of powerful magnates and bolstered by a number of Low Church bishops appointed by William. As a result, the Whigs exercised influence in the nation that exceeded their actual popularity.

The key domestic battlegrounds for the Tories and the Whigs in both Houses during Anne's reign were twofold: the struggle between Anglicans and dissenters; and the line of succession to the throne. Most Tories had supported the overthrow of James II in the Glorious Revolution, but many now repented their hasty abrogation of the divine right of kings. The rapid growth of dissenting houses throughout England was one of the results of the Revolution that these Tories most regretted. The majority of Whigs were also Anglican, yet they were not threatened by the march of religious dissent across the nation: toleration was a key component of the Whig creed.

The Tories had a further cause for regret. The 1701 proposal by Sir Edward Seymour that Louis XIV be fought until he recognised the Protestant succession to the English throne had seemed the right course at the time. However, within a year came the Act of Abjuration, requiring public office-holders to swear eternal rejection of the claims of James's

son, the Pretender, to the Crown. After the death of Anne's son, Gloucester, the implications for the Tories were stark and unsettling: to retain
power, they must turn their backs on the ousted Stuarts forever. This
had not been the plan in 1688.

Anne tried to defuse the religious and constitutional tensions with
compromise. Brought up a stolid Anglican by her tutor, Bishop Compton
– a Royalist officer in the Civil War – her limited education had left her
fearful that the Whigs were the natural descendants of her grandfather's
executioners. However, on becoming queen, Anne sought to blend
reliable Tory advisers with moderate Whigs to form a government of
consensus. At the end of 1702 one of her chief courtiers stated: 'The
Queen is resolved not to follow the example of her predecessor in making
use of a few of her subjects to oppress the rest. She will be Queen of all
her subjects, and would have all the parties and distinctions of former
reigns ended and buried in hers, and in order to it expects that those
whom she employs shall give the first example. Her Majesty's intentions
and resolutions are great and for the common good.' [2] They were also
naive.

Bi-partisan cabinets were doomed to failure. Had William allowed
Anne an apprenticeship in statecraft, she would already have known the
depth of mutual hatred that consumed Whig and Tory. Instead, she had
been excluded from real influence during her brother-in-law's reign and
so came to the throne with the misguided hope that she could bring the
parties together for the benefit of the whole country. Anne appointed
over-large cabinets to accommodate a broad political span, failing to
appreciate that such councils invariably dissolved into vicious factions.
In the hope of controlling her politicians, Anne appointed royal managers,
turning first to Marlborough. He persuaded his friend Sidney Godolphin
to become Lord Treasurer. Highly able and scrupulously honest, Godolphin was a popular first minister with his queen and he worked easily
with Marlborough. Their partnership remained intact, and in power,
until 1710.

The Marlborough–Godolphin axis proved controversial from its
inception. The High Tory Lord Rochester was an early opponent, galled

by Godolphin's appointment to the Treasury. Rochester had expected to receive the office, but was instead appointed Lord Lieutenant of Ireland. This was a prestigious posting, but one often used to remove the incumbent from the hub of Parliament. Rochester determined that he would carry out his duties from London, not Dublin, so he could still be heard on the great issues of the day. He proved himself a committed advocate for maritime war against France, peddling a Tory line popular in the shires, that Spain and France should be attacked on their weakest flanks: on the seas and in their overseas colonies. Money invested in the navy for these purposes would, he insisted, reap dividends. By contrast, sending regiments to fight in the Lowlands was risky, expensive, and would primarily benefit the Dutch. Marlborough's counter-argument chimed with Whig philosophy: peripheral gains were not going to win this war but substantial triumphs on the battlefield would. Marlborough, with the queen behind him, won these disputes; but the Tory Commons made their sympathies clear by granting the navy twice the army's financial allowance. They also defeated a bill that would have facilitated the recruitment of soldiers.

Tory jealousy of the parvenu Marlborough's status and wealth escalated as the war progressed. Anne's rewards for her captain-general at the end of 1702 were viewed as excessive. Members pointed enviously at the £10,000 annual salary that he was already receiving for leading the Dutch forces. This, together with smaller considerations from other allies, ought to satisfy this former pageboy, who had risen from obscure gentry stock to pre-eminence in the land. With his wife all but controlling the queen and the Court, and his best friend sharing the management of government, Marlborough's power seemed limitless.

Such dramatic elevation would have been acceptable to the Tories if he had used it to further their cause. However, although he shared many of their beliefs, Marlborough echoed his monarch's hope that consensus politics could prevail. 'There is nothing more certain than what you say, that either of the parties would be tyrants if they were let alone,'[3] he wrote to Sarah. 'All parties are alike. And as I have taken my resolution of never doing any hardship to any man whatsoever,

I shall by it have a quiet in my own mind; not valuing to be a favourite to either of them.'[4]

Former, Tory, colleagues resented his position, feeling snubbed by the withholding of patronage that they considered their due. If Marlborough chose not to further their interest, then they would make him feel their ire whenever the opportunity arose. At the end of 1702 the Tories started to foment a damaging slander that was to dog Marlborough for a decade: he was prolonging the war in order to enrich himself, they said. How else to explain his inability – or should they term it 'reluctance' – to bring the enemy to battle?

Early in 1703, the Tory leaders undermined the continental war. It was hard to resist the people's calls to build on the successes of the 1702 campaign and the Tories increased Marlborough's forces by 10,000 foreign auxiliaries and five new battalions of British troops. However, they also gave vent to their historic hatred of the Dutch, which stemmed from seventeenth-century naval defeats at the hands of Van Tromp and De Ruyter. It was intolerable to England, the Tories said, that while being asked to provide more soldiers to fight for the United Provinces, Dutch merchants continued clandestine trade with France. This led the Tories to: 'insist upon it with the States-General that there be an immediate stop of all ports, and all letters, bills, trade and commerce with France and Spain.'[5] It was a lot to ask of a mercantile nation and, as the Tories had hoped, the resulting row destabilised the Anglo-Dutch alliance.

While they fostered discord between the Maritime Powers, the Tories' zeal for Anglicanism threatened major ructions at home. Since James II's displacement the Tories had watched with mounting disgust the growth of Protestant dissent in England. Public office, both locally and in London, was limited by the Test and Corporation Acts, which required proof that the applicant was a practising Anglican. However, the Calvinist William had allowed standards to drift somewhat, and from 1689 a rash of dissent had spread nationwide. Furthermore, dissenters were securing office by attending the occasional Anglican service, in compliance with the letter of the law. The rest of the year they worshipped where they wished. It was here, on 'occasional conformity' – 'a religious piece of hypocrisy as even no heathen government would have endured'[6] – that the Anglicans began a concerted attack. It threatened the unity that Marlborough and Godolphin knew was necessary to keep Parliament focused on, and committed to, the foreign war.

The pair could not be seen to oppose the Occasional Conformity Bill, which was put before Parliament in January 1703. To do so would be interpreted as a denial of the supremacy of the Established Church. However, while publicly supporting the Bill, the two men expended enormous energy discreetly persuading others to vote against it. As a result, the Bill failed; but the Tories understood that cunning opponents had outmanoeuvred them, placing the pursuit of the war above loyalty to Anglican and Tory principles.

Marlborough and Godolphin realised that they must bring the extremist Tories to heel. Rochester and his allies would surely render the war untenable through their machinations unless they were checked. However, because of Rochester's blood relationship with the queen, a direct attack on him was not an option. Instead, the duumvirate persuaded the queen to insist that her uncle go to Dublin, for the proper discharge of his duties. Rochester, realising that his departure would end his influence at Court, felt compelled to resign his posts. Marlborough and Godolphin had succeeded in removing their chief opponent from office, but he was from this point a centre of opposition to them. Rochester's allies, rallying round Nottingham in the Lords, and Seymour in the Commons, now worked against the royal managers, plotting their fall, regardless of the effect this would have on the war. Indeed, they willed Marlborough's failure on campaign, in the expectation that this would lead to his dismissal.

The Whigs also turned against Marlborough and Godolphin. At the end of 1702, they were once more out of royal favour and were reduced to a small minority in the Commons. However, they hoped that the openly Whig Sarah Marlborough would use her influence with the queen to improve their position. Certainly Sarah tried to stem or deflect her mistress's Tory instincts: 'I resolved from the beginning of the Queen's reign', she later recalled, 'to try whether I could not by degrees make impressions in her mind more favourable to the Whigs.'[7] It was a mission that failed.

As their impatience grew, the Whigs channelled their disappointment into attacks on Marlborough, plodding from siege to unwanted siege in Flanders. By the end of 1703 they joined in the clamour for a defensive war. They aped the Tories, smearing Marlborough's name with the same slur that he was prolonging the war for his own gain. It was a question of how long the captain-general could withstand the dual attack at home, while leading the Grand Alliance abroad. This task was made no easier by family tragedy.

JOHN, BORN IN 1686, WAS THE only Churchill son to survive infancy. As a boy, he had been a playmate of Anne's heir, William Gloucester, the two boys sharing a passion for playing at soldiers. After leaving Eton, he went to Cambridge, where his tutor was Dr Francis Hare, later Marlborough's Chaplain-General. John was eager to fulfil his boyhood ambition and serve in the army; but Sarah, with maternal protectiveness, insisted that he complete his studies first.

While at Cambridge, John enjoyed staying at Sidney Godolphin's house in nearby Newmarket. Godolphin judged John 'the best natured and most agreeable creature.'[8] In the autumn of 1702, Newmarket was struck by an outbreak of smallpox. Godolphin wrote to reassure the Marlboroughs that he would keep John away from the town. However, on returning to Cambridge after this visit, John succumbed to the disease in its most threatening form. Sarah rushed to oversee the treatment of her son, and the queen – cruelly familiar with the agonies of watching a child in the throes of mortal sickness – sent her physicians to assist. Marlborough wrote to Sarah of his torment at the prospect of losing his sixteen-year-old son: 'If we must be so unhappy as to lose this poor child, I pray God to enable us both to behave ourselves with that resignation which we ought to do. If this uneasiness which I now be under should last long, I think I could not live. For God's sake, if there be any hope of recovery let me know it.'[9]

John died on 20 February 1703, both parents by his bedside. The

Marlboroughs were devastated, Sarah's physical and mental health both suffering. She was seen mixing with the vagrants who sought shelter at Westminster School. Marlborough was unable to help her through her crisis, for he had to leave for the new campaign in Flanders twelve days after his son's death. So close to his children, the duke shared the pain of John's loss, while questioning the purpose of accruing greater honours and riches, when he had no heir to pass them on to: 'I've lost all that is dear to me,' he confided to a friend. 'It is fit for me to retire and not toil and labour for I know not who.'[10] He arrived in the Lowlands with black crèpe on his sleeve, his household joining him in mourning. Melancholy haunted the duke throughout the campaign of 1703. 'I have this day seen a very great [military] procession,' he imparted to Godolphin, 'and the thoughts how pleased poor Lord Churchill would have been with such a sight, have added very much to my uneasiness. Since it has pleased God to take him, I do wish from my soul I could think less of him.'[11]

THE DUTCH LOOKED BACK AT THE previous year's military successes with satisfaction. No major engagement had been lost and the recapture of the Barrier Fortresses secured much of the vulnerable southeastern frontier. Furthermore, the choice of Marlborough as military commander had been fully vindicated, Athlone graciously conceding: 'The success of this campaign is solely due to this incomparable chief, since I confess that I, serving as second in command, opposed in all circumstances his opinion and proposals.'[12] However, Athlone died shortly after showing such magnanimity and it was soon clear that any hopes Marlborough may have fostered of galvanising his allies into bolder action had passed with him.

He started his campaign by besieging Bonn, setting off with 40 infantry battalions, 60 cavalry squadrons, and 100 artillery pieces, determined to make short work of the assignment. Within a fortnight of the first siege trenches being dug, and two months before the previous year's campaign had even begun, Marlborough launched a three-pronged assault on the city. This overwhelmed the defending garrison and

Marlborough took the city, thereby establishing allied control over the Rhine for 300 miles from the sea to Philippsburg. Now the Englishman's plans again diverged from the rigid parameters of his Dutch masters. Eager to disrupt French lines of communication, Marlborough advocated attacks on Antwerp and Lierre: success there would precipitate a French retreat from Brabant and West Flanders. Perhaps more importantly, it must force the French to move some of their forces from the Upper Rhine to the Lowlands, taking the pressure off the Emperor's hard-pressed forces there.

However, Marlborough was again undone by Dutch unreliability. General Coehoorn had been instructed to march on Ostend. Instead, he headed off on an expedition of self-enrichment, extracting contributions from the Flemish population in return for not destroying their property. It was disappointing in the extreme for Marlborough to have his designs again hamstrung by woeful Dutch support.

Marshal Villeroi, a recently released prisoner of war, returned to command the French Low Country armies, a post he had filled in the previous war. Marlborough wanted to bring him to battle, but the Frenchman showed reluctance to leave his defensive lines. Marlborough told Godolphin why this might be: 'At this time the strength of the French army is 118 squadrons and 61 battalions; ours consists of 125 squadrons and 59 battalions: but our battalions are stronger than theirs, so that I think we have a good deal the superiority, which is very plainly the opinion of the French, since they always decamp when we come near them.'[13] They would only engage when their numbers exceeded those of the allies.

Marshal Boufflers, with a secondary force, attacked General Opdam at Eckeren on 30 June. Opdam fled the field in disgrace, ending an uneven military career. The following day, with Villeroi and Boufflers conjoined in one army, the French transmitted their intention to fight the allied grand army. However, the marshals' resolve failed, and they scuttled back behind strong defensive lines under cover of darkness.

All the elements that had made the campaigning season of 1702 so frustrating – elusive marshals, timid Dutch politicians, fickle Dutch generals – characterised the succeeding campaign. 'Never certainly was any army better pleased with the hopes of fighting than ours, but we were disappointed,' wrote the Earl of Orkney's chaplain, Samuel Noyes, 'and now I begin to fear we shall do nothing this year, because we can't come at the enemy or any of their towns. This is the general opinion.'[14]

Exhausted by the futility of it all, Marlborough wrote to Sarah: 'I was on horseback from twelve o'clock at night till four in the afternoon yesterday, and have again marched this day. Since we had no action yesterday, I believe we shall have none this campaign, for the French are now in very strong country, and can go behind their lines when they please. Pardon the shortness of this letter, from a man that is heart and soul yours.'[15] He was tempted to retire, rather than endure these protracted trials of patience.

Marlborough's disillusionment was fed by reports from Godolphin about goings-on in Parliament. Acknowledging the Whigs' and Tories' enmity, the duke wearily replied to the Lord Treasurer: 'I am so altered in my temper, that when the queen's service will permit me to be quit of this station I am now in, I hope she will be so good as to allow of my meddling with very little business, by which I might be out of the power of the parties, for I am very sure I can please neither.'[16] In response to his stresses, he endured a succession of 'violent headaches'. 'I own to you,' he wrote to Sarah, 'my sickness comes from fretting.'[17]

The campaign was not without its successes. The town of Huy was taken in late August. The English artillery showed ruthless skill against the French keep: Samuel Noyes noted that the gunners 'Murthered them so cruelly that within less than two hours they cried out Quarter.'[18] Having lost his final stronghold, the Elector of Cologne joined Louis's list of itinerant, stateless, pensioner rulers. While reporting the capture of Huy to the States-General, Marlborough urged them on to bolder glories: 'The Allies rightly expect that we on our side should do something striking; the situation of their affairs even demanding prompt relief by a powerful diversion which would oblige the enemy to retire from the Empire.' At the same time, Marlborough reminded the States-General of the ferment back in London, whipped up against a war that was costing

England much, but delivering little. 'I can assure your High Mightinesses that this is very much expected in England and also without doubt in Holland, which would gain the greatest advantage. I can even say that in our case it is very necessary, for there are signs that people would be in a bad humour this winter with such a superiority if the campaign went by without something considerable.'[19]

Marlborough favoured a push through a weak spot that he had noted in the French lines, between the Rivers Meuse and Mehaigne. This plan was strongly supported by his generals, but was opposed by Dutch Field Deputies and commanders, who advocated instead the siege of Limburg. Marlborough was distraught at the rejection of his plan: 'When I writ last I was so very much disordered that I writ in great pain,' he complained to Sarah. 'I cannot say I am yet well, for my head aches violently, and I am afraid you will think me light-headed, when I tell you that I go to-morrow to the siege of Limburg in hopes to recover my health. But it is certainly true that I shall have more quiet there than I have here; for I have been these last six days in a perpetual dispute, and there I shall have nobody but such as will willingly obey me.'[20]

The 1703 campaign petered out, with Limburg and then Guelder falling softly into allied hands. It had been a sapping year for Marlborough, the loss of his son followed by a repetition of his Dutch allies' numbing negativity. 'I must own the conduct of Holland this summer gives but too just a handle for clamour against our great expense of carrying on this war in their country,'[21] Godolphin wrote to Robert Harley, Speaker of the House of Commons. Even Godolphin, to Marlborough's consternation, was beginning to favour a defensive war.

CHAPTER NINE

CLOSING IN

'The French King early [in 1703] had sent Marshal Villars
with 30,000 men through the Black Forest to [the Elector
of Bavaria's] assistance. The Elector had 40,000 of his own
subject troops, and both these joined together, carried all
before them that campaign.'

CAPTAIN ROBERT PARKER'S *MEMOIRS*

IF THE END OF 1703 SAW THE ALLIES divided and dissatisfied in the
north of Europe, further south matters appeared desperate. The Emperor
was faced with a rampant Hungarian insurrection and the treachery of his
son-in-law, the Elector of Bavaria. Vienna, and with it the Habsburg
hold on the Imperial crown, was now in real danger. Never had Louis
XIV looked more likely to achieve European domination.

Maximilian Emmanuel of Bavaria had finally revealed his hand in
the autumn of 1702. He had watched the start of the war without committing himself, while secretly brokering terms with the French. Louis
XIV wanted Bavarian assistance: it would provide him with a platform
from which to strike Austria. Electoral troops would have to build a
bridgehead for French forces through the rest of Germany. Ulm, Ratisbon
and Augsburg must be captured – or at least neutralised – to enable a
French advance to Bavaria.

Ulm was a powerful, fortified, presence on the Danube, manned by
its own independent armed force. The Elector secretly planned to capture

the city, realising that his best chance lay in stealth. One afternoon in early September 1702 one hundred Bavarian officers in civilian clothes, their pistols concealed, drifted through Ulm's various gateways in small, unobtrusive, groups. 'They dressed themselves up as sheep or cattle dealers, corn and beer merchants and sellers of salt and tin ware.'[1] At dusk, the infiltrators furtively unlocked Ulm's gates to allow waiting troops to pour in. The local militia was taken by surprise and the city was quickly overrun. The allies, who had been attempting to lure the Elector back to the Imperial fold through secret correspondence, now knew for certain that Bavaria was lost to Louis.

The shock of Ulm's capture was felt keenly forty miles away in Augsburg, a Free Imperial City. Its position, at the confluence of the Rivers Lech and Wertach, gave it the potential to block a French advance to Bavaria. However, Augsburg had clear memories of the horrors of warfare: it had lost half its population during the Thirty Years' War, when captured by the Swedes. Eager to avoid a similar fate, the people of Augsburg declared their city neutral. This moved the possibility of a Franco-Bavarian union ever nearer.

Six weeks later Marshal Villars trounced Lewis of Baden, an Imperialist prince and general, at the Battle of Friedlingen, on the Upper Rhine. With the fall of Ulm and the victory at Friedlingen, it was now possible for Villars to push through to the Bavarians. The combined armies could then prey on Vienna. However, it was too late in the campaigning season for Villars to penetrate the Black Forest.

The dramatic opening to 1703 seemed to seal the Emperor's fate. Villars quit his winter quarters in February, sidestepping Freiburg before moving in on Kehl. This town guarded the routes leading across the Black Forest to the Danube valley. It withstood the siege for just thirteen days, falling on 10 March. The French prepared for the final push. Marshal Tallard, the former French ambassador to London, took position in front of the lines of Stollhofen, defences covering the twenty miles between the Rhine and the Black Forest, where Lewis of Baden's army was entrenched. Villars consolidated his troops, and then, amid emotional scenes, the two generals linked up on 12 May at Dutlingen, near Villingen.

The excitement surrounding the occasion dissipated as the commanders quickly realized that they had different agendas and clashing personalities. Maximilian Emmanuel hoped to harness the power of the combined armies to enrich himself, by exacting fines and levies from surrounding cities and states. Villars, meanwhile, remained entirely focused on advancing to Vienna in order to knock the Emperor out of the war. The Elector was commander of the force, but Villars, one of the most able of Louis's marshals, would not allow Maximilian Emmanuel to divert the Franco-Bavarian force from its prime objective.

The Elector proposed a march on the Palatinate, to bring Count Styrum's Imperial army to battle. Villars, realising that the Bavarian's true intention was to pillage the Tyrol for his own gain, refused to be distracted from an attack on Vienna: the Austrian capital was known to be almost devoid of troops and there were reports that the Emperor was planning his flight. The marshal was adamant that Versailles's instructions be obeyed. After much cajoling, the Elector conceded and the move into Austria was planned for early June.

At the last moment, Maximilian Emmanuel thought better of the plan and refused to move. There was nothing that the furious Villars could do to change his ally's mind. It was a fatal delay. Meanwhile Marshal Tallard failed to block Lewis of Baden's advance to the Danube. It was clear that Vienna would not be taken in 1703. There was a significant victory, however, late in the year: in September, Count Styrum was comprehensively beaten at the battle of Höchstädt, a town on the banks of the Danube near to Blenheim. Styrum lost 5,000 men killed, and 7,000 captured. The enemy also took 37 of his cannon.

The clash between Villars and the Elector saved Emperor Leopold. The marshal wanted the Bavarian army to march for Augsburg, where Lewis of Baden's Imperial soldiers were digging in. When the Elector rejected the plan, Villars announced that the French would march by themselves, the following day. At this, the Elector went red in the face, tore off his hat and wig, threw them on the table, then exploded: 'I've commanded the Emperor's army with the Duke of Lorraine, a pretty great general, and he never treated me like this!' Villars held his ground:

'Certainly, Monsieur de Lorraine was a great prince and a great general; but I answer to the king for his army, and I will not expose it to perish because of the bad council that you seem determined to follow!' [2] The Elector temporarily backed down, before once more refusing to cooperate with Villars. Utterly exasperated, the marshal informed Louis that he could no longer remain with the army on the Danube and asked to be relieved of his command.

Villars's rare talents were now deployed against Huguenot insurgents in the French province of the Cévennes. He recommended as his replacement in Bavaria Marshal Marsin, a general of middling ability whose father had served under Condé. Marsin was known for his charm, and it was hoped that he would be able to work with the mercurial Elector. Early results were promising; in December the French and Bavarians cooperated in the capture of Augsburg and a month later, in January 1704, they also took Passau and Lintz. Control of Passau, situated at the confluence of the Rivers Danube, Inn and Ilz, strengthened the Elector's lines of communications, while securing the approaches to Upper Austria. Meanwhile, in Austria, Hungarian rebels, supported by Louis XIV, were roving the countryside menacingly. Everything looked set for a swift and conclusive march on Vienna in the spring of 1704.

PART THREE

THE CAMPAIGN

CHAPTER TEN

CUTTING THE GORDIAN KNOT

'My intentions are to march all the English to Coblenz, and to declare here that I intend to command on the Moselle; but when I come there to write to the States, that I think it absolutely necessary for saving the empire, to march with the troops under my command, that are in Her Majesty's and the Dutch pay, in order to take measures for the speedy reducing of the Elector of Bavaria.'

MARLBOROUGH TO LORD TREASURER GODOLPHIN,
29 APRIL 1704

THE COMBINATION OF HIS FRUSTRATIONS in Flanders, the backstabbing in London and the perilous state of the Habsburgs in Vienna led Marlborough to look at the prospects for 1704 with resignation: 'For this campaign I see so very ill a prospect that I am extremely out of heart,' he wrote to Sarah: 'But God's will be done; and I must be for this year very uneasy, for in all other campaigns I had an opinion of being able to do something for the common cause; but in this I have no other hopes than that some lucky accident may enable me to do good.' [1] This pessimism led him to contemplate a stunning move.

It stemmed from an idea first put to him by Count Wratislaw, the Imperial envoy to London, in February 1703. Wratislaw was an amiable figure, whose easy manner and spherical form belied a surprising strength of character and flexibility of mind. He told Marlborough that, with the Franco-Bavarians threatening on one side and Hungarian rebels massing on the other, there was only one way to keep the Empire in the war: the English commander must lead his army from the Netherlands to the Danube, and then attack the Elector and Marsin before they swamped Vienna.

As his hopes for 1703 petered out, Marlborough now addressed this extraordinarily bold proposal with increasing interest. It no longer seemed the desperate plan of a beleaguered ally, but a strategy that just might lead to the longed-for climax of decisive battle. Marlborough was convinced that this conflict could not be won in the Lowlands, where the slow attrition of siege warfare dominated. Neither was it likely to be won at all if Austria, with its German allies, was knocked out of the contest. Something spectacular was necessary, and Wratislaw's suggestion might be what was required to cut the Gordian Knot.

If the plan were to succeed, Marlborough needed to overcome a myriad of problems. First, it was certain that the cautious Dutch would stonewall the transfer of their troops to lands so far from home. Even though their frontiers were now safer than they had been since Louis's seizure of the Barrier Fortresses, the States-General were wedded to defence. Secondly, secrecy would be crucial if the 250-mile march through Europe, across the faces of Villeroi's and Tallard's armies, were not to result in annihilating French flanking attacks. Thirdly, the forces would need to be supplied while they marched, and their pace could not be rushed, if they were to arrive in a suitable condition to face the Franco-Bavarians in battle. This was a trinity of daunting challenges, each of which might have dissuaded a less determined, less exasperated, commander.

Marlborough's lieutenants confirmed that his army in the Netherlands was in good shape. 'If the recruits and clothing are in time without any accident, and prove good, Your Grace will see both Horse and Foot in a better condition than they were last year by a good deal,' wrote the exacting Lord Cutts. 'The horses in the cavalry are extremely recovered, and when the regiments have their new clothing they will appear very well.'[2] However, before he could leave England to command this promising force, Marlborough was overtaken by a debilitating domestic crisis.

Sarah Marlborough's grief at her son John's death had affected her profoundly. In her early forties, and not having been pregnant for twelve years, she nonetheless determined to have another child. Her menstrual cycle, made irregular by grief, caused the couple by turn excitement and disappointment. Finally, hope of further offspring faded.

In the spring of 1704, while staying at Holywell, their family home near St Albans, Sarah turned on John with venom. Her accusation was of infidelity, but no evidence exists to support her claim. It seems probable that Charles, Earl of Sunderland, the duchess's graceless and outspoken son-in-law, poisoned her troubled mind. Marlborough was miserable at the false accusation, writing to his wife: 'As for your suspicion of me as to this woman, that will vanish, but it can never go out of my mind the opinion you must have of me, after my solemn protesting and swearing that it did not gain any belief with you. This thought has made me take no rest this night, and forever makes me unhappy. I do call God to witness, and he may be merciful to me the last day, that when I came home this last time, I loved you so tenderly that I proposed all the happiness imaginable in living quietly with you the remaining part of my life. I do to my great grief see that you have fixed in your so very ill opinion of me, that I must never more think of being happy.'[3]

Sarah batted these protestations away and bade a curt farewell to her husband at Harwich harbour. He boarded his yacht, the *Peregrine*, without the expressions of tenderness that had marked his previous departures for the Continent. Instead, Sarah handed him a letter, since destroyed, detailing her hurt at his alleged infidelity.

The general arrived in Holland to news that increased his dejection: the Elector of Bavaria had taken the field six days earlier and the French on the Upper Rhine were moving to reinforce him. Marlborough commanded a body of Dutch troops, whom he had sent to aid the Emperor the previous year, to remain in Germany. They were to continue under the Imperial commander, Prince Lewis of Baden. On 2 May, Marlborough attended a conference with Deputies from the States-General. He had already revealed part of his hand to Grand Pensionary Heinsius, a staunch political ally. Heinsius appreciated the menace bearing down on Austria, as well as the obstructive ways of the States-General. He told Marlborough that the only hope of securing Dutch compliance in his proposal lay in presenting the States with a *fait accompli*, while being evasive about his true intentions.

Marlborough announced to the Deputies that he was to attack the French on the Moselle. This was, he explained, a logical extension of his two previous campaigns. The suggestion provoked consternation among the Dutch representatives. However, after two years of constraint, Marlborough was beyond compromise. The Dutch now saw the steel that the duke hid behind the urbane mask. His message was simple: if the States did not release their troops for the Moselle, he would do his queen's bidding nevertheless. Anne had instructed him to do whatever was necessary to preserve the Empire, and he would honour that brief by taking Britain's soldiers to the Moselle. This defiant independence astonished The Hague. In their shock, as Heinsius had predicted, the States-General agreed to the Moselle initiative, while insisting on holding back General Overkirk and his army for their protection.

Marlborough rushed to complete his preparations before the Dutch could change their minds. He persuaded the Deputies of 'the necessity of carrying with him a sufficient train of artillery with powder and ball and other ammunitions and instruments that were requisite for such service. These were likewise granted him, and his Grace ordered them immediately to be put into boats, with beds, medicaments, and other provisions for the hospitals.' [4] Happy with these arrangements, Marlborough left The Hague on 4 May, touring allied garrisons, before arriving at his Maastricht headquarters a week later.

Secrecy was imperative for the success of the real plan, the march to Bavaria. In England, only Queen Anne, her husband Prince George of Denmark, and Godolphin were aware of Marlborough's intentions. In Austria, Count Wratislaw had discussed the project with the Emperor, and with the most gifted and thrusting of the Imperial generals, Prince

Eugène of Savoy. Nobody else, apart from Cardonnel and Cadogan, Marlborough's secretary and quartermaster, was to be trusted with the expedition's true destination; not even the captain-general's brother, General Charles Churchill, was party to the secret at this stage.

Key allies were also kept in the dark. Marlborough told Lewis of Baden and the King of Prussia that the Moselle was to be the battleground for 1704. Marlborough also recommended that Baden attack the Elector of Bavaria as soon as the chance offered itself; certainly, before the French reinforcements reached Maximilian Emmanuel. The Prussians and Hanoverians were asked to send their auxiliary contingents to Coblenz, where they were to establish magazines of supplies. Given Coblenz's position at the junction of the Rhine and the Moselle, this seemed to confirm the Moselle as the intended sphere of operations. Coblenz was also a convenient launching point for a strike into the Danube valley.

Marlborough's name was a byword for penny-pinching in civilian life; but alongside this came attention to detail, his precision with supplies and a genius for administration and planning – all cornerstones of his military success. The duke entrusted one more man, after Cadogan and Cardonnel, with his scheme – Henry Davenant, the English representative in Frankfurt. This small group drew up plans for the transportation of the Anglo-Dutch forces from the Brabant, through the Black Forest, to the Danube. They established *étapes*, a system of prearranged supplies and shelter for marching troops. This would alleviate the foraging and subsistence worries of a large force on the move: the soldiers would be able to concentrate on a speedy advance, their other needs having been met in advance. The trio of deputies was helped at all stages by Marlborough's direct involvement in every aspect of the arrangements.

Marlborough recalled, from his time as one of Turenne's officers three decades earlier, that his route would be through fertile land. Provisions would be abundant. However, they would only be readily available if the population were to find the supply of their transient visitors a profitable, rather than irksome, experience. To provide for the troops on their long trek, therefore, Marlborough would need plenty of ready money: merchants and farmers would be paid for their wares en route. Moreover, his men would receive their salaries in full and on time, so keeping discipline tight among a marching force that might otherwise loot and pillage. Lord Treasurer Godolphin provided Marlborough with enough gold to finance the campaign in the field: carefully guarded coffers, known collectively as the Military Chest, would travel in convoy with the troops; guarantors of good will and fine order during a manoeuvre that, by its nature, promised extreme fatigue and continuous stress.

The rest of the accoutrements of war would be transported in 1,800 sturdy wagons, specifically designed to withstand Europe's primitive roads. These vehicles, known as Marlbrouks, were so efficient that they remained as military transport in Europe until the late nineteenth century. On Marlborough's march of 1704 they were to carry enough oats to supply the horses during the early days of the campaign, as well as military wares ranging from the soldiers' munitions, to their mobile ovens. Each oven consisted of 500 5lb bricks and was staffed by four bakers who could, when provided with the necessary grain or flour, feed 1,000 soldiers per day.

Marlborough's columns would also include Marching Hospitals. The mobile medical unit first appeared in Europe during Ferdinand and Isabella of Spain's wars against the Moors and were later a feature of the army of Henry of Navarre. William III was the first English monarch to understand the importance of field hospitals to the morale and well-being of his troops. They initially appeared during the Irish campaign of 1690, as part of the general improvements that he brought to the British army. They were a feature of William's Flemish campaigns, bringing Master Surgeons and Master Apothecaries near to the front line, in support of the rudimentary medical teams permanently attached to each regiment.

Marlborough continued this policy of medical support and chose Thomas Gardiner, former Surgeon to William's Household, as Surgeon-General for the Army during the 1704 campaign. In its current incarnation, the British military field hospital was to prove short-lived: after Marlborough's captain-generalship, they were phased out for nearly a century. Their presence in 1704 was symptomatic of the standards achieved by William and his chosen military successor. They had helped to transform the English army into a professional body whose value had only fleetingly been seen to date.

Marlborough had arrived in the United Provinces weighed down by his wife's suspicions and fury. However, before setting out on the campaign march, he was overjoyed to receive a letter from Sarah repenting her folly and expressing deepest love. He replied to it with unbridled relief:

> I do this minute love you better than ever I did before. This letter of yours has made me so happy, that I do from my soul wish we could retire and not be blamed. What you propose as to coming over, I should be extremely pleased with; for your letter has so transported me, that I think you would be happier in being here than where you are; although I should not be able to see you often. But you will see by my last letter, as well as this, that what you desire is impossible; for I am going up into Germany, where it would be impossible for you to follow me; but love me as you now do, and no hurt can come to me. You have by this kindness preserved my quiet, and I believe my life; for till I had this letter, I have been very indifferent of what should become of myself. I have pressed this business of carrying an army into Germany, in order to leave a good name behind me, wishing for nothing else but good success. I shall now add, that of having a long life, that I may be happy with you. [5]

OF THE ARMY OF 21,000 MEN that set out from Bedburg on 19 May, more than 14,000 were British and Irish, many of them recent recruits. This represented such a large proportion of the standing army that, in 1704, there were not enough guardsmen left in London to perform their traditional, ceremonial obligations at the Tower of London or at Queen Anne's principal residence, Kensington Palace.

Marlborough pushed ahead with 90 squadrons of cavalry, leaving the 51 battalions of infantry to follow. (At the start of the campaign, an English squadron consisted of 150 mounted men, and a full-strength battalion numbered 700 foot soldiers. Sickness, death and desertion could quickly pare away at these figures.) Marlborough promoted his brother, Charles, over the heads of the four other English lieutenant-generals, to the rank of general of the foot. General Churchill was given responsibility for the progress of the infantry, artillery and heavy baggage. Marlborough calculated that this body would cover, on average, about ten to twelve miles per day. With the cavalry stopping periodically to let the foot soldiers catch up, he anticipated that there would never be a distance of more than two or three days between his force and his brother's.

Marlborough needed sufficient firepower to fight on even terms, while not compromising the speed of his advance with cumbersome gunnery. Where possible, the artillery would be transported on water; yet there would be long sections of the march where primitive roads would be the only option. Sergeant Millner, one of the duke's infantry NCOs, wrote in his diary: 'In those parts the Army could march as much in one day, as the Artillery could in two.'[6] Marlborough's weapons, under the command of Colonel Holcroft Blood, were predominantly 'sakers' and 'minions', respectively 6- and 3-pounders, supported by mortars and howitzers. The largest guns weighed up to two tons and required a team of eight horses to pull them. After receiving a promise from the Emperor and the Landgrave of Hesse-Cassel that they would provide him with heavy guns in Germany, Marlborough limited his artillery train to thirty-eight weapons. The safe transport of these would dictate the allies' capabilities at the end of their long march.

MARLBOROUGH'S DESIGN WAS threatened with almost immediate abandonment. He must have felt familiar pangs of despair on receipt of a despatch from General Overkirk, one day into the march. Overkirk, commander of the force left to defend the Dutch homeland, implored Marlborough to halt. His scouts reported that Marshal Villeroi was advancing towards Namur, which suggested an attack on Huy was imminent. Marlborough must thus return with his army to see off the threat. The duke would not be diverted from his mission. His intelligence sources in the French camp were adamant that 'the enemy thought of nothing more than keeping themselves upon the defensive in Brabant, since Marshal Villeroi had orders to observe him where ever he marched.'[7] The marshal had no idea where Marlborough would strike, but suspected that an invasion of France was planned. It was Villeroi's task to be on hand wherever the allies struck. Far from acceding to Overkirk's plea for help, Marlborough asked for the Dutch to consider sending his expeditionary force reinforcements. If he was incorrect, Marlborough pointed out, and the French turned on the United Provinces, he could send his men back on boats along the Rhine at a speed of eighty miles per day.

Soon Villeroi was shadowing the allied force with 42 infantry battalions and 60 cavalry squadrons, a total of 30,000 men. The marshal appreciated that Marlborough was the key to the 1704 campaign in Europe: 'There was only danger at the point where the Duke in person stood at the head of the allied troops,'[8] he wrote to Versailles. As Marlborough had anticipated, the French force that Villeroi left in the Lowlands was not capable of threatening the Dutch.

Winston S. Churchill has described the effect that the progress of Marlborough's redcoats had on contemporary onlookers: 'A scarlet caterpillar, upon which all eyes were at once fixed, began to crawl steadfastly day by day across the map of Europe, dragging the whole war with it.'[9] Only a handful of people knew the troops' destination, but there was a general sense that Marlborough was trying something out of the ordinary. Stepney, England's envoy to Vienna, wrote to the duke on 24 May: 'This morning I received your favour of the 12th instant from Maastricht and immediately delivered the enclosed to Count Sinzendorff. I wish you a good journey and happy expedition. Nothing can promise more fairly.'[10]

Secrecy of ultimate intent was still imperative. If Villeroi, marching parallel to him, or Tallard, further south, divined his intentions, they could unite to block Marlborough's path, or send reinforcements to Bavaria. Either option would negate the genius of his plan. Marlborough bolstered the enemy's suspicions that the Moselle was his chosen field of operations. After arriving at Sinzig on 23 May, he ostentatiously left for Bonn, knowing that the French high command would soon be informed of his presence there. Bonn was the obvious launching point for an advance on the Moselle.

While inspecting Bonn's defences, Marlborough received grave news from Count Wratislaw. Marshal Tallard had delivered 26,000 men to the Elector and Marsin, at Dillingen. Tallard had evaded Prince Lewis of Baden's forces, and threaded through the Black Forest, handing his reinforcements over without any losses en route. If Wratislaw was correct, the combined Franco-Bavarian army now numbered in excess of 70,000 men. Marlborough's marching force, even when reinforced by the auxiliaries coming to join it, as well as the Imperial troops *in situ*, would not be able to tackle such an army.

This was an early indication to Marlborough of Lewis of Baden's shortcomings as a commander. For all his reputation, gained primarily against the Turks, Baden was leaden-footed in the face of the superior opposition of Louis's marshals. Soon afterwards, Baden compounded his error. Two other Imperial generals, Thungen and Styrum, reported that they had the opportunity to attack the Elector and Marsin. However, Baden insisted on coming to command the allied force in person. During the two days that it took him to reach his colleagues the Elector escaped beyond reach of the Imperialists. Tallard, astonished at his opponent's repeated incompetence, wrote to Louis XIV that Baden really should renounce his general's rank.

His ally's double failure further increased the pressure on Marlborough: it was all up to him; his expedition had to succeed or the allied cause would unravel in the wake of Habsburg defeat. Despite the dispiriting reports about Tallard's mission, Marlborough decided to press on. Even if he was to be strongly outnumbered, he had to do all he could to head off the attack on Vienna.

IT PROVED TO BE THE RIGHT decision, for Wratislaw's figures were amiss: Tallard, although he had delivered a large quantity of arms and money to his colleagues, had brought them just 13,000 men; and many of these were unpromising recruits. Marshal Marsin immediately complained to Versailles that Tallard had kept his finest regiments on the far side of the Black Forest. Tallard was indignant at Marsin's lack of gratitude. He had brought his colleague a significant infusion of fresh manpower, through difficult terrain and at great risk. The bulk of the force was composed of 7,700 militiamen but there were also 300 seasoned Irish soldiers, 1,300 veterans of the previous year's German campaigns, 2,400 cavalrymen, and 800 officers (although Tallard conceded many of these were inexperienced). At a time when Louis was fighting on so many fronts, against such a varied and numerous alliance, it struck Tallard as inappropriate that Marsin should complain about the quality of his reinforcements: 'Marshal Marsin does not seem to be happy with his recruits,' Tallard wrote to Minister of State Chamillart. 'It is certain that the men who make up the force are not to be compared with the old soldiers, who remain with the Army of the Danube; but I will add that he saw them after extreme weariness, for I had not been able to give them a rest.'[11] If Marsin did not like the look of his militiamen, then Tallard suggested that he give them the jobs of officers' servants, while transferring the latter to the ranks. Each marshal felt disgruntled and let down by the other.

After accomplishing his mission, Tallard quickly retraced his steps across the Black Forest and stationed himself at Kehl where he guarded the lines of communication between the Danube and Rhine armies. From there he anxiously listened for news of Marlborough's progress.

THE BRITISH MARCH PRESSED ahead with urgency. Marlborough arrived with all his cavalry and dragoons at Newendorff, near Coblenz, on 25 May. The infantry and artillery had fallen behind, 'by reason of the difficult and mountainous passages'.[12] The duke busied himself, while they caught up, with diplomacy and planning. He heard from the Elector of Mayence that he had sent his 'flying bridge' forward, to assist the allied troops' crossing of the Rhine. Marlborough gratefully acknowledged this support. In his reply he also asked the Elector to make supplies available to his men on their arrival in his lands, 'which should be immediately and punctually paid for, and which would be a great ease to the troops, as well as to the country, and prevent those disorders, which generally are committed in foraging and marauding.'[13]

Marlborough used this brief lull to plead with his allies for reinforcements. Arriving at Coblenz, he wrote to the King of Prussia, informing him of Tallard's successful delivery of troops to the Franco-Bavarian Danube army. Could the king help counter this advantage by sending some of his highly esteemed troops to help the allied cause? The duke also wrote once more to the Dutch, requesting the speedy dispatch of extra troops.

When Marlborough crossed the Rhine and Meuse at Coblenz, on 26 May, the French still felt sure that the Moselle was Marlborough's target. The next destination was Broubach, which Marlborough reached the following day. Here his brother, marshalling the heavy baggage and artillery, caught up with the horse. However, when told about the terrain ahead, Marlborough resolved to ride on with the cavalry, leaving the foot and cannon to follow as fast as they could. 'This was mountainous country, where one hill took up a whole day's march, and could hardly have been ascended in that time, but for the indefatigable care and pains of Col. Blood, and the other officers commanding Her Majesty's Troop of Artillery.'[14]

Marlborough now learned that the Dutch generals had persuaded their political leaders to send reinforcements. Even those who were frightened by the duke's absence from Flanders, and distrusted his audacity, realised that this march must be given every chance of success. Marlborough wrote to his wife: 'I had an express yesterday from M.Overkirk to acquaint me that they had writ to the States to desire they might immediately have power to send me twenty squadrons of horse, and eight regiments of foot; for they were of opinion that no success in Flanders could make amends for any ill accident that might happen to me for want of having more troops'.[15] Danish troops were promised, the horse to be commanded by the Duke of Württemberg, and the foot under Lieutenant-General Scholten. These reinforcements were at least a week behind Marlborough's grand army, but they were now definitely on their way.

THE MARCH REMAINED THROUGHOUT a model of calculated precision, with the men's welfare a crucial consideration. This was pragmatic as well as humanitarian; the army would be of little use if it arrived in Bavaria exhausted. Advance orders were placed for fresh footwear and other essentials, in Mayence, Heidelberg and Frankfurt. The troops were mindful of these efforts on their behalf by 'Corporal John'. They recognised that the captain-general understood not only grand design, but also the minutiae of a soldier's daily needs.

Captain Robert Parker wrote of the trouble taken to keep the soldiers fresh as they traversed challenging terrain:

> We frequently marched three, sometimes four days, successively, and halted a day. We generally began our march about three in the morning, proceeded about four leagues [a league is three miles], or four and a half each day, and reached our ground about nine. As we marched through the country of our Allies commissars were appointed to furnish us with all manner of necessities for man and horse; these were brought to the ground before we arrived, and the soldiers had nothing to do but pitch their tents, boil their kettles and lie down to rest. Surely never was such a march carried on with more order and regularity and with less fatigue.[16]

The early morning marches were not merely to save the soldiers from the heat of the day: moving long before dawn and in the half light meant that there were no clouds of dust to alert French spies to the allies' progress or direction.

Marlborough, middle-aged and no longer accustomed to long hours in the saddle, spent much of the journey in his sprung carriage. However, he was not insulated from his men's exertions. Mrs Christian Davies*, who had disguised her sex to enlist as a fighting soldier, recalled: 'I cannot help taking notice in this place ... of the Duke of Marlborough's

---

* Mrs Davies's husband had been tricked into enlisting when drunk, and was transported to the Continent immediately. She decided the only way that she could be reunited with him was by volunteering to serve the queen. Mrs Davies was wounded in the 1704 campaign, but later succeeded in tracking down her husband.

great humanity, who seeing some of our Foot drop, through the fatigue of the march, took them into his own coach'.[17] Gestures such as these buoyed up the men's morale.

The soldiers' letters and journals from the march provide snapshots of the world that opened up before them. Captain Pope wrote home with tales of the welcoming local women, 'some of them much handsomer than we expected to find in this country.'[18] Local cultures and customs were measured against familiar yardsticks. Sinzig was noted primarily for the change it brought in the liquid intake of the army: used to drinking beer, here the troops were treated to 'plenty of wine and spa water'.[19] Sergeant Millner mentions Stetten as being 'a little town most inhabited by Jews, where we had first scarcity of beer but plenty of wine.'[20] For Marlborough's senior officers, however, there was little time for such diversions. Quartermaster-General Cadogan, weighed down with responsibilities, reported to London: 'This march has hardly left me time to eat or sleep. We continue it with all imaginable diligence.'[21]

However well planned it was, however careful and considerate the commander, the march was an ordeal. The weather vacillated wildly, intense heat punctuated by driving downpours. Private Marshall Deane, of the First Regiment of Foot Guards, wrote of how: '… we halted two days and had a most terrible storm of thunder, lightning and hail and rain. The hail of such bigness that the whole army was amazed at it.'[22] We hear complaints, at the end of May, of how: 'The Artillery press'd forward in the Rear in a very tedious Road; where, the same Day, there fell a great Shower of Hail, each thereof as large as a Musket-Ball.'[23] Captain Blackader, a lugubrious Low Church Scot, who feared eternal damnation more than ever he worried about the French, recorded: 'Resting this day, not designedly, but by reason of the roads. This is like to be a campaign of great fatigue and trouble.'[24] French spies reported that rain had not only delayed the march, but had also forced Marlborough to leave 900 sick soldiers behind in Cassel, a village on the Rhine.

It was while in Hesse-Cassel that Marlborough's ruse of heading for the Moselle was laid bare as a red herring. Captain Parker noted in his diary: 'Now when we expected to march up the Moselle, to our surprise we passed that river over a stone bridge, and the Rhine over two bridges of boats, and proceeded on our march through the country of Hesse-Cassel, where we were joined by the Hereditary Prince with the troops of that country; which made our army 40,000 fighting men complete.' [25]

On the evening of 29 May Marlborough and his cavalry commander, Richard Lumley, a colleague since Sedgemoor, dined with the Elector of Mayence. Late in the evening there was a council of generals, attended by several senior allied commanders. Marlborough revealed that the Moselle was not his point of attack on the French, while not disclosing his intention of advancing to the Danube:

> And as in the project that had been laid for acting upon the Moselle, the Landgrave of Hesse-Cassel had agreed to furnish a certain proportion of heavy cannon, the Duke of Marlborough now represented to His Highness, the imminent danger with which the Empire was now threatened, and particularly the sad condition of His Imperial Majesty's affairs in Hungary; that therefore he had laid aside his thoughts of proceeding to the Moselle, since his services would be more necessary elsewhere. [26]

Marlborough asked the Landgrave to send his guns to Mannheim, under the command of his son the Hereditary Prince. There they should await his further instructions.

The force at Marlborough's disposal, reinforced by Hanoverians and Prussians, was now formidable. As it grew, so did disquiet in the French ranks. Villeroi's despatch to Versailles recognised that Marlborough had fooled them: 'There will be no campaign on the Moselle – the English have all gone higher up into Germany.' [27] Tallard wrote with equal alarm to Chamillart: 'All my spies unanimously agree that the English and Dutch cavalry crossed the Main at Cortheim near Mayence the 30th [of May].' [28] If it was not to be the Moselle, then the next obvious point of vulnerability was Alsace. It was assumed that Louis's prized conquest from the 1681 campaign, Strasbourg, was Marlborough's mark.

Marlborough encouraged this suspicion. The Hereditary Prince's move with his guns to Mannheim seemed to be the precursor to an attack on Landau. At the same time, the Governor of Phillipsburg, 50 miles ahead of the march, constructed bridges of boats across the Rhine. These promised to carry the invaders into northern Alsace. Tallard was duped by these moves and ordered his troops up the River Lauter where he hoped to repulse Marlborough's force as soon as it left Phillipsburg. He had captured Landau the previous year, and now he felt certain that he would be called upon to keep it in French hands.

Villeroi, meanwhile, prepared to come to Tallard's aid in the defence of Alsace; he sent for more units from Flanders to reinforce him. Between them Tallard and Villeroi felt they had the situation under control. On 4 June Tallard told Versailles that the enemy army would be exhausted after its long march, and would arrive in Alsace unable to do more than witness the collapse of the Habsburg Empire. In fact, the allied army was in good order. When the Elector of Mayence inspected Charles Churchill's infantry on 2 June, he was deeply impressed, particularly by the Guards regiments. These, the Elector quipped, were so finely turned out that they must already be dressed for that evening's dance.

Marlborough and the cavalry reached Ladenbourg on 3 June. Here they rested, waiting for the artillery and infantry to catch up. It was time to consolidate before the march resumed. Marlborough wrote to Godolphin the following day: 'The cannon and infantry being six days march behind me, and the troops of Luneburg, Holland, and Hesse being in several quarters, I shall halt here tomorrow, to give the necessary orders, and then shall advance towards the Danube, with what troops I have here, leaving the English and cannon to be brought up by my brother, and the Danes by the Duke of Württemberg.'[29] Several of the allied detachments reached him over the following three days. He sent messages to the Danish auxiliaries, so eagerly awaited from Holland, to hurry on. The States-General soon regretted sending this reinforcement. When they discovered that the Moselle was not, after all, to be the focus of the campaign, they conjured up more phantom perils on the home front. They sent to Marlborough, urging him to return their auxiliaries to the United Provinces. However, Marlborough insisted that his need was greater than theirs. On 6 June, realising that it would presently be common knowledge, he went further, writing to the Dutch that the Danube was his true destination.

It would soon no longer be possible to hide his intentions from his enemies. The English and Dutch, boosted by their auxiliaries, continued their trek deeper into Germany. Their move eastwards, towards Sinzheim, on 7 June, confirmed that the Danube was Marlborough's chosen battleground. The duke now informed his brother, General Charles Churchill, who was two marches behind the cavalry, of where their trek was headed. The news excited the men. They sensed the likelihood of a campaign of real importance, in contrast to the anti-climax of 1703. Captain Blackader, however, was consumed by customary pessimism, believing that his colleagues would be called to account for their profanity and faithlessness: 'When the carcasses of the one half of us are dung on the earth in Germany; then, perhaps, the other half will bethink themselves.'[30] The following three days saw the march cut through Wisloch, Erpingen and Gross Gartach, before crossing the Neckar again at Lauffen, then heading for Mindelheim.

Marlborough eased his men's passage to a crucial theatre of war with maximum care. He was conscious that failure would be disastrous for his nation, its allies, and himself. On 10 June he met up with Count Wratislaw, who was jubilant that his plan had succeeded to this point. Accompanying Wratislaw was a slight, ugly, man whose destiny was to be entwined with Marlborough's: Prince Eugène of Savoy.

CHAPTER ELEVEN

PRINCE EUGÈNE

'I confess frankly to have reached this decision only after
having tried to follow my ancestor's example of serving my
country and the Bourbon Court with all my heart, and
only after having in vain sought service many times under
the French Crown. But my mother's fate prevented me
having a career in the French Army although nothing
could ever be proved against her or me.'

PRINCE EUGÈNE'S REQUEST TO EMPEROR LEOPOLD I
TO SERVE IN THE IMPERIAL ARMY, 1683

IT IS INDICATIVE OF THE DIVIDED loyalties of the age that we find a
Franco-Italian aristocrat, born in Paris, commanding an army against
Louis XIV. Prince François Eugène of Savoy had a significant link with the
French Court: his mother's uncle was Cardinal Mazarin, first minister
successively to Louis XIII and the young Louis XIV. Mazarin had died
two years before Eugène's birth in 1663. Eugène's mother, Olympia
Mancini, was one of a trio of Italian nieces that Mazarin had brought
to France to make good marriages, and so further his position at Court.
Ironically, it was Court intrigue that was to render Eugène one of Louis's
most implacable enemies.

The Mancini girls were raised at the Palais Royal with the young
Louis and his brother Philip, Duke of Orléans. The sisters' upbringing was

barely distinguishable from that of their royal companions. Olympia Mancini was the same age as Louis, yet her domineering character gave her a hold over the boy king. An early demonstration of her influence can be seen in her sparking Louis's lifelong passion for amateur theatricals. However, Olympia's ambitions stretched beyond the Court stage: when she and Louis were both fifteen, she harboured hopes that they would marry. Louis, though, discovered in manhood that the choice of women open to him far exceeded the limits of his childhood circle. Olympia's chance to become queen slipped by, to her eternal and bitter disappointment.

In 1657 Olympia did make a royal match, but her husband was a mere scion of one of the countless houses of Italy. Prince Eugène Maurice of Savoy was a decent, but unglamorous aristocrat, whose twin passions were soldiery and the chase. He was ill-equipped to handle the exotic, scheming, and licentious Olympia. For her part, Olympia settled for this unexciting match, knowing that her husband's pursuits would absent him from their home, the Hôtel Soissons, for extended periods, allowing her to indulge in a string of adulterous liaisons, which originated through her hedonistic *salon*. Importantly for the princess, the structure of the marriage allowed Louis XIV to remain a much-valued intimate: she may have failed to become his queen, but Olympia remained at the centre of the king's private life.

It was a relationship that survived Louis's marriage in 1660. Olympia retained a key position at Court, Superintendent of the Queen's Household, which left her as purveyor of the king's entertainments, and the Hôtel Soissons as the king's favourite pleasure dome. However, when Louis took his first *maîtresse-en-titre*, Madame de la Vallière, Olympia felt usurped. Her insecurity led her to undermine the mistress, in the hope that she would be restored to power in Louis's private circle.

With the help of her friend Henrietta, Duchess of Orléans, Olympia planted forged letters, whose contents could have engineered de la Vallière's disgrace. However, Henrietta and Olympia's conspiracy was undermined by both ladies' indiscretion. The breakdown between the two led to mutual recriminations, which eventually spilled over into an unseemly, indeed spectacular, spat in front of Louis and his courtiers. Such indignities were taboo: Olympia was exiled from Court. Although the shared history of friendship with the king led to Olympia's speedy reinstatement, she never reclaimed his complete trust and confidence.

Olympia squandered her reprieve, involving herself in one of the great scandals of the Sun King's reign. The *affaire des poisons*, as it became known, was rooted in Olympia's interest in the occult and astrology, and her determination to win back Louis's favour. She became friends with Catherine Deshapes, well known for her knowledge of poisons. Through Deshapes's black arts, Olympia hoped to brainwash Louis into a renewal of their former relationship. However, Deshapes's affinity with poison was known and she was closely watched. When the two women's machinations were rumbled, Olympia's enemies at Court accused her of plotting to kill the king.

The atmosphere of suspicion opened up other possibilities. The sudden death of Olympia's husband had never been properly explained; surely the cause was now obvious? Louis realised that Olympia would have to face a trial, and that might lead to her execution. To avoid this, he gave her the opportunity to flee. She did so, leaving her children behind.

At the time of his mother's flight, in 1680, Eugène was an effeminate youth of sixteen. Contemporary gossips were unkind to him, giving him the nickname of *Madame l'Ancienne*, because of his plainness and indifference to hygiene. He was never to be distinguished in appearance. 'It is true that his eyes are not ugly, but his nose ruins his face; he has two large teeth that are visible all the time. He is always dirty and has lanky hair which he never curls.'[1] In a Court enthralled by Louis XIV's muscular triumphs across Europe, it was hard to see a role for this strange-looking son of a scandalous mother. The king decided that the young man, so keen for military service, must instead have a career in the church. Eugène was forced to receive a tonsure, to wear a cassock, and to endure Louis's references to him as *le petit abbé*.

Olympia's departure may have caused, but certainly coincided with, an extraordinary transformation in Eugène. He set aside dissolute friends and dedicated himself to a regime of self-improvement fuelled by his desire to become a soldier. The sickly boy, so reluctantly earmarked for the cloth, strengthened his physique through rigorous exercise. At the same time he developed his riding abilities and sought to improve his mind. He read and re-read Curtius's biography of Alexander the Great, and Plutarch's lives of the heroes of the Ancient World, absorbed in their tales of military glory. For more practical guidance, he studied with the mathematician, Joseph Saveur. Eugène aimed to become the complete soldier, drawing on inspiration from the past, while strengthening himself mentally and physically for the future.

Louis was unimpressed and was also displeased that the boy flagrantly flouted his royal will. He had chosen the Church as his destiny, so how dare he look elsewhere – especially towards the Army, an avenue that Louis had specifically closed to him? With the array of victories accumulated by his marshals in the 1660s and 70s, Louis felt that he knew good military material when he saw it. This ugly, puny, son of his erstwhile favourite had none of the qualities associated with battlefield heroics. Yet Eugène refused to be denied. Realising that he was unable to change the king's mind, he persuaded one of Condé's nephews, Prince Louis Armand Conti, to advocate his cause. The audience was not a success. Louis later recalled: 'The request was modest, but the applicant was not. Nobody ever ventured to stare me in the face so insolently, like an angry sparrow-hawk.'[2] Louis restated his position: Eugène was to be a priest, not a soldier. The finality of this was unmistakable: Eugène understood that he would never be allowed to serve as a soldier of France. He would, therefore, with reluctance, have to seek military employment abroad.

Angered by the treatment accorded his mother and incensed by Louis's arrogance towards him, Eugène quit France. He swore never to return, except with vengeful sword in hand. The French were to have no fiercer or more able opponent over the succeeding half century than the scorned Eugène. It seems that Louis sensed almost immediately that he had erred. After being informed that Eugène had fled into exile,

Voltaire wrote, Louis turned to his courtiers and asked: 'Do you think that with his departure I have suffered a severe loss?' The attendant sycophants assured the king that it mattered little that the prince had gone, for he would surely amount to nothing.

Eugène now embarked on a fifty-year military career that Napoleon judged to be one of the seven greatest in history. Bonaparte placed the renegade prince on a par with Alexander the Great, Caesar, Frederick the Great, Gustavus Adolphus, Hannibal, and Turenne.

IN 1683 EUGÈNE FOLLOWED TWO of his brothers into the service of Emperor Leopold (the Imperialists called him Prince Eugen). There were strong historical ties between his own and the Imperial families, Eugène sharing direct descent from the Habsburg omnipotent, Charles V. The Imperial army had a further important attraction for Eugène: the incursions of Ottoman Turks and the insurrections of Hungarian rebels guaranteed action. The Ottomans were particularly menacing at the time of Eugène's enlistment. The Sultan and the Grand Vizier had laid waste to the Balkans, before arriving at the gates of Vienna with 200,000 men. They turned back and were subsequently massacred by the Duke of Lorraine and King Sobieski of Poland. This engagement rolled back the Ottoman hordes. Eugène received his baptism of fire that day, fighting in Prince Lewis of Baden's wing. For his personal bravery Eugène received a pair of golden spurs from Lorraine, as well as the promise of his own regiment.

Eugène's startling talent was quickly recognised, a fact reflected in his rapid promotion through the senior ranks of the Imperial army. A colonel of dragoons when just 20, Louis's *petit abbé* was a major-general two years later, a lieutenant-general at 24, and a general of horse when only 26. So impressed had Lewis of Baden been with Eugène's courage and skill in the 1685 campaign against the Ottomans that he insisted on taking his young cousin to an audience with Leopold I. 'Sir,' Baden told the Emperor, 'this young Savoyard whom I have the honour to present to Your Imperial Majesty will in due course emulate all those whom the world regards as great generals.'[3] These excellent impressions were confirmed in 1687, at the Imperial victory of Mohacs, where Eugène's cavalry brigade charged through the Turkish lines in the decisive movement of the engagement. Eugène planted the Imperial Eagle in the vanquished Turks' camp, and rode off with their own precious standard, the Crescent. After the battle Eugène was rewarded for his heroics with the singular honour of taking news of the Turkish defeat to Emperor Leopold.

These years of success against the Ottomans, allied to the growing threat of Louis XIV in the west, convinced Eugène that now was the right time to make peace with the Sultan. He believed that France demanded all of the Emperor's attention. But Leopold's piety – a hangover from his early training for a career in the Church – encouraged by his Jesuit inner coterie, led him to seek further glory against the barbarian oppressors of Christianity: the Turks had harried generations of Habsburg rulers and now they could be crushed for all time. Leopold was persuaded to continue his Crusade, even though the Holy Roman Empire was neither rich nor organised enough to cope with the simultaneous threat of Sultan and Sun King.

The nine years of the War of the League of Augsburg was exhausting for all the participants. Eugène saw out the conflict on the empire's western front. From 1689 until 1697 he faced an enemy in the Italian peninsula whose backbone was comprised of Louvois's refurbished French regiments. Eugène's own troops were indolent and ill-equipped: a motley collection of Spaniards, Savoyards and Piedmontese. The officer corps was riddled with self-interest and indiscipline, leading Eugène to report to Vienna in exasperation: 'The enemy would long ago have been beaten if everyone had done his duty. They can say what they like of me and I will take no notice, because it would be wrong if the service of the Emperor and the common cause were to suffer through looking after one's private interests.' [4]

However frustrated he may have been by his men's inadequacies, Eugène sought to make the best of them. These Italian campaigns added to his reputation as one of the greatest and bravest commanders in the Imperial service. At the same time, his dynamic, mercurial and sometimes cruel tactics unsettled fellow officers. We read, in one of Eugène's despatches, of his tacit approval of atrocity in the increasingly bitter campaign of 1690, when the French raped Piedmont. After taking some of the French pillagers prisoners, 'our men did things the Turkish way, cutting off their testicles and giving no quarter.' [5] This ruthlessness was anathema to many other Imperial commanders. However, the overall tenor of Eugène's generalship was so superior that, before reaching the age of thirty, he attained the rank of field marshal.

WITH RENEWED WARFARE AGAINST the Turks, Eugène's stock rose yet higher. He was the foremost military hero of the Grand Alliance, famed across Europe. Although handicapped by the poor condition of his troops, Eugène faced an Ottoman army improved by a timely injection of French financial aid. The Turks streamed westwards, retaking many of the cities lost to the Empire in the 1680s. The Imperial War Council, unnerved by the quality and size of the enemy, gave Eugène cautious instructions to: 'forego all risks and avoid engaging the enemy unless he [Eugène] has overwhelming strength and is practically certain of being completely victorious.' [6] Eugène found these orders bewildering in their negativity.

In September 1697, in clear breach of his brief, Eugène gambled everything with an attack on the Ottomans at Zenta. 20,000 Turks were slain on the battlefield and a further 10,000 were drowned in the nearby River Theiss. The Imperial troops' ruthlessness satisfied their commander's thirst for blood, Eugène reporting in his victory despatch that his 'men could stand on the dead Turkish bodies as if on an island.' [7] The Grand Vizier, Mustafa Pasha, and four of his deputies were found among the dead. By contrast, a total of just 300 Imperial troops died in this most one-sided of battles. And yet, so pedantic was the war ministry in Vienna, so jealous were some of its members of Eugène's success, that it removed the prince from his command for failing to obey their instructions. Popular opinion overturned this pettiness, and the Emperor restored the hero to his former powers. Eugène took this chance to draw a line between past frustrations and future aspirations, stating that he would only accept reinstatement if he was allowed greater freedom on future campaigns. By the end of the seventeenth century, Eugène had become not only 'the most renowned commander in Europe' [8], but also one of the most independent.

The victory at Zenta effectively ended Ottoman hopes of expanding into central Europe. Sixteen months after the battle the Peace of Carlowitz, 'the greatest triumph in Habsburg annals' [9], was signed. The Turks recognised that their sweeping westward advances were over. At much the same time that this landmark treaty was signed, the Peace of Ryswick closed the War of the League of Augsburg. The cessation of hostilities on both fronts gave Eugène two years of peaceful respite, during which he studied his beloved history books. Louis XIV's decision to accept the Spanish throne for his grandson brought this interlude to an end.

Fighting between Louis and Leopold was underway in Italy a year before the War of the Spanish Succession ignited into a pan-European conflict. Spain and the Empire disputed the sovereignty of the peninsula's patchwork of states. The French, claiming to uphold the rights of the chosen Spanish king, marched into Lombardy and overran Mantua. They then spread through the Po valley and established their forces in a 60-mile defensive line along the Adige, reaching from Lake Garda to Venice. With outposts guarding the passes of the Tyrol, Louis's strike southwards seemed decisive: it surely guaranteed that the Italian states would either plump for neutrality, or throw in their lot with the Franco-Spanish cause.

Eugène thought otherwise. Based upon his experience as Supreme Allied Commander in Italy during the final three years of the previous war, he recommended that the Emperor make Italy his priority. At the end of May 1701, Eugène set off across Monte Baldo in the Alps, his army of 22,000 men bypassing the unsuspecting French defences, and pushing on southwards. Speed was essential if this small force was to achieve anything. Eugène determined quickly to pierce the French defensive ring that encompassed the mountain passes between the Tyrol and Lombardy in order to provoke battle. To save time, he marched through Venice, in violation of her neutrality, prepared to use every trick to wrong-foot the enemy.

The campaign became one of guerrilla warfare. The French huddled in garrisons along an increasingly extended front, never sure where Eugène and his men would strike, their nerves and resources increasingly stretched. Eugène repeatedly bettered forces that outnumbered his by a ratio of 3:2. These exploits were a fillip to the allies, John Evelyn writing delightedly in London: 'The Emperor's forces penetrate so far into Italy, as after some advantageous encounters to endanger the Milanese through the excellent conduct of Prince Eugène.'[10] Louis XIV was embarrassed by the humiliations heaped on his men, and wrote censoriously to Marshal Catinat: 'I sent you to Italy to fight a young and inexperienced Prince; he has flouted all the precepts of warfare. But you appear to be mesmerised, and let him do as he pleases.'[11] Catinat was removed in disgrace from his Italian command and was replaced by Marshal Villeroi, a good general keen to claim greatness. Villeroi felt the pressure of his sovereign's expectations, and believed that he must strike against the Imperialists early. When he learnt that Eugène's force was encamped in the fortress of Chiari, he advanced against it, confident that numerical advantage would grant him victory.

The attack came on 1 September, but Eugène was prepared for Villeroi's onslaught. He felt sure, from previous observations, that the success or failure of the earliest French attack would determine the day. He had noted that subsequent assaults by Louis's men failed to match the impetus of their first foray. If his men could withstand Villeroi's initial charge, there was a chance of seeing him off altogether. Eugène therefore ordered his troops to lie flat on their stomachs as the enemy approached: only when the French were at close range did he give the order to stand and fire. This tactic was stunningly successful, the repulsed French losing over 2,000 men, while less than 40 of Eugène's garrison perished. These heroics at Chiari captured the European imagination and proved that Louis's armies were not invincible.

The 1702 Italian campaign relied once more on Eugène's suppleness and cunning in the face of more numerous and better-equipped troops. Before the traditional fighting season had even begun, the prince had pulled off another coup of huge propaganda value. In February Eugène attempted the capture of the city of Cremona, where Marshal Villeroi and his army had their winter quarters. He filed the Imperial troops through the narrows of an abandoned canal, bringing them up into the bowels of the French position. The surprise attack, after initial promise, failed to take the city, but it did deliver Marshal Villeroi as a prisoner. This, when combined with the daring of the raid, mightily boosted the morale of the Grand Alliance. John Evelyn wrote: 'The Surprise of Cremona, and accidental quitting of it again, yet with such advantageous circumstances and taking of Marshal Villeroi, by Prince Eugène, was the great discourse of this week.'[12]

Louis shared Eugène's belief that Italy was the key military forum. He reinforced his presence there by sending Marshal Vendôme (Eugène's first cousin) there with a huge army, to put an end to the prince's colourful sideshow. In all, Louis pitched 80,000 troops against Eugène's slippery force of 28,000. Underlining this commitment, Louis insisted that his grandson Philip V of Spain personally attend the Italian campaign, to provide a focal point for the Franco-Spanish cause. However, Louis secretly remained wary of Eugène and he ordered Vendôme to avoid battle except when absolutely certain of victory.

Vendôme advanced in May 1702, his numerical advantage forcing Eugène into a tactical retreat. Vendôme cornered his army at the Crostolo and the Imperialists were soundly defeated. However, rather than flee, Eugène elected to seek battle once more. The next engagement, at Luzzara, in mid-August, was a bloody affair that both commanders claimed as their victory. Even if the result was open to interpretation, Eugène's leadership was unequivocally brilliant. He had demanded discipline and bravery from the force beaten at the Crostolo and then squared up to Philip V and Vendôme's huge army. Eugène's heroics at Luzzara added further lustre to his reputation throughout the Grand Alliance. Count Wratislaw wrote home to Austria of the Imperial commander's ever-growing celebrity in London: 'It can truthfully be said that the English revere and love the Prince like one of their own heroes.

What has been happening on the Upper Rhine or Flanders, the activities of their own Fleet – about which there is indeed much to say – all these things are looked upon with relative indifference. The eyes and ears of the English are concentrated upon Prince Eugène.'[13] From Flanders Eugène received the following effusive congratulations:

> Sir,
>
> For a long time I have wanted to do myself the honour of writing to Your Highness; but the hope of being able to send you some good news from here consistently restrained me. However, the victory which Your Highness has just won over the enemy gives me now an excellent opportunity which I cannot miss of congratulating you upon it as I indeed do from the bottom of my heart. It is a successor to the great actions in which Your Highness has participated since arriving in Italy, and which have been so valuable to the common cause. We feel the same sense of relief and deliverance as Your Highness in view of the superiority in numbers of the enemy. Your Highness's part in this encounter cannot be adequately praised, but I beg you to believe that amongst all your admirers there is none more happy or more full of respect for your Highness than I am.'[14]

It was signed: *Marlborough*

CHAPTER TWELVE

COMBINED FORCES

'Prince Eugène of Savoy met and dined with the Duke,
where they spent the Remainder of that Day in weighty
Conferences, with mutual Esteem for each other; who
were equal in Fame; Courage and Conduct in
Military Exploits; Prudence, Counsel, Dexterity, and
Address in Management of Affairs; Politeness, Temper,
and Affability in Conversation; the two greatest Men
in the Age, with great Friendship and Confidence in
each other.'

THE JOURNAL OF SERGEANT MILLNER, 10 JUNE 1704

MARLBOROUGH AND EUGÈNE were to become one of the most famed pairings in military history. It was a partnership which transcended differences of nationality, age, and temperament and which had its roots in a mutual high regard, both as soldiers, and as men. Marlborough's letter to Eugène, congratulating him on his exertions at the battle of Luzzara, was the opening salvo in half a lifetime of warm correspondence. They shared and relayed enjoyment at one another's triumphs, and in each other's company.

The campaign of 1704 brought them together for the first time, the start of a fusion of genius that was to be the despair of Louis XIV. The union of the Englishman whose talents he had applauded at the siege of Maastricht, a quarter of a century before, and of the unprepossessing princeling whose military abilities he had denied, was to be Louis's demon in his final, most testing, great war.

Both Eugène and Marlborough were outsiders who rose to the top of their respective military systems through fierce determination and rare talent. Eugène, the Franco-Savoyard émigré prince, sworn to avenge his family's humiliations at the hands of an arrogant king, stood at the pinnacle of the Imperial army in 1704. His unstinting contribution to his adoptive country earned him eternal gratitude: 'He lives in German history as one of the greatest German soldiers but also as a pre-eminent servant of the nation.' [1]

Equally impressive was Marlborough's rise. Many in London looked on the impoverished Royalist officer's son with envious suspicion. They sneered at his limited means and undistinguished provenance. His family was not of the coterie of aristocrats who believed it their right and duty to supply the lead at Court, Parliament, and in the Army. They looked for dark reasons for his advancement. Accusations of lesbianism that circled around Sarah Marlborough and Queen Anne's close friendship have remained unproven; but even Sarah was struck by the idiosyncrasy of the relationship. 'Kings and Princes, for the most part, imagine they have a dignity peculiar to their birth and station, which ought to raise them above all connexion of friendship with an inferior,' the duchess opined, in middle age. 'The Princess had a different taste. A friend was what she most coveted; and for the sake of friendship she was fond even of that equality which she thought belonged to it. She grew uneasy to be treated by me with the form and ceremony due to her rank.' [2] In a deferential age, Sarah's easy parity with the monarch was shocking to outsiders. The Marlboroughs' enemies were unwilling to concede that the duke's talents justified his exalted position. They pointed to his wife's unnatural hold over the queen, and disapproved of this, the presumed basis of his power.

Eugène and Marlborough shared much more than their unconventional rise to eminence, however. To look at the parlous state of the Imperial army at this time is to see the familiar impediments faced in England by William and dealt with by Marlborough. There was the deep obstructiveness of many politicians to modernising improvements; an acceptance by senior officers of abuses long common throughout the armies of Europe – the sale of officer ranks, and the promotion of well-connected incompetents over the heads of the less well to do and more able; and a system of recruitment that relied more on the stick than the carrot.

We find Eugène's copious correspondence to Vienna decrying the dreadful condition that his men endured on campaign. He identifies the incompetence of the military system and the lack of funds from Vienna as the fundamental handicaps facing his army. In the winter following Luzzara the hardships were such that Eugène dared to share them with the Emperor: 'We are at the end of November and the troops have not yet received their pay for the previous winter, let alone the summer. Meanwhile the men are having to go naked.'[3] There was little that Leopold could do. His finances, crippled by inefficient and dishonest bureaucracy, were further undermined when his chief banker, Samuel Oppenheimer, died deeply in debt in May 1703. But he did give his troops one great gift, of a value which was to prove immense: the following month, June, Leopold entrusted Eugène with the Presidency of the Imperial War Council.

Now Eugène could swoop on many of the parasites that compromised the effectiveness of his forces: like Marlborough, he insisted that merit be the prime consideration when promotions were considered; like Marlborough, he attempted to end the sale of officer ranks; like Marlborough, he looked to bring uniformity and order to his army. Oblivious to the jealousy of his success, and to the resentment of his candour, Eugène set about his task with purpose and vigour. The results of his overhaul surfaced later during his long tenure of office, but the respect of his men was won at once. They already recognised his rare ability against the enemy and now they witnessed his cussed commitment to them and their cause. Most importantly of all, Eugène's men felt valued and appreciated by a commander who was fluent in all the facets of warfare and who was ambitious for their success.

In the summer of 1703, Eugène fought against Hungarian insurgents who were being supported by Louis XIV and his acolyte, the

Elector of Bavaria. The Imperial forces in Hungary were as run down and neglected as their counterparts in Italy. However, the Emperor remained unable to answer Eugène's pleas for reinforcements or provisions. In a futile gesture he sent the horses of the Viennese Riding School to augment Eugène's cavalry. Leopold's income was less than one-fifth that of Louis XIV, and this disparity of wealth looked as though it might decide the war.

The opening of 1704 promised to bring an end to the Emperor's embarrassments. It seemed certain that his dynasty would be displaced before the year was out, the English representative writing from Prussia: 'The poor Empire [is] looking ripe for destruction, the head and members being either corrupt or benumbed.' [4] With the Hungarians rampant and the Elector of Bavaria free to advance on Vienna, Eugène pulled no punches: 'I hope Your Majesty will not be unmerciful if I give free play to my pen,' he wrote to the Emperor, 'for otherwise I could not answer to God. The situation seems to me to be graver than it has been at any time in Habsburg history. The state of your Army is well known to Your Majesty. Most of the soldiers have not a rag to their backs, and no money. The officers are as poor as beggars. Many are dying of hunger; and if they fall ill there is no one to nurse them. None of the fortresses has any reserves, nor supplies for more than a few days.' [5] Bold action had to be taken, before it was too late.

Vienna had escaped Franco-Bavarian occupation the preceding year, but now there could surely be no further stay of the inevitable. Eugène realised that the defence of Austria was the priority of the war. The Elector and Marsin must be stopped. If they were not, the Hungarian insurrection would become irrelevant in any case, for there would be no Habsburgs to lead the Imperial stand against the rebels.

Eugène moved to secure the Lines of Stollhofen, the barrier designed to stop French troops marching down the Rhine from Strasbourg. If Tallard and Villeroi could be kept from joining their colleagues on the Danube, then perhaps the threat of the Franco-Bavarian push could be met. The English envoy to Vienna, Stepney, wrote to Cardonnel on 24 May: 'Prince Eugène begins his Journey towards Nuremberg early tomorrow morning, and we are still willing to believe he will arrive time enough in Swabia to hinder the Elector of Bavaria from doing much mischief there.'[6] It seemed a long shot, this fending off of the enemy force aimed at the Imperial capital, but to the leaders of the Grand Alliance in Central Europe the alternative was clear and bleak.

EUGÈNE ARRIVED AT MARLBOROUGH'S headquarters of Mindelheim, mid-point between the Rhine and the Danube, on 10 June 1704. He rode into camp alongside his political ally, Count Wratislaw, the puniness of the prince contrasting with the physical hugeness of the Imperial envoy. They dined with Marlborough, and the next day conferred on the best way to conduct the campaign.

The immediate empathy between the two soldiers, aware of their onerous responsibilities, has been captured by Winston S. Churchill: 'At once began that glorious brotherhood in arms which neither victory nor misfortune could disturb, before which jealousy and misunderstanding were powerless, and of which the history of war furnishes no equal example. The two men took to one another from the outset. They both thought and spoke about war in the same way, measured the vast forces at work by the same standards, and above all alike looked to a great battle with its awful risks as the means by which their problems would be solved.'[7]

The condition of Marlborough's cavalry had impressed onlookers throughout the gruelling march south. The regiments of horse turned out for Eugène's inspection at Gross Heppach, on 12 June. They earned high praise, which betrayed a hint of wistfulness at the condition of his own, under-funded, squadrons: 'I have heard much of the English cavalry, and find it indeed to be the best appointed and finest I have ever seen,' said the prince. 'Money, of which you have no want in England, can buy clothes and accoutrements, but nothing can purchase the spirit which I see in the looks of your men. It is an earnest of victory.' Marlborough's reply was typically tactful: 'My troops are always animated with zeal for the common cause, but they are now inspired by your presence. To you we owe that spirit which awakens your admiration.'[8]

There was truth in the compliment: the British were excited to receive a man of Eugène's reputation as their guest of honour. Count Wratislaw had reported to Vienna two years earlier: 'I can say without exaggeration that in English eyes no Alexander the Great, no Julius Caesar, can compare with Prince Eugène. You cannot believe their enthusiasm [for him].'[9] It was an enthusiasm that had not waned in the interim: this was the hero whose exploits they cheered in the concluding lines of a popular wartime drinking song:

> Drink, drink, drink we then
> A flowing glass to Prince Eugen.[10]

Eugène, flattered and reassured by the tenor of his three days of discussions with Marlborough, reported to the Emperor that the English commander was 'a man of high quality, courageous, extremely well-disposed, and with a keen desire to achieve something of consequence; with all these qualities he understands thoroughly that one cannot become a general in a day, and he is diffident about himself.'[11] Marlborough, for his part, instantly felt at ease with his fellow commander, writing home to Sarah that his first impressions of the Savoyard prince were that his character exceeded the gentlemanliness and sophistication of a mutual friend: 'Prince Eugène has in his conversation a great deal of my Lord Shrewsbury, with the advantage of seeming franker.'

Eugène demonstrated his straight talking by confiding in Marlborough his grave misgivings about their fellow allied commander. 'He has been very free with me', the duke continued to his wife, 'giving me the character of the prince of Baden, by which I find I must be much more on my guard than if I was to act with prince Eugène.'[12]

WE HAVE SEEN LEWIS OF BADEN in action before: first with distinction, against the Turks in the 1680s; and then, with ignominy, earlier in 1704, when he allowed Marshal Tallard to sidestep his forces and slip through the Black Forest. This failure had permitted Tallard to deliver much needed reinforcements to the Elector of Bavaria and Marshal Marsin. The question that was now being asked, and which Eugène and

Marlborough had discussed at their initial meeting, was whether Baden was merely incompetent, or whether he was in secret league with the enemy.

An almost exact contemporary of Marlborough's, Baden had none of the Englishman's panache or daring. He had advised Leopold against war with France, knowing the state of the Imperial army and revenue. Baden trusted in the efficacy of siege warfare and ponderous, cautious, troop deployments. In the words of C. T. Atkinson: 'He abhorred manoeuvre and the attack, and clung to the defensive and the spade.' [13] This approach had proved effective against the Ottomans, whose ragged human waves could be held, and then pulverised, by disciplined musket fire. However, both Marlborough and Eugène were convinced by their experiences in Flanders and Italy, that they could only win this war against the French with knockout blows delivered in open battle. This approach was anathema to the plodding Prince Lewis.

To be fair to Baden, the 1702 campaign had seen him command the Rhine Army with some success. He had notched up a considerable feat with the capture of Landau. However, this triumph merely reaf-firmed Prince Lewis's belief that the course to victory was necessarily slow and painstaking. He viewed each besieged and taken town as a coloured stone that would eventually help form a completed mosaic representing victory. Equally unfortunate was Baden's self-importance. He hampered the Imperialist cause, during the first two years of the war, by locking horns with Count Mansfeld, Eugène's predecessor at the Imperial War Council. Jealous of his position as commander-in-chief of the Emperor's forces, Baden refused to accept orders from Mansfeld in Vienna. The two intractable men placed their squabble above the allied war effort, with Mansfeld even refusing to respond to Baden's letters. Mansfeld was replaced, but Marlborough was left to find common cause with the tetchy Baden.

Baden was coming off the back of a controversial campaign. In 1703, he had been repeatedly criticised by colleagues for the enormous length, and questionable purpose, of his marches. The commander of the Dutch contingent sent by Marlborough from the Lowlands was Major-General van Goor. He was so exasperated by the shapelessness of the Rhine Army's strategy that he refused to acknowledge Baden's command. This led to Goor's imprisonment. Further reverses helped to obliterate memories of Baden's success at Landau. The Elector of Bavaria's declaration for the Franco-Spanish cause endangered Lewis's communications with the Emperor, compelling him to fall back across the Rhine. He was subsequently defeated at Friedlingen, in October, by Marshal Villars. 1703 ended with crowning disappointment when Landau fell to Tallard in late November.

Despite his failures, Baden was quick to join the chorus of voices proffering plans for the salvation of the Habsburgs throughout the winter of 1703–4. Baden's prime concern at these councils was to ensure that he retained supreme military command so that any glory garnered against the enemy would be his. (This was the reason behind the delay that had allowed the Elector of Bavaria to evade attack by Styrum and Thungen. A swift blow by the Imperial counts might have knocked Maximilian Emmanuel out of the war.) Baden's self-serving quest for victory led him to lobby Leopold hard, in the hope of making the Rhine the centre of operations in 1704. He would not accept that the crucial priority was already, and indisputably, the defence of Vienna.

Councils of war dominated the Imperial Court in the first two months of 1704. These resonated to the clashes of the conservative, conceited, Lewis and the dashing, outspoken, Eugène. Baden, seeking to reprise his earlier success, advocated a renewed siege of Landau. This could, he argued, be followed by an invasion of France along the Moselle valley. Eugène insisted that the Landau–Moselle arena should be seen as the shield arm of the campaign, with the allied sword striking hard at the heart of Bavaria. When the Emperor received confirmation that Marlborough was coming south to his aid, Eugène's plan was pursued, while Baden's was rejected. A disgruntled Baden stated that he saw no need for his command to be amalgamated with that of any other Imperial or allied commander.

Lewis of Baden's position was undermined by his failure to stop Tallard's reinforcement of the Elector's and Marsin's forces, in May 1704.

So hopeless was his conduct, that the Emperor suspected this most senior of his princes might be working against the Grand Alliance. Leopold instructed Eugène to persevere in his junior command, but to report back any signs that Baden was colluding with the enemy. The Elector of Bavaria had fought with Baden against the Turks, and their families were related. Prince Eugène's secret message to Marlborough was shocking: it was possible that Baden's loyalties were with his old comrade in arms, rather than with the Emperor.

As THE ALLIED FORCE ENTERED the final stages of its march to the Danube, Marlborough, Baden and Eugène were compelled to work together. Their first task was to establish their individual roles in the common cause; something that was resolved before the three men met at Gross Heppach in mid-June. There were two clear allied goals: one was to hold the Lines of Stollhofen, to keep Tallard at bay in Alsace, rather than allowing him to cross again into Bavaria with reinforcements; while the other was to end the Elector of Bavaria's and Marshal Marsin's advance on Vienna, if possible through battle.

Marlborough and his grand army were to be involved in the main business of meeting the Franco-Bavarian threat. The question as to who was to work with him in this, and who was to be allotted the less glamorous command of the Lines of Stollhofen, was a matter of the utmost delicacy. Marlborough and Eugène were keen to work together, with Baden confined to the subsidiary role north of the Black Forest. However, how could they persuade their vainglorious and fractious colleague to take the peripheral role?

They could not. Not even Marlborough's silky diplomacy could distract Prince Lewis from the scent of potential glory, the possibility of clawing back some of his buffeted military reputation. Marlborough wrote to Count Wratislaw that the defence of the Lines of Stollhofen required 'a general of great experience and vigilance'; but Prince Lewis could see that his colleagues were attempting to sideline him and he would have none of it. When Wratislaw broached the possibility of Baden's going to command the Lines, Lewis's reply was blunt. 'Try to persuade the Prince to take the command,' Baden suggested, gesturing towards Eugène, 'for in the army he is the only man who could be entrusted with a command so responsible and subject to so many risks.' Eugène understood that his superior was effectively ordering him to take control of the Lines, and replied with consummate professionalism: 'The Emperor has sent me into the Empire to serve under the command of his Lieutenant-General, and as I have never made difficulties about going wherever duty called me, I am quite ready to carry out the order of the Lieutenant-General.'[14] However, he and Marlborough nursed the secret hope that they would be able to join forces later in the summer, if the opportunity arose.

The division of command reluctantly agreed, the three allied chiefs convened to work out the fine detail of the coming campaign. On 14 June they and their senior staff officers converged on the town of Gross Heppach. Here Baden, his recent failures uppermost in his mind, was a picture of penitence, greeting Marlborough with humility: 'I am come to meet the deliverer of the Empire,' he said, before referring to his recent reverses: 'You will assist me in vindicating my honour, which has been lowered in the public opinion.' Marlborough's rejoinder was perfectly pitched, both flattering and reassuring the vain prince: 'I am come to learn of Your Highness how to save the Empire. None but those deficient in judgement can depreciate the merits of the Prince of Baden, who has not only preserved the Empire, but enlarged its boundaries.'[15]

The civilities over, the allies sat in the shade of a large oak to agree the best course of action. Eugène's role on the Lines of the Stollhofen was confirmed. It was also agreed that Baden and Marlborough would split the supreme command, taking it in turns on alternate days to be the overall allied generalissimo; a structure reminiscent of his relationship with the Duke of Württemberg during his Irish campaign of 1690. Originally Baden had expected that Marlborough would join Eugène as one of his lieutenants. However, the Englishman referred back to his queen's direct instructions and made it clear that he alone could honour his sovereign's will.

After the council at Gross Heppach, Eugène set off with 28,000 troops to the Lines of Stollhofen. Marlborough's infantry and artillery had caught up with the cavalry, and now the entire force embarked on a four-day march to join Prince Lewis of Baden's main force. The two armies were unable to remain separate entities because neither was at full strength, with both generals awaiting reinforcements: Marlborough his Danes, and Baden some regiments from the Palatine. Marlborough had written to the Duke of Württemberg, now commanding the Danish cavalry, telling him to hurry on with his squadrons; the infantry could follow as best they could. Marlborough reminded the Danes, who had been noted for their lawlessness in Flanders the previous year, that they must conduct themselves honourably on their progress through Germany. The point was acknowledged by Lieutenant-General Scholten, leading the foot soldiers: 'I beg you to be persuaded, My Lord, that I will keep such order in the infantry's march, that there will be no reason for complaint.' [16]

Until the Danish cavalry arrived, Marlborough realised, the allies could not risk dividing into two. In the meantime one force lacked the flexibility to corner the Franco-Bavarians in a place where battle could be demanded. The Elector and Marsin could retire before a single, advancing, army; however, two bodies acting in a pincer movement might catch the enemy. Marlborough's hankering for a decisive battle would have to remain unfulfilled for now.

EVEN SO FAR FROM THE BRABANT, Marlborough's demons from previous campaigns made their presence felt. The Dutch Field Deputies were over 200 miles away, but their ineptitude and lack of gumption still impinged on Marlborough's planning. At the same time disgruntled politicians in England watched his foray deep into Europe with mounting disbelief and outrage. They also tingled with excitement at the possibilities that the captain-general's failure might bring them.

Marlborough had left General Overkirk in command of the Dutch army in Flanders. The States-General viewed this force as an inadequate security blanket, to be held close while Marlborough took his grand army southwards. Yet Overkirk was ambitious to make his own mark in the Englishman's absence. He was a good general, who had learnt from

Marlborough that rapid mobility disconcerted the enemy. When he discovered that the French had quit their defensive lines, he marched to occupy the vacated position. To his intense chagrin the Field Deputies vetoed the attack. 'I send now to my Lord Treasurer a relation I have received of the proceedings of our army on the Meuse,' Marlborough wrote to Godolphin, on 14 June, 'by which you will see our friends there have lost a very great opportunity. If they had made a good use of it, we might have found the effects in these parts, and every where else.' [17] If Overkirk had been permitted to attack, and had succeeded – as seemed most probable – then Villeroi would have had to return to the Lowlands. The Dutch failure allowed the marshal to hover menacingly, with the Black Forest separating his army from those of the Elector and Marsin.

As frustrating at this time, and more hurtful personally for Marlborough, were the machinations of hostile politicians in London. 1704 had opened with the Earl of Nottingham confident that he could force Queen Anne's hand to his party's advantage. This tall, whippet-thin Tory grandee, known as Don Dismal because of his humourless demeanour, presented his queen with an ultimatum: either she support his High Tory faction by offering them the key posts of government, or she must lose its support altogether. Nottingham felt sure that Anne's innate Toryism would guarantee that he would get his way. His confidence was misplaced, and his understanding of his sovereign was woefully poor. Anne tried to warn him not to pursue his plans, but the earl failed to heed the signals.

In the spring of 1704, as Marlborough prepared for his campaign on the Continent, Nottingham reiterated his clumsy political blackmail: the queen must now make the choice that she had gently rebuffed. If she did not promote Nottingham and his supporters, while at the same time dismissing their enemies from the Privy Council, she would face Nottingham's resignation as Secretary of State for the Southern Department, as well as concerted Tory opposition to her administration. Anne surprised Nottingham with her rejection of his demands. She was not a clever woman, but Anne had a keen, Stuart, sense of her duties as sovereign. Central to these was a belief that none of her subjects should ever dare to dictate terms to their monarch. She called Nottingham's bluff, and accepted his resignation.

This was not at all what the earl had expected. He hesitated to carry through a threat that would constitute a calamitous self-inflicted wound for himself and for his faction. Now Anne allowed Nottingham no escape: she dismissed his lieutenants in the Lords and in the Commons, the Earl of Jersey and Sir Edward Seymour, and awaited Nottingham's only possible move. On 18 May, the day before Marlborough set off for his historic march, Nottingham paid the price for his presumptuousness by retiring from office. Marlborough's relief at the removal of his political foes was tempered by the realisation that they would remain his implacable enemies.

It is hard to think of a project more alien to the Tories than Marlborough's trek to the Danube. The manoeuvre took British troops far from their homeland, away from defensive positions in the Lowlands, to front-line roles in the European land war. Correspondence from Godolphin and Sarah kept Marlborough appraised of the seething hostility that his actions had aroused: even after Parliament was prorogued, it was clear that when it reconvened in the autumn Marlborough would be attacked. His rash risk of British lives in this startling plan had not been sanctioned by MPs. He had exceeded his brief as commander and (a charge that was to dog Marlborough for the rest of the decade), he was undertaking this capricious venture for personal gain.

To many of Marlborough's enemies, disgruntled Whigs as well as displaced Tories, it seemed that at last the husband of the queen's favourite had overreached himself. Sir Edward Seymour savoured the prospect of the parvenu's pending downfall, claiming that if Marlborough failed, 'we will break him up as the hounds do a hare.'[18] It was widely accepted that if Marlborough failed, he would be impeached. It was even possible that the executioner's axe would follow if his enemies could present his deeds in a black enough light, so they could be interpreted as treason. Marlborough was aware of the stakes, telling Count Wratislaw: 'The issue in this matter is victory or death.'[19]

CHAPTER THIRTEEN

THE STORMING OF
THE SCHELLENBERG

*'By this march the Elector of Bavaria judged right, that
the Prince and the Duke were fully intended to attack
Donawert the next Day; whereupon, that Night, he sent to
Count De Arco a strong Detachment of the very best of his
Troops to reinforce the said Count on Schellenbergh, where
he had already made very strong Entrenchments by some
Thousands of Pioneers, employ'd thereon for several Days
before to perfect those Works which cover Donawert, on that
Point between the River Brentz and Danube, in order to
prevent our Army crossing the same, and our entering the
Country of Bavaria.'*

SERGEANT MILLNER'S JOURNAL, 1 JULY 1704

THE LAST STAGE OF MARLBOROUGH'S epic march was hard. The
soldiers trudged through the narrow defile of Gieslingen, their progress
handicapped by heavy rain. The route was punctuated with swirling
torrents of water.

Captain Blackader's gloomy diary described the arduous routine:
'Marching every day, except resting occasionally from great fatigue, or
from bad weather and bad roads.'[1] 'One thing observable,' Private Deane

wrote with pride, 'it hath rained 32 days together more or less, and miserable marches we have had for deep and dirty roads, and through tedious woods and wildernesses, and over vast high rocks and mountains, that it may be easily judged what our little army endured, and what unusual hardship they went through.'[2] Marlborough wrote to his wife of the debilitating effect of the unseasonable weather, from which even he could not be protected: 'As I was never more sensible of heat in my life than I was a fortnight ago, we have now the other extremity of cold; for as I am writing I am forced to have fire in the store in my chamber. But the poor men, that have not such conveniences, I am afraid will suffer from these continual rains.'[3]

At one point, halfway through this final leg of the trek, it took the troops two days to cover ten particularly demanding miles. Sergeant Millner recorded how the infantry marched: 'from Eysling slantingly up that steep Hill and narrow Road, where there could not go above Two in a Breast, or Three at the most, and in some Places not above One at a Time, till we arrived at the Top of the Hill.'[4] It was not until 27 June that the journey was completed. Winston S. Churchill's opinion was that: 'The annals of the British Army contain no more heroic episode than this march from the North Sea to the Danube.'[5] However, this feat would amount to nothing if Marlborough failed to capitalise on it.

The duke's and Baden's troops now combined to form an army of 85,000 men. If this force was to be able to go deep into enemy territory it needed a base where its provisions and ammunition could be stored. They could not rely on their over-extended supply lines, which passed through Nördlingen and, even further away, to Nuremberg. Such a supply post had to straddle the Rivers Danube and Lech, so that the allies could deploy their forces on either bank of the two waterways. In this way the enemy would be denied the option of avoiding battle by slipping across to the other side. The Elector and Marsin assumed that Marlborough and Baden would elect to attack either Augsburg or Donauwörth, since either would provide all the advantages required by the Grand Alliance: if one of these towns fell, there would be nothing to stop the invasion of Bavaria.

The two allied commanders selected Donauwörth. Prince Lewis advocated a structured siege of the town, but Marlborough, equally characteristically, called for a head-on assault. After some wrangling, Marlborough prevailed, and the allied army set off on a three-day march to storm the town.

As MARLBOROUGH ANTICIPATED, the Elector of Bavaria and Marshal Marsin greeted the news of the allied advance by withdrawing from their position near Ulm. They fell back to a secure camp between Lavingen and Dillingen. The two fortified towns provided strong flanks, while the River Danube protected the rear. A full deployment of artillery covered their front, protected in turn by a flooded ditch. Despite having 15,000 fewer men than the allied force, the Elector knew he was safely entrenched here, since Marlborough had been obliged to leave his heavier guns behind in Flanders. Marlborough's hopes that he might lure the enemy out of their strong defensive position, by marching temptingly across their front, came to nothing: the Elector was too canny to fall for the trick.

Ever since it had first been reported to him on 5 June that Marl-borough was on the move south from the Lowlands, Maximilian of Bavaria had feared that his principality was the duke's target. Even when others talked with confidence of Alsace or the Moselle being the Eng-lishman's destination, he had thought otherwise, and begged Louis XIV for reinforcements. The French king thought his ally was panicking unnecessarily. Weeks of stress had aggravated Maximilian Emmanuel's already poor health, leaving him more than usually open to secret nego-tiations with the enemy. Emperor Leopold was still keen to lure his former commander back to the Imperial cause. Given the Elector's earlier duplicity, Marlborough believed the best way to secure Bavaria for the Alliance was to beat its army in the field and negotiate from a position of strength. And he needed to force a battle soon, before French reinforcements could reach the area.

The Elector must have rued the poisoning of his relationship with Marshal Villars. The Frenchman had, with his customary plain speaking, and keen military eye, exhorted Maximilian Emmanuel not to be complacent about his defences: 'Fortify your towns', Villars had recommended, in 1703, 'and above all the Schellenberg, that fort above Donauwörth, the importance of which the great Gustavus taught us.'[6] However, the Elector had resented being told how best to protect his frontiers, and had neglected to make good the decaying defences that stood on the Schellenberg Heights, a huge jutting hill – 'bell-like', in the words of General Churchill's chaplain – whose bulk dominates the skyline to the north-east of Donauwörth. With its flat summit, half a mile in diameter, one flank protected by the impenetrable trees of the Boschberg wood, the Schellenberg was a natural obstacle of commanding presence. It had long been seen as the key to a town that also enjoyed the natural defences of the River Wernitz and marshes on its southern and western quarters. In the eight hundred years of Donauwörth's history, the only successful capture of the town – in fifteen attempts – had been by Gustavus Adolphus in the Thirty Years' War; and this had been achieved only after the taking of the Schellenberg. A fort erected by the Swedish warrior king remained on the heights, abandoned and rotting.

Once the Elector understood that Donauwörth was to be attacked, he charged his field marshal, General d'Arco, with bolstering the town's defences and with holding the Heights against the enemy. D'Arco, a Piedmontese soldier with a reputation for rare brilliance, was entrusted with 13,000 men, three-quarters of them drawn from Bavaria's best fighting units. These included the Elector's Guards, and his other crack unit, the regiment of the Prince Electoral. Several French regiments were sent as well, 3,500 to help on the Schellenberg, the rest to garrison Donauwörth. Among the force of 'choice troops'[7] committed to d'Arco was Colonel Jean Martin de la Colonie, a French officer of grenadiers whose personal record of the fight stands as testimony to its intensity, and its savagery.

De la Colonie and his superiors tried to divine where they were most at risk. They appreciated that they were safe from attack from the Boschberg wood, and were also sure that the flank leading down to

Donauwörth town was secure. It was now a question as to whether the eastern or western side of the Heights would be the point of attack. The Franco-Bavarians opted to give priority to the eastern defences, believing that the rough, steep terrain to the west was too difficult for the allies to assault across.

These plans were betrayed to Prince Lewis of Baden by a corporal from the regiment of the Electoral Prince, who deserted d'Arco's force and arrived at the allied camp. The traitor offered detailed knowledge of the Schellenberg's defences, and even volunteered to help with the planning of the assault. The corporal's tales strengthened Marlborough's conviction that they should attack at once, before the defences could be improved. Marlborough prepared to strike, having given orders for his medical staff in Nördlingen to muster all available surgeons in anticipation of receiving large numbers of wounded.

On the night of 1–2 July, the allies were camped at Amerdingen, fourteen miles from Donauwörth; further than the ten to twelve miles that the infantry might be expected to progress in a day's march. However, at 3 a.m. on the 2nd, Marlborough personally oversaw the advance of an assault force of 5,850 foot, drawn in groups of approximately 130 from each of the regiments under his command. He entrusted this hand-picked force to the Dutch Lieutenant-General Goor, whose clashes with Baden the previous year had resulted in his imprisonment. Thirty-two squadrons of cavalry were sent in Goor's support.

The infantry selected for the Schellenberg assault were largely English and Dutch and were predominantly companies of grenadiers. These were normally specialist constituents of each infantry regiment, but they could be brought together, as here, for operations that suited their expertise and weaponry. They were regarded as the elite of their regiment. Their armament included not just firearms, but also leather pouches of grenadoes, described by a military dictionary of 1702 as 'small shells, concave Globes or hollow Balls, some made of Iron, some of Tin, others of Wood, and even of Pasteboard; but most commonly of Iron, because the splinters of it do most execution. These are thrown by hand into places where Men stand thick, and particularly into Trenches and

Lodgments the enemy make, and are of good use.'[8] In support rode dragoons, horse-borne infantry who could combine the roles of scout, pioneer, and fighting soldier. The rest of the grand army followed behind at a less challenging pace, while this specialist vanguard pushed ahead, Marlborough eager to join battle before nightfall.

General d'Arco knew from his spies where the enemy was encamped and he was confident that he had a full day and a night, perhaps more, before the allies would be upon him. Work was proceeding on schedule, his men had already mounted guns in Gustavus's old fort, and they were now making a palisade around the perimeter of the position. After that they would dig trenches outside the breastworks, which would make the defences doubly effective. When the allies appeared, they would be confronted by a naturally strong position rendered all the more impregnable by his engineers. D'Arco was so confident that he could hold the Heights until reinforcements arrived, that he instructed his quartermasters to measure out the areas where the fresh forces would be able to camp.

At 9 o'clock on the morning of 2 July d'Arco learnt that Marlborough and Baden were on the move, heading towards Donauwörth at an angle that suggested they were aiming at his undefended flank. Alarmed, he sent to the Elector in Augsburg pleading for urgent assistance. He ordered his infantry to set to work alongside the engineers, in an attempt to help make good the defences in time. De la Colonie wrote of this scramble: 'The time left to us was too short to complete this satisfactorily; we could only place fascines one on the other, sparsely covered with earth, so as to form something of the nature of a parapet, which, moreover, was neither high enough nor wide enough to be of much use. As to the ditch on the enemy's side, from which works of this sort derive their chief strength, the Imperial forces gave us no time even to begin it.'[9]

Marlborough had no illusions: his frontal assault on the Schellenberg would be a costly affair. However, he remained convinced that the only way of achieving a speedy capture of Donauwörth was to take the Heights with a head-on attack. The Bavarian force and their French allies could strengthen the fortifications on the hill quite quickly, now that an attack was imminent. He calculated that every extra hour he gave the enemy to prepare themselves would increase his own losses by a thousand men. Despite this daunting thought, Marlborough kept calm. He told his Quartermaster-General, Cadogan, that as soon as he completed his journey to the outskirts of Donauwörth, he was to measure out land within sight of the Schellenberg, as if the allies intended a leisurely siege. D'Arco watched Cadogan's efforts through his eye-glass and fell for the deception. Safe in the belief that they had the rest of the day and the ensuing night to tighten his defences, he rode down into Donauwörth for his lunch.

FOUR DAYS OF CONTINUOUS RAIN had muddied the roads, and progress to Donauwörth was further impeded by the delaying tactics of the Elector's men, Captain Parker noting: 'The Duke was detained some hours at the River Wernitz, in repairing the bridge, and laying others for the army to pass; by which means it was four o'clock, before he reached Donauwörth.'[10] On arrival, after what amounted to three almost continuous days of marching, the infantry were immediately ordered into their battle formations. It was now they realised that their labours were merely the arduous prelude to a perilous assault.

Marlborough went forward with a cavalry detachment to inspect the enemy position for himself. He decided to attack the mid-point in the defences flanked by the Boschberg wood on the one side, and the town on the other. His tactics were typical of those he was to employ through-out the War of the Spanish Succession: choose a point of attack, and concentrate all initial efforts upon it, while holding back a reserve force; if the initial plan succeeded, and the chosen part of the enemy's front crumbled, then so much the better; however, if the enemy resistance denied him victory there, then look to see from where they had brought forward their reserves, and strike decisively at that weakened limb. Although simple in concept, this design depended for its success on the commander's touch and timing.

Marlborough's infantry prepared to march up the Heights. As he surveyed the ground, the duke saw that the retreating Bavarians had set light to Berg, a hamlet near the base of the Schellenberg. Marlborough used the smoke to mask the arrival of a battery of guns under Colonel Blood, his talented artillery commander. These cannon were now in a position from which they could inflict real damage. Blood brought the action to life with an opening salvo. D'Arco's guns replied from Gustavus's fort, and from just outside the thick trees of the Boschberg. Soon the allies' Dutch and German ordnance joined in the exchange. It was clear to onlookers from the thundering of the competing artillery that 'the Action would prove very hot.' [11]

During the cannonade d'Arco was still unaware where, in his extended lines, the main thrust of the enemy advance would be felt. His second-in-command, the Marquis de Maffei, later gave an unfavourable account of his superior's actions. D'Arco, he said, dawdled in the lead-up to the allies' attack. He then prematurely stood the soldiers to arms, when they could still have been improving the defences. However, with battle joined, d'Arco sprang into action, looking to counter the allied attack wherever it came. He ordered Colonel de la Colonie's troops into a reserve position. From here they could be sent to bolster any part of the perimeter that needed reinforcement.

The plan was flawed, because the summit of the Heights was flat and open, affording de la Colonie nowhere to hide. Colonel Blood spotted this exposed body of troops, and de la Colonie recorded the consequences: 'They concentrated their fire upon us, and with their first discharge carried off Count de la Bastide, the lieutenant of my own company with whom at the moment I was speaking, and twelve grenadiers, who fell side by side in the ranks, so that my coat was covered with brains and blood.' [12]

IT WAS EARLY EVENING AS Marlborough watched his British and Dutch infantry arranging itself into four lines, ready for the assault. This force was to follow a forlorn hope: a detachment of 50 English grenadiers under young Lord Mordaunt constituted the traditional sacrifice at such engagements. Its task was to draw the enemy fire, so that attacking commanders could establish where the defences were strongest, and where they were most vulnerable. Of this force, only Mordaunt and ten of his men were to survive the day.

At 6 o'clock the main body of infantry followed the forlorn hope up the hill at a steady walking pace, with the cavalry following behind. The foot soldiers carried with them fascines – the bundles of tightly-packed branches prepared by the dragoons from the trees of the Boschberg – which they were to cast into the defensive ditches in front of the breastworks, to speed their passage. Unfortunately no one had spotted a hollow recently worn out of the side of the Schellenberg by the summer rains. Most of the attackers mistook the gully for the Bavarians' ditch further on and hastily cast their fascines into it. They were left with no easy way of negotiating the Bavarians' trench, which they reached when within range of the defenders' musket- and grape-shot. 'There', remarked General Churchill's chaplain, sombrely, 'the enemy's shot came so thick upon them, as was no ways to be withstood.' [13]

The allied advance steadied, the British shouting 'God save the Queen!' as they came on. Then, at a signal from their officers, disciplined march gave way to furious attack: 'The enemy broke into the charge, and rushed at full speed, shouting at the top of their voices, to throw themselves into our entrenchments. The rapidity of their movements, together with their loud yells, were truly alarming,' wrote Colonel de la Colonie. At eighty paces distance, the defenders met this blood-curdling assault with a raking volley that cut through the allies, leaving many dead, including their leader, Goor, and even more wounded. Temporarily stunned, the allies then continued to move forward, pushing through the defensive ditch till they were grappling with the Bavarians in savage combat. De la Colonie recalled with horror the scene, which he likened to a representation of Hell: 'We were all fighting hand to hand, hurling the assailants back as they clutched at the parapet; men were tearing at the muzzles of guns and the bayonets which pierced their entrails; crushing under their feet their own wounded comrades, and even gouging out their opponents' eyes with their nails, when the grip was so close that neither could make use of their weapons.' [14] However, for all their tenacity and courage, the Anglo-Dutch could not penetrate the outworks, and they faltered, before falling back to their lines.

A second assault was no more successful, the demoralised assailants only being persuaded to advance once more by the bravery of their senior officers. Brigade and regimental commanders led their troops into the torrent of gunfire and grenades emanating from the summit of the Heights. The allied leader of this attack, Count Styrum, now fell, mortally wounded, a cut across his body gaping open. The allies again left piles of dead and wounded in front of the enemy palisade. They fell back, this time pursued by a Bavarian bayonet charge. Only some sterling work by retreating English guardsmen, aided by the covering fire of Lumley's dismounted cavalrymen, prevented a total rout.

It looked as though the Schellenberg might once again fulfil its historic destiny, and save Donauwörth from capture.

Fortunately for the Grand Alliance, Marlborough's unsuccessful attacks had drawn d'Arco's men away from other parts of the defences. The south-western area now had only a token defence. Critically, Donauwörth's garrison commander had failed to provide the covering fire expected by d'Arco, and, in a panic, had withdrawn his men inside the town walls. From his advanced position in a gully on the side of the Schellenberg Marlborough sent a platoon of his troops to probe this sector of the enemy parapet. The report came back that this was an area of surprising vulnerability, and Marlborough ordered eight battalions of his reserve infantry to attack it without delay. These men fought alongside the Imperialists, on the right wing of the allied attack.

Prince Lewis of Baden had entered the battle half an hour after Marlborough, and his men had avoided the battering twice experienced by their allies to the left. Baden led his men, riding his horse into the side of the savage firestorm. His men threw in their fascines, and then poured over the half-completed defences, holding their fire until inside the enemy position. Here, they engulfed a small but determined defensive force, consisting of two battalions of infantry and a smattering of cavalry. Baden's horse was shot from underneath him and he received a crushing wound in the foot which caused lasting and significant damage.

Marlborough was aware that the Imperialist troops were swarming into the Schellenberg. Now, an hour and a quarter after their first bloody assault, he exhorted his own men into a third attack up the slope. Understandably reluctant after their two recent maulings, the men moved forward with extreme caution. Lieutenant-General Lumley sent Lord John Hay with his regiment of dragoons to join the assault on foot. There was surprise and relief when the garrison commander's mistake was discovered, and no fire was felt on the English flank nearest to Donauwörth. As they moved up the hill once more, the attackers panned out, forming a broader front. The Bavarians had to spread their fire and throw their grenades across a wider range, considerably reducing the deadly effectiveness of their previous efforts.

The defenders remained hopeful that they could repel this latest assault and hold their position. They knew help was on its way, the Elector himself leading the promised relief force from Augsburg. However, many Franco-Bavarians were so caught up in the engagement that they were unaware that Baden's Imperialists were established inside the palisade. Worse, the French regiment of Nectancourt had fled the fight for the protection of the town walls. When a detachment of Bavarian dragoons tried to make good the void created by their allies' withdrawal, they were cut down by English musket fire.

General d'Arco now found himself separated from the remainder of his men, and also fled to Donauwörth, clinging to his horse as it swam the river. He later maintained that he had assumed that the rest of his command had already preceded him into the town. In this he was mistaken.

De la Colonie and his men were unaware of these developments on other parts of the battlefield. They were fighting hard when the Anglo-Dutch infantrymen in front of them stood up, making no attempt to protect themselves, or fire their weapons. 'I glanced around on all sides to see what had caused this behaviour, and then became aware of several lines of infantry in greyish-white uniforms on our left flank. From their dress and bearing, I verily believed that reinforcements had arrived for us. Having, however, made a closer inspection, I discovered bunches of straw and leaves attached to their standards, badges the enemy are in the custom of wearing on the occasion of battle, and at that very moment I was struck by a ball in the right lower jaw which wounded and stupefied me.'[15]

Baden's right wing was established at the summit of the Heights, and Marlborough controlled the left wing. The stalwart defence of the Schellenberg was over, two hours after it had begun. For the attackers, who had suffered so badly in their early assaults, it was time for vengeance. As the Bavarians and French scrambled down the hill, desperate to reach the river, throwing their weapons away, Marlborough unleashed thirty-five squadrons of English and Prussian cavalry. Their battle cry was: 'Kill, kill and destroy!'[16], and they tore after the fugitives, slashing at their backs with their sabres. No mercy was shown, the allies hunting down fugitives seeking cover in the surrounding fields. De la Colonie, who was one of the few to escape the bloodbath, 'saw a number of troops approaching ever nearer to my hiding-place, who were refusing to give quarter to the unhappy wounded they found hidden in the corn, whom they ruthlessly despatched the more easily to despoil them.'[17] The Franco-Bavarians had been merciless in their frenzied defence of the hill. Now, they could expect no quarter.

Earlier, with battle both inevitable and imminent, d'Arco had ordered his baggage-wagons to cross the single pontoon bridge into Donauwörth. However, the panic-stricken wagon drivers all bolted for safety. Their over-laden vehicles buckled the bridge of boats, before destroying it completely. As a result, at the end of the engagement, there was no easy way for the defeated to escape. Many leapt into the Danube, but most could not swim. In any case, the recent rains had made it a fast-moving torrent, making these difficult waters for those that could. Captain Parker, one of the most reliable of the soldier diarists, wrote that: 'The loss of the enemy was computed to be about 7,000 killed, 2,000 drowned, and 3,000 taken, with everything they had.'[18] Most of the survivors drifted away, rather than rejoin the Elector's and Marsin's armies, and very few of the 14,000 men who defended the Schellenberg that summer evening were to face the allies in battle again.

In his despatch to the States-General, the Prussian Lieutenant-General von Hompesch reflected on the extraordinary number of senior officers killed or wounded during the fight: 'Lieutenant-General Goor, who commanded the infantry, was killed, as was Major-General Beinheim. The wounded from the Infantry are Lieutenant-General Hoorn, in the leg, Major-General Palland, in the thigh. The cavalry wounded are the Crown Prince of Hesse, Brigadier the Prince of Saxony is wounded in the arm, but not in danger. Brigadier Bodmar is also wounded. Field Marshal the Count Styrum has a cut across his body, and his life is in danger. Field Marshal Thungen is wounded in the hand. And Major-General the Prince Alexander of Württemberg is wounded in the leg. Major-General the Prince of Bevern is killed.'[19] In all, six lieutenant-generals, four major-generals, and twenty-eight brigadiers, colonels and lieutenant-colonels were killed on the Schellenberg, with a further five lieutenant-generals wounded. This casualty rate reflected the exposed positions the senior officers had taken as they ordered their troops forward into enemy fire. No other action in the War of the Spanish Succession claimed the lives of so many generals.

There was triumph in the allied ranks. Sergeant Millner celebrated in his diary the 'undaunted Vigour, Courage, and unparallell'd Valour of the day'. He listed the victors' spoils: 'In this glorious Action we took Fifteen Pieces of Cannon, Thirteen Colours, with all their Ammunition, Tents, and Baggage, and a great Quantity of other War Utensils; besides all De Arco's Plate, and other rich Booty, which was distributed amongst our victorious Soldiers.'[20]

But the human cost of the engagement was huge. 'We gained our point, and beat the enemy from their post, and yet we have no reason to boast or think highly of ourselves,' Captain Blackader wrote. 'The British value themselves too much, and think nothing can stand before them. We have suffered considerably on this occasion, and have no cause to be proud.'[21] The duke's reliance on his British troops was evident in the list of casualties. Out of 6,000 Britons engaged, 435 were killed and more than 1,100 wounded. Allied casualties were in the region of 6,000. The number killed outright on the day was only 700, but nearly 1,000 of the badly wounded died soon afterwards, either near the battlefield or on their way back to the basic medical care awaiting them in Nördlingen. 'The moment this action was ended,' recalled Josias Sandby, Churchill's chaplain, 'it grew dark, and rained violently. This proved very fatal to the wounded.'[22]

IF A SOLDIER WAS WOUNDED IN battle at this time, the care he received was rudimentary. Nursing staff was practically non-existent in early eighteenth century Europe. Colleagues would transport the fallen back to military hospital, in wagons, and on stretchers. Rough roads rendered the journey agonising: broken thighs were particularly painful, since nobody knew how to set them in the field. Whatever the wound, the victim was often bled and purged in preparation for treatment and cure. Critical evacuation would, it was hoped, free the patient from the danger of fever, as well as drying up the moisture round the injury. In the makeshift hospitals, the wounded would – if they could swallow – be given bread, soup, and wine to strengthen them for the ordeal of surgery. Hopeless cases would be 'passed over' by the surgeons and left to expire.

The regimental medical officers had extremely limited scientific knowledge. The treatment of wounds was a mysterious business based on an uneasy fusion of common sense, tradition, and superstition. It was noted, although not universally understood, that the cleaning of wounds helped patients' prospects of survival. Medieval remedies still had their exponents in early eighteenth-century medical care; this, in an age which had recognised Dr Harvey's experiments proving that blood circulated through the body, pumped by the heart. Preying on ignorance and confusion, physicians wrote treatises confidently expounding their miraculous cures, hopeful that they would result in personal riches and kudos.

The calibre of surgeons attracted to military life was generally low. According to John Hunter, an eighteenth-century medical philosopher, and himself an army doctor, the military surgeon was likely to be a man 'who would have buried his talents and his industry in a situation where obscurity, poverty, and neglect, spread all their horrors before him. These were, for years, the portion of the army-surgeons; their situation was looked upon as the lowest step of professional drudgery and degradation.'[23] Any physician with talent or ambition opted for the more lucrative and respectable path of private practice.

Soldiers were wary of the regimental surgeon, fearing that he would rather lop off their wounded limbs quickly, than save them through time-consuming care. Amputation was common, and often immediate: 'It was very obvious to me, from chirurgical practice,' wrote Dr J. White, a naval surgeon who saw action off the Iberian coast in 1703 and 1704, 'that where amputations are requisite, they succeed ten to one better if the operation is performed immediately after the misfortune, than four or five days after. This all our surgeons in the army very well know, as well as in the navy'. [24]

Gangrenous limbs were always amputated. 'If any of the limbs of the body should be so mortified,' recommended a tract of 1700, 'that it must be cut off, which falls out, when if you cut the part you find it senseless, black and flaggy-flesh, being cold, smelling like a dead carcass, and if you support the skin from the flesh, there flows from it a green blackish matter. The manner of cutting off such mortified member is this, draw up the muscles and flesh very hard, then bind the part two inches above the place which is to be cut off, with a strong fillet; that done, with a sharp razor, or a dismembering-knife, made for that purpose, being somewhat crooked, cut the flesh round to the very bone; if this to be done below the elbow, or in the leg, then you must with your incision-knife divide the flesh betwixt the forsiles, then with the back of it take away the film or membrane which covers the bone, which is called the periostium; then with your saw take away the bone, as near the flesh as you can.' [25]

Rotting flesh was universally recognised as a grave menace. Monsieur Belloste, Surgeon-Major to the French army in Italy, acknowledged, in 1706: 'A gangrene is an accident, that occasions very much trouble in the hospitals of the Army ... we have not time to lose, but must immediately apply ourselves to stop its progress, and to avoid the fatal consequences.' However, his methods were idiosyncratic, and medically unproven. 'The remedy we used', he recalled, of his hospital days in the

War of the League of Augsburg, 'was Spirit of Nitre, or Aqua fortis, wherein crude mercury to half the quantity is dissolved: with this we have easily enough stopped mortifications in the feet or hands, applying over all the extent of the gangrene a little piece of linen wet in this liquor.'[26] Belloste relied on the medicinal properties of mercury throughout his twenty-eight-year career.

He was equally trusting of other toxic metals. 'As for leaden bullets that have not been drawn out at the first dressing, their remaining in the parts can do no great hurt, because they are friendly to Nature', Belloste advised, 'and in process of time, by their own weight, slip down between the muscles, and often appear under the skin, from whence they may be taken out, without either trouble or danger.'[27] Ignorance of lead's dangers was common. John Brown, a surgeon during the Anglo-Dutch Wars of the 1660s, declared it void of all poisons. This conclusion was based on its supposed success in other treatments: 'For lead being beaten to powder is good for old ulcers; and applied in its own metallic form and beaten thin, it does depress the lips of old sordid ulcers, and stop the increase of scirrhous tumours.'[28]

Eccentric logic caused untold pain and death in the military hospital of Louis's wars. Belloste endangered his patients through a misunderstanding of the effect of air on open wounds. He distrusted the 'nitrous' element of air, seeing this as the reason why metal rusted. 'I don't, as some do,' Belloste explained, 'take up a deal of time, in striving exactly to empty the wound, of all the matter that is in it; but as quickly as can be, I apply the dressings, to hinder, as hath been said, the action of the acid parts of the air, and the dissipation of the spirits; that the strength of the afflicted parts may be preserved as much as possible; which is very requisite, in order to enable them to bear up against the many Evils, wherewith they are assaulted on all hands.'[29] The evils of ignorant physicians were often the deadliest assault of all.

Few surgeons shared Belloste's belief that wounds were best left uncleansed: most understood the importance of picking out the detritus that accompanied musket ball or shrapnel into the body. 'The first thing to be done in order to the curing of these wounds', opined a contemporary English treatise, 'is to remove whatsoever is within the wound offending it; as linen, paper, bullets, and the like, with instruments for that purpose; as forceps, crows-bills, catch-bullets, &c. The next thing must be to staunch the flux of blood, which is done either by filling the wound with dry lint, or powders of bole-armonack, dragons blood, aloes, frankincense, the hairs of a hare cut very small, and such like.'[30] Some surgeons recommended dilating the wound, 'by thrusting into it as much lint as it could contain'[31], so as to help expel foreign bodies from the flesh.

Spirit vinegar was swabbed around wounds of the body's extremities, its antiseptic properties noted, if not understood. Soldiers who had been burnt – a common occurrence, when barrels of gunpowder were detonated by enemy fire, or when firearms exploded in the hand – were treated with ointment made from one part salt to eight parts onion juice. Burnt eyes were administered a gentler concoction, of rose water, egg white, sugar-candy, and – if available – woman's breast milk. Mouth wounds were seared closed with small cauterising irons. Severed muscles and tendons were often too complicated to cure: surgeons were advised to pull them tight, 'so that their ends, if totally divided, can be brought any thing near together, which if it be not possible to be done, which for the most part is, there is no other ill consequence, but the losing the use of that part to which it belongs.'[32]

Into this world of medical confusion, ignorance and fear strolled many a chancer. John Colbatch was a controversial medical figure who sought to profit from the misery of the battlefield at the end of the seventeenth century. William III patronised his work in the War of the League of Augsburg, inadvertently lending credibility to a charlatan. 'I began to make experiments upon dogs and other animals, wounding them in the most desperate manner I could contrive,'[33] he boasted in the introduction to his main treatise, 'A New Light of Chirurgery'. This work appeared in 1695, and still had adherents a decade later: a witness to several of the experiments with wounded animals was an intrigued Lord Cutts. What was new about Colbatch's chirurgery was his elixir, 'Vulnerary Powder'. This was, supposedly, a cure-all for any injury. 'Suppose a wound be made [by] a sword or other cutting instrument, the length or depth of which, signifies nothing, I make a solution of my powder in water, for want of which in urine, and as soon as with conveniency I can, the sooner after the wound is made the better, I either squeeze, or with a syringe, if the wound be deep, inject into the wound some of the said solution, I then close the lips of the wound together, which if wide and large, I stitch up.' [34] The sufferer was then given a diet of meat and wine. 'In all incised wounds, where my medicines have been timely enough used, and no other application preceded, they are perfectly cured in a few days, without bringing them to supparation; and I have frequently observed, that at about four days end, such wounds have been filled with a substance, much like unto Harts-horn jelly, which I have conjectured to be young flesh.' [35]

Colbatch illustrated the wonderful effects of his powder with many examples: 'A private soldier in the regiment of Colonel Collingwood, had with a broadsword his sternum or breast-bone divided, the sword likewise passed on, into the body of his lungs. From the wound rushed forth a vast quantity of blood and air together, that Mr Chombly declared that he could scarce with his hand keep on a dressing; so to bring the lips of the wound together, with a needle and thread he sowed up the wound; but the force of air was so great, the flux of blood being before stopped by my medicines, that he was forced to make his stitches in the external part of the bone, which is gristly, by reason that the skin was not strong enough to hold him.' [36]

Despite Colbatch's claims, battle wounds often resulted in death. There was no understanding of the need for antiseptic, so blood poisoning was common. Similarly, apart from a modest intake of wine, there was no anaesthetic, and shock took many during surgery. Also, many patients arrived at a battle with their immune system depressed by exhaustion, the stress of battle taking place in the wake of long marches. Undermined by inadequate diet, and weeks of hardship in challenging weather, the patient was frequently weak before receiving his injury. Psychologically, too, the badly wounded soldier knew his chances were slim; surgeons expected death to result from a broad range of wounds: 'Thus if the principal parts, as the brain and its substance, be wounded, we do judge

189

the wound to be [lethal]. If the lungs, "diaphragma", ventricle, spleen or kidneys be hurt by shot they are for the most part deadly. Of the same kind may be reckoned wounds received in the intestines or bladder; these being spermatic and membranous parts. If the fleshy parts only be wounded, and the constitution good, these may with ease be cured.'[37]

After the storming of the Schellenberg, the allied wounded were taken to Nördlingen for treatment. Marlborough had arranged for local doctors to assist in their treatment. Despite this, and even though his army was seen to have a high proportion of medical staff, the wounded died in their hundreds.

THE CASUALTY FIGURES AT THE Schellenberg shocked many in England, lending credence to the Tories' fears about the wisdom of waging war so far from home. The English poet Addison summed up the anger his compatriots felt at the battle's toll:

> How many generous Britons meet their doom,
> New to the field, and heroes in the bloom!
> The illustrious youths, that left their native shore
> To march where Britons never marched before,
> (O fatal love of fame! O glorious heat,
> Only destructive to the brave and great!)
> After such toils o'ercome, such dangers past,
> Stretched on Bavarian ramparts breathe their last. [38]

Marlborough was accustomed to bitter criticism. However, he was hurt by claims that Lewis of Baden was the real victor of the Schellenberg, and not him. At the conclusion of the battle Baden had graciously said to Marlborough: 'I am delighted that your proposal has proved such a success.' To which Marlborough had replied: 'I am thankful that you have supported me so well with your troops, and relieved the pressure on me.'[39] The exchange demonstrates a mutual appreciation of the other's role, which is borne out by their lieutenants. Hompesch, an impartial ally, paid deference to each commander's role: 'The Duke of Marlborough gave the orders throughout this action with all the promptness, calm, prudence, and presence of mind that anyone could have displayed', while 'The Prince of Baden, as everyone has said, did for his part all that a great and brave general could do.' [40]

In The Hague, though, matters were seen differently. Like the High Tories in England, the States-General were aghast at the large numbers of their compatriots slaughtered in a strange land. The Dutch cast a victory medal. It showed Prince Lewis of Baden on the obverse, while the Latin inscription on the other side, translated, read: 'The enemy defeated and put to flight and their camp plundered at Schellenberg near Donauwörth, 1704'. Of Marlborough there was no mention.

Electress Sophia of Hanover, heir presumptive to the British throne, joined in the chorus of disapproval: 'The Elector is saddened by the loss of so many brave subjects in consequences of the great general Marlborough', she wrote to her friend Gottfried von Leibniz. 'He says that the Margrave of Baden did very much better, and that without him there would have been complete failure, as on the other wing proper measure had not been taken.' [41]

Despite the criticism, Marlborough still enjoyed the confidence of his monarch. Queen Anne wrote from Windsor to Archduke Charles, the Habsburg pretender to the Spanish throne: 'I will avail myself of this occasion to tell you the news I received yesterday by an express from the Duke of Marlborough; that the Allies have gained a signal victory over the French and Bavarians, who occupied a position near Donauwörth. They entirely defeated them and took that town. I think this news will be no less pleasing to you, on account of the effect such a fine victory must have on Vienna, than it is to me, in giving me joy as much on behalf of the common cause, as because of the part taken by troops in their glorious action, under the command of the said Duke of Marlborough.' [42]

The Imperial Court appreciated the significance of the victory. Emperor Leopold broke with custom to write his congratulations to the duke in his own hand: 'Nothing can be more glorious than the celerity and vigour with which after the junction of your army and mine, you forced the camp of the enemy at Donauwörth; since my generals and

ministers declare that the success of the enterprise, which is most acceptable and opportune to me, was chiefly owing to your counsel, prudence,
and conduct, as well as to the bravery of the troops under your
command.' The Emperor celebrated what others sought to criticise:
'This will be an eternal trophy to your most serene queen in Upper
Germany, whither the victorious arms of the English nation have never
penetrated since the memory of man.' [43]

Secure in his sovereign's support, Marlborough looked to capitalise
on the taking of Donauwörth. He wrote to Queen Anne: 'I shall
endeavour to improve the happy beginning to Your Majesty's glory, and
the benefit of your allies.' [44] He was aware that lack of success in the
remainder of the campaign would make it difficult for her to continue in
her loyal support. Without it, he would be left vulnerable to the many
who wished him to fail.

CHAPTER FOURTEEN

LOOKING TO LOUIS

'I must tell you the ill news, which is, that the marshal de Villeroi has promised the Elector of Bavaria that he will send him, by the way of the Black Forest, fifty battalions of foot, and sixty squadrons of horse, as he tells him in his letter, the best troops of France, which would make him stronger than we. But I rely very much on the assurances Prince Eugène gave me yesterday by his adjutant-general, that he would venture the whole, rather than suffer them to pass quietly, as the last did.'

MARLBOROUGH TO SARAH MARLBOROUGH, 3 JULY 1704

THERE WERE MONKS LIVING IN Donauwörth in 1704 who recalled the only previous time that the Schellenberg had fallen to an enemy. Seventy-two years earlier, as boys, they had seen Gustavus Adolphus take the Heights, after a battle that had lasted two days. Marlborough and Baden's assault had proved successful in two hours. The swiftness surprised everyone. The Elector and his reinforcements arrived within sight of the battle, but only in time to witness the flight and massacre of Bavaria's finest troops. Maximilian Emmanuel had watched with tears in his eyes as the allies scythed his men down. As he withdrew, the Elector sent orders to the garrison commander to burn Donauwörth and destroy its bridge. Then he was to bring his troops to the well-protected military camp at Lavingen-Dillingen.

The departing soldiers packed bundles of straw into the town buildings to prepare them for burning. However, before the flame could
catch, the burghers intervened, tearing the faggots away with their hands.
The troops put safety before duty and fled rather than carry through
the destruction. On entering the town, Marlborough was able to report
to the States-General: 'they have only burnt the bridge, and set alight
a few magazines, and have retired at haste first thing in the morning; at
the same time we have taken possession, and have found in the town
their gunpowder store with three cannon in the arsenal, two thousand
bags of wheat, and a good quantity of oats.'[1] The allies had secured their
springboard for the invasion of Bavaria, and it was a well-supplied one.

The Elector understood the consequences of defeat. By reputation
a courageous and inspirational figure, the loss of Donauwörth left him
depressed and withdrawn. Whenever the Schellenberg was mentioned,
his face streamed with tears, and his voice choked as he recalled the fate
of his men. Maximilian Emmanuel knew that this reverse threatened
dire repercussions: unless Villeroi or Tallard – preferably both – could
reach him soon, then Marlborough and Baden would be upon him and
his countrymen would learn the full cost of their leader's treachery to
his feudal master, the Emperor.

The choice now for the Elector was simple: he and Marshal Marsin
must either hold their position at Lavingen-Dillingen or they could
retreat to a safe place, while abandoning the electorate to the invaders. He
chose the latter option, ordering a withdrawal to his camp under the
guns of Augsburg. The Elector's sense of failure as he left his people,
his estates and lucrative salt mines unprotected, was deep. Feeling that he
and Marsin had been left to their fate by Louis's marshals north of the
Black Forest, Maximilian Emmanuel began to intensify his covert negotiations with the allies. If reinforcements did not arrive soon, Bavaria
could be gained for the Grand Alliance without a further shot being fired.

THE CONFIDENCE WITH WHICH the French started 1704 should be
remembered. They had been sure that the year would bring them sufficient victories to win the war. Louis's marshals came to life in the spring,

their prime objective the domination of Austria, their secondary aim the control of Italy. In Flanders, Villeroi anticipated more thrust and parry with Marlborough, who was recognised as the most dangerous of the allied generals. On the Rhine, Tallard was instructed to intensify the Emperor's discomfort, building on his successes of the previous year. In Italy, the combined efforts of Vendôme, his brother the Grand Prior, and La Feuillade were expected to make short work of the duplicitous Duke of Savoy – Prince Eugène's cousin – who had declared himself once more for the Grand Alliance. On the Danube, Marsin was to coordinate the destruction of the Habsburg Empire with the Elector. Louis looked forward to a fighting year that promised rich and varied prizes.

Marlborough's march to the Danube stole the initiative away from the French. They were forced to monitor the duke's progress from a distance, still unaware of the expedition's destination or purpose. Villeroi and Tallard were confident they could cope with most eventualities, Tallard writing to Chamillart on 23 May: 'If the enemy wants to attack [Landau], I promise you that they will find there all that can contribute to its defence; but I doubt very much that they will try that, for Germany would be vulnerable throughout the period of the siege. If they are going on to the Moselle, as I learn Marshal Villeroi is marching there, I have nothing to say about that. If they cross the Rhine and advance into the Empire to contribute to the overpowering of the Elector of Bavaria, [that is] something that I do not wish to think about.'[2] The Danube was, to the French, the most vulnerable sphere of warfare. However, it seemed a highly unlikely destination, given its distance from the Lowlands: Marlborough would surely strike along the Moselle, or invade Alsace?

On the day in early June that Marlborough's intentions were finally revealed, Villeroi and Tallard were meeting at Zweibrücken. News that the allied army had turned towards Sinzheim confirmed that the Franco-Bavarian force on the Danube was under threat. The two marshals realised that Marlborough was trying something of real consequence. Rather than take responsibility for meeting the menace by themselves, they looked to Versailles for instruction: let Louis devise a master plan to save his and the Elector's forces.

195

The king enjoyed the deference paid to him as supreme commander of his armies, but he was unsure what to do about the allied foray into Germany. When Marlborough struck out towards the Danube, there was no obvious way of stopping him, just an unsteady raft of possibilities, none of them compelling. Louis sought the advice of his marshals on the ground. On 12 June Chamillart wrote an exploratory letter to Tallard: 'As nobody knows the said countryside better than you, and as Marshal Villeroi is very well informed about it, His Majesty knows no better than to put to you two again the choice as to what to do against the enemy.' [3]

The same day, more agitated now, Chamillart wrote once more: 'All is become doubtful and difficult. I well know that this is not your fault, but it is on these occasions that men show themselves as they are, when they have more spirit and courage than others; I have great hope that you will give new proof of this to all Europe.' [4] Villeroi and Tallard were asked to send a plan to Versailles, explaining how the Elector's and Marsin's troops could be saved from the allied advance. This crucial decision was batted backwards and forwards by the French for a fortnight, while Marlborough ploughed on, unhindered.

It was clear that the Franco-Bavarian army was now prey rather than predator, and that the electorate would feel the consequences of its ruler's treachery. However, when decisiveness was essential, the middle two weeks of June 1704 saw the French monarch and high command held in thrall. Unable to commit to one course of action, Villeroi's and Tallard's deliberations threw up four alternative strategies for the Sun King's consideration. To each was attached a list of pros and cons, underlining the two marshals' indecision. Tallard, usually so confident, opened his letter to Louis with an honesty that smacked of defeatism: 'In view of the superiority of the enemy forces between the Rhine and the Danube, assistance to Bavaria is so difficult as to appear almost an impossibility.' [5]

Louis, disappointed at his marshals' unhelpfulness, plumped for the riskiest of the four plans placed before him: an advance towards Stuttgart, while avoiding the Lines of Stollhofen. What did the two marshals think of this? The answer came in two supplementary papers, each non-committal. It was clear that the marshals would not take such an important decision: 'Your Majesty understands war better than those who have the honour to serve you,' Villeroi simpered.

Louis was paying the price for failing to listen to earlier cries of alarm from the Danube. He had ignored supplications from the Elector and Marsin in early June, when they had voiced their fear that Bavaria was to be attacked by Marlborough. On 5 June the Elector had written to Tallard: 'I am receiving at this time certain advice that all the [Allied] forces are coming to the Danube; so, Sir, there is no time to lose.'[6] The next day Marsin warned Versailles that immediate reinforcements were essential: without them, Maximilian Emmanuel might flee, with his family and gold, to join the Hungarian rebels. Louis refused to take this point seriously: surely no divinely appointed ruler would look for sanctuary with insurgents?

Having received no help, the Elector and Marsin despatched a senior representative, General Legalle, to stress in person their desperate plight. Legalle arrived at Versailles on 22 June. He alerted the king and his Council to the threat of an allied pincer movement in the open country of Bavaria which, 'in a very short time [could] devastate the defenceless land'.[7] Legalle also pointed to the Elector's weakening health: if Maximilian Emmanuel died, then Bavaria would immediately return to its historic allegiance. Her 35 battalions and 45 squadrons would then fight for the Holy Roman Emperor against France, and not vice versa.

Louis now understood that a failure to reinforce his German ally could tilt the delicate balance of the war against him. Fed up with the double talk of Villeroi and Tallard, he sent them commands that were to be obeyed without delay. On 27 June the marshals learnt that they must divide their army into three: Tallard was ordered to take 40 battalions and 50 squadrons through the mountains of the Black Forest, to reinforce Marsin and the Elector; Villeroi, with a similar number of infantry and rather more cavalry, was to pin down the allies defending the Lines of Stollhofen, while being prepared to come to the aid of the forces on the Danube; and Lieutenant-General Coignies was to take a smaller force of 8,000 men to protect Alsace. Louis felt sure that Tallard would be grateful for the fine force he was entrusting to his command:

'I have chosen the troops that must march with you,' he wrote. 'They are very good.' [8] They included three battalions each of the historic regiments of Navarre and Royal, and eight squadrons from the elite *Gendarmerie*, the pride of the French cavalry.

Louis's orders made little sense to Tallard. Baden's and Marlborough's armies would join together any day, and form a combined unit of 85,000 men. However, the king had opted to divide his army into three independent bodies, each of which would stand on the defensive while watching the enemy. French victories earlier in Louis's reign had generally been achieved through proactive aggression, not delayed reaction. Furthermore, Tallard realised that the ratio of foot to horse in his army was too high: this was a campaign which promised to be fast-paced, yet he would have to progress at the infantry's speed. Tallard remonstrated with his monarch: 'I venture to say that in the circumstances Your Majesty can come to no decision which would not encounter extraordinary difficulties in view of the numerous hostile fighting forces between the Rhine and the Danube,' he tactfully conceded, before venting his dissatisfaction. 'If the army which Your Majesty has assigned to me could maintain itself independently – that is to say, if I had fifty additional squadrons of cavalry – and if at the same time an army were stationed in the Rhine valley sufficiently large to protect Alsace and stop Prince Eugène from entering eastward, the Empire would be lost: but as Your Majesty cannot do this, it is a waste of time to discuss it. I venture only to say that with fifty squadrons of cavalry, which I am to have, a campaign cannot be undertaken. My infantry is sufficient, and in regard to that I have no misgiving.' [9] Tallard's frustration with Louis crackles from the page: he wanted some of the eighty squadrons that had been assigned to Villeroi and Coignies for himself.

On 1 July the two marshals parted. Tallard and his army of 35,000 men displayed none of the excitement and optimism that the allies had exhibited during Marlborough's march to the Danube. 'It was with deep misgivings', Winston S. Churchill wrote, that Tallard 'obeyed the commands of the King to proceed to the rescue of Bavaria. He had protested that neither the policy nor the force supplied him was suited to the occasion. He was reluctant and perplexed as he entered his coach with his son at his side.' [10]

Before setting off, Tallard received a letter from Louis, informing him of the Duchess of Burgundy's successful delivery of a son. Tallard sent three letters to France, one for Louis, one for the Dauphin and the third addressed to the infant's father. In his covering correspondence, addressed to Chamillart, he wrote: 'Nothing, Sir, approaches the joy that I have at the birth of a prince who takes away all the schisms that the Spanish succession produced; during the monarchy there has not been a circumstance where it has been so necessary to have an heir for the Crown: God grant him a life full of health!' [11]

THE WET WEATHER THAT HAD hampered Marlborough's progress also delayed the French. Three weeks of rain had churned up the roads, leaving them deeply rutted. The harness traces of the wagons and gun teams snapped as the horses tried to pull their loads free from the mud.

The summer storms dictated Tallard's route through the Black Forest: the pass at Kingzigenthal was not viable, for huge numbers of trees had fallen down, making progress dangerous and slow. Tallard set off for the pass of Walkirk. He took with him large quantities of ammunition: 4,000 cannon balls; four 24-pound cannon; and copious quantities of gunpowder. A month's grain requirements, ten days of bread rations and enough biscuit for the first five days of the march were carried in the supply train. In all, there were 8,000 wagons and carts.

Marshal and men moved forward without enthusiasm. It took two weeks to cross the mountains, narrow paths checking the soldiers' pace. Tallard's insistence on bringing two mule trains to carry delicacies and fine wine for his table made progress yet more cumbersome. Whereas Marlborough was noted for his Spartan requirements on campaign, Tallard enjoyed entertaining up to one hundred officers at mealtimes in the field.

Among Tallard's senior officers was the Count of Mérode-Westerloo. Commander of the King of Spain's Flemish troops in Alsace and Germany, the count had under his command four battalions of infantry, and three fine cavalry regiments. Mérode-Westerloo has left behind a fascinating diary of his experiences on this campaign, its one weakness being a tendency to vanity and self-importance. His everyday observations, however, and his eye for human colour, bring alive the summer of 1704.

Despite the size of Tallard's provision train, his men were often hungry. This led to indiscipline; a condition frequently associated with Tallard's troops. 'An amusing incident tickled our soldiers' sense of humour whilst we were still at Rozberg,' recalled Mérode-Westerloo. 'There were three great buildings in the camp, each easily capable of holding a hundred men … All of us – that is to say all the senior officers at least – brought our food and wine into one of the houses to make merry. It was while we were looking it over (incidentally, not a single iron nail had been used in its construction) that I found a great brass alpenhorn. Try as I might I could not get a sound out of it. Eventually everybody had a go, and at last one of them with stronger lungs than mine got the thing to work. So well did he trumpet that a moment later we heard the lowing of cattle all around in the woods, and out they came, trotting from the trees towards the fort, obeying our horn. The soldiers regarded this as manna from heaven, and in no time at all the camp resembled a slaughterhouse.' [12]

News of this spread quickly among Tallard's undernourished force. Troops started to fan out as they moved south, seeking other livestock that had been allowed to roam free. Tallard, from this point on, found it impossible to stop his men from marauding. The reprisals from German farmers were brutal: in Mérode-Westerloo's estimation, the indigenous peasantry 'killed several thousand of our men before the army was clear of the Black Forest.' [13] The contrast between the conduct of the two marching armies, Tallard's and Marlborough's, could hardly have been more pronounced.

TALLARD WAS NOT A NATURAL SOLDIER: his preferred habitat was the Court, not the campaigning tent. The gossipy Duc de Saint-Simon leaves us a lengthy sketch of Tallard, which attributed his military rank to close blood ties and friendship with the Villeroi family (Tallard's mother was sister to Nicolas Villeroi, who had preceded his son François as a marshal in Louis's army), rather than to aptitude for the battlefield. According to Saint-Simon, there were tensions between François Villeroi and Tallard: the younger Villeroi regarded his first cousin as very much his junior, his creation, despite being of similar age and equal in rank. Tallard, meanwhile, felt the implied inferiority of his own position. This made him eager to prove himself worthy of his command by virtue of ability – ability that he never truly possessed.

Saint-Simon left a full description of Tallard: 'He was a man of medium build, with slightly jealous eyes, which were full of fire and spirit, but which could see nothing; thin, pale, he stood for ambition, envy and avarice; he had lots of wit but was constantly beaten by the Devil for his ambition, his views, his intrigues, his subterfuges, and he thought and breathed nothing else. Suffice it to say that nobody trusted him, and that everyone enjoyed his company.'[14] Louis XIV certainly did, as well as valuing his intelligence. The king sent him to command his army on the Rhine.

Early results in the War of the Spanish Succession seemed to justify the king's confidence in his favoured diplomat. In 1702 Tallard captured Trèves and Trarbach, gaining for France a short cut between their forces in Flanders and on the Upper Rhine. His efforts in 1703 further helped Louis's cause: in September he took the fortress of Old Breisach, and in November Tallard defeated Prince Frederick of Hesse-Cassel (Charles XII's brother-in-law, and his successor on the Swedish throne) at Speyer-bach. This victory was followed, the next day, by the recapture of Landau, which considerably eased French communications with their army in Bavaria. However, these gains covered up tactical and physical weaknesses that later events were to expose.

Tallard, in truth, had not been ordered to attack Breisach or Landau. His instructions for 1703 had been to shadow Prince Lewis of Baden and to stop his army from slipping through the Black Forest into the Danube valley. Tallard had failed in this duty: although his two sieges were successful, and were acclaimed, his inability to block Baden had seriously inconvenienced Marshal Villars and the Elector. Indeed, the presence of this Imperialist force distracted the two commanders from their push on Vienna in 1703. By the time Baden was defeated, at the battle of Höchstädt, it was too late in the season for the Franco-Bavarians to press home their advantage.

Furthermore, Tallard's victory at Speyerbach owed more to luck than to military ability. Prince Frederick of Hesse-Cassel had been sent from the Netherlands to relieve the French siege of Landau. Saint Simon, in his pen sketch of Tallard, mentioned the marshal's very poor eyesight. At Speyerbach, as the opposing armies started to fall into their respective battle positions, Tallard asked his aides to relay to him how the enemy was manoeuvring, since he could not see for himself what they were doing. From one of the descriptions given to him, Tallard mistakenly concluded that the Imperialists were in retreat. His own army had yet to deploy in attacking formation, yet Tallard thought he must act immediately. He ordered his forces to charge. This command surprised his own commanders as much as it wrong-footed Hesse-Cassel, but they obeyed their marshal and fell upon the enemy. The two wings of the Imperial army were pushed together by the French, before falling back in disarray on their centre. The result was chaos and defeat for the Imperialists. Tallard's short-sightedness gained him a victory, and a reputation, which he did not deserve.

MARLBOROUGH AND TALLARD WERE not strangers. They had met in the aftermath of the Peace of Ryswick, when Count Tallard had been the much-fêted French ambassador at the Court of St James's and Marlborough had recently been restored to royal favour after his time in the wilderness.

Tallard cut a dash during his diplomatic mission to England, his spell as ambassador marked by lavish entertainments of which he was both initiator and recipient. While William III's favourite, the Duke of Portland, dazzled Versailles with his own displays of wealth and style, Tallard outdid him for opulence and sophistication. The house he rented from the Duke of Ormonde, in fashionable St James's Square, became famed for the French grandee's generous hospitality.

Winston S. Churchill wrote that: 'Tallard was one of the most distinguished figures in the circle of Louis XIV. Not only was he reputed
an excellent soldier with recent exploits to his credit, but his diplomatic
qualities and experience had raised him to the highest ambassadorial
posts. He might have been a Foreign Minister of France if he had not
been needed as a Marshal. He was a great gentleman, of polish, taste,
and learning, who wielded the pen, though at too great a length, as
readily as the sword.' [15]

Tallard's pen reveals him to have been a canny and observant
diplomat whose dissection of English society in the autumn of William
III's reign was lucid and clever: 'The King of England is very far from
being master here,' he reported to Louis XIV in early 1698. 'He is generally hated by all the great men and the whole of the nobility. It is not
the same with the people, who are very favourably inclined towards him,
yet less so in the beginning.' [16] In the run-up to the First Partition Treaty,
Tallard's keen political eye was unblinking, looking for every advantage
in the impending negotiations. He served his master well.

William, suspicious of Louis's plans, but keen for peace after nine
years of war, asked Tallard to be his guest of honour at the Newmarket
race meeting of April 1698. There, Tallard was flattered by the attentions of Dutch and English courtiers, Marlborough being among the
eleven earls and four dukes in attendance. Apart from the horse racing
(dominated by the king's champion mounts, Stiff Dick and Turk), there
were many other diversions for the royal house party. Guests followed
William's personal pack of hounds in the mornings, or went hawking
with the king's falcons, brought over especially from Holland. The afternoon entertainment included cockfights, which William relished: one
day he attended six in succession.

Newmarket races gave an opportunity for the king to entertain lavishly,
in surroundings removed from the formality of palace life. The gardens of
the king's lodgings were transformed during the run-up to Tallard's visit,
as evidenced by a £235 bill 'for work done at Newmarket, carriage and
digging of earth, gravel and for looking after the said gardens and fur-
nishing several trees and flowers for the use of the same.' [17] Dutch tulip

bulbs were planted there for the first time that year, to impress the house party. Tallard was placed next to the king at every opportunity. William honoured the Frenchman by drinking his health. It was the start of a relationship that touched on friendship. The goodwill between the two men greatly facilitated the subsequent negotiations between France and England, over the best way to divide up Carlos II's Spanish Empire.

The partition talks began in earnest after Newmarket. They continued throughout the summer of 1698, first in England, and then, when William went to the Netherlands in July, across the North Sea. Tallard was confident that he could extract good terms from William. However, if he was to succeed, he advised Louis XIV, then the French king must curb his frequent correspondence with his ambassador: such a volume of mail betrayed France's keenness to settle. Tallard also urged that his diplomacy be speedily concluded, for he judged that William 'is very quick-sighted, has good judgement, and will soon perceive that we are trifling with him if we protract matters too much.' [18]

Louis was happy to be led by Tallard. The short-lived Partition Treaty followed, before it was rendered obsolete by the death of the Electoral Prince of Bavaria. Louis turned again to Tallard, trusting his champion to reappear, bearing another diplomatic prize. The Second Partition Treaty ensued, a treaty that was to prove unacceptable to the Emperor, and barely palatable to the Dutch. It was Tallard's relaying of Louis's flagrant disregard for this treaty that signalled the end of his mission to London.

One of the highpoints of Tallard's time as ambassador took place in early 1699. He took pleasure in reporting to Louis that William, exhausted by a lifetime of fighting and politicking, had unexpectedly agreed to the reduction of his troops by Parliament. 'The Earl of Portland,' Tallard wrote, 'speaking the other day on this subject, said to me that the King might have put them on another footing when he was younger, and his passions were ardent; but that now he was old, he preferred calmness and mildness to what appeared to be the best for his own interest.' [19] Tallard believed this marked the end of England's incipient military role in Europe. However, Marlborough's march in the middle of 1704 disabused him of this notion, and showed him that William III had handed on the baton to an energetic successor. Tallard was on a collision course with English troops who were keen to prove their mettle.

TALLARD'S PROGRESS TOWARDS THE Danube was slow. 'I have stayed on here today, Sir,' he wrote to Chamillart from Walkirk, on 9 July, 'for two reasons: one to give time for my convoy to arrive, since its tail must stretch back three leagues, the other so that my infantry, tired by several days' march in extreme heat, can have the time to rest.' [20]

Messages had gone astray. Consequently Tallard remained unaware of the despondency that had settled over the Franco-Bavarian camp outside Augsburg. The Elector was asking five or six times a day where the French reinforcements were. Marshal Marsin wrote repeatedly, with mounting anger and desperation, urging Tallard to bring his soldiers as quickly as was possible. Referring to the taking of Donauwörth, and allied movements since, Marsin pleaded with his colleague to think of the Elector's state of mind: 'Judge, Sir, the impatience with which this prince awaits your help, which being joined to our army and his troops, will be a stronger body than the enemy's, and in a position to go to search them out wherever they may be.' [21]

Oblivious of Marsin's repeated entreaties for him to speed his men south to his aid, Tallard engaged in a siege that was to prove unexpectedly troublesome and time-consuming. He had earmarked Villingen as a town that would provide him with a useful forward-depot for his supplies, and an invaluable communications link with Alsace. Once he had taken Villingen, his plan was to march on Rothweil. A month earlier Tallard had written to Louis XIV estimating that the capture of Villingen 'by itself could not last two days.' [22] This was an over-optimistic forecast. Outside Villingen, as Tallard awaited the arrival of his ponderous supply wagons, he ordered trenches to be dug, and cannon and mortar batteries to be prepared. The townsfolk proved more resilient than the French had anticipated, Tallard writing to the king: 'Villingen is better than anyone remembered it being, the governor defends it marvellously, and he will hold me here longer than I thought. I hope in any case, Sire, that two days will conclude the business.' [23]

Tallard failed to take Villingen. French fireballs bombarded it, their cannon battered it, but it held out. The town's artillery could not be silenced, firing from towers overlooking the perimeter wall. At night the townsfolk repaired the damage done by Tallard's troops in the day. On 22 July, Mérode-Westerloo recorded: '... we were eventually forced to abandon the siege, after wasting valuable time and material; for the townsfolk and the small garrison defended the puny place so well – even though it only boasted a single ancient wall – that we had no option but to move on and join the Elector of Bavaria.' [24] Over a week, and 600 men, had been lost in this attempt to take a small town defended by a second-class fortress.

Tallard's army now struck out for Elmesing, near Ulm, which lay six days' march from Villingen. En route they came to Moesskirch, where they could ford the Danube. Whilst there, Tallard billeted himself in a castle belonging to the Fürstenberg family. Count Mérode-Westerloo was leading his column of troops out of town, past the castle, when, he recalled: 'The Marshal recognised me, and invited me in to share his breakfast chicken. He was very partial to the fine martial air imparted by receiving from a page a chunk of cold meat or a smoked tongue merely wrapped in a napkin with a hunk of bread.' It was while taking his breakfast with Mérode-Westerloo that Tallard pondered the likely result of his army's march south. 'We were standing before a window devouring chicken and watching the army roll by beneath, when he suddenly emerged from the pensive mood that had gripped him for some time and remarked, "Unless I am very mistaken, there will be a battle before three weeks are out; if one does take place it will be a very Pharsala."' [25] Here Tallard savoured his role in an engagement that would rival the decisive confrontation between Caesar and Pompey, in 48BC.

ON 18 JULY TALLARD LEARNT that Prince Eugène had slipped away from the Lines of Stollhofen with 18,000 men, leaving the Prussian field marshal Prince Leopold of Anhalt-Dessau in command. Eugène moved to Rothweil, where he could shadow Tallard's doomed siege of Villingen. This was the start of a difficult balancing act for Eugène: he must remain within range both of the Lines of Stollhofen, and of Baden's and Marlborough's grand army.

Eugène's greatest weapon was furtiveness. French spies reported to Versailles his departure from the Lines of Stollhofen. Louis correctly concluded that this move left the allied position at Stollhofen so weakened that it no longer threatened Alsace. In his most logical orders of this disjointed, perplexing period of the campaign, Louis instructed Villeroi to move towards Bavaria, where he should be prepared to join Tallard, Marsin and the Elector when required. If these four commanders had united, Marlborough would surely have been obliged to retreat to the Rhine: the alternative would have been almost certain annihilation. Eugène saved the allied plan through a series of deceptions that flummoxed Villeroi. After making a feint to the north, Eugène disappeared from French view on 27 July, leaving a detachment of cavalry to shadow Tallard. Assuming that the prince was retracing his steps to Stollhofen with his main force, Villeroi decided that he could no longer obey Louis's orders: he must, rather, remain in Alsace, in case Eugène ventured anything there.

Also duped by Eugène's northward ruse, Tallard continued his trek towards his allies. He arrived at Ulm on 29 July. His army, in contrast to the fine order witnessed among Marlborough's troops when they concluded their march, was exhausted and undernourished. The cavalry had lost many horses to 'German sickness', a fatal, contagious disease that was probably glanders.

Tallard was disappointed to find inadequate supply had been made for his men: only 6,000 sacks of flour were available for an army of 35,000. He decided to press on, Mérode-Westerloo noting: 'Leaving Ulm, we took the road to Augsburg, where the Elector was camped in company with M. Marsin, watching his country burn on the further side of the River Lech. As we approached the city we saw clouds of smoke drifting to the skies.' [26]

CHAPTER FIFTEEN

LAYING WASTE TO BAVARIA

'We shall tomorrow have all the army in the elector's country, so that if he will ever think of terms it must be now, for we shall do our utmost to ruin his country. The only hope the enemy seem to have, is the reinforcement the Marshal de Villeroi has promised them: and that they may gain time for the junction, they are strongly encamped at Augsburg, by which they abandon the greatest part of the elector's country.'

THE DUKE OF MARLBOROUGH TO LORD TREASURER GODOLPHIN, 9 JULY 1704

IN THE WESTERN EUROPE OF THE late seventeenth and early eighteenth centuries, there were no written rules of war. However, some basic thoughts about what was acceptable, and what was not, were beginning to root themselves in the common consciousness. Massive loss of civilian life and property had been one of the hallmarks of the Thirty Years' War, which had engulfed the centre of the Continent from 1618–48. Partly as a reaction to this wanton destruction, partly because the Age of Reason fostered the pursuit of greater humanity, moderation and tolerance, popular opinion began to constrain those bent on military excess.

The era of Marlborough's wars was one that was neither tied up in the religious rivalries of earlier conflicts, nor underpinned by the narrow nationalistic greed associated with nineteenth- and twentieth-century warfare. Nobody expected the Turks to conform to these expectations – they were still viewed as barbarians – but for the rest of Europe, standards were beginning to emerge. As early as 1625, the Dutch statesman Hugo Grotius had propounded, in *Of the Law of War and Peace*, that man's natural state was peaceful coexistence. Although he recognised states' essential rights and duties, he also believed that those states or leaders who transgressed God's natural law should be punished. No longer could statecraft be pursued in blameless isolation. The Oxford academic, Richard Zouche, and Samuel von Pulendorf, later in the seventeenth century, both concluded that certain acts of foreign policy could be deemed unjust.

Surprisingly Louis XIV, despite the bruising aggression of his foreign policy, found time to frame basic rules to constrain his victorious armies abroad. In 1677 he decreed that the levy exacted by France from a defeated town or province should not exceed the figure normally paid in tax by the inhabitants to their overlord. If, however, this contribution were not paid in full and on time, then it was permissible to burn houses, take hostages, and pillage possessions, until the debt was honoured. Louis's armies did not always observe his strictures, however, as we have seen: the atrocities he had allowed during his Dutch War of the 1670s, and in the Palatinate in 1674, were taken to a new pitch at the end of the 1680s when the French revisited devastation on the Elector Palatine. All the important cities, including Mannheim, Worms and Speyer, were obliterated. Louvois threatened the inhabitants with death if they attempted to rebuild their homes. In the rest of Europe such a flagrant disrespect for the conscience of the age aroused vociferous condemnation.

Marlborough's decision to adopt a policy of destruction in Bavaria should be judged in this context. The duke's logic was not in doubt: he knew the Elector of Bavaria was wavering in his allegiance to Louis XIV. If Maximilian Emmanuel's forces could be brought to battle and defeated, or if the Elector saw that his continued hostility to the Emperor would lead to the destruction of his country, then Marlborough believed Bavaria could be wrested from the party of the Two Crowns and won for the Grand Alliance. This reasoning may have been sound, but the methodology employed by the duke was flawed, and ran counter to the views of his European contemporaries. His laying waste to Bavaria was, by the standards of the age, a disgrace.

Marlborough's tactical options were limited after the taking of the Schellenberg and Donauwörth. He could not attack the Elector and Marsin at Augsburg, because the allies judged this defensive position to be so strong that, 'no Attack could be made [on it] without infinite Disadvantage'.[1] Neither did he feel confident that he could take Munich: he had left behind his largest siege guns in Flanders in order not to hinder his march south; and Lewis of Baden's promises of making good this loss, by supplying heavy artillery of his own, had proved to be fanciful, for the prince had only twelve 24-pounders to offer – not enough to bring Munich to its knees. This situation threatened to bring the whole campaign to a premature and miserable conclusion, Count Wratislaw writing with concern to the Emperor: 'Marlborough's consternation is indescribable; for if we had not had the present successes [the capture of the Schellenberg and Donauwörth], the whole campaign might have had to be ended fruitlessly owing to his departure; but now one will try to make the best of it.'[2]

Marlborough and Wratislaw wanted to lure the Elector into open battle before Tallard's reinforcements arrived. If, while trying to achieve this, Maximilian Emmanuel were to suffer for his double-dealing and treachery, the Emperor would certainly not object. In mid-May Leopold had written to Wratislaw: 'Especially have you done well in giving Lord Marlborough every possible assurance that I cannot now do anything else but seek, in every way and earnestly, to secure that the Elector of Bavaria is brought to recognise his shame and his blunders. Up to now I have not failed to exercise the utmost clemency towards him, only in order that thereby he might amend the presumptuousness and injustice with which he pursues me. But not only has there been no change in his course, but he has indeed abused my clemency. Consequently the time has at last come for him to suffer the operations of justice.'[3] We know from Marlborough's correspondence how he interpreted Wratislaw's message from Leopold: on 8 June, in the middle of his march south to the Danube, he wrote to Lord Treasurer Godolphin of his intentions on arriving in Bavaria: 'If we can hinder the junction of more troops to the Elector, I hope six weeks after we begin may be sufficient for the reducing of him, or the entire ruining of his country.'[4] A month after writing this, with Donauwörth taken and Bavaria lying vulnerable before him, Marlborough persuaded the reluctant Baden to cooperate in his policy of destruction.

Tensions between the two allied commanders had been growing since the Schellenberg. Each man felt the action to be primarily his victory (Marlborough's official despatch mentioned Baden only once; among the wounded). The difficulties inherent in shared command were exacerbated by mutual dislike: the result was visible in the confused and meandering course of the campaign throughout the rest of July.

For Marlborough, one of the most exhilarating aspects of the 1704 campaign was the comparative freedom it afforded him as military commander. On 9 July he had shared his excitement at this with his wife, writing: 'I have the pleasure to find all the officers willing to obey, without knowing any other reason than that it is my desire, which is very different from what it was in Flanders, where I was obliged to have the consent of a council of war for everything I undertook.'[5] However, the presence of Prince Lewis, with his very different ideas on warfare, cancelled out any advantage that Marlborough had gained by slipping the leash of the Dutch Field Deputies. The 1704 campaign, having started off with such dash and promise, was suffering from the compromise demanded between two commanders of totally different military creeds. The resulting indecision wasted much of the impetus gained by the heroic march across Europe. This gave the French time to scramble to the aid of Marsin's and the Elector's threatened armies.

From his position to the north Prince Eugène exhorted his allies to be bold: if a siege of Munich was not an option, then take it by force of arms! Marlborough was attracted to this idea but Baden, claiming superior local knowledge, forcefully advised against it and so it was not attempted. Eugène's further advice, to dislodge the Elector in Augsburg by moving to threaten his supply lines, again came to nothing: Marlborough and Baden spent their time allowing their grudges to fester rather than pursuing decisive advantage over the enemy.

Eugène put some of Marlborough's uncharacteristic loss of drive down to the death of Lieutenant-General Goor, who had been cut down in the first musket volley from the Schellenberg's defences. Goor had been seen as a positive influence on his commander, a Dutchman whose fierce energy Marlborough had found infectious. The duke wrote to Sarah, after the taking of Donauwörth: 'Since this action I have hardly had time to sleep, for Lieutenant-General Goor helped me in a great many things, which I am now forced to do myself, till I can find some other officer I can rely on for it.' [6] With Goor dead, Marlborough's camp had become less dynamic, more uncertain. For the first time in his military career the duke was responding to situations, rather than setting their pace.

In a mirror image of Tallard's tarrying outside Villingen, Marlborough and Baden wasted valuable time besieging the town of Rain. It was important to control Rain since together with Donauwörth and Neuburg it formed an Orion's Belt of crossing-points that allowed Marlborough and Baden to deploy with equal ease on either side of the Lech and the Danube. However, the time that it took to subdue a force of less than 1,000 men (half of whom were survivors from the Schellenberg, led by de la Colonie) was deeply troubling and again exposed the allies' weakness in heavy artillery. Happily for Marlborough the surrender of Rain on 16 July was to result in the capture of 'Twenty Four Brass Cannon, some Ammunition, a great Quantity of Corn, and other Provisions, which did much assist our Army.' [7] Welcome though this infusion of weaponry and supplies was, it was scant reward for the grand army's week-long exertions.

More regrettable than this delay was the policy that accompanied it. Throughout July Marlborough sent allied troops deep into Bavaria, to burn and destroy the population's buildings and crops, hoping that this would bring the Elector either to battle, or to terms. Bavaria had not experienced warfare in its borders since the last three years of the Thirty Years' War, when the French and Swedish armies had caused widespread damage. This had been partly as vengeance against Maximilian I, Maximilian Emmanuel's grandfather, who had been the Catholic Imperialists' military commander. He had crushed the Bohemians, seized the Upper Palatinate, and been raised from ducal to electoral rank as a reward. The intervening half-century had seen decades of peace. The allies found that Bavaria was unable to resist their sweeping raids of destruction.

Eugène, so impressed by Marlborough when they had met a month before, and aware of Prince Lewis's earlier military record, was troubled. He wrote candidly of his misgivings to his kinsman, the Duke of Savoy: 'Up to now everything has gone well enough between them, but I fear greatly that this will not last. And, to tell the truth, since the Donauwörth action I cannot admire their performances. They have amused themselves with the siege of Rain and burning a few villages instead of, according to my ideas, which I have put before them plainly enough, marching straight upon the enemy. To put things plainly, your Royal Highness, I don't like this slowness on our side. The enemy will have time to form magazines of food and forage, and all our operations will become the harder. The Duke is more than a little hesitating in his decisions.' [8] Marlborough's indecision was particularly puzzling to Eugène, who understood that military failure would be catastrophic for the duke, back in London: 'If he has to go home without having achieved his objective, he will certainly be ruined,' [9] was Eugène's stark summation.

In fact, Marlborough was ill. The migraines had returned, as they were wont to do during periods of intense stress. He was weighed down by the strain of his massive responsibilities and the horror of the losses he had seen at the Schellenberg. He wrote to his duchess, on 13 July: 'My blood is so heated, that I have had for the last three days a violent headache; but, not having stirred out of my chamber this day, I find myself much easier, so that I hope to-morrow morning to be very well.' [10] At the same time he confessed the unease he felt at his policy of spoliation: 'You will, I hope, believe me, that my nature suffers when I see so many fine places burnt, and that must be burnt, if the Elector will not hinder it. I shall never be easy and happy till I am quiet with you.'[11] Marlborough had never before held command during such a bloody and consequential campaign.

At the same time his brutal policies were bearing bitter fruit. The Bavarians were terrified of the allied raiding parties, and many fled to the cities for safety, taking with them exaggerated tales of terror in the countryside. After the fall of the Schellenberg and Rain, de la Colonie fell back to Munich. He was scornful of the alarm he found amongst the cowed civilian population. 'The idea that all the country-side of Bavaria had been reduced to ashes, owed its origins simply to fear and panic. I do not deny that some houses were burnt, but the enemy's generals had no part in this; it was the work of marauders and camp followers who, disgusted in finding the peasants' houses abandoned, burnt some of them, and as is usually the case with a people wild with fear, they carried the panic with them.'[12] De la Colonie underestimated the allies' ruthlessness, and could not understand why the Bavarian people were so traumatised.

Maximilian Emmanuel's Electress, Maria Antonia, a daughter of Emperor Leopold's from his first marriage, had long advocated her husband's return to the Imperial fold. Now, genuinely moved by the privations of the peasantry, she begged him to divest himself of the French alliance, and repair the damage his treachery had caused to his people. In public, the Electress joined with the Council of State in seeking divine help in the face of the allied assault: 'Public prayers and religious processions were ordered, Her Highness taking part in the latter bare-footed and with exemplary devotion.'[13] Despite being heavily pregnant, she went to her husband in Augsburg, to plead with him to break with Louis before further disasters overtook Bavaria.

Maximilian Emmanuel was moved by his wife's wish to help her adoptive people. However, he deferred his decision until he knew whether France was to send him another army. On 22 July Marshal Marsin wrote to Tallard: 'His Royal Highness charges me with begging again on his behalf, Sir, as I have done with all my earlier letters, that you come to join him as diligently as possible, since that is the only way of delivering his country from these evil hosts, him from the pain of seeing it burn before his eyes, as well as from the continual persecutions that are at this time afflicting his family and his subjects.'[14]

The Elector's concerns were largely selfish. His priority was to protect his personal assets. He sent the majority of his army to stand guard over his country estates and income-producing salt mines. Lieutenant-Colonel de la Colonie suspected that this scattering of troops was tactically unsound, for: 'There were hardly any Bavarians left with the army at Augsburg except a few regiments of cavalry, the rest being dispersed in various directions.'[15]

Playing on the Elector's greed, the Emperor revived the covert lines of communication between Vienna and Augsburg. He hoped to be able to welcome the Prodigal Son back to the Imperial fold. With the situation looking grim for the Habsburg cause in Italy and Hungary, Leopold was prepared to pay substantially for Bavaria's renewed friendship. He offered Maximilian Emmanuel a full pardon, the restoration of all of his territories, the additional lands of Pfalz-Neuburg and Burgau, and a subsidy of 200,000 crowns. Furthermore, the allies would pay for the use of 12,000 Bavarian troops in the hard-pressed arena of Italy. In reply, Maximilian Emmanuel was asked to agree to two points, which Leopold communicated via Count Wratislaw: 'You must and shall at all times reject the claim to the title of King, and also refuse the French troops permission to depart freely.'[16] Wratislaw asked the Elector to come to the monastery of Fürstenfeld, where acceptance of this agreement could be confirmed. With no sign of French reinforcements arriving in Bavaria, the Elector greeted these overtures with interest.

It was now that Marshal Marsin's entreaties finally persuaded Tallard away from the siege of Villingen. So worried was Marsin that the Bavarian alliance was about to dissolve, that he called a council of his senior officers to meet with him and the Elector, so that they could feel the way forward together. The Marquis de Blainville, Colbert's son, captured the pervading mood in the French High Command: he said the best that his compatriots could hope for was Bavaria's neutrality while they evacuated the electorate; to look for more than that was, Blainville thought, dangerous delusion. Marsin was equally concerned by the situation, but adopted a more bullish approach: if the Elector were to defect, then the French would destroy the Bavarians' baggage trains before leaving the country for good.

The letter that decided the Elector to continue in Louis's cause was smuggled from Tallard to Maximilian Emmanuel in the button of a messenger's coat. This flimsy strip of paper contained reassuring news: Tallard was en route through the Black Forest; he and 35,000 men would soon be in Bavaria; and this union of forces would help to roll back the allied invaders. 'Upon this', wrote Captain Robert Parker in his memoirs, the Elector 'broke off the treaty abruptly, and let our Generals know, that he would serve as a dragoon under the King of France, rather than as General of the Emperor's Forces'.[17] Instead of meeting Wratislaw to sign the agreement at the monastery, the Elector sent the message that his 'honour' – until this juncture, a slippery commodity – would not allow him to desert confederates who were making such valiant efforts to come to his aid.

The allies were angry that their hopes of negotiating with the Elector proved to be nothing more than skilful time-wasting by a wily, unprincipled, renegade. If Maximilian Emmanuel were to remain an enemy, Marlborough decided, then his people would have to suffer for their master's decision. He ordered the ravaging of Bavaria to be intensified.

As well as wanting vengeance, the duke feared that he and his men would be obliged to quit Bavaria as soon as Tallard arrived. If this were so, he did not want to leave supplies for the advancing French forces. This time the destruction was truly significant: 'A great number of Parties were sent out far and near, who burned and destroyed all before them; insomuch, it was said there were 372 Towns, Villages, and Farm-houses, laid in ashes; and it was a shocking sight to see the fine Country of Bavaria all in flame.'[18] On 29 July Count de la Tour, general of the Imperial horse, and the Count de Costfrize, lieutenant-general of the Dutch cavalry, set off with 5,000 mounted men 'to plunder and burn the Country up to Munich,' recalled Josias Sandby. 'The like was done at the same time, in other places of Bavaria, so that the Elector in his own camp, might see his country in flames round about him.'[19] Two days later the Duke of Württemberg took 2,000 more men to add to the destruction.

Many historians have apportioned the blame for the laying waste of Bavaria equally between Marlborough and Baden, but this is unfair on Prince Lewis. A mediocre general, Baden was nevertheless a proud soldier. He hated the policy which required him to behave, in his words, 'like a hussar' – the hated Hungarian cavalryman, with a reputation for vulpine savagery. (De la Colonie referred to hussars as 'properly speaking, little more than bandits on horseback'.[20]) This remained his view even though, fifteen year earlier, the French sacking of the Palatinate had spilled over into his territories. It was with disgust that Baden wrote to the Emperor: 'As a result of the ravaging, the fires, and the forced contributions, in a short time there may be little of Bavaria left. I hope that I have taken the right course of Your Majesty's service in accepting other people's opinion.'[21] Relations between Baden and Marlborough had, by this stage, deteriorated to a point of mutual contempt.

Marlborough's mood lifted, though, when he heard that Prince Eugène was on his way: it had long been the duke's intention to have this sympathetic, daring, figure by his side, should the Franco-Bavarians be made to fight. Eugène, having shadowed Tallard since Villingen, sent word that he was approaching the Danube, with 70 cavalry squadrons and 20 battalions of foot. The Lines of Stollhofen would have to fend for themselves, for Eugène was homing in on the area of Bavaria between Ulm and Donauwörth, where he aimed to lend support to Marlborough's army. Both men hoped that they might bring the enemy to battle.

CHAPTER SIXTEEN

BATTLE LOOMS

'From the heights of Biberbach we shall see what the enemy will do and regulate our own movements accordingly until the thirteen battalions and sixteen squadrons with which the Elector has undertaken to strengthen his army have enabled us to grip the enemy tighter, and then we shall not let them get off cheaply.'

MARSHAL TALLARD TO LOUIS XIV, 5 AUGUST 1704

EUGÈNE REACHED HÖCHSTÄDT ON 5 August, the next day riding over to Marlborough's camp in Schrobenhausen to discuss their military options. One of the commanders' primary concerns was what to do about Prince Lewis of Baden. With the climax of the campaign now imminent, Marlborough and Eugène agreed that it was imperative to sideline Prince Lewis before he compromised their aims. They knew that the pace of the succeeding days would need to be fast and fluid, in contrast to Baden's plodding, pedestrian, ways.

In the event, Prince Lewis engineered his own removal from the key sphere of operations. Ever since Rain fell, midway through the previous month, he had been advocating the siege of Ingolstadt, a city with a proud history of strength in defence; indeed, it had never been taken by force. If it could be captured now, Ingolstadt would give the allies control of the Danube all the way to Passau. More importantly to Baden, a siege here would allow him to put some distance between himself and

Marlborough, returning the prince to an independent command – and one which promised glory even greater than the plaudits reluctantly shared after the storming of the Schellenberg.

Marlborough was not confident that Baden would take Ingolstadt. 'It is the strongest place in this country, which makes me very much apprehend the success; for I am very sure that one-half of what will be promised [by Baden] will not be performed,'[1] he wrote to Godolphin. However, given the importance of the city, there was a possibility that the Elector might break cover, in an attempt to lift the siege. This could give the opportunity for battle that Marlborough and Eugène desired. The prospect of this, and the joy of being rid of an increasingly irascible colleague, led the duke to endorse Baden's proposal. To his surprise, neither Marlborough nor Eugène tried to discourage him in his desire to oversee the siege.

On 7 August, the first of Baden's men started off for Ingolstadt, the main body following two days later. It says something of their low opinion of their colleague that Marlborough and Eugène were prepared to see him depart with 15,000 Imperialist soldiers at a time when Tallard had arrived at Augsburg with his reinforcements: the two commanders preferred to be at a numerical disadvantage without Baden, than enjoy superior numbers with him by their side.

Eugène and Marlborough now separated, heading back to their respective armies, eager for battle.

ON THE DAY THAT EUGÈNE REACHED Höchstädt, 5 August, Tallard arrived at Augsburg. He was frustrated by the situation that had greeted him in Bavaria. 'It is a terrible thing', he wrote to Chamillart, 'to arrive mid-campaign in a place where the enemy have been master, and where they have taken all the positions which could be most favourable to them.'[2]

The Elector and Marsin greeted him with relief, tempered by confirmation of Eugène's presence in Bavaria. Louis had just written to Tallard: 'I hope that when all my troops are united you will have sufficient forces to continue the war at an advantage during the rest of this campaign.'[3] However, it was not to be: the three allied commanders – Marlborough, Baden and Eugène – could now put 80,000 men in the field. The Elector, Marsin and Tallard had 60,000 between them.

The Franco-Bavarians would have enjoyed parity, had the Elector not dispersed his native troops around his country. Eight battalions were in Augsburg, six in Ulm, two in Memmingen, and one in Lavingen, with lesser detachments elsewhere. Marsin wrote to Versailles that Eugène's arrival: 'makes it necessary for M. Tallard to press to the utmost his Electoral Highness to recall some of his troops who are in Bavaria to make this army equal in number to the enemy, and even if possible stronger, so that we can go where we like. The Elector has 35 good battalions and 43 squadrons of good troops, of which since the enemy entered into Bavaria he has had 23 squadrons and 5 battalions with the army, the rest being spread about in his properties in small bodies, which produced no effective result, and which would be much more useful for the service of the King and of the Elector in reinforcing the army.'[4] The Elector agreed to recall his variously dispersed units, but this would take some time.

Marsin's phrase 'so that we can go where we like' is significant: it is evidence that the Franco-Bavarians were not contemplating imminent battle, even when their forces outnumbered those of the Grand Alliance. Louis had written to Tallard explaining that his main task was to keep the allies out of Italy, where they might undermine French efforts. The marshals and their host merely sought freedom of movement, assuming that this would persuade the allies to move back to the Lines of Stollhofen, and beyond. The Franco-Bavarian High Command believed that Marlborough had failed to capitalise on the dizzying effect of his march from the Danube: he had captured Donauwörth and Rain but, crucially, he had not succeeded in attacking Marsin and the Elector when they were alone. Now that Tallard had finally appeared, the Englishman would surely have to withdraw northwards, to protect his extended lines of communication? If all went well, during his retreat, Marlborough might leave himself vulnerable to attack in flank or rear.

On 9 August, the Franco-Bavarians set out for their old fortified camp at Lavingen-Dillingen. From there they could either strike out at Eugène's small army or wait for the Elector to reconvene his forces, watch the enemy, and fall on him as he retired. It seemed that Louis's forces had regained the initiative.

THE EARL OF ORKNEY, ONE OF Marlborough's lieutenants and a veteran of King William's wars, wrote home: 'Prince Luis (sic) of Baden, having marched the 9th [August] with 22 battalions and 34 squadrons all imperial to besiege Ingolstadt, the Duke of Marlborough took post between the Paar and Danube, so as either to cover the siege or be ready to join Prince Eugène in case the Elector should pass the Danube.'[5] No sooner had Marlborough taken this position, than Eugène rode into his camp to tell him that the enemy was on the move, heading towards Dillingen. Marlborough immediately sent the Duke of Württemberg with twenty-seven squadrons of Imperial cavalry to support the prince. At the same time he ordered his brother, General Churchill, to follow with twenty battalions of infantry and the allied artillery.

The grand army followed this vanguard on the morning of 10 August, heading for the Rain environs while Eugène dropped back to a less exposed position near Donauwörth. Marlborough was conscious of the pressure on him, and on the Emperor: Hungarian rebels were threatening Vienna; and Marshal Villeroi could strike southwards through the Black Forest at any time. The duke's message to Godolphin stressed that something must be chanced, so as to alleviate the situation for the Grand Alliance as a whole: 'If we find a fair occasion we shall be glad to embrace it, being persuaded that the ill condition of our affairs in most part require it.'[6] An urgent despatch received from Eugène that evening made it clear that that occasion was to hand:

Monsieur,
The enemy have marched. It is almost certain that the whole army is passing the Danube at Lavingen. The plain of Dillingen is crowded with troops. I have held on all day here; but with 18 battalions I dare not risk staying the night.

221

Everything, milord, consists in speed and that you put yourself forthwith in movement to join me to-morrow, without which I fear it will be too late. In short, all the army is there.

While I was writing sure news reached me that the whole army has crossed. Thus there is not a moment to lose and I think you might risk making the march by the Lech and the Danube. That will shorten it a good deal, and the road is better. I await your answer, to make my dispositions. [7]

In response to this thrilling news, Marlborough urged his men on for their union with Eugène's Imperialists. At noon on 11 August General Churchill's vanguard reached the prince, finding his infantry digging in on the Schellenberg Heights, and his cavalry deployed along the River Kessel. Within twelve hours the rest of Marlborough's army arrived at their new position between the Kessel and the Danube. They were now united, just three miles from the Elector and the two marshals.

THE PACE IN THE FRANCO-BAVARIAN ranks had been a little less frantic. Their generals had been surprised, on 10 August, to find that the fortifications at Lavingen-Dillingen, where they had expected to entrench their troops, were no more. They discovered that Marlborough had ordered them to be levelled the previous month, as soon as the Elector's retreat to Augsburg had left them empty and exposed. There was no panic, however, for there was no thought that the allies would attack. As Winston S. Churchill wrote: 'In this warfare of marches and countermarches battles were so rare that if reasonable precautions were taken, and the military movements were correct, they might almost be ruled out.' [8] The Franco-Bavarians were sure that they could avoid battle merely by sticking to the conventions of contemporary war: they would form a camp that demanded respect, rather than inviting attack.

Of more immediate interest to the three Franco-Bavarian commanders was the news of Eugène and Marlborough: they still hoped that a frustrated enemy was assembling as a prelude to retreat out of Bavaria.

The Elector now found himself in a familiar position, at loggerheads with his French counterparts. Keen to avenge his country's ravaging over the previous six weeks, he argued strongly for an immediate advance on the allied armies. However, Tallard was less hasty, preferring to await the arrival of the recalled Bavarian detachments. When the Elector persisted, Tallard replied icily: 'If I were not so convinced of Your Highness's integrity, I should imagine that you wished to gamble with the King's forces without having any of your own, to see at no risk what would happen.'[9] This persuaded the Elector not to attack. The French and Bavarians pushed forward three miles to Höchstädt, capturing the allied fort there, and taking the 100-man garrison prisoner. Outside the town, on 12 August, they established a new camp. Tallard wrote to Louis: 'I dare assure Your Majesty that Marshal Marsin and I have every intention of sustaining with honour the dignity of Your Majesty's armies.'[10]

The two marshals decided against digging defensive positions around the perimeter. The site, on a hill, was already protected by the 300-foot width of the Danube to the right; and a boggy tributary of the river, the Nebel, 'thought unpassable, as it afterwards was found in several Places'[11], ran across its four-mile front. The left flank was screened by thick woodland, which was militarily impenetrable. Besides, there was a string of villages in front of the main position, bringing further cohesion to the defences. These were Lutzingen, Oberglau, Unterglau and Blindheim, the last of which the allies knew as Blenheim.

CONTEMPORARY MILITARY CONVENTION dictated that an army should never attack an enemy superior in numbers. Tallard, Marsin and the Elector assumed that the army of the Grand Alliance still outnumbered theirs by a ratio of 4:3. This misapprehension was reinforced by the testimonies of planted 'deserters', who drifted over from the allied position six miles down the valley on the 12th. They claimed that Baden had marched through the night to return to his colleagues' side. 'Three or four prisoners taken one after the other have confirmed the same thing,'[12] Tallard informed Louis. The ruse was necessary to stop the Franco-Bavarians from falling on the allies that day, before they were prepared to fight.

223

Marlborough and Eugène, whose intelligence service was consistently superior to their enemies', were aware that the Franco-Bavarian army was stronger than their force: it had 60,000 troops and more than 100 cannon, against the allies' 52,000 men and 60 guns. The only allied advantage was in cavalry. However, Marlborough knew the conservatism of his enemies, and he had recently written to Godolphin that he was: 'very confident they will not venture a battle.'[13] He was also sure that his men were better than the enemy's; a constant belief of his, as shown in a letter written fourteen months earlier, also to the Lord Treasurer: 'I know not where the French get their men,' he had commented then, 'but it is certain they have six battalions in their army more than we have, though most of ours are stronger than theirs.'[14] Unlike the huge majority of his contemporary commanders, Marlborough was untroubled by an enemy advantage that rested simply in a superiority of numbers; such was his belief in the men whose training he had overseen.

On 12 August Eugène and Marlborough ascended the church tower in Tapfheim. From this vantage point, using spy-glasses, they made notes of the terrain before them, and of the precise layout of the two opposing armies. They decided that this was the battleground they both had hankered after.

The two allied generals were delighted to see the French quartermasters measuring out the land between Blenheim and Lutzingen as a camp. They were further pleased to note that the enemy lay in a most unusual format, reflecting the failure of the Elector's and Marsin's force to amalgamate with Tallard's. As a result, instead of the infantry being between two wings of cavalry, as was the custom, the Franco-Bavarian army was drawn up in a disjointed front, of: cavalry-infantry-cavalry-cavalry-infantry-cavalry. Marlborough and Eugène noted this with great interest, for a double cavalry wing in the centre of a battlefield was a soft core, ripe for exploitation.

They decided to strike before the enemy could organise effectively, well aware that 14 battalions of Bavarian reinforcements were heading towards Höchstädt. Messengers had arrived from further afield with news that Marshal Villeroi was making for the duchy of Württemberg: this threatened the allied communications with Nördlingen, Philippsburg, and Mayence. Attack or vulnerable withdrawal were the only options left to Marlborough and Eugène. The duke remembered Turenne's dictum: 'The conqueror has as much reason to seek for an occasion of fighting, as much as he that is upon the defensive has to avoid it.'[15]

It was too late to attack on the 12th so in the evening they gave orders to prepare for combat on the morrow. Josias Sandby recalled: 'No body can express the courage and joy with which both officers and soldiers showed, when they thought they should come to an engagement.'[16] 'And all that night,' Sergeant Millner wrote in his Journal, 'the most of our Army kept in a moving Posture, making ready, posting and putting themselves in good Order, Horse, Foot and Artillery, for the Battle.'[17] It was helpful to keep busy, rather than to dwell on the coming battle: despite the excitement, this engagement promised death and mutilation for thousands.

FOR THE FRANCO-BAVARIAN HIGH Command, the evening of 12 August was a time of relaxation and optimism. All were convinced that the allies would soon retreat. Even reports that enemy pioneers had been spotted levelling a ravine between Tapfheim and Blenheim caused no alarm. The three commanders each retired to their quarters in the surrounding villages – Tallard to Blenheim, Marsin to Oberglau, and the Elector to Lutzingen. There was no moon that night, or wind, just a heavy mist.

PART FOUR

THE BATTLE

CHAPTER SEVENTEEN

BATTLE JOINED

'It would be impossible to imagine a more magnificent spectacle. The two armies in full battle array were so close to one another that they exchanged fanfares of trumpet-calls and rolls of kettle-drums. When ours stopped, their music struck up again.'

THE COUNT OF MÉRODE-WESTERLOO

THE COUNT OF MÉRODE-WESTERLOO enjoyed 'a good hot plate of soup' with fellow senior officers on the evening of 12 August and returned in high spirits to the barn outside Blenheim that his servants had requisitioned for him. He sunk contentedly into his campaign bed. 'I slept deeply until six in the morning,' he later recalled, 'when I was abruptly awoken by one of my old retainers – the head groom in fact – who rushed into the barn all out of breath. This fellow, Lefranc, shook me awake and blurted out that the enemy were there. Thinking to mock him, I asked, "Where? There?" and he at once replied, "Yes – there – there!", flinging wide as he spoke the door of the barn and drawing my bed-curtains. The door opened straight on to the fine, sunlit plain beyond – and the whole area appeared to be covered by enemy squadrons.' [1] Hastily downing his morning cup of chocolate, and pulling on his uniform, Mérode-Westerloo rushed to warn Tallard of the approaching peril. 'There was not a single soul stirring as I clattered out of the village: nothing at all might have been happening. The same sight met my gaze when I reached the camp – everyone still snug in their tents – although the enemy was already so close that their standards and colours could easily be counted. They were already pushing back our pickets, but nobody seemed at all worried about it.' [2] The French had been taken completely by surprise.

Soon their camp was abuzz, Sergeant Millner of the 18th Royal Irish noting with satisfaction: 'We saw all their camp in motion, their Generals and their Aides de Camps galloping to and fro to put all things in order.' [3] The Franco-Bavarian troops quickly fell into position, the legacy of Martinet and Louvois evident in their disciplined response to this unexpected attack. Still trying to grasp the early morning's events, Mérode-Westerloo stopped to take in the view before him: 'The brightest imaginable sun shone down on the two armies drawn up in the plain. You could even distinguish the uniforms of each successive unit … it was an almost indescribably stirring sight.' [4]

Captain Robert Parker was among the myriad uniforms – Austrians and Dutch in contrasting greys, British, Hessians and Hanoverians in scarlet, Prussians in dark blue – that Mérode-Westerloo could see advancing towards Blenheim. 'We had upwards of three leagues to march to the enemy; when we came in sight of them their whole camp was standing; but as soon as they perceived us, they fired three [other eyewitnesses say two] cannon to call in their foragers; so little did they expect a visit from us this morning.' [5] The French 24-pounders had been brought into action by Mérode-Westerloo's quick-thinking aide-de-camp, their booming report recalling all the troops to the camp. As they fell back, the French burned the hamlets of Berghausen, Schwenenbach and Weilheim, in order to deprive the advancing enemy of cover.

THE ALLIED TROOPS HAD BEEN ON the move for four hours when Mérode-Westerloo's head groom had spotted them. Since their visit to Tapfheim church tower the previous day, Eugène and Marlborough had been preparing for a pre-dawn advance against the enemy. Two brigades – one Brigadier-General Rowe's, the other Major-General Wilkes's – were pushed forward. They secured the passage of the Reichen, a tributary of the Danube two miles from Tapfheim, en route for the Franco-Bavarian camp. Four hundred pioneers were also sent ahead, to improve the roads during the night. French pickets had encountered this force on the evening of the 12th without appreciating their significance.

Marlborough spent much of the night in prayer, attended by his chaplain, Archdeacon Hare. In the early hours of 13 August he received the sacrament, before resting briefly. On rising he held a quick meeting with Eugène, to establish 'the various arrangements for a battle, which appeared to involve the fate of the Christian world.' [6]

The strength of the enemy position, and their clear superiority in numbers – especially in artillery – led many senior officers to plead with Marlborough not to attack. Lieutenant-General the Earl of Orkney said nothing, but silently doubted his commander's plan: 'for, I declare, had I been to give my opinion, I had been against it, considering the ground where they were encamped, and the strength of the army.' [7] However, conscious that the alternative of retreat along his threatened lines of communication was also fraught with perils, and mindful of the wider allied need for victory, the English captain-general overruled those reservations that were voiced: 'I know the danger,' he conceded, 'yet a battle is absolutely necessary, and I rely on the bravery and discipline of the troops, which will make amends for our disadvantage.' [8]

AT TWO O'CLOCK ON THE MORNING of 13 August, all the tents and baggage were sent from the allied camp back to Reitlingen. At the same time a vanguard of forty squadrons was sent forward, towards the enemy position. The main allied force, in eight columns, followed at 3 a.m., pushing forward over the Kessel. Marlborough was towards the rear of this advance, in his campaign carriage, his Knight of the Garter ribbon adorning his scarlet uniform.

When the eight columns passed the Reichen, Rowe's and Wilkes's brigades fell in step with them to provide a ninth arm. This was now placed under the command of 'the Salamander', Lord Cutts. Mist that had fallen the previous evening provided cover for the march, the route having been marked out by scouts working in advance of the grand army.

They reached Schweningen, two miles from Blenheim, at six o'clock, and here Marlborough and Eugène made their final plans for the day, before separating their armies into two wings. The commanders, accompanied by forty cavalry squadrons, inspected the lines of the enemy, looking for any changes since their church-top inspection the previous day. It was important to get a feel for the terrain. During this final reconnaissance they consulted Major-General Natzmer, a Prussian who had been taken prisoner during the previous year's defeat at the nearby battle of Höchstädt. They found that he retained an excellent knowledge of the area. Bearing Natzmer's advice in mind, the battle plan was agreed: Marlborough, with 36,000 troops, would attack Tallard's equal force on the left, in the process attempting the capture of Blenheim village; while Eugène, leading 16,000 men, would fight the Elector and Marsin's combined army of 24,000 troops, to the right.

Not only was Eugène to be outnumbered, he was also to face the ablest of the three enemy commanders, the experienced and accomplished Maximilian Emmanuel of Bavaria. In addition, Eugène had to perform a complex initial manoeuvre, deploying his men across the plain in a protracted arc, in order to face the Elector's and Marsin's position. Marlborough's larger wing would have to wait until this was achieved before the general engagement could begin.

TALLARD'S EYESIGHT WAS SO WEAK that he could not make out the appearance of the allied cavalry for himself. Anxious aides-de-camp informed him of the enemy's progress, and waited for their commander's instructions.

The marshal failed to grasp that he was under attack. He believed, rather, that the strong display of enemy squadrons simply confirmed his suspicions: Marlborough was engaged in a humiliating withdrawal from Bavaria. This show of force was merely a smokescreen, behind which the main allied army would slip away to safety. At the moment when Marlborough and Eugène parted, to head up their respective wings of attack, Tallard wrote confidently to Louis XIV: 'This morning before daybreak the enemy beat the *générale* at two o'clock, and at three the *assemblée*. They can now be seen drawn up at the head of their camp, and it appears they will march today. Word in the country is that they are going to Nördlingen. If that is so, they will leave us between them and the Danube, and consequently they will have difficulty in sustaining the places that they have taken in Bavaria.' [9] Tallard – courtier, diplomat and wit – was beginning to reveal his inadequacies as a soldier.

Barely had the marshal's messenger left for Versailles, than his mis-interpretation of events became clear. A little after seven o'clock, Tallard was informed that the entire enemy was heading for the Franco-Bavarian camp. It was a baffling move. Tallard asked the Elector and Marsin to join him in Blenheim, to help make sense of unconventional but bold enemy tactics.

It was nine o'clock when the three commanders climbed Blenheim's church tower to plan their final manoeuvres. Their deliberations were underpinned by the misinformation that Baden was advancing with Marlborough and Eugène against them: only numerical superiority could explain the allies' rash assault of their strong defensive position. Tallard proposed, and his colleagues accepted, that it would therefore be best to fight a defensive action, allowing the enemy to come to them. Most importantly, both flanks of the Franco-Bavarian line must be held, whatever the cost. Blenheim village started to attain a crucial position in the battle plan.

Situated at the extreme right of the line, this settlement of 300 houses lent itself to concentrated defence: it certainly seemed capable of holding a flank. Lieutenant-General the Marquis de Clérambault was given command of the village, and to him were entrusted the cream of the French infantry. This included the regiment of Navarre, formed in the mid-sixteenth century, one of the four senior units of foot in Louis's army. Supporting it were the brigades of Languedoc, Groder, Royal, and Allemagne. Sixteen battalions occupied Blenheim village, while eleven more stood in reserve, several hundred yards behind the village. In support were twelve squadrons of dragoons under the Count de Hautefeuille. They were dismounted, since many of the troopers had lost their horses to glanders. They deployed behind a line of wagons, providing covering fire from the banks of the Danube to Blenheim's perimeter.

Clérambault's instructions were to hold the village at all costs. Tallard was told that Lord Cutts's redcoats were filing towards Blenheim. He knew their reputation as the cream of Marlborough's storm troopers: this was the force that had astonished Europe by taking the Fort of St Michael, in Venlo, 'so that no one that was there could with modesty express, nor no one that was not believe.'[10] Clérambault was to see that their success was not repeated.

THE FRANCO-BAVARIAN LEFT FLANK was less of a concern to the three commanders. Marsin and the Elector, who controlled this wing, realised that attack was impossible through the woods to their north: any force that succeeded in penetrating the thick trees would be cut down by their cavalry before forming for battle. However, to solidify this wing, Tallard recommended that the Elector and Marsin commit eight battalions to garrisoning the village of Oberglau. This would provide further ballast to the defensive front.

To the rear of Oberglau stood another thirty battalions, including the brigades of Champagne and of Bourbonnais, two more of France's senior foot regiments. They were supported by the 'Wild Geese'. These were units from the 25,000 Irish soldiers who had left their homeland, to serve under French leadership, following William III's victories in their homeland in the 1690s. The Wild Geese were renowned for their bravery and resilience, and were among the most effective of Louis's diverse selection of foreign mercenaries. To the left of Oberglau were two lines of the Elector's horse, and the bulk of Marsin's cavalry.

Further to the north, near the smaller village of Lutzingen, were Count d'Arco and five elite battalions of Bavarians. These had been reconstituted and rearmed, during the six weeks since the fall of the Schellenberg. They held the sector from Lutzingen to the dense woodland to the north.

The deployment of so many prime infantry regiments in and around the three villages left Tallard with just nine battalions of inexperienced foot at the centre of his line. Many of these were from new regiments that Louis had hastily formed at the start of the War of the Spanish Succession. They had been trained well, but this was their first real combat. A few hours earlier, they had been asleep, confident that the enemy was planning to withdraw from the Danube. Now they looked across the fields and saw that they were to be attacked by a determined foe in his tens of thousands. Their terror is easy to imagine.

Tallard knew that, whatever its inadequacies in infantry, his centre had an impressive cavalry strength. Here he amassed eighty squadrons, eight of which were from the elite regiment of the *Gens d'Armes*, the Household Cavalry of France whose talismanic presence had long been valued by the monarchy. Their oldest company dated from 1422, and King Francis I had described them as 'the arm that carries my sceptre.'[11] Louis XIV was honorary captain of their first four companies. Other members of the royal family held all the most prestigious ranks in the regiment, while the troopers were drawn from the aristocracy of France. Every man in the regiment enjoyed officer rank in the line cavalry and their uniforms displayed their exalted status: a red tunic coat with silver buttons, the cuffs and hat trimmed with silver lace, the company captain's coat of arms embroidered into their housings.

The French cavalry, with the *Gendarmerie* at its core, had carried all before it in the War of the League of Augsburg. It remained to be seen how it would cope with the British cavalry, restructured by Marlborough in the intervening years.

With his basic deployment agreed, Tallard looked at how best to use the Nebel, the stream of four yards' breadth, whose marshy banks he had felt sure would deter the allies from attack. He saw two options: either maximise its potential as a natural impediment and make it unbreachable, or allow them to clear the water before hurling them back in fatal confusion. With this second plan, the French cavalry could charge downhill, annihilating a disordered enemy. Meanwhile the Blenheim garrison could fire from the flank, before joining in the slaughter with fixed bayonets. Tallard sacrificed military common sense in the pursuit of greater personal glory. For years belittled as Villeroi's favoured cousin, here was a chance to show that he was a leader in the vein of Condé and Turenne. He feared that the successful holding of the Nebel would send the allies into premature retreat and so cheat him of decisive victory.

The voluntary surrender of such an effective advantage was a dangerous tactic that Marsin and the Elector strongly opposed. All would depend on timing: if the cavalry were sent too late, the Elector pointed out, then the enemy might prove impossible to dislodge. Tallard, 'a proud, conceited Frenchman', in Captain Parker's estimation, 'puffed up with the success of his former campaign thought the Elector took upon him to dictate to him; and told him that was not the way to obtain a complete victory, which now offered; and that the utmost that could be made of it in their way, was only a drawn battle: whereas he was for drawing up the army at some distance from the morass; and then the more that came over to them, the more they should kill.'[12] 'Beware of these troops,' the Elector warned, with the Schellenberg in mind: 'They are very dangerous: you cannot afford to concede anything [to them].' Tallard, annoyed at this negativity, countered: 'Well, then, I see that to-day the victory will be my own.'[13]

Tallard does not seem to have considered a third way of using the Nebel to good effect, even though it was one that had proved useful a year before, in the same place. As the Duke of Saint Simon was to comment: 'The first battle of Höchstädt afforded a lesson which ought to have been studied on this occasion … either take up a position behind the brook, and parallel to it, so as to dispute its passage with the enemies, or to take advantage of the disorder they would be thrown into in crossing it by attacking them then. Both these plans were good; the second was better; but neither was adopted.'[14] Even a soldier-courtier of Saint-Simon's limited range could see the pitfalls of Tallard's plan: far better to attack when the allies were struggling to establish a foothold on the Franco-Bavarian bank, than when they were able to organise themselves into a defence.

However, the marshal was blind to the potential problems. He kept his men high up on the hill overlooking the Nebel, in effect beckoning the allied High Command to cross over unimpeded. This invitation was to be accepted by the allies as their initial suspicion gave way to disbelief. Tallard was prepared to risk all in pursuit of his Pharsala.

IT WAS JUST AFTER SEVEN O'CLOCK in the morning when Marlborough's men began their first approach towards the Nebel. Dragoons were in the forefront, with orders to find where the river was passable. Pontoons were prepared and fascines were cut, to aid the troops in what promised to be a laborious crossing.

The movement of massed infantry, except on the flattest of terrains, was still at a rudimentary stage in the early eighteenth century. Huge delays were inevitable as blocks of men were pushed into their new positions by hectoring NCOs. As Winston S. Churchill observed, this left manoeuvring infantry vulnerable to cavalry attack: 'Although their firepower was growing, they must still depend largely upon their strict array and their bayonets, while all around, close at hand moved the flashing squadrons which upon the slightest disorder could crumple them almost instantaneously. Thus passing even a small hedge or ditch, which unarmed men could easily jump or perhaps step over, was in the presence of the enemy a most anxious business, and every movement, even of 100 yards, had to be judiciously foreseen as to the ground and timed as to the enemy.'[15]

The Nebel proved to be a substantial impediment, and it cost the allies much of the advantage gained by their early morning advance. The stream, with its marshy banks, was only fordable intermittently, the safest passage being via a damaged bridge near Oberglau, or near to two mills to the north of Blenheim. Any further crossing-points would need to be provided by the allied engineers' pontoons. Furthermore, it was soon clear that those crossing the Nebel would have to withstand heavy musket fire from the tightly packed garrisons of Blenheim and Oberglau. If Tallard had chosen to defend the Nebel stoutly, it is hard to see that the battle could have ended in anything but allied defeat.

As was then customary in battle, the artillery delivered the opening shots at Blenheim. Marlborough's biographer, Archdeacon Coxe, claimed the bombardment began at eight o'clock in the morning, the first cannon balls emanating from the French right wing. Captain Robert Parker recalled the moment well, for the battery was pointing at his men: 'The first shot the enemy fired was at our Regiment, and it fell short; the second killed one man, which was the first blood drawn that day.'[16]

Marlborough called for his artillery commander, Colonel Blood,* and told him to choose ground for allied counter-batteries. The duke inspected these positions, before ordering the guns to return fire. This was the start of a gunnery duel that dominated the morning. Sergeant Millner recalled that: 'Both Armies cannonaded each other very smartly and vigorously with several Batteries, from Eight in the Morning till past Twelve at Noon, with great Loss.'[17]

Forty miles away, outside Ingolstadt, Prince Lewis could hear the rumbling of the artillery as he composed a letter to Emperor Leopold. He added to it a surprisingly tender postscript for one so indisposed to his English colleague: 'The Prince and Duke are engaged to-day to the westward. Heaven bless them.'[18]

The French ordnance was led by four booming 24-pounders, placed above Blenheim village. The remainder of their guns were spread evenly across the Franco-Bavarian front, sheltering their cavalry, and protecting the battalions holding Oberglau and Lutzingen. Tallard's artillery nearly pulled off a spectacular coup early in the engagement. Sandby

---

* While the French artillery was a beneficiary of the Louvois-Le Tellier reforms, with a professional structure, the English artillery was still essentially an amateur part of the forces: its civilian contractors were hired on a seasonal basis for campaigning. These civilian operators gained a reputation, among the regular troops, for self-preservation: a charge that ignored their vulnerability to advancing enemy soldiers. In 1683 Charles II had tried to bring some order to an arm of the fighting unit whose potential was clear, issuing 'Instructions for the Government of our Office of Ordnance'. However, it was not until after Queen Anne's reign, in 1716, that four permanent artillery companies were created. Despite this, artillery officers' ranks remained separate from those of the main body of the army for another generation.

recorded Marlborough's lucky escape with a shudder: 'His Grace now rode along the lines to observe their posture, and the countenances of his men, and found both them and the officers of all nations of the allies very cheerful and impatient of coming to closer engagement with the enemy. And as he was passing a large cannon ball from one of the enemy's batteries grazed upon a ploughed land, close by his horse's side, and almost covered him with dust. He never altered his pace for this, but moved on.'[19]

BEFORE MARLBOROUGH'S CAPTAIN-generalship, cannon were generally used for the opening salvoes of a battle. They then provided covering fire for the initial troop movements, before falling silent, and often becoming unimportant players in the engagement. Marlborough, however, was convinced that the artillery should contribute to every phase of his battle.

The English guns arrived at the battlefield of Blenheim, together with their Dutch counterparts, escorted by Lord Cutts's column, from which point Marlborough showed a keen interest in their deployment. A powerful battery was established on high ground above Unterglau, which was the midpoint of the engagement. As a result of this nurturing of his resources – only 175 men, controlled by 13 officers, operated Blood's cannon – Marlborough compensated for the French superiority in heavy guns throughout the battle. To give his main force an opportunity of crossing the Nebel without heavy flanking fire from the south, Marlborough needed to subdue the village of Blenheim. He sent several of his cannon to support Cutts's infantry regiments in their assault on a defended position that looked impregnable.

BLENHEIM VILLAGE

*'About 3 o'clock in the afternoon our English on the left
was ordered by my Lord Duke to attack a village full of
French called Blenheim which village they had fortified
and made so vastly strong and barricaded so fast with
trees, plants, coffers, chests, wagons, carts and palisades
that it was almost an impossibility to think which way
to get into it.'*

PRIVATE JOHN MARSHALL DEANE, *A JOURNAL OF
MARLBOROUGH'S CAMPAIGNS DURING THE WAR OF THE
SPANISH SUCCESSION, 1704–11*

MARLBOROUGH HAD AGREED TO wait for word from Eugène before
ordering his own men to advance across the Nebel. It was important for
the two allied wings to coordinate their attacks, in order to stop either
one being swamped by the superior numbers of the enemy. Marlborough had expected to hear from Eugene that he was ready for the attack
by eleven. However, Eugène's Prussian and Danish infantry encountered unexpected delays, as they scrambled across the difficult terrain
that lay between them and the position from which they could strike at the
Elector's and Marsin's forces. 'The ground being extremely broken,
covered with brush-wood, and intersected by ravines and rivulets ...'[1],
the Imperialists' slow progress left them vulnerable to intense artillery
fire.

240

Sandby noted that Eugène 'was obliged to sustain the enemy's great shot, all the while he was drawing up, and could not bring his own field pieces to bear against them, because of a great many ditches, and the badness of the ground, from one end of the wing to the other.' [2] Even though fascines were used to help the men cross the pitted ground, Eugène's guns could not be brought forward to answer those of the enemy. Meanwhile, Marlborough and his men also remained exposed to the Franco-Bavarian cannon, unable to move forward until the Imperialist wing was in position.

Marlborough's wait was partially relieved by the need to attend to final details. Part of his soldiers' devotion to their captain-general stemmed from his care for their wounded. After his high losses at the Schellenberg, Marlborough was doubly keen to have the medical staff primed to receive the injured. John Hudson and John Goldie, director and senior surgeon of the Blenheim field hospital, and fifteen fellow British surgeons, were told to prepare for large numbers of battlefield casualties. These would be transported back from the front line in waiting carts, driven by orderlies who were guarded by armed man-servants.

The resident surgeon for each regiment would perform the basic operations, including amputations, assisted by his surgeon's mate. The mate was an apprentice with staff officer rank, whose grasp of medicine was often very limited. We know of the ordeal by ignorance that was the injured soldier's lot. Each man would have realised that any bone protruding from a wound was likely to be cut away; and that even an apparently clean injury could result in prolonged suffering and death. 'Gunshot wounds are acknowledged by all to be very troublesome,' wrote a contemporary surgeon, 'because of the tearing, and of the disordering of the flesh, occasioned by the bullet, the stop put to the circulation so far as they reach, the havoc that attends them, and the obstructions they occasion; all which are but too able to produce very grievous accidents, fluxions, [and] mortifications.' [3] How to mend these wounds safely remained, for the most part, a mystery.

The duke also insisted that his men receive Christian blessing before the battle. This was a standard method of galvanising frightened troops

241

into action; and of appeasing their souls on what, for thousands, would be their day of death. Each regiment had its own chaplain, who now stood at the head of his men, offering them the consolation afforded by their faith. With such a polyglot, multi-cultural, army, the allied ranks contained a broad cross-section of faiths: Calvinist Dutch stood next to Anglican English, with Catholic Imperialists adjacent to Presbyterian Scots. Captain Blackader, the God-fearing Scottish diarist, was one of many lifted by spiritual faith that day: 'In the morning, while marching towards the enemy, I was enabled to exercise a lively faith, relying and encouraging myself in God, whereupon I was easy, sedate, and cheerful. I believed firmly that his angels had me in their charge, and that not a bone should be broken.' [4]

Blackader's optimism was all the more startling, given the heat of the French artillery throughout the morning. The allies were forced to endure it, waiting in their formations for the command to attack, as the cannon balls came skidding across the plain, then ploughed into their ranks. The screams of the wounded were terrible.

The French marshal Vauban, the great siege master and engineer, had perfected ricochet shot. These cannon balls did not simply land and explode, but remained intact, bouncing along and sending splinters and earth flying with each hop before finding their mark. Captain Robert Parker remembered an occasion from the 1702 campaign in Flanders when he had been quick-witted enough to see a cannon ball heading straight for him, for they were not fast projectiles, just deadly ones. As he nimbly stepped aside, the projectile killed the man behind him.

Wincing at the sight of such carnage now, Marlborough sent a series of messengers to Eugène, to find out what was delaying him. He was anxious to establish how long it would be before he could send his men forward, to take their chance in proper combat, rather than remaining at the mercy of the French gunners. The reply kept coming back that Eugène was not ready, that he was reordering his line, and that he needed to engage his reserve. Finally, at noon, 'Colonel Cadogan returned, and gave his Grace an account that Prince Eugène had posted his infantry in two lines to the right of all, and his cavalry joining to their left, were drawn up in the same manner, and that his highness's *corps de réserve* were to fill up the intervals, occasioned by the extension of the line.'[5]

Eugène was ready to advance. Marlborough now mounted his horse, and calmly said to his generals: 'Gentlemen, to your posts.'[6]

FOR THE WAITING LORD CUTTS, THE task ahead was a daunting one: he was to advance his fifteen squadrons and twenty battalions on Blenheim. The village lay 250 yards from the Danube, behind the Nebel, its stone houses standing about its focal point, the church. Such picturesque arrangement belied its function now: Tallard had designated Blenheim as the key stronghold for the French against the allied attack. Any force that Marlborough chose to send across the Nebel, and which strayed within range of its cannon and muskets, would feel its heat. Cutts did not know how many enemy were inside Blenheim, but his orders were to take the village.

He had organised his ninth column into six lines of men, the first four of foot, the remaining two of horse. The first and third lines of the infantry were British – the brigades of Rowe and Ferguson – while the second line was Hessian, and the fourth Hanoverian. The horse were all British, Ross's dragoons preceding Wood's cavalry. Mid-morning, Cutts sent the van of this formation, Rowe's British brigade, to gain a bridgehead over the Nebel.

These troops first pushed back the two battalions of French soldiers who had been holding the area surrounding the two water mills. They then forded the water at its shallowest point, and awaited the arrival of the rest of Cutts's ninth column. Meanwhile, Rowe's men had to endure the heavy fire of the four French 24-pounders. Two other large guns joined in the bombardment. Cover was limited (Sergeant Millner recorded that, 'they posted themselves in a bottom'[7], 150 yards up from the Nebel), and their casualties were horrific. With enormous courage, they remained steady under fire, cut off from their colleagues, and within easy range of the enemy.

When Marlborough ordered a general advance, the remaining lines of Cutts's column crossed the Nebel to join Rowe's beleaguered brigade.

As they moved forward, they were hit by musket fire and partridge shot – an anti-personnel case-shot used by artillery at ranges of less than 200 yards. However, they reached Rowe's position. Cutts now ordered his brigadier forward, to attack the village.

The French had been tightening Blenheim's defences all morning: garden fences were transformed into barricades, and the 'openings between the houses and gardens were closed with boards, carts, and gates.'[8] The Royal Brigade and that of Languedoc stood ready to greet the attackers, with Lieutenant-General Zurlauben's horse and the brigade of Montroux in reserve.

THE BRITISH INFANTRYMEN WERE armed with muskets, to which socket bayonets were attached. Bayonets had become increasingly common since the 1670s, developing from the plug device, a simple affair which was shoved into the end of the barrel and so transformed the discharged musket into a shortened pike. The introduction of the socket bayonet, which could be attached to the rifle's end without stopping the musket's use as a firearm, rendered the pike-man – that survivor of medieval warfare – obsolete: from now on the infantryman was to be both musketeer and pike-man. In 1705 European armies recognised the demise of the pike, and the bayonet has remained an infantry fixture ever since.

While the bayonet evolved, the flintlock musket was introduced, improving on the old matchlock mechanisms, being lighter and very much more reliable. The flintlock misfired only once every five shots, insignificant compared with the wildly temperamental matchlock. The introduction of the flintlock coincided with the improvement of the loading drill, and the use of paper cartridges, which meant that a well-practised infantryman could fire up to two shots per minute: a generation earlier, the anticipated rate of fire was one shot every three to four minutes. The French were the last troops to embrace the flintlock. Whereas the Anglo-Dutch forces had used it throughout the War of the League of Augsburg, Louis only authorised it in 1700, and it took many years for it to become standard issue.

ROWE LED HIS MEN FORWARD AT one o'clock. He knew that it would not be possible for them to fire more than one round each during this assault as any loss of momentum would be fatal. Rowe ordered his men not to fire until he had struck the village palisade with his sword. After that, they must get inside the enemy defences and kill with their bayonets and swords.

The massed ranks of Frenchmen inside the village, supported by the dragoons on the flank, waited until the slowly advancing British were thirty yards from the ends of their barrels before discharging their fusils simultaneously. The noise of the volley was thunderous. When the smoke from the burnt gunpowder blew away, the French saw that they had slain dozens of their attackers and wounded many more. As at the Schellenberg, a disproportionate number of officers fell. 'But yet that did not discourage that gallant officer Brigadier Rowe from marching directly to the very pales,' wrote Sandby, 'before he suffered a man to fire a piece; and then our men gave the first volley in the teeth of the enemy.' [9]

The French recoiled in turn, but their numbers were such that fresh musketeers could push to the front of their defences, and fill the void. Their repeated volleys forced the British back, one musket ball shattering Rowe's thigh, and leaving him slumped against the palisade. A lieutenant-colonel and a major from his regiment ran to his aid, but both were shot dead at point-blank range before they could carry their stricken commander away. In this first attack, which lasted minutes, one in three of Rowe's assault force were killed or wounded. The British fell back in confusion, crashing into the Hessian brigade which made up the second line of attack.

The Blenheim garrison, their blood up, now cheered on three squadrons of their famed *Gens d'Armes*, assisted by gun-toting *carabinier* horsemen, as they fell on Rowe's rebuffed force. The French cavalry swooped, and plucked the regimental colours from the chaos. They ploughed on, eager to slice through the Hessians beyond. However, the Hessians stood firm, allowing the British through their ranks before firing into the pursuing *Gens d'Armes*. They checked the French horsemen with the steadiness of their fire, and the *Gens d'Armes* retreated in turn. The Hessians returned Rowe's regimental colours to their British allies, the first of many heroic feats they performed that day.

BLENHEIM OCCUPIES AN OPEN plain, and Cutts could see that the Hessians had won only brief respite for his men: it was evident, from their troop movements, that the French were going to use more cavalry attacks to blunt his infantry advance. He sent a messenger to Lumley, one of Marlborough's lieutenant-generals of horse, requesting reinforcements to protect his men from the impending threat.

Lumley sent Colonel Palmes over the Nebel, near the two burning mills, with five squadrons of dragoon guards. Zurlauben, the Swiss-born commander of Tallard's cavalry, saw this small British force advancing out on a limb, and decided to pulverise it. He gave the order for all eight squadrons of the *Gens d'Armes* to follow him in attack.

In any of Louis's previous wars, the Sun King's elite cavalry charging a smaller enemy force would have been a one-sided affair, ending in predictable triumph for the Frenchmen. However, this trend had been less marked in the first years of the War of the Spanish Succession. Just one year earlier, at the battle of Eckeren, 1,500 French cavalry had been driven from the field by a plucky charge from 40 Dutch troopers, commanded by the Prussian general, Hompesch. Now, at Blenheim, something equally astonishing took place.

Zurlauben, pushing his two wings slightly forward, aimed to outflank the British cavalry, while launching his main thrust into their centre. Captain Parker saw what happened next: 'Palmes perceiving this, ordered Major Oldfield, who commanded the squadron on his right, and Major Creed, who commanded that on his left, to wheel outward, and charge those squadrons, that were coming down on them; and he, not in the least doubting but they would beat them, ordered them when they had done that, to wheel in upon the flanks of the other squadrons that were coming upon him, while he charged them in front.'[10] To the amazement of the French, Palmes, instead of turning heel, ordered his squadron commanders to meet the '*Gens d' Armes*'. 'Those of the enemy,' wrote

Sandby, 'gave their fire at some distance, but the English squadrons marched up to 'em sword in hand, broke 'em to pieces, and put them to flight.'[11]

Palmes's men now overreached themselves, pursuing the enemy with slashing swords. In their excitement, they crossed the Maulweyer, a stream that flowed through Blenheim. This rashness brought them within range of the massed French infantrymen in the village, whose repeated volleys slew many of the dragoons. Nonetheless, the effect of Palmes's flair and bravery was felt throughout the battlefield: if the *Gens d'Armes* could be broken, then surely none of the Sun King's army was invincible? The reverse startled the Franco-Bavarian High Command. 'This was a great surprise to Tallard,' wrote Captain Parker, 'who had placed such confidence in his troops, that he verily thought there were not any on earth able to stand them.'[12] Tallard later wrote about the incident with disbelief, still unable to accept an equation that seemed flawed: 'Although there were eight squadrons on our side, the five enemy squadrons sustained their shock and made them recoil.'[13]

The Elector, who was riding with Tallard's wing at the time, was similarly confounded. 'What! There is the *Gendarmerie* running away? Is it possible?' Then, turning to his aides-de-camp, he ordered: 'Go, gentlemen, tell them that I am here in person. Rally them and lead them back to the charge.'[14] However, there was to be no reprise for the *Gens d'Armes*: the remnants of their shattered force attached themselves to the *Royal Etranger* regiment. The vast majority had been eliminated from the battle, including their wounded leader, Zurlauben.

This episode had a huge effect on French morale. Mérode-Wester-loo later commented on the way in which the *Gendarmerie* had been 'flung back in rude disorder.'[15] The Count watched with sadness as: 'The broken, disordered cavalry poured through the intervals between my own squadrons; the *Gendarmerie* was undoubtedly soundly beaten.'[16] The watching garrison in Blenheim village witnessed the rout from up close, and was also shaken by the sight of their champions' defeat. For the first time many defending the palisades appreciated the quality of the enemy.

As for Tallard, Parker reckoned that, having seen his 'squadrons so shamefully beaten [he] was confounded to that degree, that he did not recover himself the whole day, for after that, all his orders were given in hurry and confusion.'[17]

TALLARD'S ORIGINAL ORDERS HAD specified that two large forces of infantry should be deployed inside Blenheim itself, one to fight in the front line, the other to be held in reserve. He had appreciated that placing more than this quantity of troops in an enclosed area would be counter-productive: there was a limit to the space available for firing and reloading muskets; and also these men might be needed at short notice on other parts of the battlefield. Both reasons explain the positioning of his third force outside the village, nearer to the centre of the French front: it was his intention that the brigades of Artois, Gueder and Navarre should be available as a high-level reserve, when required.

Clérambault, however, panicked. Seeing the perseverance with which the allies attacked his position in Blenheim, and mindful of Tallard's insistence that it be held at all cost, he took a fateful decision. Without consulting Tallard, Clérambault pulled the reserve infantry brigades, and Hautefeuille's dismounted dragoons, into the village. Mérode-Wester-loo later wrote bitterly about the move: 'At this stage I saw two lines of our infantry forming up behind the village of Blenheim, with their right flank on the Danube's bank. If only they had stayed there, and left the defence of Blenheim's gardens, hedgerows, houses and barricades to smaller detachments – constantly reinforced or replaced as the need arose – things would have gone much better. However, the whole for-mation was eventually drawn into the defences.'[18] Tallard, it is recorded, heard what Clérambault was doing, and yet failed to countermand his orders.

This was dramatically to influence the course of the battle, for it upset the balance of troops under Tallard's command. Also, at a stroke, it made irrelevant the numerical superiority that the Franco-Bavarians had brought into the engagement. Sixteen allied battalions had an enemy force nearly twice their size ensnared in a trap of their own making.

Marlborough, spotting the French error, told Cutts not to attack further: it would be enough if he could keep the enemy contained in the village. Cutts, on the point of leading his Hanoverian troops in a third attack, stood the men down, and then sent them to join the main action at the centre of the battlefield. He then ordered the remainder of his men to fall back 80 yards from the French entrenchments. If any of the enemy tried to break out through the allied ring, they were to be shot.

It was half past two in the afternoon, and elsewhere matters were going less promisingly for the allies.

CHAPTER NINETEEN

GENERAL ENGAGEMENT

'During this period the engagement spread over the whole field of battle, and firing broke out everywhere from one end of the armies to the other.'

THE COUNT OF MÉRODE-WESTERLOO

AS CUTTS'S MEN HEADED FOR Blenheim village, Marlborough and Eugène began their general advance across the Nebel. Prior to attack Marlborough had arranged his men in an unusual tactical formation, designed to cope with the dangers of crossing water and marshland in the face of a strong enemy. He ordered his brother to draw up the infantry in two lines: the first of these, of seventeen battalions, was to spearhead the river crossing, with the second, of eleven battalions, following in the rear. In between the infantry formations rode seventy-one squadrons of cavalry, again divided into two lines.

This protective sandwiching of the cavalry was recognition of the comparative stability of foot soldiers during a fragile and exposed manoeuvre. The first line of infantry would secure a foothold on the French side of the stream, while the leading cavalry squadrons picked, or swam, their way across the Nebel. The second line of foot would support the operation from the allied bank, a bulwark of musketry providing covering fire. Meanwhile the troopers of the second line of cavalry would aid the crossing by hurling bundles of bound branches onto the marshland. Infantrymen and pioneers would place planks on top of these fascines. The attack was to be one in which infantry and cavalry worked closely together.

While his grand army prepared for the crossing, Marlborough ordered his pioneers forward to repair the stone bridge at the hamlet of Unterglau. The French had tried to destroy it earlier in the day, as they fell back before the allied advance. However, it was a substantial structure, supporting the main road between Höchstädt and Donauwörth, and the French sappers had only disabled the bridge, not destroyed it. Marlborough's engineers were confident they could make it serviceable again.

A single crossing point would not suffice. Allied officers were sent forward to determine where the allies' mobile pontoon bridges should be placed. Pioneers began to assemble five of these structures; one to the north of the broken bridge at Unterglau and the other four further downstream, between Unterglau and Blenheim. While they strained to span the water, the engineers found that they had become the favoured target of the enemy's gunnery, and suffered severe casualties. However, there was a substantial stretch of front that could only be strafed by cannon, and remained out of the reach of flanking musket fire. The two-mile gap between their heavily garrisoned villages presented a problem to the Franco-Bavarian defenders; one that Marlborough noted.

THROUGHOUT THIS PERIOD OF waiting – waiting for the bridges to be usable, and waiting for Eugène's forces to be ready for their push against the Elector and Marsin – Marlborough's division remained within range of the French artillery. In the summer sunshine the men ate their lunchtime rations, sitting and lying in formation on the stubble, the cavalry dismounted. Tallard's guns continuously disgorged cannon balls into their tightly packed ranks. 'We were excited by the extraordinary effects produced by our fire,' one of the French artillery officers, Baron de Quincy, wrote, 'each discharge piercing their battalions, and some slant-ways; and from the very order in which the enemy were posted, every shot told.' [1] The allies withstood this pounding, accepting it as part of the battlefield lottery. Their training told them that there could be no escape; all they could do was will their commanders to order them forward, releasing them from their static vulnerability.

This forbearance demonstrates the growth in discipline in Europe's professional armies during the late seventeenth and early eighteenth centuries. Holding firm while your neighbour is decapitated, or your officer disembowelled, is not a natural reflex. The fact that repeated horrors, witnessed at close proximity, did not lead to mass flight, is testimony to the soldiers' discipline. They had surrendered their freedom of thought to demanding NCOs and officers. Gruelling exercises in winter quarters and training camps paid dividends on the battlefield. Obedience under such an onslaught was total: it had to be, for the alternative was panic, chaos, and certain defeat. The contemporary French marshal, Catinat, was almost dismissive about the self-sacrifice demanded of his men during such situations: 'One prepares the soldier to not fire, and to realise that it is necessary to suffer the enemy's fire.' [2] Two thousand allied troops were lost in the morning bombardment at Blenheim, before closing with the enemy.

AT LAST, THE BRIDGE AT UNTERGLAU was repaired, the pontoons were in place and Eugène had relayed his readiness to attack. Marlborough ordered General Churchill to take his infantry forward. They marched through the blazing remains of Unterglau and across the pontoons beyond. Churchill's two multinational lines of foot were each led by British lieutenant-generals, Ingoldsby and Orkney. Ten battalions of Hanoverians were detached from the attack through Unterglau, and placed in reserve under the command of Major-General the Prince of Holstein-Beck.

The allies expected fierce resistance to their crossing of the Nebel. Tallard's cavalry was visible at the top of the opposing hill, but it was assumed that these squadrons would fall on Marlborough's men as soon as they traversed the stream. Brigadier-General Kane, present at the crossing, recorded later how his men 'passed over as well as they could and formed as fast as they got over, Tallard all this while as a man infatuated looking on.'³

The Prince of Hesse commanded the two allied lines of cavalry. His three lieutenants, Württemberg, Lumley and Hompesch, rode at the head of their respective Danish, English, and Dutch squadrons. When they reached the river banks Lumley sent ahead Colonel Palmes's dragoons to aid Rowe's men after their drubbing outside Blenheim village. When Palmes's initial success against the *Gens d'Armes* was undone by overconfidence and descended into retreat, Marlborough sensed that Tallard would unleash his forces quickly, denying the allies a foothold on the far side of the Nebel. He therefore 'resolved to pass the rivulet immediately, and come to a general engagement', Sandby recalled: 'Accordingly they began to pass as fast as the badness of the ground would permit them.'⁴

Sergeant Millner remembered the allies' astonishment and relief when Tallard failed to cut them down as they established themselves on the hostile bank: 'The enemy gave us all the time we wanted for that purpose, and kept very quiet on the hill they were possessed of, without descending to the meadow towards the rivulet; insomuch that even our second line of horse had time to form themselves.'⁵

Lumley's Englishmen, on the left of the allied advance, had the worst of the crossing. Their sector was opposite Blenheim village, with its heavy defences. Also, this was the point where the Nebel divided into twin tributaries: a double impediment, which also added to the bogginess of the ground. The squadrons eventually crossed, but were greeted by Blenheim's concerted artillery and musket fire. As Marlborough had anticipated, shocked at the *Gendarmerie*'s flight from Palmes's dragoons, Tallard now sprang into action. He belatedly ordered his cavalry to charge the allied foothold on his side of the river.

Tallard's assault was fierce, an eyewitness recalling that 'they attacked with a great deal of fury'.⁶ The French troopers fired their pistols and carbines, before hitting the static enemy with a momentum enhanced by the downward slope of the hill. The front line of allied cavalry, which had pushed ahead of the infantry, was winded and dazed, and started to fall back towards the river in confusion. Lumley's sector was particularly hard hit, faltering under the simultaneous attacks from cavalry, infantry and artillery. However, some of Tallard's men had failed to join in what was meant to be a general cavalry attack. This left his squadrons unable to follow up their initial success, for they lacked numbers, and now came up against the united firepower of the two lines of allied infantry.

THESE FRENCH TROOPERS NOW experienced at first hand some of William III's and Marlborough's tactical improvements from the previous decade. This was a period in which French musket drill, for so long unmatched in Europe, had flirted with, but ultimately rejected, change. Louis's infantry persisted with a firing formation of five parallel lines, the musketeers taking it in turn to stand, stoop, kneel, and – after firing – lie prone. Each line discharged a simultaneous volley. The result was a thin scatter-gun smattering of musket-balls emanating from the entire length of the French infantry. There was no premium on marksmanship, and supervision by officers or NCOs was often distant, resulting in ill-directed and largely uncontrolled fire.

While William and Marlborough gave their musket-fire focus, Louis remained convinced that the cavalry decided the outcome of a battle. However, the commanders of his Anglo-Dutch enemies during his two final wars explored ways of maximising the fighting effectiveness of the foot soldier. If used properly, William and Marlborough were sure, the infantry could be more than the secondary limb of an army. Indeed, it could independently turn the balance of an engagement.

After much experimentation, Marlborough concluded that his men were at their most destructive when deployed in three lines. In this formation they fired as individual platoons, under the direct command of their superiors. The officers and NCOs could concentrate the men's fire where it was most needed, monitoring both accuracy and effect. The soldiers were told to aim at their opponents' stomachs, maximising the chances of striking the enemy in a telling spot – hopefully, puncturing a vital organ.

This arrangement gave Marlborough hard-hitting pockets along the allied line, disgorging their united firepower into the most vulnerable sectors of the advancing enemy. The results of these simple modifications were devastating: whereas the French system scattered musket balls along a wide front, the Anglo-Dutch method cut down large swathes of their opponents in a moment.

One of our soldier-diarists, Captain Parker, witnessed the differing effects of the French and allied armies' gun drill. His troops encountered some French-trained mercenaries at the battle of Malplaquet in 1709. Otherwise evenly matched, the two parties of soldiers adopted the firing tactics common to their respective armies. An exchange of volleys followed, killing forty of Louis's mercenaries, but only ten of Parker's men. As the captain concluded: 'The French at that time fired all by ranks, which can never do equal execution with our platoon-firing, especially when six platoons are fired together. This is undoubtedly the best method that has yet been discovered for fighting.' [7]

TALLARD'S CAVALRY CHARGE PUSHED back the first line of allied horse, but then foundered on the dense volleys from the supporting infantry's flintlocks. 'This check', Captain Parker wrote, 'allayed that fire, which the French have always been so remarkable for in their first onsets: it was observable, that they did not make such another push that day; for when they are repulsed, their fire immediately abates.' [8] As they hovered indecisively, the French cavalry was met by the concentrated charge of the sword-wielding squadrons of Lieutenant-General von Bülow, the 'Commander in Chief of the Luneburgh Troops', as Sergeant Millner recorded. Bülow 'brought up from the second line his own regiment of dragoons, and two others of the troops of Zell, viz. Major-General Villars's, and Brigadier-General Bothmar's, who charged the enemy with such vigour, that they broke them, and drove them beyond the second rivulet, called Meulweger, and from thence to the very hedges of Blenheim.' [9]

Marlborough and Tallard both expected the cavalry to decide the day. The duke knew that, if his first line of horse failed, it would be immensely difficult to prosper elsewhere. He therefore instructed Villars's and Bothmar's men to remain with Lumley's force. He then committed a further five squadrons of dragoon reserves to the front line. The Prince of Hesse placed these troops on his hard-pressed left. The allied cavalry now pressed forward, free of the Nebel, ready to meet the enemy.

The French artillery continued to fire, the retort of its guns punctuating the screams of the dying and wounded. The cannon smoke draped a pungent haze over the action. Regimental officers struggled to keep control over their units, their aides-de-camp galloping across the field as they conveyed and received orders. Fighting was hand-to-hand, desperate, and frenzied. Ordnance played, muskets and pistols fired, while sword and bayonet clashed. Musketeers' hands burned on heated barrels, the repeated impact of their volleys bruising their shoulders. Some moved their weapon to the other shoulder, to spread the pain of the discharge; others fired with the stock pressed to their chests.

Where possible, the injured had their wounds staunched before being dragged to the back of their lines for the rough journey to surgery. Arteries were tied with straps or ligatures, to try to stem the bleeding. Blood and filth were mopped away from the wounds, and obvious detritus – pieces of garment, wadding, or shattered bone – was extracted. It was best to do this immediately, 'in any wound made either by shot, splinter of bullet … while the parts seem as if they [are] stupefied or benumbed.'[10]

The combatants fought, hand to hand, in the dozens of mêlées that engulfed both fronts, while the high command of both sides looked to see where help was most needed. So much of the skill of generalship lay in touch and timing, in understanding the nuances and vagaries of conflict and in realising when a key juncture in the fight had been reached. Committing reserves wisely, bolstering a position effectively and being flexible in the face of the unforeseen; this was the currency of the successful commander. The mayhem of combat could be expected to supersede the well thought out design, and it was how a general reacted to developments that counted.

Tallard's battle plan had involved forays of infantrymen from

Blenheim village falling on the flanks of the allied advance. However, these forays failed to materialise, because the French battalions could not escape Cutts's muskets. This was the first hint for Tallard that the proposal he had presented so confidently to the Elector and Marsin in the church tower that morning may have contained a deep flaw. For now, he could console himself with the knowledge that elsewhere on the battlefield there seemed to be less cause for concern, and much reason for confidence.

BY TWO O'CLOCK THE FIGHTING WAS spread along the entire four-mile battlefront. From Blenheim and the Danube, through to Lutzingen and the wooded hills, five armies – Tallard's, Marsin's, the Elector's, Eugène's and Marlborough's – were immersed in a series of struggles for ascendancy. At the centre of all this stood the village of Oberglau, whose garrison was commanded by the French general, the Marquis de Blainville. Like Clérambault in Blenheim, Blainville's instructions were to hold his strategically important village at all costs, and he was equipped with a sizeable force to ensure his success.

The Duke of Württemberg's Danish cavalry, assisted by Hanoverian horse, led the allied attack on Oberglau. However, Marsin's right infantry wing pushed hard against this advance, pushing Württemberg back over the pontoons. The allied squadrons reformed, and crossed once more; but, without infantry reinforcements, it was clear that Württemberg's squadrons would be repulsed again, leaving the centre of the field in Franco-Bavarian hands.

Marlborough ordered the Prince of Holstein-Beck, only recently arrived in the allied camp, to cross the Nebel with ten battalions. The prince descended from the high ground near Weilheim, where he had been directing artillery fire, and started to lead his men over to the enemy bank of the Nebel. He had attained his first foothold, with just the battalions of Goor and Beinheim, when nine hostile battalions charged out of the village, the Wild Geese at the forefront. They 'debouched with loud shouts out of the village'[11], and savaged the allied force, their rapid mobility and disciplined musket fire inflicting serious damage. When

Holstein-Beck looked up from this slaughter, he saw utter disaster pending: Marsin's cavalry, having broken through the Danes and Hanoverians, was preparing to bear down on him in a flanking charge which threatened devastation.

An aide-de-camp galloped to Major-General Fugger, a senior courtier to the Habsburgs, whose brigade of Imperial Cuirassiers was the nearest source of aid. Fugger refused support: he could not, the message came back, use his men as reinforcements without Prince Eugène's permission. Holstein-Beck would have to fend for himself.

Fugger's failure to help was immediately disastrous for Holstein-Beck and his force. The French and their Irish mercenaries cut down Holstein-Beck's two battalions, and captured the prince. He was severely wounded, with several wide cuts soaking his uniform in blood. He was thrown into the back of a cart and transported back behind the Franco-Bavarian lines. His force was now leaderless, and unless its position could be retrieved, a gaping hole would be formed in the allied centre: from this void the Franco-Bavarians would be able to strike both left and right, holding the centre of the battlefield and separating Marlborough's and Eugène's wings. Tallard was later to record that: 'At this moment I saw the hope of victory.'[12] Fugger's pusillanimous hesitation had handed the marshal the chance to divide and destroy the allied army.

Marlborough was alive to the overwhelming importance of the moment. He rode forward from his position near Unterglau to take personal command of the relief operation. First, he called forward three of Holstein-Beck's reserve battalions of Hanoverians, under Brigadier-General Bernsdorf. He ordered them to follow him across the Nebel, and posted them himself. Next, he summoned Colonel Blood and his cannon from the battery at Weilheim: they must also clear the Nebel, if the allied position was to be salvaged. The guns were needed to cover the right flank of the allied cavalry, which had been left unprotected after Holstein-Beck's reverses. The artillery's journey was both difficult and dangerous, the gunnery crews straining to roll their 6-pounders across the marshland. Given the problems experienced by men on foot or horseback in traversing the mud and water of the Nebel, the efforts of the gun teams in reaching the enemy side of the stream were remarkable. On their arrival, the duke and the colonel placed the cannon in tight formation. They then fired with withering effect at the Wild Geese and their French allies, forcing them to fall back out of range of the guns.

Given this breathing space, Holstein-Beck's infantry managed to regroup in battle order, and they were soon fighting effectively once more. However, Marlborough realised that his unsupported battalions were still in danger. He sent to Eugène, asking him to release Fugger and his cuirassiers, so that they could help to meet Marsin's cavalry incursions. Eugène, although extremely hard-pressed on his own wing, immediately ordered Fugger to ride to Marlborough's aid. The ease of the two allied commanders' relationship, the mutual respect and understanding they had enjoyed since first meeting, rescued their combined armies from cataclysmic danger.

Fugger was just in time. Marsin's horse were already charging forward when taken from the side by the Imperial cuirassiers – armoured heavy cavalry – and their momentum struck hard against the enemy, derailing their forward motion. The French were forced to look to their own safety, rather than thundering down upon Holstein-Beck's vulnerable foot. This furious cavalry encounter spun away from the centre of the field, caught up in its own energy, Marsin's squadrons gradually falling back, no longer a threat to the allied battalions. The battle for Oberglau was now an infantry contest, and Marlborough had posted his foot soldiers: 'so advantageously that their fire raked the [enemy] column as it recoiled from the charge, and occasioned dreadful slaughter.'[13] Colonel Blood's battery added to the bloodshed: with partridge shot strafing them, the Franco-Irish force fell back further, retreating to inside the village of Oberglau, and beyond. The duke then: 'kept those within [Oberglau] besieged', while the remainder of his own army could 'march before it and attack the cavalry of the enemy with great liberty.'[14] Marlborough's timely intervention, with telling artillery support, had saved the allied centre from destruction; but his success had only been made possible by Eugène's selfless loan of the Imperial cuirassiers.

AFTER SIX HOURS OF CANNONADE, and two of fierce fighting, the battle in Marlborough's sector was, perhaps, slightly tilted in the allies' favour. True, they had failed to take Blenheim or Oberglau; but the Franco-Bavarian garrisons cooped up in each village contained quantities of men that Tallard, the Elector and Marsin needed for deployment elsewhere. Also, Marlborough had denied Tallard's opportunity to drive a wedge through the allied front; while the French cavalry had already expended its premium energy in an unresolved tussle that had seen a clear demonstration of the effectiveness of Anglo-Dutch infantry firepower.

On Eugène's wing, the prince was fighting valiantly against superior forces, but here Marsin and the Elector held the advantage, repeatedly throwing Eugène's advances back across the Nebel. By mid-afternoon victory was possible for both sides, whereas a little earlier in the day allied defeat had loomed as a probability. Josias Sandby, the chaplain, was later to confide: 'Before three [o'clock] I thought we had lost the day.'[15] After that point, balance was restored to the battlefield.

Survivors of Blenheim were to recall how, in an engagement where frantic fighting had consumed the entire front, there was a moment in the afternoon when the two exhausted, bloodied, armies drew breath and took stock before entering what all present knew would be the decisive period of the engagement. Captain Parker noted how: 'The cavalry had this breathing-time, in which both sides were very busy in putting their squadrons and lines in order.'[16] Marlborough used this lull to return from his rescue of Holstein-Beck's beleaguered men to his central command post midway between the two garrisoned villages of Oberglau and Blenheim. As he made his way back he ordered one of his aides-de-camp, Lord Tunbridge, to ride to Prince Eugène, to inform the prince that all was well again in the middle of the battlefield and to enquire how the prince had been faring on the right wing.

THE ACCOUNT IN SERGEANT MILLNER'S diary makes Eugène's path to this temporary lull sound straightforward: 'Prince Eugène caused the right wing to march along the wood, to fall on the flank of the Elector, who extended his left proportionately, to prevent Prince Eugène's gaining his flank.'[17] However, Eugène's task up to this point had been an even more demanding one than that faced and met by Marlborough. It was only the prince's dynamic presence that had prevented the superior forces of the Elector and Marsin from putting his troops to flight, and so bringing about allied defeat.

Eugène's force comprised the right-hand four of the eight allied columns that had arrived before the Franco-Bavarian camp in the dawn mist. The two outer columns were cavalry, with the infantry marching to the immediate right of Marlborough's division. This force had first been espied by the two marshals and the Elector when spread along the raised ground beyond Berghausen. From there the men had been surprised by the difficulty of their passage to their battle positions, and they had been forced to take 'a greater circuit, through the woods upon the right, and to extend the wing further than was first thought of'.[18] The ground up to the wooded hills on the Franco-Bavarian flank was 'so embarrassed with brambles, hedges, and other encumbrances that there was no marching by columns.'[19] There was no cover from the Imperial artillery while they fell into position, and transporting the guns forward across such difficult terrain was a time-consuming business. In the meantime, the Elector's cannon had free rein. They pounded into Eugène's ranks, causing some of the heaviest casualties of the day. Because they were detached from the main allied body, the wounded had a long and circuitous route back to the surgeons. Many bled to death making this journey. Others were carried or dragged across the pitted ground, the rough treatment of their unset, broken, limbs adding to their distress.

Eugène's infantry was two-thirds Prussian, and one-third Danish (although many of the latter had been recruited in Germany). The Prussian army was credited throughout Europe with extreme hardiness, and it added to its reputation at Blenheim, taking the brunt of the firepower without wavering. When their own guns were finally in place, and the signal to cross the Nebel in front of Lutzingen was at last given, Eugène's infantry rushed to overwhelm the battery of six guns that had been their chief tormentor. Some Prussians then dug in to hold this captured position, while the rest of the infantry streamed forward, surprised by the ease of their progress so far, the Danes sweeping up to the outskirts of the woods on the hill.

The first line of Imperialist cavalry sustained the initial impetus of Eugène's attack, overwhelming the Bavarian force arrayed against it. However, the combined success of foot and horse now tempted the Imperial forces to overreach themselves; forgetting their numerical inferiority, they pushed too far ahead, without consolidating their position. The disordered Franco-Bavarians regrouped while the Elector – who, throughout the battle, repeatedly confirmed the leadership qualities that both parties had vied for over the previous two years – sent his second line of cavalry into battle. The artillery position was retaken from the Prussians; and then Eugène's cavalry was rolled back in disarray, across the Nebel to the woods from which they had started their charge.

Standing exposed, unaided by horse, Eugène's infantry fought as best it could against the trinity of the enemy's artillery, infantry and cavalry. While their cannon fired from a deadly range of just 200 yards, the Franco-Bavarian muskets raked the allies' front, and the Prussians were attacked in flank by Marsin's probing squadrons. The pressure of the incessant firepower eventually told, and Eugène's infantry also fled to the allied side of the Nebel. Some headed for the cover of the woods to the north of the fighting, hoping to find sanctuary from the enemy volleys there. The Danes, witnessing the speedy withdrawal of their allies, also started to waver. It looked as though all of Eugène's men would dissolve into flight. Given the desperate position of his wing, it is testimony to Eugène's generosity as a general that he was prepared to allow Marlborough the use of Fugger's Imperial Cuirassiers at this juncture. In truth, Eugène could not afford the loan when so hard-pressed himself, but he accepted that the duke would not have made such a request lightly and that his need must be even greater than his own.

IT WAS THE LEADERSHIP QUALITIES of Eugène and the Prussian commander, Prince Leopold of Anhalt-Dessau, that kept the infantry of the Imperialist division from quitting the battlefield altogether. Prince

Leopold was one of the founding fathers of the Prussian military machine, known to subsequent generations of his compatriots as 'the Old Dessauer'. Later, he invented marching in step, and the iron ramrod. A dashing, moustachioed figure, he had murdered the fiancé of the girl he loved, so that he could marry her instead. He brought the same level of clinical ruthlessness to the battlefield, expecting his men to give all for their cause.

The two princes' personal bravery was a source of inspiration to the dejected, outnumbered, Imperialist force. Their combined strength of personality managed to control the men, and prevent them from fleeing the field altogether. Bellowing instructions to their officers, and exhorting their troops to choose courage over dishonour, the two commanders brought order back to their ranks, and regrouped them for further fighting. While the infantry prepared to re-enter the battle, Eugène led his cavalry forward once more, just half an hour after their earlier charge. Once more they enjoyed initial success before suffering a serious reverse, this time when caught between the gunfire of Lutzingen and Oberglau. As they faltered in the storm, the Elector and his Bavarian squadrons fell on them, the impact of this assault again pushing the Imperialists back across the Nebel to the safety of the woods.

It was due to one of the Dutch commanders, Brigadier-General Heidenbrecht, that Eugène's men were able to extract themselves. Heidenbrecht had advanced from Marlborough's wing to a point above Oberglau, where his brigade had dug in. From here he could protect one of the prince's flanks, while firing down upon the Franco-Bavarians in the village. Without Heidenbrecht's assistance it is unlikely that Eugène's men could have remained in the battle, for the gunfire from Oberglau would surely have annihilated much of his force, and sent the rest into headlong retreat.

Delivered from defeat, Eugène redoubled his efforts in attack. The prince was now in full warrior mode, very far removed from the *petit abbé* of Louis's fancy. His colleagues noted the transformation that overcame the Savoyard during combat, when he: 'became possessed with a sort of warlike fury; his eyes lighted up; he rushed hither and thither, raging; he shrieked curses and encouragement, yelling and harking his bloody war-dogs on, and himself always at the first of the hunt.'[20] Fired up, Eugène now harangued his men into regrouping for a third cavalry charge. However, even though the prince managed to take the cavalry forward again, the task was beyond his drained and demoralised men. This attack soon faltered, the horse scrambling once more for the safety of the allied bank. Winston S. Churchill described the exhaustion that overcame Eugène's wing after repeated rebuffs, just as the action on Marlborough's approached its lull: 'The whole of Eugène's attack had come to a standstill. For nearly three quarters of an hour the two lines of cavalry in this quarter stood facing each other at sixty yards' distance, neither of them able to move forward or strike another blow. In vain did Eugène on one side and the Elector on the other ride along the ranks animating, commanding, entreating, and taunting their exhausted and shaken soldiers to a renewed effort.'[21]

Eugène was disgusted at the repeated failure of his men, at one point shooting dead two of his troops as they ran from the battlefield. A commander who asked so much of himself expected sacrifice and complete dedication from his men: instant, ruthless, retribution was the penalty for those who failed to obey his martial code. Having witnessed the triple failure of his horse, the prince handed command of the cavalry to the Prince of Hanover and the Duke of Württemberg, telling them to restore the disordered lines as best they could. Eugène then went to seek out his infantry, to see if they could provide the means for victory that his spent horsemen had denied him.

The prince soon discovered that the situation for the foot soldiers was as challenging as the one he had just left. The superior numbers of the Franco-Bavarians made progress agonising. Eugène's appearance in their ranks gave heart to his men, but they could do no more for him than hold their position in the face of ceaseless enemy pummelling. The Count of Mérode-Westerloo, watching from across the valley, reported with satisfaction: 'Over on the Elector's side, Prince Eugène and the Imperial troops had been repulsed three times – driven right back to the woods – and had taken a real drubbing.'[22]

It was intense fighting and casualties were high. The prince narrowly avoided joining them when one of the Elector's dragoons, on the point of shooting Eugène, was run through by an Imperialist blade. It was one of many close calls for the prince, a Prussian observer later reporting that: 'Eugène and Marlborough exposed their persons repeatedly. Eugène went so far that it is almost a miracle that he escaped with his life.'[23] Inspired by Eugène's valour, his infantry remained firm on the field, holding the superior numbers arrayed against them with stoic discipline. Anhalt-Dessau's Prussians were especially impressive in their resilience, their steady rifle fire giving backbone to Eugène's infantry formation. They stood their ground against the enemy cavalry, their volleys rolling out in a steady, deadly, rhythm. However, the superior numbers of the enemy made Eugène realise that his men could not, for now, triumph in this quarter. They could hold on against Marsin and the Elector, and yield nothing to their attacks, but beyond that they could only wait for an advantage to be handed to them; either by an error on the enemy's part, or by progress on Marlborough's wing. In the meantime, the lot of Eugène, whose every instinct was for the bold attack, was to be firm in defence, biding his time.

The Count of Mérode-Westerloo wrote later that the battle was completely in the balance, at this juncture: 'Thus from a church tower you would have seen the enemy repulsed on one flank and we on the other, the battle rippling to and fro like the waves of the sea, with the entire line engaged in hand-to-hand combat from one end to the other – a rare enough occurrence.'[24] However, it was impossible for this momentum to be maintained by either army, and Eugène's wing of the battle joined in the general lull that now descended on the field of Blenheim.

CHAPTER TWENTY

CAVALRY CHARGE

*'The Duke now finding the enemy very backward in
renewing the battle, and, as it seemed, rather in a tottering
condition, sent orders to all his troops to advance gently,
until they came pretty near them, and then to ride on a full
trot up to them.'*

CAPTAIN ROBERT PARKER

WITH EUGÈNE'S WING PINNED down on the right, and large numbers
of French troops cooped up in the villages of Blenheim and Oberglau, it
was clear that if there was to be a positive conclusion to proceedings it
would have to be found in the battlefield's centre. Furthermore, given the
terrain lying between Marlborough and Tallard, and the way in which
the armies had thus far been deployed, it was clear who would be called
upon to decide the day: 'Here was a fine plain without hedge or ditch, for
the cavalry on both sides to show their bravery; for there were but few
foot to interpose, these being mostly engaged at the villages.'[1] The
defining encounter of the day was to between the horsemen of the two
main armies.

Marlborough, son of a Royalist cavalry colonel, and disciple of Prince
Rupert and Cromwell, knew that the cavalry charge frequently determined the outcome of battle. He coolly ordered his squadrons to
assemble in two lines. Many of these had been kept in reserve until this
point, and came as fresh additions to an action that had already consumed

so many of their colleagues. Behind the front line of horse Marlborough drew up pockets of General Churchill's infantry, arranged in blocks. Large gaps were deliberately left between these units, through which the allied horse could pass to safety if the French managed to reverse their attack.

The second line of cavalry was deployed behind the infantry, thus protected from any mishap that might overtake their colleagues to the fore. Colonel Blood, still an intricate part of Marlborough's battle plans at this late stage, brought up his guns to boost the allied attack, and to bolster any necessary defence. Even though the action was primarily to be the cavalry's, the captain-general was keen to involve his other two arms, as both cover and support, should all not immediately go to plan.

Tallard waited as this unified force began to cross the Nebel. The marshal was able to call on sixty cavalry squadrons, most of which had already seen action that day, to counter Marlborough's fresh men. Despite this disadvantage, Tallard remained confident that his horsemen could repel the allies, for under his command he had what was believed to be the flower of Louis XIV's army: 'The French horse, 10,000 strong, stood their ground at first firmly,' wrote one Victorian historian, embracing this moment of high drama in a battle that thus far had exhibited the bruising characteristics of a fist fight: 'the choicest and bravest of their chivalry were there: the banderols of almost all the nobles in France floated over their squadrons.' [2] It remained to be seen how these inheritors of Turenne's and Condé's bequest would cope with Marlborough's less aristocratic, self-made, military heritage.

In truth, Tallard should not have attempted to stand his ground like this. He faced overwhelming odds and his cavalry had already shown itself unworthy of its proud heritage. It is likely that the marshal's short-sightedness might have stopped him from appreciating the size and the condition of the force that was about to fall upon him. Tallard's reasoning is not properly known: whether through ill-placed bravery, myopia, or simple misjudgement, his army was about to be exposed to a deadly attack, unaided either by the Elector's and Marsin's men on the other wing, or by the huge force still bottled up in Blenheim village.

267

TALLARD'S CHARGING CAVALRYMEN had been stunned earlier in the day when hit by the platoon-firing of the allied infantry straddling the Nebel. Now they were to be equally wrong-footed by Marlborough's choice of cavalry tactics. The French liked to use the armed horseman initially as a mounted bearer of carbine or pistol. He was sent at the trot towards the enemy, to discharge his weapon from close range, before either entering into a charge, or retiring to reload. This was a form of fighting common in central Europe a century before, when the *Reiter* (German cavaliers) had employed their wheel-lock weaponry from the saddle. Louis XIV had adopted this technique for his own cavalry's use. The king retained his faith in a system of engagement that had served France well during the early campaigns of his mammoth reign.

There had been a period that spanned the Dutch War and the War of the League of Augsburg – which, significantly, coincided with Louis's greatest triumphs – when the French cavalry turned more readily to the sabre and the charge than to the hand-gun and the measured tread. However, the outbreak of the War of the Spanish Succession saw a reversion to the old method of trot and fire. This was partly because of Louis's innate tactical conservatism, but also because the French army, drained after decades of almost continuous warfare, and expanded beyond its own capabilities at the outset of this latest conflict, could no longer provide its troops with mounts strong enough to maintain the physical demands of the repeated charge. Huge numbers of horses were needed to cope with the explosion of new cavalry regiments. The king accommodated this requirement with a renewed faith in simpler, time-honoured manoeuvres.

Unfortunately for the French, their reversion to outmoded practices and their abandonment of the all-out charge were ill-timed. The tactics of the audacious English captain-general rendered them dangerously out of date. The Duke of Marlborough wanted his cavalry to be free from distraction whilst in the saddle: the demands of cumbersome and unreliable firearms could only, he was sure, detract from a squadron's fighting effectiveness. As one of Marlborough's officers, Brigadier-General Kane, recorded, the commander believed it important for the cavalry to 'handle their swords well, which is the only weapon our British Horse makes use of when they charge the enemy; more than this is superfluous.'[3] To underline his point, Marlborough issued the horsemen with just three pistol rounds per trooper, per campaign. The cavalryman was only to use his hand-gun if surprised into defensive action – for instance, if ambushed while foraging. The pistol was not part of the battle drill.

In this different approach to tactics, strategy and armaments lay the subtle fault lines exploited by Marlborough at Blenheim. The French, proud of a long list of past battle honours, confidently peered down from the ridge of their hill, as sure of eventual victory as their forebears had been for sixty years. Meanwhile the allies had crossed over on to the hostile bank of the Nebel, rallying under the banner of a commander of limited battle experience. Nonetheless Marborough was determined to bring down this haughty enemy, which had provided him with invaluable military apprenticeship in his youth. The French, before this day, neither fully appreciated Marlborough's understanding of, and belief in, his men's capabilities; nor his fine grasp of French vulnerabilities.

He was driven by ambition born of years of professional frustration. Here, on a Bavarian field, against imposing odds, was the opportunity that Marlborough had longed for, initially as an outcast in the Court of William III and, later, as the repeated victim of the debilitating timidity of the Dutch Field Deputies. He wanted to prove himself as a commander endowed with gifts that merited the title of captain-general. He wanted, equally, to slough off the slurs of those who attributed his advancement to his wife's friendship with the queen. When Marlborough ordered his trumpeters to sound the advance, the duke would embark on a course that promised to be the defining point of his life. At the same time, this cavalry engagement would decide if Louis XIV could cling to the aura of invincibility that had held Europe in a thrall of suspicion and fear for more than half a century. Personal and political destinies hung in the air as the allies prepared to engage.

IT WAS FOUR O'CLOCK AS Marlborough's men prepared for their advance. The cavalry was in two lines, supported by twenty-three battalions of infantry. This large force, engaged along the two-mile front stretching between the villages of Blenheim and Oberglau, moved slowly from the marshland of the Nebel up the hill towards the enemy. It covered this broad expanse with purposeful menace, ready to lock horns with the enemy squadrons.

On approaching his position, General Charles Churchill noticed that Tallard had pulled the nine battalions of his reserve infantry into his own second line of horse. This promised to provide a solid cornerstone from which the French cavalry regiments could launch themselves. Churchill asked Marlborough to call forward some of his own troops, in a mirror of Tallard's shrewd move. Three battalions of Hanoverians were summoned, along with a battery of Blood's cannon, under Captain Gibbons.

By skilful consolidation of his reserves, Marlborough now enjoyed numerical advantage in this sector of the battle, both on horse and on foot. Satisfied that he had all his men correctly deployed, Marlborough moved forward; it was five o'clock when he drew his sword, and ordered his trumpets to sound the advance. At the very outset of the engagement Marlborough had uttered the words, 'This day I conquer or die.'[4] Now was the moment when the choice would be made: the fate of his bold dash across Europe, designed to save a key ally's empire, would soon be known.

THE FRENCH MOVED DOWN THE hill towards the allies, loosing off their firearms, before breaking into a charge, hoping to push the allies from the field through sheer impetus. The first line of Marlborough's cavalry, which was moving at a measured pace, buckled under the impact. One of Tallard's generals later recalled their excitement at what transpired next: 'All our Brigades charged briskly, and made all the Squadrons they attacked give way.'[5] However, thanks to Marlborough's forward planning, the retreating allied cavalry could exit to safety, through the orderly fissures in the supporting banks of infantrymen.

Marlborough, in the thick of the fighting, was perplexed to see one of his most senior officers making to flee the battlefield after this initial reverse. Not for him the knee-jerk justice of a shot in the coward's back, favoured by Eugène across the valley; rather, the icy courtesy that leaves this most accomplished of generals a man of indecipherable character: 'Mr —-,' he called, 'You are labouring under a misapprehension. The enemy lies that way. You have nothing to do but face him and the day is your own.'[6] The anonymous officer rejoined the battle, falling in with the other disordered troops as they regrouped.

Churchill's flintlocks and Blood's cannon covered the cavalry's retreat. They fired repeatedly on the pursuing French until they, too, were obliged to fall back. The allies then pushed forwards, and reached the crest of the hill that had remained French until now. However, Tallard's infantry refused to yield further ground, bravely holding their position until Marlborough pushed forward his foot and artillery in support. Brigadier-General Kane was to recall, with masterly under-statement, the carnage that ensued: 'Our foot and Colonel Blood with nine field pieces came up, which kept [the enemy] employed.'[7]

One of Marlborough's lieutenant-generals was the Earl of Orkney, a veteran of the War of the League of Augsburg, who had been seriously wounded at the siege of Namur. He wrote of his role in this desperate sequence of fighting: 'By this time I had got over about nine battalions of foot which were left with me, and marched to sustain the horse, whom I found repulsed, calling out for foot, being pushed by the gendarmerie. I went to the head of several squadrons and got 'em to rally and form upon my right and left and brought up four pieces of cannon, and then charged both foot and horse. The [enemy] horse were put to flight.'[8] Tallard had not had the forethought to leave gaps in the second line of his cavalry, and a general confusion engulfed the French forces. The repulsed squadrons wheeled back and forth in front of their unyielding colleagues. The ensuing pandemonium gave the allies the opportunity to steal more ground, their advance up the hill gathering momentum.

Another of Blenheim's ominous pauses now ensued, eventually punc-tuated by the long-range opportunism of both sides' cannon and the renewed duel of their musketry. Exhausted men prepared for the next phase of battle. Captain Blackader looked to his religion to summon his remaining energy: 'During all the little intervals of action, I kept looking to God for strength and courage, and had a plentiful through-bearing, both to keep up my own heart, and help to discharge my duty well in my station.' [9]

The cavalry remained in limbo for 'some time, neither advancing against the other'.[10] The two forces were taking this opportunity to regroup, both assuming that the next attack would come from the allies. To counter this, Tallard pushed his reserve battalions forward. He hoped that their line volleys would prove as effective against Marlborough's horse as the allies' platoon-fire had been against his own. However, Tallard's second line of cavalry, in which his infantry was embedded, was gradually forced to retreat. The foot were left exposed to the combined attacks of Marlborough's infantry and artillery. The allied cavalry hovered, waiting for its chance to hack down the remnants of the force.

These French and Italian foot units – the brigades of Robecq, Belleisle, and Beuil – were filled with novice soldiers; but these young men had shown an unswerving discipline already that day. Now they remained in formation as Colonel Blood sent Captain Gibbons and his cannon into position, 'within half a musket's shot of the enemy's position', and fired 'cartouche shot upon them, which was done with good success, and made a great slaughter of the enemy,' wrote Sandby: 'Notwithstanding this, they yet stood firm, and closed their ranks as far as they were broke: till this being terribly weakened, and put into disorder, they were forced to give way, and then our squadrons fell in among them, and scarce suffered any of 'em to get off, but cut them down in whole ranks, as they were shown lying after the battle was over.'[11] Their courageous stand was noted with pity and respect, on a day when hideous death was everywhere. Captain Robert Parker watched with sadness as the abandoned French foot soldiers were: 'cut to pieces to a man, such only excepted, as threw themselves down among the dead.'[12] The Earl of Orkney recalled the enemy infantry's final stand with the respect of a seasoned soldier: 'Their foot remained in *bataillon carré* in the best order I ever saw, till they were cut to pieces almost in rank and file.'[13]

Looking on, Tallard realised that the battle was almost certainly lost. His priority now was to prevent the complete destruction of his army. 'At this time Count Tallard rallied his broken cavalry behind some tents that were all this time standing in his camp,' recalled Sergeant Millner, 'and then seeing things in this desperate condition, resolved to draw off his dragoons and foot out of Blenheim, and sent orders by one of his Aid de Camps to Marshal Marsin at Overklaw [Oberglau], to face the enemy with some troops on the right of the said village, to keep them in play, and favour the retreat of his infantry that was in Blenheim.'[14] It was all in vain: the Blenheim garrison reported that it 'could neither help him or themselves',[15] for it was still pinned down by Cutts's massed infantry fire. Meanwhile Marsin 'sent him word, he had too much work on his own hands',[16] to offer any help. This response was in stark contrast to Eugène's generosity to Marlborough earlier in the engagement. Despite Tallard's entreaties, Marsin felt unable to send his colleague reinforcements, wrongly judging that Tallard's want could not exceed his own. Tallard was left to face the decisive moment of the battle alone.

MARLBOROUGH WATCHED AND WAITED. Now he judged that the enemy cannonade and fusillade were flickering in the face of his own concerted firepower. As one of his officers later wrote, the captain-general by now felt confident that the French cavalry, after repeated repulses, 'had no great stomach for renewing the battle, but rather seemed in a tottering condition.'[17] Marlborough beckoned to his men to follow him once more in attack, his sword raised as the trumpeters again sounded the charge. This time, it was not the extended stride of walking squadrons that confronted Tallard, but the allied cavalry at full trot, knee-to-knee, swords at the ready. This wall of horse and horsemen moved with ever-increasing speed and aggression and with an irresistible momentum. 'Those of the enemy presented their fusils at some distance, and upon discharging them, wheeled about, broke one another in pieces, and betook themselves to flight.'[18]

The sight of an entire French army fleeing the field had not been seen in Europe for over half a century. The allies could barely contain their disbelief at having trounced a nation for so long considered invincible. Even the *Maison du Roi*, Louis's Household Cavalry, wilted in the face of Marlborough's horsemen. Captain Parker later recalled the moment he realised that: 'The French fire was quite extinguished,' and 'they made not the least resistance, but gave way and broke at once. Our squadrons drove through the very centre of them, which put them to an entire rout.'[19] Marlborough now sought to maximise the effect of this unprecedented phenomenon, the Sun King's army in eclipse. He must drive home his advantage, and transform the French defeat into an undiluted humiliation.

THE VAST MAJORITY OF THE FRANCO-Bavarian fugitives attempted to head for nearby Höchstädt, the town that had lent its name to their victory over the allies ten months earlier. Marlborough despatched Hompesch and thirty squadrons to pursue them. Bothmar was sent to block their escape, but a few of the French cavalry succeeded in getting away: some forced their way through the brigadier-general's dragoons, while others used the contours of the ground to evade detection. However, the greater part of those seeking the safety of Höchstädt never reached it, plunging instead into the Danube. Panic, an inability to swim, and the river's width all combined to send thousands to their deaths. Their defeated comrades watched their drowning gasps from the river-bank.

Hompesch thundered on after the broken enemy. The French tried to regroup to face their pursuer, and formed a line after crossing the Brennen. But their morale was in shreds, and the sight of allied horse again closing in on them persuaded the cavalry to bolt for freedom. Two battalions of infantry laid down their arms, rather than die in futile resistance.

A SMALLER FORCE – PERHAPS 2,000 men – decided against the Höchstädt escape route. It tried to make, instead, for Sonderheim, via a
pontoon over the Danube. 'But the bridge', Captain Parker observed,
without emotion, '(as it frequently happens in such cases), broke under
the crowd that rushed upon it, and down they went. At the same time our
squadrons pursued close at their heels, cutting down all before them;
for in all such close pursuits, it is very rare that any quarter is given. In
short, they were almost all of them killed or drowned; and the few that
reached the far side of the river, were killed by the boors of the villages
they had burnt.'[20]

One of the survivors from this group of fugitives was Mérode-Westerloo. Since his dawn awakening by his head groom, he had had an active
day, which had reached its zenith when attacking Marlborough's final
advance. He had joined in this manoeuvre's initial success, 'and I had
the good luck to defeat my adversaries and push them back to the brink
of the stream.'[21] However, he had then experienced the rapid about-face
that overtook the French forces: having failed to spot the lines of allied
infantry poised close to the Nebel, he had unwittingly led his men to
within range of the enemy muskets before: 'they killed and wounded
many of our horses at thirty paces'.[22] Mérode-Westerloo's horse was
slain then, felled by two musket balls; but some sharp-eyed attendants,
recognising the count, had rescued him with a fresh mount.

He galloped on to Blenheim village in an attempt to bring some of
its stranded battalions into the central fighting zone. Frustrated by the
negativity of the French commander there, the count rejoined the main
action with the remnants of his scattered squadrons. They were successful against the Prince of Hesse's forces, but there was no time to
celebrate their advantage. It was now that the thumping wave of
Marlborough's main charge fell on Tallard's horse, sending Mérode-
Westerloo spinning away from the battlefield. He was then caught up
in the relentless rhythm of the allied cavalry assault:

Hordes of the enemy were pushing our flanks, and we soon found
ourselves faced by numerous squadrons on no less than three sides –

and we were borne back on top of one another. So tight was the press that my horse was carried along some 300 paces without putting hoof to ground, right to the edge of a deep ravine: down we plunged a good twenty feet into a swampy meadow; my horse stumbled and fell. A moment later several men and horses fell on top of me, as the remains of my cavalry swept by, all intermingled with the hotly pursuing foe. I spent several minutes trapped beneath my horse.

After managing to extricate himself from under his exhausted mount, Mérode-Westerloo pushed his way out from under a pile of dead and dying horses:

> I had barely found my feet when a passing hussar fired his pistol at me. The next moment a huge English horse grenadier – a whole head and shoulders taller than I – came up. He dismounted and came forward to take me prisoner in a leisurely way. I noticed his lack-adaisical air, and grasped my long sword, which was dangling from my wrist, keeping it pressed well into my side. When he was within two paces I lunged at him, but I then discovered my left knee was injured, so I stumbled and missed my stroke. The Englishman raised his sword to cut me down, but I parried his blow and ran my sword right through his body up to the hilt. I wrenched my blade free, but as he fell he slashed at me again, but only succeeded in cutting the thick edge of my boot, which did me no harm. I put my foot on his head and plunged my sword through his throat.'[23]

This time one of his valets rescued Mérode-Westerloo – with yet another horse – before falling dead, riddled with shots from Marlborough's rampaging cohorts. The count clung to the horse, and plunged it into the Danube, intent on making for Höchstädt. Once on land again, he removed his white cockade from his hat and relied on his indeterminate nationality to bluff his way through various allied units:

> When I reached some windmills on a small stream, not far from Höchstädt, some of these soldiers advised me not to go any closer, as the

enemy were still in possession of the town. I replied that we would soon have them all in our clutches, and pretended I was going closer for a reconnaissance. As I approached my objective, someone fired several shots at me, but I got past and into the town. Reaching the barrier, I walked my horse for a short distance before being challenged: "Who goes there?" "French general officer!," I replied. An officer then let me enter. I went into the square, where I found several French generals who had the nerve to tell me I was pretty late. I retorted that they, for their part, had arrived too soon. We then all had a drink at the fountain. [24]

TALLARD'S FLIGHT FROM THE battlefield proved less successful than Mérode-Westerloo's. After his desperate, final, rally behind his camp's tents, the marshal had found himself caught up in the rout and pushed down towards Sonderheim. He arrived at the bridge there, only to find it broken. Accompanied by several of his senior officers, he headed up the river towards Höchstädt, realising that he now had the unenviable choice of trying to swim the Danube, or surrendering to the encircling enemy. His mind was made up for him when a squadron of Hessian troopers surrounded his small but distinguished force as they approached a mill. One of them recognised the enemy commander by the Order of the Saint-Esprit that he had worn into battle. Tallard handed his sword in surrender to Lieutenant-Colonel de Boinenburg, the Prince of Hesse's aide-de-camp. He was immediately taken to Marlborough.

Bleeding from a wound in the hand, and shocked by news that his son had been gravely wounded, Tallard cut a very different figure to the French grandee who had dazzled the Court of St James's a few years earlier. The architect of the ill-fated Partition Treaty and the man who had informed William III – with an arrogant flourish – of his master's determination to accept Carlos II's Will, Count Tallard now had the ignominy of being a prisoner of war. Marlborough paid courteous attention to the marshal, and offered him use of his own carriage. Tallard accepted, and was escorted away to begin his captivity.

I<small>T WAS SIX O'CLOCK IN THE EVENING</small>; just one hour since Marlborough had ordered his troops forward in the crucial advance of the day. Surveying the destruction before him, and seeing signs that the Elector and Marsin were leaving the field, Marlborough called for paper and pen. An aide tore him a sheet from a book, on one side of which was a tavern bill. On the reverse the duke wrote one of the most celebrated field despatches of British military history. It was addressed to his wife, Sarah, and read:

> 'August 13 1704. – I have not time to say more, but to beg you will give my duty to the queen, and let her know her army has had a glorious victory. M. Tallard and two other generals are in my coach, and I am following the rest. The bearer, my aide-de-camp, Colonel Parke, will give her an account of what has passed. I shall do it in a day or two, by another more at large. – Marlborough'.

CHAPTER TWENTY-ONE

VICTORY

'My faith was so lively during the action, that I sometimes said within myself, Lord, it were easy for thee to cause thy angels to lay all these men dead on the place where they stand, or bring them in all prisoners to us. And for encouraging our regiment, I spoke it aloud, that we should either chase them from their post, or take them prisoners; and I cannot but observe the events at seven o'clock at night, when they laid down their arms to us.'

CAPTAIN BLACKADER

VICTORY WAS ASSURED BUT INCOMPLETE when Marlborough's aide-de-camp, Colonel Parke, left for England with the victory despatch. Marsin and the Elector were still fighting on even terms with Prince Eugène on the other wing; Marsin making some progress while the Elector was struggling to hold his own. Meanwhile, twenty-seven battalions of French soldiers continued to hold Blenheim village, many of them the cream of Louis's infantry. They were hemmed in, but they were still armed, spirited, and proud in a tradition of military glory that had forgotten how to recognise defeat. However, the destruction of Tallard's army had made the allied position insuperable. Marlborough now looked to capitalise on his troops' achievements at the centre of the engagement, by pushing home his advantage across the entire battlefield.

The Elector and Marsin immediately realised that Tallard's disintegration left their wing's right flank vulnerable. They swiftly transformed their battle plan from one of wearing attrition to urgent self-preservation. The Franco-Bavarians had been clinging on to their village strongholds of Oberglau and Lutzingen with admirable resolve. However, they had been increasingly hard-pressed by Eugène's latest advance. This, the fourth of the day for the Prussian and Danish infantry, had once more been inspired by the determined leadership of Eugène and Prince Leopold of Anhalt-Desau. Prince Leopold had led his men forward against the enemy ranks while carrying a banner aloft. Despite only having two squadrons of cavalry in support, Eugène's men had gradually gained the upper hand. The sight of Tallard's rout turned Marsin's and the Elector's barely tenable situation into one that threatened complete catastrophe.

The Bavarians were the first to feel the effect of Tallard's defeat. Marlborough called back some of his pursuing squadrons, and led them in a charge that hit the enemy's unprotected side: 'The army of the Elector, entirely unsupported, and taken in flank by the English, wavered in its turn,' Saint Simon chronicled in his secret diary. 'All the valour of the Bavarians, all the prodigies of the Elector, were unable to remedy the effects of this wavering. Thus was seen, at one and the same time, the army of Tallard beaten and thrown into the utmost disorder; that of the Elector sustaining itself with great intrepidity, but already in retreat; and that of Marsin charging and gaining ground upon Prince Eugène. It was not until Marsin learnt of the defeat of Tallard and of the Elector, that he ceased to pursue his advantages, and commenced his retreat.'[1]

The Elector and Marsin turned towards Lavingen, nine miles upstream, where there was a good crossing-point over the Danube. Their withdrawal was achieved with maximum efficiency, especially when one considers the shock the two commanders must have experienced at seeing Tallard's sudden and complete defeat, across to their right. Captain Parker was mightily impressed by the enemy duo's good generalship, in these most difficult of circumstances: 'they instantly, and with great dexterity and expedition, formed their troops into three columns, and marched off with the greatest despatch and order imaginable.'[2] Sandby also noticed the Elector 'retiring in very good order, but in great haste, with his squadrons and battalions interlined.'[3] Torching Oberglau and Lutzingen as they fell back, they used the smoke from the burning villages to screen their retreat.

However orderly their withdrawal, there can be no denying Marsin's and the Elector's defeat at Blenheim. They had failed to overwhelm a much smaller force, sent to attack them while they occupied a strong defensive position where their superior cannon were well placed to wreak maximum damage. Add to this the military experience and ability of the Elector of Bavaria, and one conclusion becomes clear: Marsin and the Elector failed, because a superior commander had denied them victory.

Eugène had stiffened the allied resistance and led by the example of his reckless personal courage. He deserves huge credit for holding his army together. He absorbed repeated reverses, each of which could have broken a lesser commander. The prince was still at the forefront, leading his infantry in their fourth push forward, when the Franco-Bavarians began their retreat. He had already forced the Bavarian extreme left-hand wing back beyond Lutzingen and was awaiting any further slackening in the enemy's resolve before pushing home his gains. Indeed, the Imperialists were making as good progress as the rough terrain would allow them when they saw the smoke rising above Oberglau and Lutzingen. A cry of triumph went up through their ranks, the men recognising the fires as signals of victory: the enemy was quitting the field of battle.

One of Eugène's nineteenth-century biographers wrote of the prince that he 'was one of those real generals who hold that a victory not followed up is a victory thrown away.'[4] The prince now ordered his men to reform, and to prepare to pursue the retreating enemy. He was adamant that the broken Franco-Bavarians should share the fate of their colleagues in the middle of the field: pursuit followed by capture or death. Eugène was unaware that Marlborough had despatched Hompesch's thirty squadrons of horse, to follow up their hounding of

Tallard's fugitives with an attack on Marsin's and the Elector's retreat. The inability of the two wings to communicate their intentions to one another now gave rise to the greatest stroke of luck that the vanquished experienced during the battle of Blenheim.

The disintegration of Tallard's army had been so sudden, and his colleagues' decision to retreat had followed so swiftly, that the allied commanders had been unable to coordinate their pursuit. Both wings were keen to maximise the advantage of the day before nightfall. However, the failing light, and the thick smoke from the torched villages, conspired to create a debilitating confusion. Hompesch could see Eugène's men 'at some distance behind the Elector and appearing to be part of his army'.[5] He stopped to check the identity of this force: if these troops were, as Hompesch not unreasonably suspected, Marsin's rear guard, then they might outflank his planned charge and destroy his squadrons. At the same time – again the victim of the evening gloom – Eugène faltered in his pursuit: he believed Hompesch's horsemen to be Franco-Bavarian. After all that his men had endured that day, and taking into account the small cavalry force still available to the prince, Eugène's caution is understandable.

By the time both allied generals realised their mistakes, it was too late: Marsin's troops – joined by the remnants of the Elector's men, and two fleeing battalions from Tallard's army (this latter force was eventually taken prisoner, near Höchstädt) – had already placed the marshy River Merselingen between themselves and the allies. If pursued now, in light that had turned from murky to poor, then another whole engagement beckoned, in circumstances that would not favour the attacker. Nobody wanted to risk diluting the massive victory that the allies already knew to be theirs. Besides, the allied troops were exhausted. They had not slept the night before, and their day of fighting had been preceded by hours of marching. Marsin and the Elector, egging their men on, managed to slip away from Blenheim without suffering the savaging that had ripped apart Tallard's army.

Captain Parker looked on the escape of Marsin and the Elector with magnanimity, and resignation: 'Our troops were much fatigued, and night drew on, all which favoured their retreat. Or perhaps it might rather be said, that Providence interposed, which seeing the slaughter of the day, thought it sufficient: otherwise few, if any, could have escaped.'[6] Eugène viewed it as inevitable that the enemy would elude his pursuit, after the rigours of the day. The Earl of Orkney recalled a conversation with Eugène after the battle, and, 'by what the Prince told me, he had enough to do with them, having repulsed several times, and been several times repulsed himself both horse and foot, especially the horse; but at last gained ground and forced them to retire, which they did in good order; nor did he think to push them too hard with his troops, who were much fatigued with the many engagements he had had.'[7] Only those who chose to disregard his troops' exertions earlier in the day could criticise Eugène for failing to follow through the victory.

AS HOMPESCH'S CAVALRY RODE OFF in pursuit of the broken enemy, General Charles Churchill and his twenty-three battalions moved to tighten the stranglehold on Blenheim village. This was now the only remaining point of French resistance on the entire plain. With him went two experienced lieutenant-generals, Orkney and Ingoldsby, who quickly crossed over the small river that bisected Blenheim. Before them lay a bastion bristling with troops, but also with indignation at its enforced isolation from the heart of the battle. The garrison was confused as to what had transpired elsewhere during the day. It had also been hampered by the inadequacies of its commander, the Marquis de Clérambault, who had been panicked by the ferocity of Cutts's assaults earlier and had pulled all the battalions that Tallard had placed in support of the village into Blenheim itself. As the afternoon progressed, Clérambault had rigidly insisted that this outsized force be kept inside the village perimeter. This was his blinkered interpretation of his order to hold Blenheim at all costs.

The result had been, from the first, militarily unsatisfactory, rendering idle many useful men. By the evening, Clérambault's actions threatened to turn the heavy defeat of Tallard's centre into a disaster for the French army. The Count of Mérode-Westerloo had noticed earlier in the afternoon that: 'The men were so crowded in upon one another that they could not even fire, let alone receive or carry out any orders. Not a single shot of the enemy missed its mark, whilst only those few of our men at the front could return the fire, and soon many of these were unable to shoot owing to exhaustion or their muskets exploding from constant use.' [8] Later Mérode-Westerloo rode across, to try to draw off a dozen of Blenheim's battalions. He intended to form a fresh defensive line along the banks of the Nebel as a bolster to Tallard's overextended forces. Mérode-Westerloo would support this new deployment with what remained of his cavalry squadrons, as well as with his four pieces of artillery. At first, his proposal was received with enthusiasm in Blenheim: 'The brigades of Saint-Ségond and Monfort were setting out to follow me,' the count recalled. However, when Clérambault heard of the plan, he rushed over to block the move, 'and shouting and swearing drove them back into the village'. [9]

Clérambault's insistence on confining his huge force to the village was to seal its fate. Blenheim made a very fine defensive position but a poor launching pad for offensive manoeuvres. Each time the French tried to quit the village, they failed: 'As they were necessarily thrown into confusion in getting over their trenches,' wrote Captain Parker, 'so before they could form into any order for attacking us, we mowed them down with our platoons in such numbers, that they were always obliged to retire with great loss; and it was not possible for them to rush out upon us in a disorderly manner, without running upon the very points of our bayonets.' [10] The allied troops denied the French an exit from Blenheim throughout the afternoon. Now, with Tallard captured and his cavalry in flight, it was time not merely to contain, but to kill or capture the twenty-seven battalions of Frenchmen still contained in the village.

THE FRENCH WERE NOT HELPED by the sudden loss of their commander, soon after Churchill's forces began to fan out around Blenheim. As far as his colleagues were concerned, Clérambault had simply and inexplicably disappeared. In fact he had realised that his nervous insistence on keeping his men so tightly bound inside the village had guaranteed Tallard's defeat. Overcome by the consequences of this ill judgement, Clérambault ordered his groom to accompany him to the Danube's edge, with two horses. These were to be used for escape, because the marquis could not swim. The groom went first, and made it safely to the far side of the river. Clérambault followed, 'But,' as Winston S. Churchill recorded, 'the swirl of the Danube mercifully extinguished a life for which there was no room on earth.'[11]

The groom later revealed that Clérambault had told him that, realising his military career had ended in disgrace, he intended to live as a hermit. More kindly, it was claimed in his defence that he was reconnoitring an avenue of escape for his men on the bank of the Danube when an allied cannon ball made his horse shy, hurling him into the river to his death. Whatever the reason, Clérambault's disappearance left the densely-packed, hard-pressed garrison of Blenheim leaderless. This at a time when the allies were tightening their grip around the part of the battlefield they had largely left alone while the main issue of the day was settled elsewhere.

GENERAL CHURCHILL'S TROOPS quickly closed down the escape routes from Blenheim village to the Danube. The vigorous efforts of Lord Cutts and his men had already pushed the French back into the core of the village. The Salamander's first line was close to the enemy entrenchments, and Sandby watched as it 'continually discharged in platoons, and the other lines relieved this, and each other successively.'[12] The extensive defensive limbs, constructed of overturned wagons, carts, and household furniture, were gradually abandoned, as the French sought refuge from Cutts's fire.

It was just after seven o'clock in the evening when Brigadier-General Webb and the Queen's Regiment were despatched to man one of these abandoned barriers. Their orders were to stop any of the garrison from fleeing to freedom. On taking up his position, Webb spread out his force so it also controlled the most direct path running from the village to the Danube. Instantly his decision paid off, for several hundred French soldiers were encountered slipping away down this route and were taken prisoner. It was a similar story with Prince George's Regiment: no sooner had they taken control of another track leading from Blenheim to the river, than they found themselves delivered of a large group of escapees.

Meanwhile Lord John Hay and his dragoon regiment duped the main body of French defenders. They maintained steady fire from high ground above the village, and were so deployed that the enemy thought them the advanced guard of a large detachment. In fact, they were all the troops the allies could muster at that time. Brigadier-General Ross simultaneously blocked off the opposite side of the village, with eight squadrons – five of dragoons, and three of horse – from Lumley's cavalry. General Churchill appreciated that the village must be taken before darkness, since a night breakout would be difficult to contain. Despite the men's exhaustion after a day of continually firing their muskets, he commanded the British Brigade to make a third frontal attack on the French stronghold. Churchill ordered Ingoldsby and Orkney to attack the village in flank and rear, while Cutts was told to make a simultaneous attack on the front, 'if his troops were not too much spread, or at least to make a feint of doing it'.[13]

Cutts's men went forward against the formidable weight of French muskets, past the piles of dead comrades who were strewn along the approaches to the village. This time they broke through the enemy defences and engaged in vicious hand-to-hand combat. Meanwhile Churchill sent Orkney and Ingoldsby to assault Blenheim from two other sides. Orkney had a mixed force of three infantry battalions, Hay's dragoons, the 5th Dragoons and four cannon. These guns were unable to cross the Maulweyer, the rivulet passing through Blenheim, but they provided helpful flanking fire from the far bank, which pounded the French. Churchill was hopeful that the strength of his three-pronged attack might wring a plea for surrender from the defendants.

The French were not yet thinking of capitulation. Many of them belonged to regiments that were the pick of Louis's army and were aware of the proud traditions inculcated by Le Tellier, Louvois, and Martinet. Furthermore, these isolated troops had yet to receive confirmation of the defeat of their main force, or word of the withdrawal of Marsin and the Elector. They remained determined in defence, expecting that their colleagues would soon come to their relief.

Orkney and Ingoldsby led their men into the concerted French fusillades. Both attacks penetrated the village perimeter, only to find strong resistance from every part of Blenheim. The French had transformed the high stone wall of the churchyard into a bastion of blazing musketry. Their firepower was so intense that the British were forced to retire. Before falling back, Orkney's men set light to the few buildings that remained intact. Allied cannon had fired furiously upon the village all afternoon, from 'within musket shot'. Marlborough's howitzers had added to Blenheim's devastation by igniting its barns and houses. Private John Marshall Deane, of the 1st Regiment of Foot Guards, wrote later of how he and his colleagues had 'fought our way into the village which was full of fire, and our men fought in and through the fire and pursued others through it, until many on both sides were burned to death.'[14] These flames pushed back the frightened defenders. They also provided Colonel Blood's gunnery officers with illumination in the evening gloom. French resolve started to waver.

An hour after Clérambault's absence was noted, Camp-Marshal Blansac took command of the village garrison. He had restored an element of discipline to an otherwise chaotic situation; but Blansac's was not a firm voice in a crisis. Deeply troubled by the plight of his men, and increasingly aware of the desperation of his position, Blansac looked for guidance from his marshal. He sent an aide-de-camp to find Tallard, to learn what he was expected to do. Being so isolated, Blansac was unaware that Tallard was already in Marlborough's carriage as a prized prisoner of war. He remained in the dark because his messenger was captured before completing his mission. Blansac was left frightened and confused in his position of unaccustomed authority.

Meanwhile Tallard learnt of the sorry predicament of the French troops in Blenheim. The captured marshal sent word to Marlborough, with a suggestion: Tallard would command his garrison to lay down its arms, provided Marlborough guaranteed the defeated men safe passage from the battlefield. Marlborough's inner steel briefly flashed bright in his reply to this proposal: 'Inform Monsieur de Tallard that in the position in which he now is, he has no command.'[15]

There was to be no respite for the French now. Orkney's men resumed the attack with torches blazing and muskets and bayonets poised. 'This we could easily perceive annoyed them very much,'[16] the earl dryly observed. Giving way to the pressure from all sides, two French brigades – the *Régiment Royal* and Saint-Ségond's regiment – tried to flee Blenheim, but they were quickly surrounded. Orkney, facing the trapped *Régiment Royal*, exhorted the French to lay down their arms. As he did so, he tried hard to hide his concern at the enormous number of enemy soldiers that he could see inside Blenheim. He had had no idea that the village contained so many thousands. Equally, he was frightened that his exhausted men would not be able to fight on for much longer. He sent his aide-de-camp, Sir James Abercrombie, to parley with the enemy. 'Upon which,' Abercrombie later wrote, 'I rode up to the Royal Regiment and pulled the colours out of the ensign's hands, and was slightly wounded by him. I asked them if they did not hear what the general offered; but his lordship was come up by this time, without giving any fire, and ordered them to lay down their arms, which they did, asking quarter.'[17]

The brigadier-general commanding the *Régiment Royal* was the Marquis Denonville. A great favourite of the Duke of Burgundy's, the handsome and outspoken Denonville agreed to immediate surrender, provided his men were treated with respect, and not plundered. Orkney readily accepted this condition, for he was eager to achieve a swift conclusion to the fighting. The Frenchmen laid down their arms, and joined the swelling bank of prisoners of war.

Further success followed with the men of Saint-Ségond's brigade, a new creation formed in 1702 in Agen and Condom; and one of the units that Mérode-Westerloo had tried to extricate from the village earlier in the day. They surrendered on similar terms to their colleagues. Ingoldsby next sent Lieutenant-Colonel Belleville, a Huguenot officer, to parley with the French. Belleville emerged from Blenheim with his own brother – a French dragoon captain – as well as Blansac, and another general. While both sides sought a mutually acceptable end to the fighting, Orkney spoke to the senior officers among the French prisoners. He was perturbed to find that his fears about the enemy's numbers were well-founded: 'After having taken these two brigades, I enquired of Mon. De Nonville what remained in the village. St-Ségonde answered more than twenty battalions and twelve squadrons of dragoons, which I own struck me, since I had not above seven battalions and four squadrons commanded by Brigadier Ross, which were of great use to me. However, I made the best countenance I could and desired the same brigadier to return along with my ADC to the Marquis de Blansac, marishal de camp, who commanded the whole (Monsieur Clérambault lieutenant-general being drowned), [to ask if he] would come out and speak with me.'[18]

Orkney aimed to bluff the senior French officers. They must believe their situation so desperate that surrender became the only option. If Blansac and his commanders realised that the allies were fully extended in a thin encirclement of the village, they would undoubtedly elect to fight on. Furthermore, a mass break-out would be impossible to contain. The Count of Mérode-Westerloo later wrote that the key to this contest within a contest would have been: 'organising the twenty-seven battalions and fourteen dragoon regiments into a square to fight their way out. Good infantry, well disciplined and highly trained, could easily have done this.'[19]

Fortunately for the allies, Denonville proved to be a willing and malleable go-between. With surprising ease Orkney convinced the Frenchman that his mission was noble and humanitarian: it was for him, as an officer of high rank, to deliver his men from certain death. What else could await them, when the might of Marlborough's army was unleashed against the village's battered defences? To underline his point, Orkney made much of the fate that had befallen Tallard's main force earlier in the day. There was no need, surely, for the French to suffer further huge casualties when their cause was clearly lost? What use to Louis were dead soldiers when survivors might have the chance to fight for him another day? They might be able to retrieve their reputations in more promising circumstances; but they could achieve nothing if dead.

Denonville returned to Blenheim a convert to the need for total and immediate surrender. Abercrombie rode beside him, waving a handkerchief to signal the continuing ceasefire. To the diarist Saint Simon's disgust, the bumptious French brigadier-general betrayed his cause immediately on re-entering the village: 'Instead of speaking in private to Blansac and the other principal officers – since he had undertaken so strange a mission – Denonville, who had some intellect, plenty of fine talk, and a mighty opinion of himself, set to work haranguing the troops, trying to persuade them to surrender themselves prisoners of war, so that they might preserve themselves for the service of the King.'[20] The effect was immediate: many of the soldiers, harried by Churchill's three-pronged attack, unnerved by the howitzers, and accepting the evidence of wider defeat, chose self-preservation over needless self-sacrifice. Blansac shouted at his men not to listen to Denonville, but to resume their defence of the stronghold. However, only the distinguished regiment of Navarre, to whom the thought of surrender was anathema, applauded their commander's words of defiance.

Abercrombie witnessed the demoralising effect of Denonville's words with quiet relief. He then made his way through to the far side of Blenheim, where he slipped back into the allied ranks, asking to be taken to Lord Cutts. Abercrombie advised Cutts to halt his attacks immediately, since the French seemed certain to capitulate. Cutts stood his force down from what would have been their fifth attack of the day. The British infantry commanders then waited to see what their French counterparts would decide to do.

BLANSAC CALLED HIS SENIOR OFFICERS to a council of war, hoping to form a consensus on how best to proceed. A heated debate followed, the participants divided between fighting till the death, or mass surrender.

Orkney now rode forward and requested a meeting with the French acting commander. He confirmed to Blansac that the French were completely surrounded, that Tallard's army had been destroyed and that the Elector and Marsin were in headlong retreat. The camp-marischal should disabuse himself of the hope that anyone would be riding to his assistance. Orkney advised Blansac again to consider his duty, in these desperate circumstances. In a calculated gamble the earl then claimed: 'that the Duke of Marlborough ... was already above a leg in pursuit of their horse, and that he [had] sent me word that I should have twenty battalions to sustain me, with all our cannon.' The earl was to record of his ruse: 'It bore weight, and made us soon finish matters; though,' he later conceded, ruefully, 'to tell truth, it was a little gasconade in me.'[21]

It was nine o'clock at night when the Blenheim garrison finally lay down its arms. The entire force – twenty-seven battalions of infantry, four regiments of dragoons and half a battalion of bombardiers – became prisoners of war. In protest at such shame, the soldiers of the Navarre regiment burned their colours. In several other units the men buried their weapons, while some officers refused to add their signatures to the declaration of surrender. Symbolic acts of resistance were futile. The truth was that many of Louis's most feared military units – not only the regiment of Navarre, but also those of Languedoc, and the celebrated *Régiment du Roi* – were now captive. 'Without vanity,' Orkney wrote, when looking back at this feat, 'I think we did our part.'[22]

As the British began to process their 10,000 prisoners from the village, Durelle, one of Marlborough's aides-de-camp, appeared. He had come directly from the captain-general's side. Unaware of the latest developments, Durelle passed on Marlborough's urgent instructions: Blenheim village must be sealed up for the night, with every avenue of escape plugged. The attack could resume in the morning. Durelle was informed that this would not be necessary: Blenheim had already fallen.

PART FIVE

THE AFTERMATH

CHAPTER TWENTY-TWO

'QUE DIRA LE ROI?'

*'News of the defeat was received at the same moment that
the celebratory bonfire in honour of the Duchess of
Burgundy was being prepared, the engraving of which
I have sent to you. As the weather seemed to be tending to
rain, the men charged with watching over the fireworks set
about covering them. A passer-by, seeing them stretching
out their cloths, shouted at them: what are you doing?
One of them replied immediately: "We are packing up the
bonfire to send it to the Emperor, there's no longer any
need for it here".'*

LETTER OF *MADAME*, SISTER-IN-LAW OF LOUIS XIV,
31 AUGUST 1704

THE FALL OF THE VILLAGE MARKED the end of the battle of Blenheim.
The casualties had been high for the allies: 4,542 killed and 7,942
wounded. Of these, the largest proportion – 2,234 out of their 10,786
combatants – fell to the British; this on top of the losses sustained at
the Schellenberg, six weeks earlier. Nearly 300 out of the 716
British officers present were either killed or wounded. The losses of
individual regiments reveal where the fighting had been at its harshest:
Rowe's, Ingoldsby's and Howe's infantry regiments, so instrumental
in closing down the enemy position at Blenheim village, lost two-thirds
of their officers; while Wood's, Wyndham's and Schomberg's dragoon

295

guards, active in the centre of the battlefield, lost half of theirs.

Unlike the Schellenberg, the list of senior allied officers killed was limited. The Prince of Holstein-Beck was recaptured from the French, but he was miserably wounded and died soon after. Brigadier-General Rowe was likewise mortally injured. Major-General Count Noailles, and Brigadier-Bielk, a Dane, were killed outright during the fight. Lord North and Grey was seriously wounded, but survived. Lieutenant-Colonel Dormer, a bookish and popular soldier, died in Sandby's arms at six that evening, three hours after being shot in the thigh. He haemorrhaged to death, in agony.

Among the minor casualties was Captain Blackader, who had been confident that God would watch over him that day. He 'got a small touch of a wound in the throat' during the second of Cutts's infantry charges on Blenheim village. Surprisingly, for a time of medical ignorance, such wounds were correctly considered quite unimportant: 'All the Ancients agree in this,' wrote the French Surgeon-Major, Belloste, 'that wounds of the neck, though passing quite through, are easily enough cured, provided the great vesels, and spinal marrow be not hurt.'[1] Blackader's was just such a wound.

The captain reached a characteristicly dour conclusion as to why his compatriots had suffered such grave losses: 'This victory has indeed cost a great deal of blood, especially to the English,' he wrote. 'I was always of opinion that the English would pay for it in this country; and when I consider, how, on all occasions, we conquer, yet with much blood spilt, I am at a loss to know what the reason may be. Perhaps it is that our cause is good, and therefore God gives us success in our enterprises, but our persons very wicked, and therefore our carcasses are strewed like dung upon the earth in Germany.'[2]

For the French and Bavarians, the casualty figures made for doleful reading. Marlborough intercepted reports sent from Duttlingen to the French court by survivors. These conceded that 40,000 of Louis's and the Elector's men had been killed, wounded or captured at Blenheim. Among these were 3,000 German mercenaries, from Greder's and Zurlauben's regiments. They became turncoats after their surrender, rather than face imprisonment for the remainder of the war. Marsin recorded that all that was left of the Franco-Bavarian army were the 62 squadrons and 31 battalions that now followed him to Ulm and Augsburg. This was less than 20,000 men – a third of the force that had contested the field – and many of these were wounded. Perhaps most revealing is the statistic calculated by Marlborough's biographer, Archdeacon Coxe: of the 4,500 Franco-Bavarian officers who fought at Blenheim, only 250 were not killed, wounded, or captured.

The number of prisoners – 'infinite', in Saint Simon's estimation – was too great to be processed immediately, so: 'The British troops at Blenheim formed a lane wherein the prisoners stood all night, and they on the watch over the same.'[3] Orkney was so encumbered with captive generals that he was obliged to hand over his quarters to some of them. He had no roof over his head again until he reached the allied camp at Munster. Marlborough's last order of the day reflected the massive number of prisoners that had been taken: all allied soldiers were to sleep on their weapons, in case there was an attempted break-out by the captives. It was still barely comprehensible to the high command that so many of Louis's proud army had laid down their arms rather than fight on.

IN RECOGNITION OF THE ARTILLERY'S heroic exertions throughout the battle, Marlborough ordered Colonel Blood to collect and sort through the battle's spoils. The capture of 129 colours and 110 standards reflected the enormity of the French defeat. Sergeant Millner itemised the rest of the plunder: 'seventeen pair of kettle-drums, fifteen pontoons, twenty-four barrels, eight cases of silver, thirty-four fine coaches, three hundred loaded mules, and three thousand six hundred tents, standing or struck.'[4] The allies used the enemy's tents for cover that night. They were delighted to find that they contained great quantities of herbs and cabbage. And nearer to the Danube there lay about 100 fat oxen ready skinned, which were to have been delivered on this day to the enemy's army. 'These', noted Josias Sandby, 'were no unwelcome booty to our soldiers.'[5]

While they dug in for the night, the allies tended their many wounded. 'And now,' Sandby noted, 'His grace took an especial care to have all the wounded men sent to the hospital. For this purpose he ordered all the country round about to bring in wagons and carriages, upon pain of military execution, and the sergeants of all the regiments were commanded to take up and send away their own men.' [6] Less respect was shown for the dead: as Marlborough rode towards his accommodation in a nearby mill, he noted that pillagers had already stripped every body on the field, allied or enemy.

Hompesch, the Prussian lieutenant-general in charge of the Dutch cavalry, wrote his report for the States-General on the night of the battle. He recorded how the French prisoners were bewildered by the astonishing reverse their army had suffered. They had begun the day willing the allies to attack, so confident were they in their defensive position. Now they were victims of one of the most comprehensive defeats in French military history. In his despatch Hompesch underlined the personal courage of the leading allied generals in their glorious triumph: 'The Duke of Marlborough gave his orders for this enterprise with great steadiness. He was everywhere in the heat of battle, and acted in all things with great presence of mind. Prince Eugène for his part did all that he could do; and the Prince of Hesse-Cassel was also in the heat of all the action, and greatly distinguished himself.' [7] Hompesch was too modest to mention his own part in the victory: he had inspired his men during the crossing of the Nebel, and his final cavalry pursuit killed and captured many Franco-Bavarian fugitives before they could escape the battlefield.

The prize trophy of the day, Marshal Tallard, was moved from Marlborough's coach to the Prince of Hesse's quarters. Here he received a late visit from Marlborough, Eugène, and Wratislaw; the three men whose combined efforts, military and diplomatic, had brought about his defeat. Several of the senior allied generals were also present at this encounter; as well as Josias Sandby, General Churchill's chaplain, who has left an eyewitness account: 'Reaching the Marshal's quarters, they found him very much dejected, and wounded in one of his hands. His grace humanely inquired how far it was in his power to make him easy under his misfortune, offering him the convenience of his quarters, and the use of his coach. The Marshal thankfully declined the offer, saying, he did not desire to move, till he could have his own equipage.'[8] During the hour's conversation that followed, Tallard insisted that he and the Elector had planned to engage the allies on 14 August. He also confirmed that he would have struck on the 12th, had it not been for the false testimony of the 'prisoners' planted by Marlborough. Their claims that Prince Lewis of Baden had linked up with the main allied force had dissuaded Tallard from attack: Marlborough's simple subterfuge had worked.

THE CAPTAIN-GENERAL'S OTHER conspiracy, readily entered into with Prince Eugène, had involved Prince Lewis of Baden. They had managed to keep him away from the crux of the campaign, immersed in the siege of Ingolstadt. With the Franco-Bavarian force soundly defeated, there was no hope of rescue for Ingolstadt's defenders: it was evident that Baden was to achieve his ambition of taking this previously unconquered city. However, this was no consolation for the prince when he learnt of his colleagues' glorious victory. Participation in a triumph such as Blenheim would have rescued his compromised military reputation. Now, instead of being party to the battle honours, he realised that Marlborough and Eugène had forfeited 15,000 men to guarantee his absence, preferring to be outnumbered than saddled with him. His anger resonated throughout Europe.

The Count of Mérode-Westerloo heard it, in the French camp: 'At this time we learnt of the fall of Ingolstadt and of Prince Lewis's rage when he learned of the trick Prince Eugène and the Duke of Marlborough had played him. It is quite certain that there would have been no battle had the Prince been with them; he was not the sort to risk all to gain all. If no battle had taken place, the English could hardly have wintered in Germany, and I don't know what might have befallen before they could have returned, as we would have enjoyed superiority of numbers.'[9] Baden presented himself as a man robbed of a share of the victory laurels. His enduring bitterness was intensified by pain from the foot that had been badly wounded at the storming of the Schellenberg.

He never forgave Marlborough and Eugène. Even when they flattered Baden by asking him to judge the fair division of their prisoners, he remained hostile and distant towards the two commanders who were now the toast of the Grand Alliance.

THE ALLIED HIGH COMMAND designated the first Sunday after the battle a day of Thanksgiving. Marlborough wrote to his wife: 'This day the whole army has returned their thanks to Almighty God for the late success, and I have done it with all my heart; for never victory was so complete, notwithstanding that they were stronger than we, and very advantageously posted. But believe me, my dear soul, there was an absolute necessity for the good of the common cause to make this venture, which God has so blessed.'[10]

After their religious service, the allied troops enjoyed traditional, martial, celebrations: a volley of muskets was followed by a triple discharge of cannon. Tallard and his three senior captive officers were obliged to ride out to see the victory festivities. The marshal, an extremely reluctant witness to the proceedings, was nevertheless granted the honour of inspecting the troops. Marlborough, who had ordered his men to pay Tallard the same level of respect that they showed to him, watched as the allied officers saluted their enemy commander as he passed. Marlborough then asked Tallard how he liked the look of the allied troops. Tallard shrugged and replied gracelessly: 'Very well, but they have had the honour of beating the best troops in the world.' Marlborough retorted tartly: 'What will the world think of the troops that beat them?'[11]

Tallard's army was destroyed at Blenheim. Sergeant Millner calculated that: 'It appears that not one of the forty battalions, with which Count Tallard joined the Elector of Bavaria some few days before the battle, escaped; ten thereof were entirely cut to pieces in the intervals of their horse, in the heat of the action: two taken in their precipitate retreat to the other side of Höchstädt, and twenty-eight taken prisoner of war in the village of Blenheim.'[12] Marlborough met some of the captives from Tallard's force, and enjoyed a memorable encounter with a disgruntled private. 'If the King of France had many men like you,' the duke said, 'he would soon be victorious.' The soldier, within earshot of some of his superiors, replied: 'It is not men like me he lacks, but a general like you.'[13]

The French officers smarted with humiliation. Josias Sandby was instructed by General Churchill to 'take a list of the French generals and other officers', and walked into a room containing sixty or seventy men of middling and junior rank, of which 'some were blaming the conduct of their own Generals, others were walking with their arms folded, others were laid down lamenting their hard fortune and complaining of want of refreshments, till at last, abandoning all reflections of this nature, their chief concern was for their king, abundance of them muttering and saying, "Oh que dira le roi?".'[14]

AT FIRST THE KING DID NOT KNOW what to say, for there was marked hesitation in informing His Majesty of what had transpired on the Danube. 'The true account of this battle was concealed from old Lewis [Louis] for some time,' related Captain Robert Parker, 'but when he came to know the truth of it, he was much cast down; it being the first blow of any fatal consequence, his arms had received, during his long reign.'[15] There were initial rumblings that a battle had taken place at Höchstädt, and that the outcome had not been as favourable as that of its predecessor. However, beyond that, there was silence.

Eventually, eight days after the battle, a despatch arrived from Villeroi, giving bald confirmation of defeat: 'By this courier the King learnt that a battle had taken place on the 13th; had lasted from eight o'clock in the morning until evening; that the entire army of Tallard was killed or taken prisoners; that it was not known what had become of Tallard himself, or whether the Elector and Marsin had been at the action.'[16] Louis, impatient to learn more, insisted that all letters home from participants in the battle be opened and read by his agents, so that a more complete picture of the humiliation could be pieced together. He wrote anxiously to Marsin: 'Cousin, the news I have received from Stuttgart, from Basle, and from various towns along the Rhine, added to the large number of letters from my army officers who are prisoners of war leaves me no room to doubt that an action took place at Höchstädt on the 13th, in which the enemy must have gained a considerable advantage. I do not understand how it is possible that I have not had any news about this from you, neither from Marshal Tallard. I will wait for it keenly, and I very much hope that matters are not in as bad a state as the enemy has made out; give me the detail, as soon as you can.'[17]

When the scale of the disaster was established, Louis was distraught. 'The grief of the King at this ignominy, and this loss, at the moment when he imagined that the fate of the Emperor was in his hands, may be imagined.'[18] He shielded the depth of his despair from all but his most intimate confidants. One day, when the courtiers had retired, Louis turned to his mistress, Madame de Maintenon, and asked her what she made of the massive defeat. Her view was that Louis must submit more to the will of God; then he would be immune from such reverses. The king seemed distracted: 'Ah! Madame, thirty battalions of French prisoners of war!' As he reflected on this humiliation, Louis looked up to see that one of his priests had arrived, to offer consolation. 'Father!' he said, 'It is not possible always to be lucky: God is punishing France, and it is necessary for us to submit to his will.'[19]

THE COURT GREETED NEWS OF THE defeat less philosophically. Louis's sister-in-law, *Madame*, reacted to the first inklings of disaster with disbelief: 'Someone has just told me some strange and bad news. I think my people have misunderstood; they say that the enemy have captured twenty-six of Marshal Tallard's battalions, and they are not sure that he himself was not taken. In this state, Marshal Tallard will hardly be able to render service to the Elector of Bavaria. I understand nothing by this news. The word also is that the Elector of Bavaria has beaten ten thousand men, but no one knows yet where or how; time will tell.'[20]

Consternation was the theme. Courtiers learned of sons and brothers who had been taken prisoner, wounded, or killed. There was widespread sympathy for Marshal de Clérambault, whose son's death was learnt of, before his disgrace was understood. The old marshal had only one other son, a celibate priest, so his loss was thought particularly cruel, for it marked the end of the family line. The Princess de Conti was stricken by the death of her youngest cousin, le chevalier de la Vallière. Mothers bustled around Versailles, eager for information about their sons. 'The commotion was general', according to Saint Simon: 'There was scarcely an illustrious family that had not had one of its members killed, wounded, or taken prisoner.'[21] Gradually the mood changed from sadness to censure: 'The public sorrow and indignation burst out without restraint. Nobody who had taken part in this humiliation was spared; the generals and the private soldiers alike came in for blame.'[22]

Marshal Villars had no time for apologists who sought to exonerate the defeated:

> What better could the Blenheim troops have done, say some idiots, than to surrender in order to save themselves for the King! I reply to them like ancient Horace, learning that his son had taken flight; and I say like Corneille to those who ask me, 'What do you wish this corps to have done?'
>
> > Let it die,
> Rather than save itself in a keen despair.
>
> It is thus that at the battle of Rocroi, the Spanish infantry, commanded by the old Count of Fuentes, preferred to perish rather than ask for quarter. Shouldn't the soldiers and officers at least have attempted to open a path for themselves, sword in hand, and shouldn't they have preferred a glorious death to the shame of dying of starvation in a prison? I blush for the French for such dishonourable conduct.'[23]

Survivors of the defeat were quick to apportion blame. Baron de Montigny Langnat, wounded at Blenheim, wrote twelve days after the battle: 'It is certain that the *gendarmerie* and the cavalry of M. Tallard are the cause of the loss of this great battle; as well as the fact that we had too many battalions on our right [in the village], and those in the centre missed them.'[24] There was also strident criticism of Tallard's belief that the Nebel would dissuade the enemy from attacking in the first place: it was a stream, not a river. The marshal was seen to have compounded his mistake by failing to use the Nebel as a defensive line during the battle. Why had he allowed the enemy to cross? Why, also, had he committed so many battalions to the defence of Blenheim village?

Marlborough allowed Tallard to give his own account of the defeat. The Marquis de Silly was granted a two-month licence, during which time he was to relay the marshal's words to Louis XIV, before reverting to his imprisonment of war. In early September Tallard followed up this representation with a written account of the battle, addressed to Chamillart. This contained a broad examination of the failings of his men and his allies, with barely an acknowledgement that his generalship might be to blame. 'The heavy cavalry did badly, I have to say very badly, because they never broke one squadron of the enemy,' Tallard wrote, before adding: 'I saw besides an instant in which the battle was won by the brigade of Robuq and that of Albaret [who were part of the 9 battalions that were cut down in Marlborough's decisive charge] if the cavalry that had been pushed forward nearer the enemy than it had been before, for the protection of the infantry, had not suddenly turned, and abandoned this poor infantry.' [25]

Tallard was particularly critical of the Elector: he had found Maximilian Emmanuel every bit as obstructive as the exasperated Villars had said he had been during the 1703 campaign: 'This shows clearly, sir,' Tallard wrote to Chamillart, 'what is the effect of such diversity of counsel, which makes public all that one intends to do, and it is a severe lesson never to have more than one man at the head of an army. It is a great misfortune to have to deal with a prince of such a temper as the Elector of Bavaria.' [26] The Elector's reluctance to bring his troops to the front was indicative of a profound selfishness: 'In addition, there was the total ignorance of the enemy's strength, and the Elector of Bavaria having all his troops, except five battalions and about twenty-three squadrons, spread about the country to cover his salt-works, a gentleman's private estate in fact, instead of what they should have guarded – his frontiers.' [27]

The Court heard Tallard's words with embarrassment and suspicion. He was responsible for a military calamity that had touched all their lives.

A WEEK AFTER HIS CAPTURE, Tallard set off under guard for England. He had asked to be imprisoned there, because he knew the country well from his time as ambassador, and because he felt confident that Marlborough would see he was well-treated: it had quickly been noted by the French that the duke's prisoners were better looked after than those allotted to the Imperialists. Sergeant Millner recorded how: 'Count Tallard, with the rest of our share of prisoners of distinction, etc., were sent from Höchstädt under a guard of forty English horse, towards Hanau and Frankfurt.'[28] *Madame* wrote to a friend how her half-sister Amèlie had visited most of the captured officers, as they passed through Frankfurt, but: 'Tallard did not want to see her. She writes that he is talking to himself; something he has only done all of his life. Thus, at the king's supper, he likes to stand up and start to speak all alone. The Duchess of Burgundy and I often laughed about it last winter.'[29] Tallard, for so long an awesome Court figure, was now subject to ridicule. He was depicted as a partridge that had buried its head in the sand when confronted by the allied assault. He should have acted decisively and strongly. Instead, it was said that he had panicked.

The English formed a similar view of Tallard's responsibility for the outcome of Blenheim. Captain Richard Pope, in the aftermath of victory, wrote home: 'To give you my opinion how this great matter was brought about – next to overruling Providence – it is owing to two things: first, a very good disposition of our troops, which, as it is reported here, was concerted betwixt my Lord Duke and Prince Eugène only; and, secondly, a very great fault committed by Marshal Tallard.'[30]

Meanwhile Tallard and his senior officers continued on their way to English imprisonment. A docket details their final journey:

'London the 16th December, 1704.
This day the Mareschal de Tallard with the other French officers that came over with him in the Katherine and William and Mary yachts landed at the Dock Yard at Blackwall, from whence, after having been Entertain'd at Dinner they set out in the afternoon in several Coaches provided for them for Barnet in their way to Nottingham and Lichfield, where Her Majesty has thought fit they should Reside.' [31]

Tallard was destined for Nottingham. With him went the cream of his officers: the general of horse, the Marquis de Monperoux; the general of dragoons, the Marquis de Hautefeuille; and the commander of Blenheim village, the Comte de Blanzac. There were also five titled major-generals, and two brigadier-generals – one of them Saint-Ségond, who had been compromised by Ingoldsby and Orkney when attempting a break-out from Blenheim. Seventeen other senior officers were sent to Lichfield. A further nine waited to find out which of the two towns was to be their gaol. Among this group was Denonville, whose disgrace in France had been complete: Louis knew of the weasel words with which he had exhorted an entire army to surrender, and stripped the marquis of his commission. The king cashiered a further fourteen brigadiers, and two *maréchaux de camp*. However, he never publicly criticised Tallard for his part in the defeat.

There was much interest in England in the high-ranking prisoners. A year after they had passed through Market Harborough on their way north to Nottingham, their innkeeper was to recall: 'The French gentlemen have all their victuals dressed by their own cooks, who make in particular excellent soup. They travelled but few miles in a day, having a great equipage with them.'[32] On reaching Nottingham, Tallard resided in Newdigate House, for which he paid a fifty-shilling weekly rent. A pretty house, it was a far cry from the sumptuous ambassadorial residence that he had enjoyed when previously in England. However, a man called Bailey, writing in Nottingham in 1853, recalled that: 'The Count here cultivated a very beautiful garden, which was the admiration of the whole neighbourhood for the variety and splendour of the flowers grown therein, as well as for the taste and elegance of the design with which it was laid out.'[33] Tallard's famed love of soup led him to cultivate root vegetables. He sent his chefs to look for suitable plants for his kitchen garden. They were delighted to find wild celery growing locally and thus Tallard, marshal of France, is widely credited with having introduced the delights of celery to England's northern Midlands.

The marshal became known locally as 'the Great Man at Nottingham'. Daniel Defoe, passing through a generation later, noted that

Tallard's legacy was not merely horticultural: '''Tis said, likewise, that this gallant gentleman left behind him here some living memorandum of his great affection and esteem for the English ladies.'[34] He had plenty of time to develop such relationships. Writing to Marlborough a month after arriving in Nottingham: 'You do not doubt, Sir, that I desire my liberty, [and] I am ready to enter into all the expedients that will be able to procure it, be that by ransom or some other means.'[35] He remained a prisoner until 1711.

MARSIN'S AND THE ELECTOR'S retreat was uncomfortable. From Blenheim, they headed for Ulm. They took with them 1,000 wounded officers and 6,000 wounded men. Mérode-Westerloo, despite three injuries, regrouped what he could find of his Flemish forces: 'I could not hold myself responsible for what might happen if we came within a mile of Prince Eugène, for the troops in their present nervous condition were likely to bolt if a hare got up. I then marched on: midnight tolled from Lavingen as we passed by. There the Elector's cavalry caught up with me. We pressed on in complete silence until daybreak, when I calculated we had put some eight miles between ourselves and the enemy, after passing very close to his right wing.'[36] He left the infantry and baggage behind, and 'At last we reached Ulm about seven in the evening and marched into the town, trumpets and kettle-drums playing. The day's march had been no less than 42 miles. I went to rest after being in the saddle for thirty hours with neither sleep nor food, and only one drink of water.'[37] The count was fortunate to reach safety. 'Most of them', Sandby noted, of the retreating Franco-Bavarians, 'never reached so far as Ulm, for both Gondelfingen and most of the villages our army marched through were full of graves.'[38]

At Ulm, Marsin and the Elector rested for three days, before leaving behind nine lesser battalions, who had particularly suffered at Eugène's hand. To them were entrusted the worst of the wounded: they were instructed to negotiate terms with the pursuing allies, which must include provision for these injured men. Among them was the Marquis de la Beaume, Tallard's son. Marlborough asked the French to hand him over, so he could be reunited with his father and treated by allied doctors. He was surrendered, but his injuries were severe and he died soon afterwards.

Marsin pushed on westward from Ulm, his pace quicker now that he had jettisoned the seriously wounded, but he was still harried all the way: 'All our hussars, with several parties of horse, went in pursuit of them,' Sandby noted, 'and they with the country boors cut off all that could not keep up with their army. So that there was yet a greater slaughter made of them, than appeared at first.'[39] Marshal Villeroi came to the aid of this broken army. Louis had ordered him to attack the Lines of Stollhofen; but he ignored the king and set off to help his colleagues. Ten days after the battle, on 23 August, Villeroi met up with Marsin and the Elector and found them at the head of just 16,000 men – 13,000 French and 3,000 Bavarian. They had scrambled across the Black Forest in disarray. Now the presence of Villeroi's army imparted a modicum of discipline to their ranks, without staunching the haemorrhage of casualties that followed heavy defeat. By the end of the month, 12,000 survivors reached the Rhine, and crossed over to Strasbourg. This was all that was left of the three armies who were supposed to have stolen the Imperial crown. Unaware of what had transpired a few days earlier, one of Louis's advisers, M. de Chamlay, wrote a report at Versailles on 17 August: 'One thing that the Elector and the French generals who are with him must have, in my view, particularly recommended to them, is to separate from one another as little as possible: as long as they have their forces together, one can say without flattery that they will be in some way invincible.'[40] The pathetic remnants of the three armies proved this to be misplaced arrogance.

LOUIS'S CONDUCT AFTER BLENHEIM failed to chime with the expectations of his traumatised people. The king had chosen to greet the news from the Danube with a veneer of easy resignation. However, the impact of military defeat fell heavily on a nation used to victory. Madame de Cornuel summed up the Court's sudden dissatisfaction at Louis's warmongering: 'The *Te Deum* of the great princes are often the *De Profundis* for the private citizens.'[41]

Louis misjudged the mood of the country. His determination to carry on as usual, rather than humble himself before national catastrophe, was inappropriate. Saint Simon wrote scornfully of the king's decision to ignore his people's suffering, while continuing to celebrate family blessings: 'In the midst of all this public sorrow the rejoicings and the *fêtes* for the birth of the Duke of Brittany, son of Monseigneur the Duke of Burgundy, were not discontinued. The City gave a firework *fête* upon the river, that Monseigneur, the Princes, his sons, and Madame the Duchess of Burgundy, with many ladies and courtiers, came to see from the windows of the Louvre, magnificent cheer and refreshments being provided for them. This was a contrast which irritated the people, who would not understand that it was meant for magnanimity.'[42] Even when deeply humiliated, his people consumed by the unaccustomed agonies of defeat and personal loss, it seemed that the Sun King's reflex was to seek consolation in rich pleasure.

CHAPTER TWENTY-THREE

VINDICATION

'The wicked are estranged from the womb: they go astray as
soon as they be born, speaking lies.
'Their poison is like the poison of a serpent: they are like the
deaf adder that stoppeth her ear ...
'Break their teeth, O God, in their mouth ...
'The righteous shall rejoice when he seeth the vengeance: he
shall wash his feet in the blood of the wicked.
'So that a man shall say, Verily there is a reward for the
righteous: verily he is a God that judgeth in the earth.'

EXTRACTS FROM PSALM 58, THE TEXT CHOSEN FOR THE
SERVICE OF THANKSGIVING FOR THE VICTORY AT BLENHEIM,
AT ST PAUL'S, LONDON, SEPTEMBER 1704

IN ENGLAND THE NEWS OF BLENHEIM was greeted with an extraordinary outpouring of national rejoicing. It was nearly three centuries since Henry V's victory at Agincourt had given cause to celebrate a significant victory on the Continent. Sarah Marlborough had received her husband's messenger, Colonel Parke, at St James's on 21 August. Overjoyed by the contents of his despatch, she urged the colonel to carry her husband's hastily written words on to Queen Anne, at Windsor Castle. There, Parke found his monarch seated in the bay window of the Long Gallery. He fell to his knees, and handed her the note that gave the merest outline of what had transpired at Blenheim. It was enough to assure her that British troops had been party to a stunning victory.

After reading the despatch, Anne asked Parke what she could give him, to reward him for the joy of his message. Tradition entitled the bearer of such tidings to a bounty of 500 guineas, but Parke averred that instead of financial reward he would prefer a miniature portrait of his queen. Anne, flattered by this, and ecstatic at the vindication of her support for Marlborough's command, gave Parke his miniature. She also gave him 1,000 guineas.

The cannon of the Tower of London thundered their applause for the army. Church bells pealed and bonfires blazed as the message of celebration spread throughout the land. On a beautiful September day, a service of Thanksgiving was held at St Paul's. Londoners cheered the corpulent Queen Anne as her eight-horsed coach processed from palace to cathedral. Sarah Marlborough shared the carriage with Anne and her Danish consort. Mounted grenadiers preceded the monarch. Behind walked the Archbishop of Canterbury and all the lords, courtiers, and judges of England. From Charing Cross to Temple Bar, the Trained Bands of London stood in a double line.

Boyer wrote that: 'The rejoicings were suitable to the great occasion and her Majesty's subjects gave all the demonstrations imaginable of their affection to her Majesty's person and zeal for her government.' [1] In the evening, fireworks and bonfires continued the celebrations of this rare English triumph.

THE STATES-GENERAL WROTE TO Marlborough: 'This action will make known to France, that her forces are not always invincible, and will deliver her a blow, the likes of which the reigning king has never felt during all his long reign.' [2]

Marlborough's senior officers were proud to have pierced Louis's aura of invincibility. They could appreciate Blenheim's significance as a turning point in Continental affairs. Major-General Wood wrote: 'You have given joy to Europe in shaking of a crown, that long has stood firmly fixed on the head of a saucy monarch.' [3] Brigadier-General Howe spoke of his delight at a victory, 'over so powerful an enemy, which appears greater every post and is the more wonderful to all mankind, for certainly such a victory was never gained before over an army equal in number and composed of old and disciplined troops; I do from my soul rejoice at the great glory and reputation the Duke of Marlborough has gained in this last victory as also the whole campaign, as much as I do for the vast advantage all Europe does and will find by it.' [4]

The British, although they numbered just a fifth of the allied force, had furnished the overall commander, and paid for many of the allies' auxiliaries. They quickly claimed the victory as their own, calling it Blenheim, while the rest of Europe remembered it as the Battle of Höchstädt. The Bishop of Salisbury's wife, Mrs Burnet, trilled her delight at the resulting lift in national mood: 'I cannot defer letting your grace know the joy I see in every one I meet', she wrote to Sarah Marlborough. 'The common people, who I feared were grown stupid, have and do now shew greater signs of satisfaction and triumph, than I think ever saw before on any good success whatever; and after the first tribute of Praise to God, the first cause of all that is good, every one studies who shall most exalt the Duke of Marlborough's fame, by admiring the great secrecy, excellent conduct in the design, and wonderful resolution and courage in the execution.' [5]

The queen was quick to note the unifying effect of Blenheim, writing to Marlborough: 'You will very easily believe that the good news Colonel Parke brought me yesterday was very welcome, but not more, I do assure you, than hearing you were well after so glorious a victory, which will not only humble our enemies abroad, but contribute very much to the putting a stop to the ill designs of those at home.' [6] Anne was delighted that her moderate party manager's military skills would quieten some of her more troublesome subjects.

However, self-interested political prejudice could not be silenced altogether, even in the afterglow of awesome triumph. The Tories in the House of Commons were caught up in the surge of patriotism yet they chose to differentiate between the victor and the victory, celebrating the success of their country rather than that of an individual whom they intensely disliked. One of their newspapers, *The Observator*, had written, early in 1704: 'No men are more mischievous to a State than favourite men of war.' [7] The Tories would have welcomed Marlborough's failure in a campaign that ran so directly counter to their preferred foreign policy.

Marlborough's continued resistance to the Occasional Conformity Bill increased their hatred. The Tories were deeply concerned by the rise in licensed meeting houses (by 1710, there would be nearly 4,000 of these assembly halls across England), as well as the creation of Dissenting academies. Marlborough's refusal to stand against this proliferation caused fury in the Tory ranks. Sarah believed an objective onlooker might think that 'the battle of Höchstädt had been gained over the Church of England and not over the French.' [8]

The efforts of Admiral Rooke, in the mouth of the Mediterranean, were much more to Tory liking. In the summer of 1704, Rooke captured Gibraltar and then saw off the enemy's attempt to wrest it back at the battle of Malaga, the only large naval engagement of the war. These seaborne triumphs allowed the High Tories to bracket their praise for Marlborough with warm applause for Admiral Rooke. Daniel Defoe wrote to Robert Harley, Marlborough's ally in the Commons: 'The victory at sea they look upon as their victory over the Moderate party & [Rooke's] health is now drunk by those here who won't drink the Queen's nor yours. I am obliged with patience to hear you damned & he praised, he exalted & her Majesty slighted & the sea victory set up against the land victory.' [9]

But the Whig-dominated House of Lords was effusive in its praise for Marlborough, and tight-lipped about the naval victory achieved by the Whig admiral. 'We can never enough admire your wisdom and courage,' they told Queen Anne, 'in sending that seasonable and necessary assistance to the Empire, and we cannot too much commend the secrecy and bravery with which your orders were executed.' [10] Marlborough wrote to Sarah of his detachment from this political in-fighting: 'I do assure you as for myself, my pretending to be of no party, is not designed to get favour, or to deceive any body, for I am very little concerned what any party thinks of me; I know them both so well.'[11]

The Tories overreached themselves late in the year. The nation and the monarch were keen to build on the success of Blenheim, and make the 1705 campaign even more telling: the mood was for increasing supply to Marlborough's army. However, Nottingham and Bromley presided at a meeting of 150 Tory MPs in a London tavern, and initiated an inflammatory move: they would only agree to the continued funding of the war, through the Land Tax Bill, if Parliament and the queen would approve their addendum. This was, effectively, another Occasional Conformity Bill. Queen Anne was so incensed by this placing of party above national interest that she broke with the High Tories. 'Our enemies have no encouragement left but what arises from their hopes of our divisions,' she scolded. 'It is therefore your concern not to give the least countenance to those hopes. I hope there will be no concentration among you but who shall most promote the public welfare.'[12]

MARLBOROUGH'S ROUTE HOME TO London from the Danube was a circuitous one. Already exhausted by the campaign, and further drained by the battle, he wished to be home with his wife. 'For thousands of reasons I wish myself with you. Besides I think if I were with you quietly at the lodge, I should have more health, for I am at this time so very lean, that it is extremely uneasy to me, so that your care must nurse me this winter, or I shall certainly be in a consumption.'[13] Instead of this gentle homecoming, he was forced to attend to his broad duties as captain-general of the queen's forces, and his wider diplomatic role within the Grand Alliance. The campaigning season still had several months to run, and he and Eugène were keen to press hard against an enemy so utterly demoralised by defeat. If further progress could be made, the allies could mount an attack on French soil in 1705.

It was now that Prince Lewis of Baden rewarded his allies for their earlier subterfuge. Marlborough and Eugène were eager to sweep the French out of Germany. However, instead of agreeing to this, Baden insisted on following up the fall of Ingolstadt with another siege. The allies set off at the end of August to invest Landau. Owing to Baden's muddled tactics, it failed to fall until November.

Marlborough did not allow these months to go to waste. He built up a position in the Lower Moselle and beyond which could be used as a launching pad for the following year's fighting. The duke could see that here was a theatre of war made for free-flowing fighting. It was an attractive contrast to the Lowlands, Captain Parker writing that Marlborough 'considered that the Netherlands were crowded with a number of the best-fortified towns in Europe, and that they were surrounded with lines almost impregnable; from hence he concluded it next to an impossibility to penetrate into France that way. His scheme therefore was to carry on the war along the Moselle, and having proposed it to Prince Eugène, he immediately approved of it. Whereupon they went to the siege, where, in a council of war, the King of the Romans, the Prince of Baden and all the general-officers fell into it at once.'[14] In the autumn and winter Augsburg, Ulm, Trèves and Trarbach joined Ingolstadt and Landau as allied prizes.

Marlborough was optimistic that the advantages gained in 1704 would be of both immediate and lasting significance. To his friend and political fellow traveller, Lord Treasurer Godolphin, he wrote: 'France is now of that condition, that if her Majesty's arms have good success this next year, she will have it in her power to make such a peace as may make Christendom quiet as long as it may please God to bless us with her life.'[15] To secure that goal, the members of the Grand Alliance must redouble their efforts, and commit more soldiers to the common cause.

The victor of Blenheim had an easy path through the courts of Germany. The Emperor made good an earlier promise, and rewarded Marlborough with an Imperial title: he was greeted on his tour of England's allies as the new Prince of Mindelheim (his principality extended to just fifteen square miles). Response to Marlborough's requests for auxiliary troops for the 1705 campaign was markedly more straightforward than in previous negotiations, now that further glory seemed attainable.

Marlborough had seen the impressive fighting power of the Prussian troops. They had sustained Eugène's wing at a time when the Imperial cavalry's inadequacies had threatened disaster. The King of Prussia was delighted with the plaudits that his subjects' efforts had garnered from around Europe. He was equally happy to profit financially from the standing of his troops (his grandson, Frederick the Great, was to refer to him as 'the mercenary king'). Marlborough concluded his visit to Berlin by agreeing a levy of 8,000 extra Prussian troops. These would assist the beleaguered Duke of Savoy, Prince Eugène's cousin, in northern Italy.

In Hanover, where grave misgivings had been aired at the heavy casualties of the Schellenberg, Marlborough charmed his hosts. The venerable Electress Sophia had her head turned by the duke's exquisite manners. She wrote to the mathematician Leibniz, her close friend: 'Never have I become acquainted with a man who knows how to move so easily, so freely, and so courteously. He is as skilled a courtier as he is a brave general.'[16] While in Hanover, he received confirmation of Landau's and Trarbach's fall. This marked the end of the 1704 campaign.

On his way home, via Holland, Marlborough received hasty congratulations from unexpected quarters. First, the burghers of Amsterdam, traditionally the most Francophile of the United Provinces, sent word to him that they would be honoured to receive him, and show their gratitude to the conqueror of Louis XIV's armies. This was symptomatic of an about-turn by the Dutch States-General as a whole. For so long the force that had held Marlborough back when he had urged bold attack, now they welcomed the hero with fulsome praise and lavish gifts, which included a gold basin and ewer. Grand Pensionary Heinsius, for years a confidant of William III, felt that his confidence in Marlborough had been vindicated by the victory. Blenheim thus helped to bind together the disparate forces within the United Provinces, and keep them committed to the War of the Spanish Succession. There was broad hope that, after so much suffering over so many decades, the Englishman would tame France.

As in Hanover, Marlborough's Dutch visit was untroubled by memories of the slaughter at the Schellenberg. Now, when there was need to refer to that bloody day, a bright revisionism bloomed: 'After the first blow you gave them at Schellenberg', the States-General claimed, 'we had reason to expect something greater would follow; but never dared to carry our hopes so far, as to think of so glorious and complete a victory as you have gained over the enemy. The action of that day has placed your merit in its true lustre. A day whose glory might have been envied by the greatest captains of past ages, and whose memory will endure throughout all ages to come.'[17]

The States-General might truthfully have added how elated William of Orange, their erstwhile ruler, would have been at the outcome of Blenheim. Elated and, perhaps, a little jealous. This was victory on a scale that had eluded the Dutch prince throughout a lifetime of soldiery, but which had fallen to Marlborough at the first opportunity. However, William should be credited for all those years of military struggle: his efforts had drained France, while alerting the allies to the standards of military professionalism required to win against such a foe. In commemoration of the triumph, in which more Dutch soldiers had been engaged than Englishmen, the States-General struck a medal that showed Marlborough and Eugène in the likeness of Castor and Pollux.

In mid-December, after nearly eight months overseas, Marlborough returned to England with Tallard and the more illustrious French prisoners. In the House of Lords the duke was welcomed with a congratulatory address. 'This most honourable house', the Lord Keeper said, 'is highly sensible of the great and signal services Your Grace has done her Majesty this campaign, and of the immortal hour you have done the English Nation; and have commanded me to give you their thanks for the same.'[18] Marlborough deflected much of the praise to others: 'I must beg, on this occasion, to do right to all the officers and soldiers I had the honour of having under my command; next to the blessing of God, the good success of this campaign is owing to their extraordinary courage.'[19]

The British soldiers' excellence at Blenheim was marked by a parade two weeks later, from the Tower of London, along the Strand and Pall Mall, to Westminster. Thirty-four regimental standards were carried by the cavalry, with 128 colours following behind, borne by the infantry. This victory harvest was then placed on public show in Westminster Hall. The dark shade of suspicion that the English had harboured for their soldiery was replaced by an unashamed pride in a feat so spectacularly achieved, so far away from home.

ANNE BESTOWED REWARDS ON Marlborough to match his heroism. She promoted him to the prestigious post of Colonel of the First Guards, a sinecure that had added worth for the recipient, this being the regiment in which he had first gained his commission. She also decreed that her earlier gift of £5,000 per annum to the duke should be granted to his heirs in perpetuity. The queen looked for a more tangible reward for Marlborough's success, so future generations could remember 'the greatest and most glorious action that had happened in several ages.'[20] There was talk of making part of London a living testimony to the victory, with statues of Marlborough and the queen standing tall on plinths. This worried Godolphin, whose instincts were that no subject should be ranged equal to his monarch.

Eventually, Anne settled on a rural prize for her champion. The Royal Manor and Park of Woodstock had been the sovereign's property since Henry I's enclosure of the land, five hundred years earlier. It was home to his menagerie of lions, leopards, and camels. Woodstock had been a popular home for subsequent monarchs, although Elizabeth I, when a princess, had unhappy associations with the place: it was here that her sister, Queen Mary, had her imprisoned for a year. In February 1705, the estate was gifted to Marlborough and his heirs. The queen declared that the 15,000 acres of land were to be cleared and ordered the removal of the ruined manor house so that a castle could be built for the duke. Parliament agreed to fund the project, and allotted £240,000 for the task. Anne chose Sir John Vanbrugh, architect of Castle Howard, to plan a suitably magnificent house. Marlborough busied himself in this project: it appealed to his sense of destiny, and his love of grandeur. He was also delighted with the £6,000 annual income from the estate. The avenues of trees nearest the mansion were planted out in the same deployment as the allied troops had formed on Blenheim's battlefield. However, the building work was to become a project that ran away with itself. Its escalating costs were deemed unacceptable by a less friendly political administration and by a monarch whose favour the Marlboroughs had dissipated. The duke was never to see the completion of the magnificent building that became known as Blenheim Palace.

MARLBOROUGH'S VICTORY WAS ALSO commemorated in verse. Joseph Addison wrote 'The Campaign' in 1705, presenting Marlborough as a hero in the ancient mould, acting with the blessing of a Christian God:

> Twas then great Marlborough's mighty soul was proved,
> That in the shock of charging hosts unmov'd,
> Amidst confusion, horror, and despair,
> Examin'd all the dreadful scenes of war:
> In peaceful thought the field of death survey'd,
> To fainting squadrons sent the timely aid;
> Inspir'd repuls'd battalions to engage,
> And taught the doubtful battle where to rage.
> So when an angel by divine command,
> With rising tempest shakes a guilty land;
> Such as late o'er pale Britannia past,
> Calm and serene he divines the furious blast;
> And, pleas'd the Almighty's orders to perform,
> Rides in the whirlwind, and directs the storm.

Eugène's role was given rather less emphasis:

> Famed Eugenio bore away,
> Only the Second Honours of the Day.

However, Eugène's part in the battle was secondary because that was the role he had agreed to. The prince had always known his calling was to be a great soldier, and now he had proved his abilities against the man who had denied him his vocation. Louis knew now that he had handed his enemies a field marshal of the highest calibre.

There were rumblings after the battle that Eugène had let slip the chance to destroy the enemy army by failing to pursue it during its withdrawal towards Lavingen. Even Marlborough punctuated his paeans of praise for the prince with a private misgiving, written to his wife, contrasting the successes of the two allied wings: 'the army of M. de Tallard, which was what I fought with, is quite ruined; that of the Elector of Bavaria, and the Marshal de Marsin, which Eugène fought against, I am afraid has not had much loss, for I can't find that he has many prisoners.'[21]

This seems to be a clear criticism of Eugène. However, it can also be seen as a note of disappointment directed at the Imperial cavalry, whose performance had been poor throughout the day: indeed, Marlborough decided against writing an official despatch to the Emperor about Blenheim because this would have obliged him comment on the part played by Leopold's horse. He had no wish to insult the lynchpin of the Grand Alliance in the wake of so great a triumph. The day after the battle Marlborough wrote to Harley, in London: 'I cannot say too much in praise of the Prince's good conduct.'[22] That is doubtless a fairer judgement of Eugène, and a clearer reflection of the duke's admiration for his brother-in-arms.

The Emperor was delighted with Eugène's part in Blenheim. Having seen his family's Imperial role unexpectedly retrieved, Leopold was generous to his deliverers. To Eugène, whose second love after warfare was architecture and art, the Emperor gave a Viennese palace, the Stadtpalais. He also paid 6,000 gulden to the city to meet all future taxation, and guaranteed that the palace should never have troops billeted on it.

THE ELECTOR OF BAVARIA WAS NOW, in John Evelyn's words, 'quite beaten out of his Country'.[23] His gamble to usurp the Holy Roman Emperor had been dashed on the battlefield and it was with good reason that he had been heard to exclaim on the night of the defeat: 'The Devil take me if I know what to do now!'[24] His country had already suffered for his treachery, with Marlborough's devastation of the towns and villages leading to Munich. After the defeats at the Schellenberg and at Blenheim, it was effectively without an army. Maximilian Emmanuel's choices were either to seek a return to the Imperial fold, as a prodigal son; or to break the links with the Empire altogether. This he could do by removing to Brussels, and concentrating on his role as Viceroy of the Spanish Netherlands. In that capacity he could continue to fight for and with Louis, against his liege lord.

Louis was generous to his ally. On receiving confirmation of the disaster at Blenheim, he wrote to Marshal Marsin:

> The state in which the Elector finds himself gives me far greater pain than the loss that I have suffered. If he finds the occasion to make an accommodation, or to preserve his family and his country – such as it is – it will be more advantageous than seeing it be ravaged, which it would not be able to avoid after what has happened.
>
> Assure him that, even if he takes that course, I will not change my feeling toward him at all, and that I will maintain all the promises I have made with him.
>
> If he finds the enemy determined not to offer him any conditions, the only course that is open to him is to cross the mountains with my troops.
>
> He will go to Flanders where he will continue the war with more ease and luck, and he will wait for a general peace which may allow him to enjoy the advantages that he deserves. [25]

Although the Emperor wished to punish Maximilian Emmanuel for his 'base revolt', Marlborough was keen to secure the Elector's services. 1704 had proved desperately difficult for the Grand Alliance in Italy. Prospects for the coming campaign would be greatly enhanced if the Elector could be given command in the peninsula, in place of the unreliable and untalented Duke of Savoy. However, having had dealings with Maximilian Emmanuel before, Marlborough held out almost no hope that his overtures would be successful. As he confided to Sarah: 'Prince Eugène and I have offered [the Elector] that if he will join in the common cause against France, he shall be put in possession of his whole country, and receive from the queen and Holland 400,000 crowns yearly, for which he should only furnish the allies with 8,000 men; but I take it for granted he is determined to go to France and abandon his own country to the rape of the Germans.'[26] Marlborough was correct: the Elector had not changed. The allies awaited Maximilian Emmanuel's word through his spokesman, Baron de Sorgestein. 'But when this gentleman returned to the place appointed him,' remarked Sandby, 'the Elector would not vouchsafe to come to him, as he had promised, nor so much as send his secretary, but only sent this message, that he was so watched by the French that neither himself, nor his secretary, could stir.'[27]

The Elector abandoned his country, his wife and his five children, in order to fight with Louis XIV in the Spanish Netherlands.

There was widespread gloating at Maximilian Emmanuel's dramatic fall. Inflated ambition had consigned one of the key princes of the Holy Roman Empire to the role of an exiled mercenary. A contemporary Dutch newspaper, *Les Nouvelles des Cours d'Europe*, speculated on the thoughts of the famous warrior prince as he faced his new situation: 'Let us remember that this prince, who is today believed lost, saw himself with one foot on the throne of Bohemia, and the other on the throne of the Empire. The question currently being asked is what will happen to His Highness? This is a very rapid fall. It is a famous and new example of those hackneyed phrases, that the more one approaches the top of the hill, the more frightening is the sight of the precipice beyond; that the highest trees are those most exposed to the storm; that the tallest towers fall with the greatest violence and impact, and that the mountains that stretch to the skies are often destroyed by lightning.'[28]

Maximilian Emmanuel left his Electress, Maria Antonia, as ruler of Bavaria. She sent her confessor to negotiate with the allies. By the Treaty of Ilbersheim, signed on 7 November 1704, the Wittelsbach family was granted continued lordship over Munich. The rest of the electorate, however, was placed under Austrian military rule. For the allies, one of the happier consequences of the battle of Blenheim was the removal of Bavaria from the war.

CHAPTER TWENTY-FOUR

LESSONS LEARNED

*'The French Armies' former fiery Courage daily abated,
and they were quite dishearten'd, and still retain'd a Fear
of being beat by our worthy Hero and courageous and
victorious Army, wherever they met therewith; the which
all along every where accordingly happen'd, and ours were
fully satisfied and transported with the Hopes thereof: That
wheresoever they met them, they were able to beat them; so
that in short, during our Abode in the War, the grand
Allied Armies remain'd the Conquerors, and the French
the conquered.'*

SERGEANT MILLNER'S *JOURNAL*

BLENHEIM WAS THE TURNING POINT for Louis XIV. He had developed an addiction to the glory of war early in life, and this had been fed to surfeit in his middle years. However, the whipping that his troops received in Bavaria made the ageing monarch understand the cost of defeat, and place value in peace. This astonishing reverse was the forerunner to a steady rhythm of defeat and humiliation that played for France over the next five years. Thanks to a plethora of allied misjudgements, and the focused brilliance of Marshal Villars's generalship, Louis emerged from the war with Philip of Anjou still on the Spanish throne; ostensibly the reason for the contest. However, the intervening trial of strength was an unacceptable drain on the French nation and a telling watershed in the country's military fortunes.

Blenheim was reviewed with a shudder at Versailles. It was the revelation of the rot that had taken hold, unseen, even when the victory *Te Deum* had become a regular part of the Court year. It was a defeat that was greater in scope and meaning than any inflicted by Condé, Turenne or Luxembourg, during Louis's winning years. Europe would have to exhume the bloodied corpses of Gustavus Adolphus's enemies to find battles that resonated with such consequence. For, at Blenheim, the balance of power in Europe, the Holy Grail of William of Orange's foreign policy, had been upheld. The cloak of invincibility that had hung easily around France's shoulders had been torn away, to provide a vision of shaming vulnerability; not only in the shattering destruction of French soldiers, but also through the humiliation of mass surrender. Louis's prime regiments – units that had been famed for their fighting qualities throughout the Continent – had chosen shameful captivity over continued resistance. This had been the final action of a day dizzying in its detail, and bewildering in its implications.

It was soon followed by further disaster, Guizot recording in his *History of France*: 'The defeat of Höchstädt in 1704 had been the first step down the ladder; the defeat of Ramillies on the 23rd of May, 1706, was the second and the fatal rung.'[1]

1705 was a year of grave disappointment for Marlborough. His hopes of marching into France to end the war came to naught, because of inadequate support from the Grand Alliance. Prince Lewis of Baden, still seething with resentment, was obstructive and difficult. Brigadier-General Kane wrote of Baden that he 'never could forgive' Eugène and Marlborough for 'robbing him of a share of the late victory.'[2] 'But however that was,' Captain Parker remarked, 'the Duke was greatly chagrined at the disappointment, as he had conceived great hopes of penetrating into France that way, which must have obliged the French Court to alter their measures.'[3]

The Dutch, reverting to type, impeded Marlborough's ambitious designs. These included a plan to attack Villeroi's disadvantaged army on the field of Waterloo. Here was a chance to free the Netherlands from the French menace for the remainder of the war. General Slangenberg failed to provide promised artillery to the captain-general in time. He delayed the guns in favour of his personal baggage, to which he gave precedence on the narrow road to the allied lines. Slangenberg was dismissed, but an allied victory over the French at Waterloo was deferred for 110 years.

Eugène decried the restrictions placed on Marlborough: the prince could see that domestic political interference and international military constraints were stopping him from advancing the allied cause. 'It is extremely cruel,' he wrote to the duke, 'that opinions so weak and discordant should have obstructed the progress of your operations, when you had every reason to expect a glorious result. I speak to you as a sincere friend. You will never be able to perform anything considerable with your army unless you are absolute, and I trust your Highness will use your utmost efforts to gain that power in future. I am not less desirous than yourself to be once more united with you in command.'[4] However, Eugène could not be spared from his duties in Italy and at home; both spheres where the Imperial cause remained under pressure.

In the spring of 1706, Marlborough cast off the weight of disappointments and frustrations handed him since Blenheim. He opened his campaign, eager for battle in the Lowlands. Significant success early in the fighting season could be built upon in the summer and autumn: he hoped to break the cycle of grinding war that Flanders nurtured. He must seize the advantage for the Grand Alliance; and this must not be an isolated success, but part of a cohesive approach to winning the war.

Marlborough was relieved to find Marshal Villeroi and the Elector of Bavaria ready to fight, both keen to avenge the defeat at Blenheim. Louis, who was eager to distract his people from domestic difficulties, egged them on. The king also wished to reach a position from which peace could be favourably negotiated. He urged the Elector and Villeroi to find a suitable site for battle. 'At this time they examined all the ground from Louvain to the River Mehaigne, and finding the ground around Ramillies the fittest place to draw the Duke of Marlborough to a battle, they ordered the engineers to draw a plan of it, and the order of battle, and sent it to the Court for their approbation. The plan was highly approved of, and such a number of troops sent them as they required; and among them were as many of the Household Troops, as could be spared.'[5]

Louis sent instructions that played into Marlborough's hands: the Elector and Villeroi must establish where the English troops were deployed, since it was clear from events at Blenheim that these were exceptional soldiers. Thus when Marlborough ordered his troops to make a feint towards the weaker wing of the Franco-Bavarian line, Villeroi and the Elector reinforced this sector. By cunning use of the terrain, Marlborough halted his advance and pushed the men, unseen, along the length of a ridge. When these men suddenly appeared in another quarter, and fell on the surprised enemy, Villeroi and the Elector's soldiers fled the field. In the duke's greatest personal victory, 12,000 Franco-Bavarians were killed or wounded, and a further 10,000 taken prisoner or deserted. His own casualties were 4,000 men. Whereas Blenheim had lasted all day, Ramillies was decided in an hour: time enough for Philip V to lose two-thirds of the Spanish Netherlands, and Louis to squander another army.

On the same day that he learnt of the defeat at Ramillies, Louis was informed of a major reverse in Spain. The Habsburg claimant to the Spanish throne, Archduke Charles, had landed in Catalonia the previous autumn, making Barcelona his capital. On 11 May 1706, Philip V tried to recapture the city, but an Anglo-Portuguese army saw him off. That day there was a total eclipse of the sun: the superstitious read this as a divine signal that the Sun King's era of triumph was at an end.

Prince Eugène now dealt Louis's Italian ambitions a thundering blow. The prince and his cousin, the Duke of Savoy, attacked Marshal Marsin and the Duke of Orléans as they besieged Turin. French survivors revealed that on hearing of Eugène's approach Marsin was paralysed by fear. Despite outnumbering the Imperialists by two to one, he allowed Eugène to attack his positions. Eugène again relied on Prince Leopold of Anhalt-Dessau's Prussian infantry, and again he led his men courageously against a larger army. Marsin, who had foretold his own death prior to battle, was indeed mortally wounded. After bitter fighting, Eugène eventually carried the day. He lost a tenth of his men, but this was an acceptable cost for driving Louis XIV's armies out of Italy: the French troops fled towards home. With them went their Spanish allies, who had dominated the peninsula for generations. On 13 March 1707, the king's representatives signed a treaty by which they agreed that all French forces would quit Italy the following day.

Saint Simon gives us a vivid picture of the effect of these defeats on Louis: 'He was nothing more', wrote the duke, 'than an old and wrinkled balloon out of which all the gas that inflated it has gone. He went off to Paris having lost all the varnish that made him glitter and having nothing more to show but the under-stratum.'[6] Family tragedies rained down on Louis, further crushing him. The Duke of Brittany, whose birth had appeared to confirm God's love for the Bourbons, failed to survive infancy. The baby's parents, the Duke and Duchess of Burgundy, also died young. It seemed to Louis that he was being divinely castigated for past errors.

Further humiliations followed. Marlborough and Eugène joined to record a second victory, at Oudenarde, in 1708. At one point in this engagement Eugène was about to be swamped by the French. Marlborough, unbidden, sent reinforcements to extricate the prince from the crisis, quietly repaying the debt of the loan of Fugger's Imperial Cuirassiers which had been so pivotal at Blenheim. Oudenarde saw the Netherlands delivered from a French invasion that had threatened to sweep the allies from Dutch soil.

Marlborough's tactics were similar during his three greatest victories. Five years after Blenheim, at the battle of Malplaquet, Marshal Villars unravelled the Englishman's game plan, with rude effect. Marlborough, Villars realised, concentrated his attack on a point in the French line that, if carried, would win the day. If it did not immediately succeed, then Marlborough looked to the sector from which the enemy commander had taken men to shore up his defences. Marlborough would then fire in his body blow at this exposed solar plexus. However, even after anticipating Marlborough's moves at Malplaquet, and inflicting hideous casualties on the allies – this was the bloodiest European battle for nearly a century – Villars was still forced to quit the field; an acknowledgement of defeat, even if Marlborough's was only a pyrrhic victory.

1709 was the bleakest year of Louis's reign: failed harvests brought famine, his coinage was devalued by 30 per cent and the army was in rags, its morale equally frayed. He was actively, if secretly, seeking to extricate himself from this war that had consumed his armies, and ground his people down. After Malplaquet, where 11,000 French soldiers were slain, the king became deeply depressed. Madame de Maintenon reported that: 'Sometimes he has a fit of crying that he cannot control, sometimes he is not well. He has no conversation.'[7] Although proud of Villars's brave resistance, Louis was keener than ever to sign a peace treaty.

BLENHEIM WAS THE CATALYST FOR king and courtiers to think seriously about concluding the war. 'From the moment when Louis XIV realised, as he was the first to realise, the new values and proportions which had been established on August 13th, he decided to have done with war', wrote Winston S. Churchill: 'Although long years of bloodshed lay before him, his object henceforward was only to find a convenient and dignified exit from the arena in which he had so long stalked triumphant. His ambition was no longer to gain a glorious dominion, but only to preserve the usurpations which he regarded as his lawful rights, and in the end this was to shrink to no more than a desperate resolve to preserve the bedrock of France.'[8]

Louis understood that something dangerous and unstoppable had been unleashed in this latest war. He knew that he had been served notice of the change at Blenheim. There would be no more strikes, during his lifetime, at the heart of the Holy Roman Empire. On the Continent's fringe, his warships were in irreversible decline, with no money available to restore them. They could not challenge the English Navy, or even the depleted Dutch fleet. His interference in British affairs was now the troublesome meddling of an awkward neighbour rather than the menacing threats of a potential overlord. It was hard to believe that Louis had once held the king of England in his financial thrall, his pension ensuring neutered subservience. Blenheim demanded that France now respect her island neighbour.

England's healthy finances had loosened the nation's sinews, preparing her for contests on foreign fields. Godolphin's coffers had eased the march to the Danube, allowing the allies to pass through territory made friendly by prompt payment. The good conduct of the soldiers as they passed through Germany was the result of ready money: there was no need to pillage when all needs were catered for. The contrast with Tallard's marauding foragers, stealing from an indigenous population who became eager for vengeance, is clear.

WILLIAM OF ORANGE BROUGHT England into the Grand Alliance. He had no love for his new kingdom, but he appreciated the advantages that its wealth and its navy would bring his cause. William only lived to see England fight in allied reverses, but this was the apprenticeship that her army required, after centuries of military underperformance. The king overcame his distaste for Marlborough to entrust him with control of the English army. Marlborough was a talented soldier – that much was clear; but he was also assured of Anne's support. This, William appreciated, was essential in a country whose political classes were predominantly Tory, and reluctant to fight on the Continent.

Queen Anne agreed to support this war that, as she was quite aware, she had inherited from William along with the crown. Louis now faced an enemy who could lend generalship, finances, and manpower – both her own, and hired auxiliaries – to the exhausted Empire and the ailing United Provinces. Provoking a fight with such an adversary was Louis's misjudgement. England had begun a climb that would see her eventually enjoy imperial status. Blenheim hastened this process. Winston S. Churchill did not exaggerate when he wrote: 'The destruction of the Armada had preserved the life of Britain: the charge at Blenheim opened to her the gateways of the modern world.'[9] It was a seminal moment in the nation's history.

WHY HAS BLENHEIM BEEN LARGELY forgotten? It ranks as one of the most important battles in European history, marking the moment when Louis was finally brought down, and made to realise that the Continent would not become his fiefdom. France would not recover her military status until Napoleon gifted her his extraordinary talents. It was also the occasion when British and Prussian troops gave an indication of the forces they would be, in the subsequent centuries. At the same time, it was the opening performance of Eugène and Marlborough, as gifted a pair of generals as has ever worked in concert.

Surely Blenheim deserves to be remembered? Napoleon certainly felt so. He was a great admirer of the two allied generals, and was amazed by English reticence about Marlborough's great achievements. The French Emperor ordered his historians to correct the enemy's oversight. *L'Histoire de Jean Churchill, Duc de Marlborough*, was published by the Imprimerie Impériale in 1805. Napoleon is believed to have contributed, anonymously, to this work. We know that Bonaparte hummed 'Marlbrouk s'en va t'en guerre', a tune that tells of dread respect for the duke's name, as he crossed the Niemen, at the start of his Russian campaign of 1812.

Marlborough enjoyed the respect of his foreign enemies. He could be less sure of his compatriots. Tory resentmentment of his policy grew, as Sarah Marlborough's influence over Queen Anne waned. This left the duke vulnerable and unsupported. When the Whigs were driven from office in 1711, Marlborough was dismissed from his command. He was accused of having prolonged the war to his own advantage; a charge refuted by the evidence of his private correspondence, in which he clearly longs to settle with his wife in quiet retirement. The force of Tory opprobrium, whipped up by a vicious press, drove him into exile on the Continent. George I restored him to his positions, but the duke was old and unwell by then. In 1722, after a series of strokes, he died, with Sarah by his side.

Subsequently many denigrated Marlborough's reputation, Swift and Macaulay slandering him repeatedly. Their impetus was more political than personal, but the combined effect was devastating. The perceived import of the battle of Blenheim diminished as Marlborough's name suffered. It is difficult to understand Marlborough the man. He was enigmatic, focused, and brilliant. He was also avaricious, and – as we know from his correspondence with the Jacobites – capable of double-dealing. However, his men adored him, and knew his incomparable military worth: they were proud to point out that he never lost a battle, or failed to take a city that he besieged.

He was the main architect of his first great battle, Blenheim. There he secured a decisive victory for democracy over absolutism. He saved the Habsburg dynasty and humbled Louis's Bourbon line. He handed England military eminence in Europe, and destroyed the notion of France's invincibility. The future of the United Provinces was guaranteed, while renegade Bavaria was punished for her leader's treachery. Blenheim was the vindication of William's creed: Louis must be, and could be, stopped.

If you visit the battle site today, there is little to commemorate the engagement whose scale and consequence thrilled contemporary Europe. The village green has a small plaque recalling the barest details of the day's events. Yet, at the time, Emperor Leopold was quick to realise the scale of the humiliation that his historic adversary, Louis le Grand, had suffered. He ordered a plinth to be erected on the battlefield at Blenheim with a short inscription: 'Let Louis XIV know that no man before his death should be called either happy or great'.

SOURCES

Prologue

1 Letter of Louis XIV to the Cardinal de Noailles, 25 June 1704. Recorded in *Les Nouvelles des Cours de l'Europe*, 'Tome XI', July 1704

2 *Memoirs of the Duke of Saint Simon*, vol. II, translated by Bayle St John, p. 7

3 *Louis XIV*, Vincent Cronin, p. 225

4 *Saint Simon*, ibid., p. 8

Chapter One

1 Winston S. Churchill, *Marlborough: His Life and Times*, vol. I, p. 258

2 Louis XIV's *Mémoires*, quoted by René Chartrand, in *Louis XIV's Army*

3 Extract from the Treaty of Dover, 1670, quoted in *The Stuart Age*, Barry Coward, p. 263

4 Silvius, cit. Grew, *William Bentinck and William III*, p. 28

5 Quoted in *William and Mary*, Henri and Barbara van Zee, p. 81

6 *Saint Simon*, ibid, vol. III, p. 228

7 Voltaire, I, p. 327

8 John Evelyn, *Diary*, 27 February 1704

9 Wiliam of Orange, quoted in *William and Mary*, H. and B. van Zee, p. 185

10 Evelyn, ibid, 2, 413 (15 July 1683)

11 Matthew Prior, quoted in *William and Mary*, H. and B. van Zee, p. 442

12 Evelyn, ibid, 3, 8 (3 November 1685)

Chapter Two

1 W. S. Churchill, *Marlborough: His Life and Times*, vol. I, p. 180

2 *The Letters of Philip Stanhope, 2nd Earl of Chesterfield*, vol. II, London, 1837, p. 237

3 Louis XIV's letter to James, Duke of York, quoted in *History of His Own Time*, Gilbert Burnet, vol. II, p. 124

Chapter Three

1 Quoted in *William and Mary*, van der Zee, p. 102

2 Pierre de Ségur, *Le Maréchal de Luxembourg et Le Prince d'Orange*, p. 105

3 Duchess of Orléans, *Correspondance Complète de Madame*, trans. M. G. Bruner, vol. II, p. 94

4 A. L.Rowse, *The Churchills*, p. 62

5 Quoted in Christopher Hibbert, *The Marlboroughs*, p. 7

6 Quoted in Kate Fleming's *The Churchills*, p. 45

7 Quoted in John A. Lynn's *Giant of the Grand Siècle: the French Army, 1610–1715*

8 C. T. Atkinson, *Marlborough and the Rise of the British Army*, p. 50

9 Ibid, p. 57

10 Quoted in C. Hibbert, *The Marlboroughs*, pp. 74–5, from *Mémoires relatives à la Guerre de Succession*, Sicco van Goslinga, pp. 42–4

11 BL Add. MS 61427, fo. 93. John to Sarah Churchill, 3 January 1680

12 BL Add. MS 61427, fo. 101. John to Sarah Churchill, 24 January 1680

13 BL Add. MS 61453, fo. 124. Lady Tyrconnel to Sarah Churchill, 5 April 1699

14 BL Add. MS 61427, fo.117. John Churchill to Sarah Churchill, July 1684. Also in *Rule of Three*, Iris Butler, p. 59

15 Rutland Papers, H.M.C., xii, Part II, 81

16 G. M.Trevelyan, *England in the Reign of Queen Anne*, vol. I, 1930–4, p. 167

17 BL Add. MS 61414, fo. 3: Anne to Sarah Churchill, 1683

18 Quoted in C. T. Atkinson's *Marlborough and the Rise of the British Army*, p. 78

19 Quoted in *Monmouth's Drill Book: An Abridgement of the English Military Discipline*, ed. John Tincey

Chapter Four

1 Ordinance of 23 December 1680, quoted in *Histoire de Louvois*, Camille Rousset

2 Sir Edward Creasy, *The Fifteen Decisive Battles of the World*, pp. 394–5

3 *Memoirs of the Duke of Saint Simon*, quoted on p. 82 of *Giant of the 'Grand Siècle': the French Army 1610–1715*, John A. Lynn

4 *The History of France*, vol. IV, M. Guizot, p. 421

5 Louis XIV, *Mémoires de Louis XIV*, ed. Charles Dreyss, vol.II, p. 250

6 *The History of France*, vol. IV, M. Guizot, p. 420

7 W. S. Churchill, *Marlborough: His Life and Times*, vol. I, p. 402

8 Nicholas Luttrell, *A Brief Historical Relation of State Affairs, 1678–1714*, vol. II, p. 466

9 *The History of France*, vol. IV, M. Guizot, p. 350

10 Anonymous correspondence of Fénelon, quoted in *The History of France*, vol. IV, M. Guizot, p. 350

11 *Memoirs of the Duke of Saint Simon*, vol. II, trans. Bayle St John

12 *The Stuart Age*, Barry Coward, p. 347

13 James Ralph, *The History of England During the Reign of King William*, vol. II, p. 761

Chapter Five

1 Quoted in *Louis XIV*, Vincent Cronin, p. 309

2 Voltaire, quoted in *Louis XIV*, Philippe Erlanger, pp. 282–3

3 *Memoirs of the Duke of Saint Simon*, vol. III, p. 16

4 John Evelyn's *Diary*, 17 November 1700

5 Quoted in *The Spanish Bourbons: the History of a Tenacious Dynasty*, John D. Benjamin, p.28

6 *The Fifteen Decisive Battles of the World*, Sir Edward Creasy, p. 401

7 Quoted in *Prince Eugen of Savoy*, Nicholas Henderson, p. 55

8 *Memoirs of the Duke of Saint Simon*, vol. II, pp. 397–8

9 *Introduction aux documents relatifs à la succession d'Espagne*, M. Mignet, pp. 360–1

10 Nicolaas Japiske, *Prince William III*, pp. 415–16

11 W. S. Churchill, *Marlborough: His Life and Times*, vol. I, p. 492

12 *Mémoire pour M. Poussin*, 15 April 1701, in R.O. transcripts, quoted by W. S. Churchill, vol. I, p. 509

13 *Handboek* vol. I, Groen van Prinsterer, p. 445, quoted by van der Zee, p. 463

14 BL Add. MSS 21, 489, fo. 51. Ambassador Stanhope to Secretary at War Blathwayt, 23 September 1701

Chapter Six

1 Letter of Count Wratislaw to the Earl of Marlborough, sent from Vienna, 4 May 1701, quoted on p. 120 of Coxe's *Memoirs of Marlborough*

2 *Memoirs of an Old Campaigner, 1692–1717*, M. de la Colonie, trans. Walter C. Horsley, p. 80

3 *The Churchills*, Kate Fleming, p. 34

4 W. S. Churchill, vol. II, p. 294

5 From *The Lives of the Two Illustrious Generals*, quoted in W. S. Churchill, vol. I, p. 350

6 *The Diary of John Evelyn*, 24 January 1692

7 *Memoirs of Sarah, Duchess of Marlborough*, ed. W. King, p. 53

8 From *The Lives of Two Illustrious Generals*, quoted in W. S. Churchill, vol. I, p. 495

9 Quoted in *Prince Eugen of Savoy*, N. Henderson, p.12

10 *Memoirs of an Old Campaigner*, M. de la Colonie, p. 75

11 BL Stowe MSS. 222, fo. 118: William III to the Duc de Ploen, 20 December 1701

12 *Letters*, Lord Chesterfield, vol. I, 221 and 222, quoted in W. S. Churchill, vol. I, p. 478

13 *History of France*, Guizot, vol. IV, p. 366

14 Queen Anne to the Directors of the Circle of the Upper Rhine, St James's, 17 March 1702. [S.P. 104/201, f.127. In Latin.] Quoted in *The Letters of Queen Anne*, ed. Beatrice C. Brown, pp. 82–3

Chapter Seven

1 *Memoirs of the Most Remarkable Military Transactions*, Captain Robert Parker, ed. David G. Chandler, p.18

2 Daniel Defoe, quoted in *The Churchills*, Kate Fleming, p. 45

3 Letter from Marlborough to Godolphin, 13 July 1702, quoted in Coxe, *Memoirs of Marlborough*, vol. I, p.171

4 Quoted in Coxe, vol. I, p.176

5 *Memoirs of the Most Remarkable Military Transactions*, Captain Robert Parker, ed. David G. Chandler, p. 20

6 *Mémoires de Berwick*, vol. I, p. 187

7 Letter of Marlborough to Sidney Godolphin, 27 August 1702, quoted in Coxe, vol. I, pp. 180–1

8 Marlborough to Sarah, July 1702, quoted in Coxe, vol. I, p. 176

9 Brigadier-General Row, Mar. MSS, p. 266

10 Quoted from the *London Gazette*, 428, quoted in W. S .Churchill, vol. I, p. 281

11 KWC, SP/8/5, f.95, quoted in *The Art of Warfare in the Age of Marlborough*, David G. Chandler, p.112

12 Quoted in W. S. Churchill, vol. I, p. 413

13 Contemporary pamphlet quoted by Ralph, *History*, vol. ii, p. 422

14 Christophe de Dohna, *Mémoires Originaux*, 1883, pp. 151–2. Quoted in W. S. Churchill, vol. I, p. 350

15 Millner's *Journal*, 8 OS June 1702, p. 7

16 Millner, quoted in C. T. Atkinson, p. 487

17 C. T. Atkinson, p. 509

18 Parker, p. 22

19 Ibid

20 Ibid, p. 23

21 R. Pope to T. Coke, Coke MSS., III, p.16

22 Ibid

23 Parker, p. 25

24 Disp., I, 48; cf. Portland MSS., IV, 49. (Atkinson.)

25 Marlborough to Sarah Marlborough,

28 October 1702, quoted in Coxe, p. 194

26 Quoted in Coxe, p. 193

27 Marlborough to Sarah Marlborough, 6 November 1702, quoted in Coxe, vol. I, p. 206

28 John Evelyn's *Diary*, 30 December 1702

29 W. S. Churchill, vol. II, p.168

Chapter Eight

1 Quoted in J. P. Kenyon, *Revolution Principles*, p. 72

2 Sir John Leveson-Gower, 26 December 1702 [HMC XII, App. 5, p.173], quoted in *Queen Anne*, David Green, p. 112

3 Marlborough to Sarah Marlborough, 14 June 1703, quoted in Coxe, vol. I, p. 274

4 Marlborough to Sarah Marlborough, 30 September 1703, quoted in Coxe, vol I, p. 278

5 Quoted in G. Holmes, *British Politics*, p. 68

6 Quoted in J. P. Kenyon, *Revolution Principles*, p. 92

7 Sarah Marlborough: *Correspondence*, vol. II, p. 147

8 Quoted in Coxe, vol. I, p.114

9 Marlborough to Sarah Marlborough, quoted in Coxe, vol. I, p.114

10 Conversation between Marlborough and Lord Ailesbury, quoted in Coxe, vol. I, p. 115

11 Marlborough to Godolphin, 9 April 1703, Coxe, vol. I, pp. 226–7

12 Quoted in Coxe, vol. I, p.196

13 Marlborough to Godolphin, 31 May 1703, Coxe, vol. I, p. 247

14 *Letters of Samuel Noyes*, ed. Major S. H. F. Johnston, 15 July 1703

15 Marlborough to Sarah Marlborough, 28 June 1703, quoted in Coxe, vol. I, p. 251

16 Marlborough to Godolphin, 11 June 1703, Coxe, vol. I, p. 271

17 Marlborough to Sarah Marlborough, Coxe, vol. I, p. 279

18 Noyes, ibid

19 Coxe, vol. I, pp. 284–5

20 Marlborough to Sarah Marlborough, early September 1703, Coxe, vol. I, p. 284

21 Godolphin to Harley, 26 September 1703, quoted in *Marlborough and the Rise of the British Army*, C. T. Atkinson, p. 182

Chapter Nine

1 *The Chronicles of an Old Campaigner 1692–1717*, M. de la Colonie

2 *Histoire de France*, Anquetil, vol. XI, p. 342

Chapter Ten

1 Marlborough to Sarah Marlborough, 22 February 1704, quoted in *Prince Eugen of Savoy*, Nicholas Henderson, p. 96

2 Lord Cutts to Marlborough, 15 March 1704. Blenheim Papers, Vol. LXII, ADD MS 61162

3 Marlborough to Sarah Marlborough, April 1704 (day not known), quoted in W. S. Churchill, vol. I, pp. 723–4

4 Journal of Josias Sandby (known as *Hare's Journal*), Chaplain to General Charles Churchill, pp. 76–7. Blenheim Papers, Vol. CCCVIII, British Library, ADD MS. 61408.

5 Marlborough to Sarah Marlborough, 5 May 1704, W. S. Churchill, vol. I, p. 322

6 Sergeant Millner's *Journal*, 28 May 1704, p. 83

7 *Hare's Journal*, p. 81

8 Villeroi to Chamillart, 18 May; Pelet, quoted in W. S. Churchill, pp. 324–5

9 W. S. Churchill, vol. I, p. 324

10 Blenheim Papers, Vol. CCCXII, British Library, ADD MS. 61412

11 *Campagne de Monsieur le Maréchal de Tallard en Allemagne*, vol. 1, p. 203

12 *Hare's Journal*, p. 86

13 Ibid, p. 88

14 Ibid, p. 90

15 Marlborough to Sarah Marlborough, 27 May 1704, quoted in Coxe, vol. I, p. 328

16 *Memoirs*, Captain Robert Parker, pp. 80–81

17 *The Life and Adventures of Mrs Christian Davies*, p. 60

18 Captain Pope, Cowper Papers, HMC, vol. III, p. 36, quoted in W. S. Churchill, vol I, p. 335

19 Millner, quoted on p. 193, C. T. Atkinson

20 Millner, quoted on p. 195, C. T. Atkinson

21 ADD MSS. 22, 196 – the Correspondence of Cadogan and Lord Raby, 1703–10, entry dated 30 May 1704, quoted in Chandler, *Marlborough as Military Commander*

22 *A Journal of Marlborough's Campaigns*, John Marshall Deane, 27 May 1704, ed. David G. Chandler, p. 2

23 Millner's *Journal*, 30 May 1704, p. 83

24 *Life of Blackader*, Andrew Crichton, pp. 212–3, 18 May 1704

25 Parker, 29 May 1704

26 *Hare's Journal*, p. 90

27 *Pelet and Le Vault*, Villeroi, vol. IV, pp. 470–2

28 *Campagne de M. le Maréchal de Tallard*: Tallard to Chamillart, 4 June 1704, p. 228

29 Marlborough to Godolphin, quoted in Coxe, p. 333

30 Journal of Captain Blackader, 28 OS May 1704. From *Life of Blackader*, Andrew Crichton, p. 214

Chapter Eleven

1 *Correspondance Complète de Madame, Duchesse d'Orléans*, ed. G.Brunet, quoted in Henderson, p. 8

2 Quoted in Henderson, p. 11

3 *Histoire du Prince François Eugène de Savoye*, E. Mauvillon, vol. I, p. 43

4 Eugène to Graf Tarini, 2 August 1691, A. Arneth, *Prinz Eugen von Savoyen*, vol. I, p. 455, quoted in Henderson, p. 32

5 Eugène to Graf Tarini, 30 September 1690, A. Arneth, vol. I, p. 452, quoted in Henderson, p. 31

6 Instruction to Eugène from the Imperial War Council, 5 July 1697. A. Arneth, *Das Leben des Kaiserlichen Feldmarshalls Guido von Stahremberg*, pp. 187–8. Quoted in Henderson, p. 40

7 *Feldzüge*, I Ser., II, Suppl. ñ Heft, p. 52, quoted in Henderson, p. 42

8 *Lectures on Modern History*, Acton, p. 259, quoted in W. S. Churchill, p. 536

9 *Marlborough and the Rise of the British Army*, C. T. Atkinson, p. 196

10 *The Diary of John Evelyn*, p. 1073, 3 August 1701

11 Louis XIV to Catinat, 10 August 1701, *Feldzüge*, I, Serg., III, p. 239, quoted in Henderson, p. 59

12 *The Diary of John Evelyn*, p. 1078, 8 February 1702

13 *Der Fall des Hauses Stuart*, O. Klopp, vol. X, p.185. Quoted p. 74, Henderson

14 *The Letters and Dispatches of John Churchill, First Duke of Marlborough from 1702–1712*, ed. General Sir George Murray, vol I, p. 30

Chapter Twelve

1 *Prinz Eugen*, Kurt von Priesdorff, p. 5, quoted in 'Prince Eugène of Savoy and Central Europe', by Paul R. Sweet, 'The American Historical Review', vol. 57, no. 1, October 1951, p. 50

2 *A Vindication of the Conduct of the Duchess of Marlborough*, Gilbert Burnet, Bishop of Salisbury, pp. 13–14

3 Eugène to the Emperor, 21 November 1702, A. Arneth, vol. I, p. 185

4 Baron Raby to Stepney, 29 March 1704, BL Add. MS 31, 132, fo.120

5 Eugène to the Emperor, 12 January 1704, A. Arneth, vol. I, p. 23. Quoted in Henderson, pp. 89–90

6 Stepney to Cardonnel, 24 May 1704, BL Blenheim Papers, Vol. CCCXII, ADD MS. 61412

7 W. S. Churchill, vol. I, p. 773

8 *Hare's Journal*, quoted in Coxe, vol. I, p. 337

9 Count Wratislaw to Vienna, O. Klopp, *Der Fall des Hauses Stuart*, vol. X, p. 185. Quoted in Henderson, p. 74

10 G. M. Trevelyan, *England under Queen Anne*, vol. I, p. 152

11 Eugène to Emperor Leopold, *Feldzüge*, vol. VI, Supp. p. 131

12 Marlborough to Sarah Marlborough, 15 June 1704, quoted in Coxe, Vol. I, p. 341

13 C. T. Atkinson, *Marlborough and the Rise of the British Army*, p. 196

14 O. Klopp, XI, p. 128, quoted in Henderson, p. 99

15 *Hare's Journal*, quoted in Coxe, p. 338

16 Lieutenant-General Scholten to Marlborough, 9 June 1704, Blenheim Papers, Vol. CLX, ADD MS. 61260, fo. 13

17 Coxe, vol. I, p. 340

18 Sir Edward Seymour quoted in N. Henderson, p. 104

19 Letter of Wratislaw to Prince Lewis of Baden, 6 May 1704, quoted in W. S. Churchill, vol. II, p. 304

Chapter Thirteen

1 *Life of Blackader*, Andrew Crichton, p. 214, extract from diary entry dated 12–23 June 1704

2 *A Journal of Marlborough's Campaign*, Deane, 26 June 1704

3 Marlborough to Sarah Marlborough, 25 June 1704, quoted in Coxe, p. 345

4 Millner's *Journal*, p. 90, 26 June 1704

5 W. S. Churchill, *Marlborough, His Life and Times*, p. 314

6 *Vie du Maréchal Duc de Villars*, vol. I, p. 289

7 Millner's *Journal*, p. 94

8 *Military Dictionary, A*, Anon., quoted in *The Art of Warfare in the Age of Marlborough*, David G. Chandler, p. 69

9 *The Chronicles of an Old Campaigner*, M. de la Colonie, trans. W. C. Horsley, p. 179

10 *Military Memoirs of Marlborough's Campaigns*, ed. David G. Chandler, p. 32

11 Millner's *Journal*, p. 95

12 De la Colonie, p. 182

13 *Hare's Journal*, p. 112

14 De la Colonie, p. 185

15 De la Colonie, p. 191

16 Rutland Papers, H.M.C., ii, p.181, quoted in W. S. Churchill, p. 388

17 De la Colonie, p. 195

18 Parker, *Military Memoirs of Marlborough*, p. 33

19 Lieut-Gen Baron von Hompesch to the States-General, quoted from pp. 117–8 *Nouvelles des Cours de l'Europe*, July 1704, Tome XI

20 Millner's *Journal*, pp. 95–6

21 *Life of Blackader*, Andrew Crichton, 2 July 1704

22 *Hare's Journal*, p. 115

23 Quoted in *Military Surgery*, John Hennen, p. 2

24 J. White, MD, *De Recta Sanguinis Missione*, quoted in *Military Surgery*, John Hennen, p. 48

25 *A new Tract for the Cure of Wounds made by Gun Shot or otherways, fitted for the meanest Capacities, exceeding useful in times of War and Peace*, anon. BL Rare Books. 1507/1802

26 *The Hospital Surgeon, or a New, Gentle, Easie Way, to Cure speedily all sorts of Wounds, and other Diseases belonging to Surgery*, Mr Belloste, Surgeon-Major to the Hospitals of the French King's Army in Italy, pp. 207–8

27 Ibid, pp. 8–9.

28 *A Compleat Discourse of Wounds*, John Brown, pp. 98–9

29 *The Hospital Surgeon*, Belloste, pp. 217–8

30 *A New Tract for the Cure of Wounds*, anon., p. 1

31 *The Hospital Surgeon*, Belloste, p. 97

32 Ibid, p. 35

33 *A New Light of Chirurgery*, John Colbatch, London, 1695, introduction to the reader

34 Ibid, pp. 28–9

35 Ibid, p. 32

36 Ibid, p. 54

37 A *Compleat Discourse of Wounds*, Brown, pp. 99–100

38 Addison, *The Campaign*

39 Imperial Official Report, *Feldzüge*, vi, p. 837, quoted in W. S. Churchill, p. 389

40 Von Hompesch to the States-General (see above), p. 120

41 Leibniz's *Werke*, 1873, vol. IX, p. 91, quoted in W. S. Churchill, vol. I, p. 807

42 Letter of Queen Anne to the King of Spain, Windsor, 14 July 1704, S.P. 104/108, f.86, in French

43 Emperor Leopold to Marlborough, quoted in Coxe, pp. 363–4, trans. from the original in the Blenheim Papers

44 Marlborough to Queen Anne, 3 July 1704, quoted in Coxe, p. 359

Chapter Fourteen

1 Letter of Marlborough to the States-General, 4 July 1704, quoted in *Nouvelles des Cours de l'Europe*, July 1704, Tome XI

2 Tallard to Chamillart, 23 May 1704. *Campagne de Monsieur le Maréchal de Tallard en Allemagne*, Vol. I, p. 174

3 Chamillart to Tallard, 12 June 1704, *Campagne de Tallard*, p. 253

4 Chamillart to Tallard, 12 June 1704. *Campagne de Tallard*, p 264

5 Quoted in W. S. Churchill, p. 343

6 Elector of Bavaria to Tallard, 5 June 1704, *Campagne de Tallard*, p. 299

7 W. S. Churchill, vol. II, p. 344

8 Louis XIV to Tallard, 23 June 1704, *Campagne de Tallard*, pp. 312–3

9 Tallard to Louis XIV, 29 June 1704, *Campagne de Tallard*, p. 341.

10 W. S. Churchill, vol. II, p. 411

11 Tallard to Chamillart, 29 June 1704, *Campagne de Tallard*, pp. 327–8

12 Mérode-Westerloo, from *Memoirs of Marlborough's campaigns, 1702–1712*, ed. David G. Chandler, pp.159–60

13 Ibid

14 *Mémoires complets et authentiques du duc de Saint-Simon sur le siècle de Louis XIV et la Régence*, Tome VII, ed. H.-L.Delloge

15 W. S. Churchill, vol. II, p. 411

16 Tallard to the King, *Letters of William III and Louis XIV and of Their Ministers*, ed. Paul Grimblot, vol. I, p. 466

17 John Philip Hore, *The History of Newmarket*, vol. III, p. 231

18 Tallard to the King, 8 July 1698, Grimblot, vol. II, p. 54

19 Tallard to the King, Grimblot, vol. II, p. 236

20 Tallard to Chamillart, 9 July 1704, *Campagne de Tallard*, p. 20

21 Marsin to Tallard, 9 July 1704, *Campagne de Tallard*, p. 15

22 Tallard to the King, Lauterburg, 16 June 1704, Pelet, vol. IV, p. 481

23 Tallard to the King, 18 July 1704, *Campagne de Tallard*, p. 56

24 *Mérode-Westerloo*, ed. David G. Chandler, p. 160

25 Ibid, p. 162

26 Ibid, p. 161

Chapter Fifteen

1 Millner's *Journal*, p. 105

2 Wratislaw to the Emperor, Ebermergen, 4 July 1704, *Feldzüge*, I, Ser. VI, p. 841

3 The Emperor to Wratislaw, 15 May 1704, *Feldzüge*, VI, p. 824

4 Marlborough to Godolphin, 8 June 1704, quoted in Coxe, vol. I, p. 336

5 Marlborough to Sarah Marlborough, 9 July 1704, quoted in Coxe, vol. I, p. 370

6 Marlborough to Sarah Marlborough, 4 July 1704, from Donauwörth. Coxe, vol. I, p. 366

7 Millner's *Journal*, p. 103

8 Eugène to the Duke of Savoy, *Feldzüge*, VI, supp. p. 131, O. Klopp, op. cit. XI, pp. 164–6, undated, quoted in Barnett, *Marlborough*, p. 101

9 Eugène to the Duke of Savoy, ibid, O. Klopp, XI, p. 166

10 Marlborough to Sarah Marlborough, 13 July 1704, quoted in Coxe, p. 371

11 Marlborough to Sarah Marlborough, undated, Coxe, p. 376

12 M. de la Colonie, p. 206

13 Ibid, p. 206

14 Marsin to Tallard, *Campagne de Tallard*, pp. 103–4

15 M. de la Colonie, p. 210

16 Emperor to Wratislaw, 23 July1704, *Feldzüge*, vol. VI, p. 845, quoted in W. S. Churchill, p. 399

17 *Memoirs*, Captain Robert Parker, p. 84

18 Ibid, p. 85

19 *Hare's Journal*, p. 38

20 M. de la Colonie, p. 159

21 Prince Lewis of Baden to the Emperor, Roder, vol. II, p. 65., quoted in W. S. Churchill, p. 408

Chapter Sixteen

1 Marlborough to Godolphin, Friedberg, 3 August 1704

2 Tallard to Chamillart, 4 August 1704, *Campagne de Tallard*, p. 12

3 Louis XIV to Tallard, 2 August 1704, *Campagne de Tallard*, pp. 124–5

4 Marsin to Chamillart, 8 August 1704, Pelet, vol. IV, p. 550, quoted in W. S. Churchill, p. 429

5 'Letters of the First Earl of Orkney during Marlborough's Campaigns', English Historical Review, vol. 19, no. 74, April 1904, pp. 307–21

6 Marlborough to Godolphin, Nieder Schonfeldt, 10 August 1704

7 Eugène to Marlborough, 10 August 1704. Camp of Munster. Quoted in W. S. Churchill, pp. 426–7

8 W. S. Churchill, vol. II, pp. 431–2

9 Tallard to Chamillart, 4 September 1704, Pelet, vol. IV, p. 564

10 Tallard to Louis, 12 August 1704, *Campagne de Tallard*, p. 139

11 Millner's *Journal*, p. 111

12 Tallard to Louis, 12 August 1704, *Campagne de Tallard*, p. 139

13 Marlborough to Godolphin, Nieder Schonfeldt, 10 August 1704, Coxe, p. 382

14 Marlborough to Godolphin, 18 June 1703, Coxe, p. 249

15 Turenne, quoted in *Hare's Journal*, p.151

16 *Hare's Journal*, p. 147

17 Millner's *Journal*, p. 112

Chapter Seventeen

1 Mérode-Westerloo, from *Military Memoirs of Marlborough's Campaigns, 1702–1712*, ed. David G. Chandler, p.166

2 Ibid, pp.166–7

3 Sergeant Millner, quoted in *Marlborough and the Rise of the British Army*, C. T. Atkinson, p. 217

4 Mérode-Westerloo, p. 168

5 Captain Robert Parker, *Memoirs*, (British Library), pp. 86–7. (Also Chandler, p. 37)

6 Coxe, p. 386

7 'Earle of Orkney from ye Camp at Steinheim', to John, Lord Hervey (later 1st Earl of Bristol), 17 August 1704, quoted from EHR, vol. 19, no. 74, April 1904, pp. 307–21

8 Coxe, p. 386

9 W. S. Churchill, vol. II, p. 437

10 Coke, MSS., III, p.16, quoted by C. T. Atkinson, p. 170

11 *L'Ecole de Mars*, M. de Guignard, quoted by David G. Chandler, *The Art of Warfare in the Age of Marlborough*

12 Parker, p. 87

13 Quoted in W. S. Churchill, p. 441

14 *Memoirs of the Duke of Saint Simon*, trans. Bayle St John, vol. II, p. 9

15 W. S. Churchill, pp.111–2

16 Parker, ed. David G. Chandler, p. 38

17 Millner, p. 115

18 Prince Lewis of Baden to the Emperor, 13 August 1704, quoted in W. S. Churchill, vol. II, p. 438

19 *Hare's Journal*, p. 158

Chapter Eighteen

1 Coxe, p. 400

2 *Hare's Journal*, p. 158

3 *The Hospital Surgeon*, Belloste, pp. 254–5

4 *Life of Blackader*, ed. Andrew Crichton, p. 223

5 *Hare's Journal*, p.157

6 W. S. Churchill, vol. II, p. 444

7 Millner's *Journal*, p. 115

8 Coxe, p. 395

9 *Hare's Journal*, p. 160

10 *Memoirs*, Captain Parker, p. 41

11 *Hare's Journal*, p. 163

12 *Memoirs*, Captain Parker, p. 41

13 Tallard, December 1704, from Pelet, vol. IV, p. 575, quoted in W. S. Churchill, p. 447

14 Pelet, vol. IV, p. 586, quoted in W. S. Churchill, p. 448

15 Mérode-Westerloo, quoted in David G. Chandler, p. 169

16 Ibid, p. 170

17 *Memoirs*, Captain Parker, p. 41

18 Mérode-Westerloo, quoted in David G. Chandler, p.168

Chapter Nineteen

1 Letter from Baron de Quincy to Chamillart, 18 September 1704; Pelet, IV, p. 576, quoted in W. S. Churchill, p. 443

2 Marshal Catinat, quoted in *L'Infanterie au XVIIIe siècle: la tactique*, Jean Colin, p. 25

3 Brigadier-General William Kane, *The Campaigns of King William and Queen Anne*, p.110

4 *Hare's Journal*, p. 163

5 Millner's *Journal*, p. 117

6 Ibid, p.117

7 Parker, *Memoirs*, quoted in *The Art of Warfare in the Age of Marlborough*, David G. Chandler, p.120

8 Parker, *Memoirs*, ed. David G. Chandler, p. 41

9 Millner's *Journal*, p. 117

10 *A Compleat Discourse of Wounds*, John Brown, p. 107

11 *The Life of Marlborough*, Archibald Alison, vol. I, pp. 171–2

12 Marshal Tallard, quoted in W. S. Churchill, vol II, p. 450

13 *The Life of Marlborough*, A. Alison, p.172

14 *Military History*, vol. I, p. 159, quoted in C. T. Atkinson, p. 228

15 *Hare's Journal*, quoted in W. S. Churchill, vol. II, p. 450

16 Parker, *Memoirs*, p. 42

17 Millner's *Journal*, p. 115

18 *Hare's Journal*, p. 157

19 *Military History*, vol. I, p. 159, quoted in C .T. Atkinson, p. 228

20 Quoted from the *History of Henry Esmond*, Thackeray

21 W. S. Churchill, p. 451

22 Mérode-Westerloo, quoted in *Military Memoirs of Marlborough's Campaigns*, ed. Chandler, p. 172

23 *Feldzüge*, vol. I, Ser. Bd. VI, p. 521

24 Mérode-Westerloo, quoted in *Military Memoirs of Marlborough's Campaigns*, ed. Chandler, pp. 172–3

Chapter Twenty

1 Millner's *Journal*, p. 117

2 *The Life of Marlborough*, Archibald Alison, vol. I, p. 174

3 Kane, W. S. Churchill, vol II, p. 110

4 Quoted in W. S. Churchill, vol. II, p. 435

5 Lediard, vol. I, p. 429, quoted in W. S. Churchill, p. 453

6 Quoted in C. Hibbert, p.151

7 Kane, quoted on pp. 229–30, C. T. Atkinson

8 The Earl of Orkney, EHR, vol. 19, no. 74, April 1904, p. 308

9 Diary of Blackader, *Life of Blackader*, ed. Andrew Crichton, p. 223

10 Millner's *Journal*, p. 118

11 *Hare's Journal*, p. 166

12 Captain Robert Parker, *Memoirs*, ed. Chandler, p. 43

13 Earl of Orkney, EHR, p. 308

14 Millner's *Journal*, pp.118–9

15 *Military History*, quoted on p. 225 of C. T. Atkinson

16 Captain Parker, p. 42

17 Kane, quoted on pp. 229–30, C. T. Atkinson

18 *Hare's Journal*, p. 166

19 Captain Parker, p. 42

20 Ibid, p. 42.

21 Mérode-Westerloo, p. 171

22 Ibid, p. 172

23 Ibid, pp. 174–5

24 Ibid, p. 175

Chapter Twenty-One

1 *The Memoirs of the Duke of Saint Simon*, translated by Bayle St John, vol. II, p. 11

2 Captain Robert Parker, *Memoirs*, ed. David G. Chandler, p. 42

3 *Hare's Journal*, p. 167

4 *Prince Eugen of Savoy*, Colonel G. B. Malleson, p. 69

5 Millner's *Journal*, p.123

6 Captain Parker, p. 43

7 *Earle of Orkney from ye Camp at Steinheim, 17 August 1704. Account of the Battle of*

Blenheim: EHR, vol. 19, no. 74, April 1904, p. 319

8 Mérode-Westerloo: ed. David G. Chandler, p.169

9 Ibid, p. 172

10 Captain Parker, pp. 89–90

11 W. S. Churchill, vol. II, p. 460

12 *Hare's Journal*, p.168

13 *Hare's Journal*, p.169

14 Private John Marshal Deane, p. 11

15 Quoted in C. Hibbert, p. 152

16 Orkney, EHR p. 309

17 Orkney, EHR vol. 19, No. 74, April 1904, p. 309

18 Orkney, EHR p. 309

19 Mérode-Westerloo, p. 174

20 *The Memoirs of the Duke of St S.*, p. 12

21 Orkney, EHR p. 310

22 Quoted in W. S. Churchill, vol. II, p. 462

Chapter Twenty-two

1 *The Hospital Surgeon*, M. Belloste, p.100

2 *The Life of Blackader*, Andrew Crichton, pp. 223–4

3 Sgt Millner, quoted in W. S. Churchill, vol. II, p. 462

4 Sgt Millner, quoted in C. T. Atkinson, p. 236

5 *Hare's Journal*, p. 170

6 Ibid, p.174

7 Hompesch to States-General, *Nouvelles des Cours de l'Europe*, August 1704, p. 234

8 *Hare's Journal*, quoted in Coxe, vol. II, p. 2

9 Mérode-Westerloo, p.180

10 Marlborough to Sarah Marlborough, 18 August 1704. Coxe, vol. II, p. 8

11 Parker, ed. David G. Chandler, p. 45

12 Millner's *Journal*, p. 121

13 Quoted in W. S. Churchill, p. 471

14 *Hare's Journal*, p. 170

15 Parker, ed. David G. Chandler, p. 44

16 *Saint Simon*, vol. II, trans. Bayle St John, p. 14

17 Louis to Marsin, 21 August 1704, *Campagne de Tallard*, p.166

18 *Saint Simon*, vol. II, trans. Bayle St John, p.16

19 *Mémoires et Lettres de Madame de Maintenon*, Tome V, M. de la Beaumelle

20 *Lettres de la Princesse Palatine*, trans. A-A. Rolland, pp. 248–9

21 *Memoirs of the Duke of Saint Simon*, vol. II, p. 15

22 Ibid, vol. II, p. 1

23 Lettre de Maréchal Villars, *Hist. de Marlborough*, vol. I, pp. 400–401

24 Lettre de M. le Baron de Montigny Langnat, 25 August 1704, *Histoire Militaire*, IV, p. 588. Quoted in A. Alison, p. 175

25 Tallard's official account, in *Histoire Militaire*, IV, p. 568, quoted in A. Alison, p. 175

26 Tallard to Chamillard, quoted in Guizot, vol. IV, p. 372

27 Tallard to Chamillard, 4 September 1704; Pelet, IV, p. 565, quoted in W. S. Churchill, vol. II, p. 429

28 Millner's *Journal*, p. 130

29 *Lettres de la Princesse Palatine*, trans. A.-A. Rolland, pp. 257–8. Letter from Fontainebleau, 27 September 1704

30 Captain Richard Pope, 16 August 1704, quoted in *Count Tallard's Exile in Nottingham*, Alfred Stapleton, p. 7

31 BL ADD. MS 61318, f.147

32 *A Journey to Edenborgh in 1705*, quoted in *Count Tallard's Exile in Nottingham*, p. 8

33 Quoted from p. 12 of *Count Tallard's Exile in Nottingham*

34 *Tour through Great Britain*, Daniel Defoe, 1724–6, quoted on p. 15 of *Count Tallard's Exile in Nottingham*

35 ADD. MS 61271, ff.1.18. Tallard from Nottingham to Marlborough, 31 January 1705 **36** Mérode-Westerloo, ed. Chandler, pp. 177–8

37 Ibid, p. 178.

38 *Hare's Journal*, p. 177

39 Ibid

40 *Campagne de Tallard*, p. 146

41 Madame de Cornuel. Quoted in a letter from 'Madame', p.257, *Lettres de la Princesse Palatine*, 7 September 1704

42 *Saint Simon*, vol. II, trans Bayle St John, p. 16.

Chapter Twenty-three

1 Boyer, *Annals*, quoted in *Queen Anne*, David Green, p. 131

2 States-General to Marlborough, August 1704. ADD MS 61265B: *Nouvelles des Cours*

de l'Europe, September 1704, Fo.1–19

3 Major-General Cornelius Wood to Marlborough, 2 February 1705, Blenheim Papers, vol. LXII, BL ADD MS 61162, Fo.1.18

4 Brigadier-General E.Howe to Marlborough, 22 August OS 1704, Blenheim Papers, vol. CCCXIII: BL ADD MS. 61413 (fl.39)

5 Mrs Burnet to Sarah Marlborough, 23 August 1704, quoted in Coxe, vol. II, p. 38

6 *The Letters of Queen Anne*, edited by Beatrice C. Brown, pp. 149–50. To the Duke of Marlborough: Windsor, 21 August 1704

7 *The Observator*, ii, No. 82, 15–9, January 1704, quoted in *England in the War of the Spanish Succession*, John B. Hattendorf, p. 210

8 Sarah Marlborough, quoted in W. S. Churchill, vol. II, p. 512

9 Defoe to Harley, HMC Portland IV, 28 September 1704, quoted in *Anne*, Trevelyan, p. 131

10 *Parliamentary History*, vi, p. 356, quoted in W. S. Churchill, vol. II, p. 512

11 Marlborough to Sarah Marlborough, 20 October 1704, Coxe, vol. II, pp. 44–5

12 Queen Anne, quoted in *Anne*, Trevelyan, p. 12

13 Marlborough to Sarah Marlborough, 10 October 1704, Coxe, vol. II, p. 28

14 Captain Robert Parker, ed. David G. Chandler, p. 48

15 Marlborough to Lord Godolphin, 3 November 1704, quoted in Coxe, vol. II, p. 48

16 Electress Sophia to Leibniz: *Werke*, Leibniz, 1873, IX, p.112, quoted in W. S. Churchill, p. 510

17 Parker, ed. David G. Chandler, p. 46

18 Lediard, vol. I, p. 470

19 Lediard, vol. I, p. 470

20 Captain Pope, Coke MSS, iii, 40, quoted in *Marlborough and the Rise of the British Army*, C. T. Atkinson, p. 239

21 Marlborough to Sarah Marlborough, quoted in Coxe, I, pp. 213–4

22 Marlborough to Harley, *The Letters and Dispatches of John Churchill, First Duke of Marlborough from 1702–1712*, ed. General The Right Hon. Sir George Murray, vol I, pp. 391–2

23 John Evelyn's Diary, 27 August OS 1704

24 Quoted in W. S. Churchill, vol. II, p. 474

25 Louis to Marsin, 21 August 1704, *Campagne de Tallard*, pp. 166–7

26 Marlborough to Sarah Marlborough, 21 August 1704, quoted in Coxe, vol. II, p. 13

27 *Hare's Journal*, p. 176

28 *Les Nouvelles des Cours de l'Europe*, September 1704, p. 240

Chapter Twenty-four

1 Guizot, *History of France*, vol. IV, p. 373

2 Brigadier-General Kane, quoted in *Marlborough and the Rise of the British Army*, C. T. Atkinson, p. 240

3 Captain Robert Parker, ed. David G. Chandler, p. 52

4 Eugène to Marlborough, 13 September 1705, Coxe, vol. I, p. 322

5 Captain Robert Parker, ed. David G. Chandler, p. 59

6 Saint Simon, quoted in Guizot, p. 373

7 Quoted in *Louis XIV*, Vincent Cronin, p. 322

8 W. S. Churchill, vol. II, pp. 478–9

9 Ibid, p. 518

APPENDICES

APPENDIX A

The senior officers of the Army of the Grand Alliance at Blenheim

Captain-General: The Duke of Marlborough

Imperial Field Marshal: Prince Eugène of Savoy

Generals of Horse: Prince Maximilian of Hanover, the Prince of Hesse, the Duke of Württemberg and Count de la Tour

Generals of Foot: Prince Leopold of Anhalt-Dessau, and Charles Churchill

Lieutenant-Generals of Horse: the Prince of Durlach, Hompesch, von Bülow and Lumley, the Marquis de Cazani, the Prince of Bareuth and Count Oost Frieze

Lieutenant-Generals of Foot: Lord Cutts, the Earl of Orkney, Ingoldsby, Scholten and Hoorn

Major-Generals of Horse: Count Fugger, Natzmer, Noyelles, Erbach, Schulenburg, Aurochs, Wood, Caraffa, Bibra, Vittinghof, Villiers, and the Prince of Hesse Homburg

Major-Generals of Foot: Fink, the Prince of Holstein-Beck, Withers, Herbeville, Wilks, Rantzau, St Paul and Luc

Brigadier-Generals of Horse: Baldwin, Ross, Brockdorff, Groevendorff and Bothmar

Brigadier-Generals of Foot: Bielk, Heidenbrecht, Wulfen, Hulsen, Rowe, Fergusson, Rebsdorff, Canitz, Bernsdorff, Steckendorff and Webb

APPENDIX B

British and Irish Regiments who fought at Blenheim, with their later names

INFANTRY

Queen of England's Guards – 1st Battalion, 1st Guards – The Grenadier Guards

Orkney's – 1st and 2nd Battalions, 1st Foot – The Royal Scots

Churchill's – 3rd Foot; the Buffs (Royal East Kent) – The Queen's Regiment

Webb's – 8th Foot; the King's Regiment (Liverpool) – The King's Regiment

Howe's – 15th Foot; the East Yorkshire Regiment – The Prince of Wales's Own Regiment

Derby's – 16th Foot; the Bedfordshire & Hertfordshire Regiment – The Third Royal Anglian Regiment

North & Grey's – 10th Foot; the Royal Lincolnshire Regiment – The Second Royal Anglian Regiment

Ingoldsby's – 23rd Foot – The Royal Welch Fusiliers

Hamilton's – 18th Foot; the Royal Regiment of Foot of Ireland – disbanded

Marlborough's – 24th Foot; the South Wales Borderers – The Royal Regiment of Wales

Rowe's – 21st Foot; the Royal Scots Fusiliers – The Royal Highland Fusiliers

Fergusson's – 26th Foot; the Cameronians – disbanded

Meredith's – 37th Foot – The Royal Hampshire Regiment

CAVALRY

Lumley's – 1st King's Dragoons Guards – The Queen's Dragoon Guards

Wood's – 3rd Dragoon Guards – The Royal Scots Dragoon Guards

Wyndham's – 6th Dragoon Guards; the Carabiniers – The Royal Scots Dragoon Guards

Schomberg's – 7th Dragoon Guards; Princess Royal's – 4th/7th Dragoon Guards

Cadogan's – 5th Dragoon Guards; Princess Charlotte of Wales – 5th Royal Inniskilling Dragoon Guards

Ross's – 5th Royal Irish Dragoons – The 16th/5th the Queen's Lancers

Hay's – 2nd or North British Regiment of Dragoons; the Royal Scots Greys – The Royal Scots Dragoon Guards

Strength of each unit, according to the 'Blenheim Roll':

Queen of England's Guards:	36 officers and 553 men
Orkney's: 1st Battalion,	38 officers and 601 men
2nd Battalion,	37 officers and 540 men
Churchill's:	31 officers and 559 men
Webb's:	35 officers and 704 men
Howe's:	39 officers and 545 men
Derby's:	31 officers and 632 men
North & Grey's:	40 officers and 540 men
Ingoldsby's:	33 officers and 487 men
Hamilton's:	36 officers and 542 men
Marlborough's:	35 officers and 489 men
Rowe's:	36 officers and 593 men
Fergusson's:	40 officers and 613 men
Meredith's:	32 officers and 543 men
Lumley's:	25 officers and 457 men
Wood's:	25 officers and 288 men
Wyndham's:	25 officers and 286 men
Schomberg's:	24 officers and 246 men
Cadogan's:	14 officers and 135 men
Ross's:	26 officers and 298 men
Hay's:	25 officers and 315 men

2,234 of these men died on 13 August 1704

APPENDIX C

The regiments brought into Bavaria by Marshal Tallard

INFANTRY REGIMENTS (nationality of those not French, shown in *italics*):
Navarre (3 battalions) – captured at Blenheim village
Royal (3 battalions) – captured at Blenheim village
Languedoc (2 battalions) – captured at Blenheim village
Greder Allemand (2 battalions), *German* – captured at Blenheim village
Zurlauben (2 battalions) *Walloon* – captured at Blenheim village
Nice (1 battalion)
Boulonnois (2 battalions) – captured at Blenheim village
Aunis (2 battalions) – captured at Blenheim village
Artois (2 battalions) – captured at Blenheim village
Agenois (1 battalion) – captured at Blenheim village
Provence (1 battalion) – captured at Blenheim village
Robecq (2 battalions)
Montrou (1 battalion), *Italian* – captured at Blenheim village
D'Albaret (1 battalion)
Auxerrois (2 battalions)
Lassay (1 battlion) – captured at Blenheim village
Baudeville (1 battalion)
Tavannes (1 battalion)
(Second de) Condé, Ulm (1 battalion)
(Second de) Xaintonge, Ulm (1 battalion)
(Second de) Foix, Ulm (1 battalion)
(Premier de) Blaisois (1 battalion) – captured at Blenheim village
(Premier de) St. Segond (1 battalion), – captured at Blenheim village
Chabrillant (1 battalion)
Milan Espagnol, Augsburg (2 battalions), *Italian and Spanish*
Montfort (2 battalions), *Spanish and Walloon* – captured at Blenheim village
Santerre (2 battalions) – captured at Blenheim village

CAVALRY REGIMENTS
Gendarmerie (8 squadrons)
Mestre de Camp General (3 squadrons)
Bourgogne (3 squadrons)
Orléans (3 squadrons)
Du Roi (3 squadrons)
St Pouange (3 squadrons)
Noailles (3 squadrons)
La Baume (2 squadrons)
Ligondez (2 squadrons)
Montrevel (2 squadrons)
Tarneau (2 squadrons)

Croy Espagnol (2 squadrons), *Spanish*
Gaetano (2 squadrons), *Italian*
Berenghen (3 squadrons), *German*
Grignau (3 squadrons)
La Vallière (2 squadrons)
Framla Espagnol (2 squadrons), *Spanish*

DRAGOONS
Mestre de Camp Général (3 squadrons)
La Reine (3 squadrons)
Vasse (3 squadrons)
Chevalier de Rohan (3 squadrons)

ARTILLERY
Royal Artillerie (90 cannon, of which 35 were captured by Marlborough's Wing, 18 by Eugène's, 18 were retrieved by Marsin, and the rest destroyed)

The combined **Franco-Bavarian casualties** were approximately 20,000 killed and 14,190 taken prisoner, including 40 generals

The following senior French officers were sent to England as prisoners of war in December 1704:

TO NOTTINGHAM
The Comte de Tallard – Marshal
The Marquis de Monperoux – General of Horse
The Comte de Blanzac – Lieutenant-General
The Marquis de Hautefeuille – General of Dragoons
The Marquis de Valseme – Major-General
The Marquis de Seppeville – Major-General
The Marquis de Silly – Major-General, and Quartermaster-General
Chevalier de Croissy – Major-General
The Marquis de la Vallière – Major-General
Monsieur de St Seconde – Brigadier-General
The Marquis de Vassey – Colonel of Dragoons

TO LICHFIELD
The Marquis de Marivaux – Lieutenant-General
Monsieur de la Messilière – Brigadier-General
Monsieur Joly – Brigadier-General
Monsieur d'Amigni – Brigadier-General
Monsieur de St Maurice – Brigadier-General
Comte de Lionne – Colonel of Foot
Marquis de Salsey – Colonel of Foot
Baron d'Elst – Colonel of Foot

Monsieur de Balincourt – Colonel of Foot

Monsieur Saulveboeuf – Colonel of Foot

Monsieur de Montenay – Colonel of Foot

Monsieur de Gallart – Colonel of Foot

Monsieur de Cressy – Colonel of Foot

Monsieur de Ligondais – Colonel of Horse

Baron de Heyder – Colonel of Horse

Monsieur de Prie – Colonel of Horse

Monsieur D'Aurival – Colonel of Horse

RELEASED ON PAROLE in late 1704, before going to England as prisoners of war:

Monsieur Denonville – Brigadier-General

Monsieur de St Pouange – Colonel

Monsieur de Carmain – Colonel

The Comte de Tavannes – Colonel

The Comte de Montfort – Colonel

The Comte de Sepack – Colonel

The Duc Glopis de Châtillon

Destined to be prisoners of war in England, but **too badly wounded to travel:**

Monsieur de Signier – Brigadier-General

Monsieur D'Auvet – Colonel

.

BIBLIOGRAPHY

Alison, A., *The Life of Marlborough, vol. I,* London and Edinburgh, 1852

Anderson, M. S., *War and Society in Europe of the Old Regime,* New York, 1988

Anquetil, L.-P., *Histoire de France, vol. xi,* Paris, 1805

Ashley, Maurice, *James II,* London, 1977

Atkinson, C. T., *Marlborough and the Rise of the British Army,* London, 1921

Barnett, Correlli, *Britain And Her Army,* London, 1972

Barnett, Correlli, *Marlborough,* London, 1974

Barraclough, Geoffrey, *The Origins of Modern Germany,* Oxford, 1972

Belloc, Hillaire, *The Tactics and Strategy of the Great Duke of Marlborough,* Bristol, 1933

Belloste, Surgeon-Major, *The Hospital Surgeon,* London, 1706

Black, Jeremy, *European Warfare, 1660–1815,* New Haven, CT, 1994

Brown, Beatrice C., (ed.) *The Letters of Queen Anne,* Cassell, 1935

Brown, John, *A Compleat Discourse of Wounds,* London, 1678

Chandler, David G., *The Art of Warfare in the Age of Marlborough,* Spellmount, 1976

Chandler, David G., *Marlborough as Military Commander,* Batsford, 1973

Chandler, David G., (ed.) *Military Memoirs of Marlborough's Campaigns, 1702–1712,* London, 1998

Chartrand, René, *Louis XIV's Army,* Osprey, 1988

Childs, John, *Armies and Warfare in Europe, 1648–1749,* Manchester, 1982

Childs, John, *Warfare in the Seventeenth Century,* Cassell, 2001

Churchill, Winston S., *Marlborough, His Life and Times, vols i and ii (of four),* London, 1933–8

Colbach, John, *A New Light of Chirurgery,* London, 1695

Coward, Barry, *The Stuart Age,* London and New York, 1980

Coxe, Archdeacon, *Memoirs of John, Duke of Marlborough, vols i and ii (of six),* London, 1820

Creasy, Sir Edward, *The Fifteen Decisive Battles of the World,* London, 1895

Cronin, Vincent, *Louis XIV,* London, 1965

Crichton, Andrew, *The Life and Diary of Lieutenant-Colonel J. Blackader,* London, 1824

Defoe, Daniel, *The Life and Adventures of Mrs Christian Davies,* London, 1743

Delloge, H.-L., (ed.), *Mémoires complets et authentiques du duc de Saint-Simon sur le siècle de Louis XIV et la Régence, tome vii,* Paris, 1840

De Genlis, Mme, *Journal du marquis de Dangeau,* Paris, 1817

De la Beaumelle, M., (ed.), *Mémoires et Lettres de Madame de Maintenon, tome v,* Maastricht, 1778

De la Colonie, Jean-Martin (trans. W. C. Horsley) *The Chronicles of an Old Campaigner,* John Murray, 1904

Doyle, William, *The Old European Order, 1660–1800,* Oxford University Press, 1978

Du Crest, Sabine, *Des Fêtes à Versailles,* Paris, 1990

Evelyn, John, *The Diary of John Evelyn,* Oxford University Press, 1959

Falkner, James, *Great and Glorious Days: the Duke of Marlborough's Battles, 1704–1709,* Spellmount, 2002

Fleming, Kate, *The Churchills,* Weidenfeld and Nicolson, 1975

Frey, Linda and Marsha, *A Question of Empire,* Columbia University Press, New York, 1983

Green, David, *Queen Anne,* London, 1970

Grimblot, Paul, (ed.), *Letters of William III and Louis XIV and of Their Ministers, vol. ii,* London, 1848

Guizot, M., *The History of France, vol. iv,* London, 1875

Harris, Frances, *A Passion for Government: The Life of Sarah, Duchess of Marlborough,* Oxford, 1991

Hattendorf, John B., *England in the War of the Spanish Succession,* New York and London, 1987

Henderson, Nicholas, *Prince Eugen of Savoy,* Weidenfeld and Nicolson, 1964

Hennen, John, *Military Surgery,* Edinburgh, 1818

Hibbert, Christopher, *The Marlboroughs,* London, 2001

Jones, J. R., (ed.) *The Restored Monarchy, 1660–1688,* London, 1979

Kane, Brig-Gen Richard, *Campaigns of King William and the Duke of Marlborough,* London, 1735

Lynn, John A., *Giant of the 'Grand Siècle': the French Army, 1610–1715,* Cambridge University Press, 1997

Lynn, John A., *The Wars of Louis XIV,* Longman, 1999

Macaulay, Thomas Babington, *Macaulay's History of England, vols i and ii (four vols),* Everyman's Library, 1906

Marlborough, Sarah, *Private Correspondence of Sarah, Duchess of Marlborough, vol. I (two vols),* London, 1838

Mignet, M., *Introduction aux documents relatifs à la succession d'Espagne*

Millner, Sergeant John, *Journal of all the Marches, Famous Battles, Sieges, And other most note-worthy, heroical, and ever memorable Actions of the Triumphant Armies, of the ever-glorious Confederate High Allies, In their late and victorious War Against the Powerful Armies of proud and lofty France,* London, 1733

Mitford, Nancy, *The Sun King,* London, 1969.

Parker, Captain Robert, *Memoirs of the most Remarkable Military Transactions from the Year 1683 to 1718,* Dublin, 1746

Peterkin, A., and Johnston, W., *Medical Officers in the British Army, 1660–1960, vol. I,* Wellcome Library, 1968

Plumb, J. H., *The Growth of Political Stability in England, 1675–1725,* Macmillan, 1967

Rey, Marc-Michel, *Campagne de Monsieur le Maréchal de Tallard en Allemagne, two vols*, Amsterdam, 1763

Rolland, A-A, (ed.) *Lettres de la Princesse Palatine*

Rowse, A. L., *The Churchills*, New York, 1956

Saint Simon, Duc de, (trans. by Bayle St John), *The Memoirs of the Duke of Saint Simon*, Chapman & Hall, 1857

Tincey, John (ed.), *Monmouth's Drill Book: An Abridgement of the English Military Discipline*, Partizan Press, 1986

Trevelyan, G. M., *England Under the Stuarts* (vol. v of *A History of England*, ed. by Sir Charles Oman), London, 1938

Trevelyan, G. M., *England Under Queen Anne: Blenheim*, London, New York, Toronto, 1930

Van der Zee, H. and B., *William and Mary*, London, 1973

Contemporary pamphlets and periodicals:

A New Tract for the Cure of Wounds made by Gun Shot, Anon., 1700

Nouvelles des Cours de l'Europe, tome XI, The Hague, July 1704

Nouvelles des Cours de l'Europe, tome XII, The Hague, August 1704

Nouvelles des Cours de l'Europe, tome XIII, The Hague, September 1704

Twentieth-century journals and magazines:

The American Historical Review, vol. 57, No.1, October 1951: *Prince Eugène of Savoy and Central Europe*, Paul R. Sweet

Biographical Tracts, 1904–1908: Count Tallard's Exile in Nottingham, Alfred Stapleton

The English Historical Review, vol. 19, No. 74, April 1904: *Letters of the First Lord Orkney during Marlborough's Campaigns*

EHR, vol. 8, No. 29, January 1893: *Villars*, William O'Connor Morris

French Historical Studies: vol. 18, No.4, Autumn 1994, *Recalculating French Army Growth during the Grand Siècle, 1610–1715*, John A. Lynn

FHS: vol. 6, No. 3, Spring 1970, *The Functioning of Ambassadors under Louis XIV*, William J. Roosen

Journal of the Society for Army Historical Research: A Journal of Marlborough's Campaigns During the War of the Spanish Succession, 1704–1711, by John Marshall Deane, ed. David G. Chandler, Special Publication no. 12, 1984

JSAHR: Letters of Samuel Noyes, Chaplain of the Royal Scots, 1703–4, ed. Major S. H. F. Johnston, vol. 37, 1959

Manuscripts:

The Blenheim Papers, British Library: this huge collection formed the core of my primary research. The source notes to each chapter identify which manuscripts have been used in my text. Many more, being communications between Marlborough, his officers, allies and enemy, added to the general narrative.

One of the most important manuscripts in *The Blenheim Papers* is '*Hare's Journal*'. There has been a question mark over the authorship of this work. I have fallen in line with the view of Dr Frances Harris that this was not written by Marlborough's chaplain-general, Francis Hare, but by General Charles Churchill's chaplain, Josias (also known as Josiah) Sandby. To read further on this debate, see: *The Authorship of the Manuscript Blenheim Journal, Bulletin of the Institute of Historical Research, LV, 1982, pp. 203–6.*

INDEX